IN ONE'S BONES

IN ONE'S BONES:
THE CLINICAL GENIUS
OF WINNICOTT

Dodi Goldman, Ph.D.

JASON ARONSON INC.
Northvale, New Jersey
London

This book is set in 10 pt. Goudy by Lind Graphics of Upper Saddle River, New Jersey, and printed and bound by Haddon Craftsmen of Scranton, Pennsylvania.

Library of Congress Cataloging-in-Publication Data

In one's bones : the clinical genius of Winnicott / [edited by] Dodi
  Goldman.
      p. cm.
    Consists partially of papers from various sources including
  fourteen of D.W. Winnicott's papers.
    Includes bibliographical references and index.
    ISBN 1-56821-020-5 (pbk.)
    1. Winnicott, D. W. (Donald Woods), 1896–1971. 2. Psychotherapy.
  I. Winnicott, D. W. (Donald Woods), 1896–1971. II. Goldman, Dodi.
    [DNLM: 1. Psychoanalytic Therapy. 2. Psychoanalytic Theory.
  3. Psychoanalytic Therapy—collected works. 4. Psychoanalytic
  Theory—collected works.   WM 460 I35 1993]
  RC438.6.W56I5 1993
  616.89'14'092—dc20
  DNLM/DLC
  for Library of Congress   93-16205

Manufactured in the United States of America. Jason Aronson Inc. offers books and cassettes. For information and catalog write to Jason Aronson Inc., 230 Livingston Street, Northvale, New Jersey 07647.

To Alex,
for a friendship
spanning years and seas

CONTENTS

FOREWORD

THIS IS THE SECOND VOLUME that Dodi Goldman has contributed to the series that investigates the relationship of Freudian and Object Relations theory. It is clear from the introduction that he provides, and the editorial choices that he has made, that his first volume was certainly no fluke. Winnicott is in his bones. Goldman weaves together an array of clinical, developmental, and biographical material that again increases our understanding and our feeling for this extraordinary human being (and psychoanalyst). If I didn't know Goldman's age I would assume that he must be a colleague of Winnicott's. All of his choices fit together to form a Winnicottian tapestry that we all will delight in again and again. I must say that this book makes the reading of Goldman's first volume all the more rewarding.

—Steven J. Ellman, Ph.D.

INTRODUCTION

FOR D. W. WINNICOTT, THE CLINICAL encounter—whether in the form of standard psychoanalysis, psychotherapy, consultation, or squiggle technique—was always a mutual experience. "In order to use the mutual experience," he once averred, "one must have in one's bones a theory of the emotional development of the child and the relationship of the child to the environmental factors" (Winnicott 1971a, p. 3). A single statement, and yet opening so many Winnicottian doors: use of an object, maturational processes, facilitating environment. As Keats once noted: "Every point of thought is the centre of an intellectual world."

But what does it mean to have a theory of emotional development "in one's bones"? Certainly it must contain the notion that one's therapeutic work must come from deep within, from an authentic part of the therapist's own self. Furthermore, Winnicott offers an important antidote to the current proliferation of self-help techniques and the "therapizing" of popular culture: treatment, to be effective, must be grounded in a developmental theory of emotional growth. One is also immediately faced with the seemingly effortless, inspiring, and inimicable way Winnicott works. Could the kind of therapeutic work he performed—and Winnicott certainly enjoyed performing—be done only by him? Can one learn or be trained to work from one's bones? A common reaction to Winnicott's work is to see it as so singularly personal and intuitive as to dismiss its relevance or integration into psychoanalytic thinking. Is it not a contradiction even to envision a Winnicottian technique, let alone an orthodoxy? Can there be such a thing as a "school" of open-mindedness? But Winnicott is actually sending a paradoxical message: clinical work must be an authentic reflection of the therapist and grounded in shared theory; it requires both discipline and inner freedom.

As a result of the harsh political struggles within the British Psycho-Analytical Society, Winnicott remained a lone and somewhat quixotic figure for many decades. He was denied teaching positions because of his reluctance to align himself with either the Freudian or Kleinian camp. Today, however, especially in France and the United States, there is an upsurge of interest in his creative contributions. It is quite ironic how after so many years of being held in suspicion he is today being claimed by adherents of every school. Increasingly, clinicians are struck by the way his vision cuts across traditional polarizing dichotomies: people are both innovative symbol makers and biologically driven organisms, accounts of human behavior include both maturational processes and the facilitating environment, analytic understanding includes both drives and object relations, object relations are both internal and external, the self is both a content of mental apparatus and an overarching locus of experience.

The growing interest in Winnicott is also the result of the powerful metaphors he fashioned, such as *holding environment, good-enough mother, transitional object,* and *True and False Self.* Winnicott's ideas were rarely expressed as exact logical concepts; rather, in Guntrip's words, they were "imaginative hypotheses that challenged one to explore further" (1975, p. 155). These "imaginative hypotheses" seem strikingly apt for the kind of patients seen by the majority of clinicians today. These patients do not come to treatment ready to freely associate and overcome resistances through a therapeutic alliance dedicated to self-understanding. As a rising number of clinicians are faced with the reality of treating individuals who do not fit the classical neurotic mold, Winnicott's metaphors become increasingly appealing as a way of understanding clinical material.

The danger of such an appeal, however, particularly within our commercial culture, is that Winnicott's metaphors can become quickly fashionable—a cheap intellectual currency, so to speak—and the complex substance of his ideas subsequently lost. Ours is an era with potent anit-intellectual trends. Winnicott's deceptively simple, compressed, intuitive, and evocative style creates, at times, the illusion of understanding in the absence of concerted intellectual effort. He can, therefore, be easily idealized or poeticized beyond recognition. No doubt, he would have found such sentimentality quite repugnant, in that it entailed a denial of unconscious reservoirs of cruder emotions. This, then, is one of the paradoxes of Winnicott's legacy: the deceptive appeal of his ideas clouds the depth and precision of his thought. As a result, many of his inventive ideas are flagrantly misappropriated, parroted by people devoid of his imagination and clinical sophistication. At the same time, Winnicott would have preferred people creatively transforming his ideas, using them for their own needs, rather than adhering to them as a new orthodoxy.

Winnicott had a profound need to approach matters in a very personal way, which felt original and real to him. He dreaded the lack of authenticity and creativity of clinical ventriloquism. Even theory was somewhat of a transitional phenomenon for him, offering him concepts that he then reinvented in accordance with his own sensibilities. As M. Gerard Fromm noted, Winnicott seems to "ignore serious inquiry as to whether his use of a particular concept is something he made or something he found" (1989, p. 5). This tendency, what F. Robert Rodman has called his "insistence on being himself" (1987, p. xix) and what Masud Khan refers to as his "inviolable me-ness that enabled him to be so many different persons to such diverse people" (1975, p. xi) helps explain why Winnicott is both enormously appealing to some and ignored, if not mistrusted, by others. Winnicott's personal strivings were so consistently echoed in his theoretical conceptualizations that one cannot easily disentangle his creative concepts from the person that he was. As Khan, who was both a former patient of Winnicott's and the driving impetus behind the publication of many of his writings, noted: "His theories are abstractions of that constant happening which was Winnicott the living person and clinician" (1975, cp. xi).

It is precisely because Winnicott's originality of thought and his originality as a person were so inseparable that he appears, at times, too "idiosyncratic," "obtuse," or "difficult to link with other approaches" (Davis and Wallbridge 1981, p. xi). It is the reason, for example, that Raymond Cahn has argued that Winnicott's "theoretical neologisms" and "neo-concepts" have a "specificity that cannot be integrated into other theories" (Clancier and Kalmanovitch 1987, p. 114). His reluctance to employ terms in a conventional way, his proclivity for using language in a personal way to arrive at innovative concepts, and his failure to clearly acknowledge modifications in theory or the sources from which some of his own ideas derived all contributed to the reservations that many psychoanalysts have had about him. Winnicott's ideas, many believe, cannot be easily coordinated with the conceptual language of traditional theory.

Another criticism frequently levied against Winnicott is that he tends to underemphasize sexual fantasy and ignore the role of the father in development. This criticism is, at times, somewhat overstated, given the nature of the particular material Winnicott chose to elucidate. After all, Winnicott was struggling to make a genuine contribution regarding the importance of earliest infancy. At the time of his writing, the real mother's significance was often denied, either by an exclusive focus on the technique of bodily care, which could be performed by nurses as well as by mothers, or by singular emphasis on intrapsychic libidinal gratifications. Winnicott wished to shift the focus to the emotional development of the infant as it evolved through the facilitating gestures of the caretaker. His emphasis is really more on the maternal *function* than on the woman as mother. Furthermore, he was writing in a cultural setting wherein infant care was assumed to be a woman's prerogative. In his mind, the father, at the earliest stage, was a duplicate mother.

Still, there is definitely what could be called a maternal bias that permeates Winnicott's writings. Fathers and sexual identity are but small sideshows in development. The father's main function is to enable the mother to be the best mother she can possibly be. As Phillips (1988) points out, the father's coming between the child and the mother is of far less interest to Winnicott than the transitional space from which the father is absent yet which "initially both joins and separates the baby and the mother" (Winnicott 1971b, p. 121). The real drama is the one dominated by the maternal. In fact, Winnicott possessed such a strong maternal identification that Katherine Whitehorn, in an article in *The Observer* based on an interview with him, went so far as to describe him as a "Madonna."

It is common knowledge that Winnicott maintained a sustained counterpoint between pediatrics and psychoanalysis throughout his career. People who knew and observed him were deeply impressed with his astonishing powers with children. But the same qualities that made Winnicott uniquely accessible to children were at the root of his ability to work successfully with psychotic or regressed adults as well. Many of the adult analyses he conducted were with highly disturbed individuals who had had unsuccessful analyses with others (Little 1990). Apparently, he was profoundly open to the rawness of human experience; he could tolerate the painful exposure of undiluted impulses or the chaos of unbridled fantasies. It was these kinds of experiences, no matter what the age of the patient, to which Winnicott was naturally attuned.

Still, Winnicott's particular genius with children has been noted by nearly everyone who has watched him work (Gillespie 1971). He enjoyed being a hands-on pediatrician. He understood in a deep way that children are able to communicate with some urgency once they feel that there is someone who might possibly understand. His unassuming and direct manner and his uncanny ability to quickly grasp the core of a child's psychological difficulties strengthened a child's belief in being understood. Eventually, people were to come from around the world for consultations with him. In the decades of his association with Paddington Green Children's Hospital and The Queen's Hospital for Children he was to see over 60,000 cases. During the Second World War he served as a consultant psychiatrist to the Government Evacuation Scheme, which entailed supervising close to 300 delinquent children being housed in a group of five hostels. After the war, despite his heavy weekly work load, he spent many of his Sundays driving to a school for maladjusted children in the countryside. There is probably no other figure in the history of psychoanalysis with such a volume of practical experience with children.

There can be no doubt that the continuity of Winnicott's practical experience with children had a major impact on his theorizing. He began his independent medical practice as a pediatrician and, as he put it, he "never cut loose" (1975, p. ix). As a physician in a children's hospital, he had the valuable experience of having to meet the reality of social pressures. At The Queen's Hospital for Children in the decade 1922–1933 he was in charge of the Rheumatism Clinic, which dealt with rheumatic fever, chorea, and concomitant heart disease. Before the advent of penicillin, he dealt with large epidemics of encephalitis lethargica, summer diar-rhea, and various polio epidemics.

Pediatrics strengthened Winnicott's conviction that there are natural processes that should not be interrupted. Life's roots (the word *root* appears frequently in his writing) are organic, not something that can be calculated or contrived. Children, he concluded, cannot be made to develop; at best they can be provided with a relatively unintrusive, but supportive, setting in which they may flourish. "We cannot even teach them to walk," he once wrote to an anthropologist working in Tanzania, "but their innate tendency to walk at a certain age needs us as supporting figures" (Rodman 1987, p. 186). And to a group of midwives he proclaimed that:

> One general idea goes right through what I have to say: that is that there are natural processes which underlie all that is taking place; and we do good work as doctors and nurses only if we respect and facilitate these natural processes. [Winnicott 1957, p. 107]

Winnicott had great faith – perhaps exaggerated – in the "silent integrative forces" of natural growth processes.

Unlike some child analysts, Winnicott was as consistently attuned to the practical problems of management as he was to the unconscious processes of the child. His therapeutic consultations were predicated on the assumption that there was an "average expectable environment to meet and to make use of the changes that have taken place in the boy or girl in the interview, changes which indicate a loosening of the knot in the developmental process" (Winnicott 1971a, p. 5). Winnicott always took into account the child's physical development, the resources of the social class from which the child came, and the availability and capability of the parents to facilitate the maturational process. The evacuation experience brought him into daily contact with the devastation brought by the break-up of families. When he took on the evacuation consultancy, he knew he would have to turn his attention to issues of care and management. The overburdened local staffs were desperate for practical advice (Winnicott 1984).

Winnicott genuinely believed in the value of an uninterrupted dialogue between the clinical data obtained through pediatrics and the clinical data of psychoanalysis, feeling that "the proper procedure is obviously to get all we can both from observation and from analysis, and to let each help the other" (Winni-cott 1941, p. 61). Following his own muse, he straddled both disciplines, frequently seeing himself as a "pediatrician who has swung to psychiatry, and a psychiatrist who has clung to pediatrics" (Winnicott 1948, p. 157). Winnicott noted how "odd flashes of insight from parent and child remind the analyst of material patiently acquired in analytic work" (Winnicott 1942, p. 82). Occasionally, he went even further and claimed to have "learned much that is of value in analysis from the therapeutic consultation, and from the study of other non-analytic material" (Winnicott 1942, p. 82).

Pediatric practice allowed Winnicott to carefully observe the somatic processes of children interacting with caretakers. This was the basis of his conclusion that mother and infant were a single unit. "The mother's milk does not flow like an excretion," he said,

> it is a response to a stimulus, and the stimulus is the sight and smell and feel of her baby, and the sound of the baby's cry that indicates need. It is all one thing, the mother's care of her baby and the periodic feeding that develops as if it were a means of communication between the two — a song without words. [Winnicott 1957, pp. 111–112]

Winnicott creatively transformed many of these concrete observations into potent metaphors for the working of the mind. Watching what mother and baby did together contributed to his understanding of what went on inside baby's mind. An infant's experience of breathing, which appears to come from both within and without, was seen by Winnicott as the basis for the conception of spirit, soul, or anima (Winnicott 1945). *Holding, handling, object presenting,* and *transitional objects* are all metaphors for psychic processes rooted in concrete phenomena observed in child–parent interactions. His observation that midwives frequently interrupt the delicate initiation of breast-feeding by impatiently shoving the breast into baby's mouth, and that baby responds by instinctive withdrawal (Winnicott 1957), was probably the backdrop to his notion that the infant needs to "create" the breast.

Winnicott's transformation of concrete observations into metaphors for psychic processes is consistent with his natural proclivity for working from his own body ego. As he once reflected: "To some extent, I always listen with my throat" (Winnicott 1963, p.83). Winnicott was always elaborating what he believed were the somatic origins of self, fantasy, and abstract ideas. "The basis of a self," wrote Winnicott, "forms on the fact of the body which, being alive, not only has shape, but which also functions" (Winnicott 1970, p. 270). When a patient would reveal fantasy material in regard to the transference, Winnicott would invariably ask about the "accompanying orgastic bodily functioning" (Winnicott 1989, p. 26).

Nevertheless, psychoanalysis, not pediatrics, was the primary vehicle for both Winnicott's clinical understanding of children and his formal theorizing. Although pediatrics concerns itself with the care of the developing child, it was actually psychoanalysis that provided Winnicott with a developmental point of view.

The year Winnicott received his first appointments at The Queen's Hospital and Paddington Green, 1923, was also the year he undertook a personal analysis with Strachey that was to last for ten years. This analysis enabled Winnicott to see children for the first time as real people rather than as merely anatomic or somatic beings. Having undergone analysis enabled Winnicott to see the child through the eyes of the analyzed adult. As he later recalled:

> It was only through analysis that I became gradually able to see a baby as a human being. This was really the chief result of my first five years of analysis, so that I've been extremely sympathetic with any paediatricians or anybody who can't see babies as human, because I absolutely couldn't, however I used to try. [Winnicott 1967, p. 574]

In his mind, psychoanalysis was the vehicle for understanding even infancy, because it was the most precise instrument available for studying human nature objectively. He was absolutely convinced that the elucidation of the earliest stages of emotional development must come chiefly from psychoanalytic treatment "whether it be used in the analysis of small children or of regressed adults or of psychotics of all ages" (Winnicott 1952, p. 221). These were the main sources of data from which Winnicott inferred the subjective life of infants. "If from various analyses certain common factors emerge," he wrote, "then we can make definite claims"(Winnicott 1952, p. 221). Or, as he said in his paper, "The Theory of the Parent–Infant Relationship":

> Indeed it is not from direct observation of infants so much as from the study of the transference in the analytic setting that it is possible to gain a clear view of what takes place in infancy itself. This work on infantile dependence derives from the study of the transference and counter-transference phenomena that belong to the psychoanalyst's involvement with the borderline cases. [Winnicott 1960b, p. 54]

Even when he attempted to understand the mental state of infants immediately after birth, Winnicott turned to an analysis of the dreams of his adult patients (Winnicott 1949). Psychoanalysis, where regression is a key feature, takes priority over the objective study of infants and the infant–mother relationship when it comes to understanding even the birth traumas of infants. And in his paper, "The Observation of Infants in a Set Situation," which is the closest Winnicott ever comes to a controlled observational study, he writes:

It is illuminating to observe infants directly, and it is necessary for us to do so. In many respects, however, the analysis of two-year-old children tells us much more about the infant than we can ever get from direct observation of infants. This is not surprising; the uniqueness of psycho-analysis as an instrument of research, as we know, lies in its capacity to discover the unconscious part of the mind and link it up with the conscious part and thus give us something like a full understanding of the individual who is in analysis. [Winnicott 1941, p. 61]

For his own psychological reasons, Winnicott felt compelled to defend his fierce personalism and to guard against what he perceived as threats to his unique sensitivity. A poignant example of this occurred in the 1920s, when, after having been an outpatient physician at Paddington Green, he was finally assigned inpatient bed privileges. At first, Winnicott was excited by his newly won status. But soon he began to avoid the inpatient unit, handing over the inpatients to a junior associate. In a private letter to Margaret Torrie he explained why:

I knew at the time why I was doing this. I said to myself: the distress of babies and small children in a hospital ward, even a very nice one, adds up to something terrific. Going into the ward disturbs me very much. If I become an in-patient doctor I shall develop the capacity not to be disturbed by the distress of the children, otherwise I shall not be able to be an effective doctor. I will therefore concentrate on my O.P. work and avoid becoming callous in order to be efficient. So I lost the status symbol but that didn't matter somehow. [Rodman 1987, p. 168]

Winnicott was consistently cautious in choosing his case load so as to maximize his strengths and preserve his receptivity. For years, he deliberately avoided taking on cases of delinquents because he feared being sidetracked into a time-consuming endeavor promising little benefit. When he worked with severely regressed patients, he understood that he must be able to have the inner resources to tolerate another individual's regression to dependence. Appreciating both the enormity of the task and the extent to which one's countertransferential reactions play a role, Winnicott was careful to take on only one such patient at a time.

Winnicott was what one might call a graceful narcissist and a natural performer. He took delight in people watching him conduct therapeutic consulta-tions or listening to his case presentations. He thrived on the opportunity to present his ideas to audiences of all kinds.

At the same time, he allowed himself latitude with patients that would not have been tolerated in less prominent clinicians. The license he took was part of a pattern of making the therapeutic enterprise feel personally real for him. He refused to define psychoanalysis based on frequency or regularity of sessions. Instead, he believed in a form of "psychoanalysis on demand" (Winnicott 1977, p. xv), in which his motto was often "How little need be done?"(Winnicott 1962, p. 166). He saw the actual person of the therapist and a personal technique as essential ingredients in therapy. At times, he went so far as to imply that psychoanalysis was not *what* was done but *who* was doing it (Winnicott 1958a).

Winnicott offered tea to patients, sought one out in a public restaurant to change an appointment, held another's hands for a long period of the analysis, and even gently rocked a patient's head. He was frequently late to his appointments at Paddington Green, which he nicknamed his "psychiatric snack-bar." Eric Trist (1992) recalls seeing him shout advice across a crowded room to a mother whom he had overheard having a discussion with another woman. Winnicott often agreed to see children on an irregular basis rather than transfer them to more available colleagues. As Katharine Rees, a psychiatric social worker who worked with him at Paddington Green, remarked: "It is as if he felt that an ounce of Winnicott was worth a pound of pedestrian psychotherapy." As a result, at least some of the children were sorely "short-changed" (Rees 1991). He obviously felt special or unique, such that he allowed himself to do whatever felt right to him at the very moment.

Winnicott's narcissism remained healthy in the sense that it did not preclude a capacity to imaginatively enter into other people's lives. It did not have the dead-end quality of more pathological forms of narcissism. Although his overt behavior might have appeared, at times, to be narcissistic, he genuinely enjoyed being used by others and not exploiting them. As much as he wanted to be himself, he wanted others to be themselves. As he wrote once to Augusta Bonnard: "Let's enjoy being ourselves and enjoy seeing what we do when we meet it in the work of others" (Rodman 1987, p. 117). If anything, Winnicott's narcissism caused him to underestimate the difference between himself and others (Riley 1991). He was obviously blessed with a genius for quickly and intuitively grasping other people's core conflicts and communicating them in a way that the person could take in. He took it for granted that others were equally competent. As a result, he was not particularly concerned with how the formal structure of analysis might serve as a safeguard against potential abuses.

Winnicott also gained obvious pleasure from gently but firmly knocking up against classical doctrine, striking at it, tearing it down, and, in the process, appreciating its resilience. Periodic expressions of defiance were obviously crucial for his sense of himself as real. What is more, his staunch antidogmatism made him allergic to the tendencies to canonize and idolize certain facets of theory. One senses in Winnicott a constant impulse to animate technical discussions; presumed knowledge was a dead end. A poignant example appears in a private letter he wrote to Gabriel Casuso, a Cuban psychoanalyst, in 1956. Casuso had written a paper in which he discussed his one-year-old son's discovery of his penis. In response, Winnicott playfully and defiantly turned conventional wisdom on its head by amusing himself with the question: "What is the penis symbolical of?" Winnicott wondered if, perhaps, to some extent the penis might be symbolical of "a snake or of a baby's bottle or of the baby's body as it moved in the womb before the arms and legs became significant. . . . Or, of other more fundamental objects as, for instance, the toothbrush, or some toy or . . . of the fish or reptile" (Rodman 1987, pp. 99–100). This was Winnicott's way of letting his colleagues know that he felt one should never presume one knows these things for certain.

The narcissistic aspect of Winnicott's temperament, his subtle displays of entitlement, never diminished the genuine respect he expressed toward those with whom he worked. Clare Winnicott said that frequently he would come bounding up the stairs exclaiming, "I have learned so much from my patients today!" (Grosskurth 1986, p. 399). At the end of supervision he would often thank a student for helping him. Jean-Marc Alby, professor of psychiatry and medical psychology at the Faculté de Médecine Saint-Antoine in Paris, had come to know Winnicott during a series of Anglo-French psychoanalytic meetings. Reflecting on Winnicott's modesty he commented:

> He did not believe himself to be omnipotent with his patients. He did not ask of them what they were not capable of giving. Thus he did not expect mothers to be very good or even good, but simply good enough; he sustained those who had difficulties with their children, telling them to do at least what they could, whereas Freud said that whatever mothers do it will be bad in any case." [Clancier and Kalmanovitch 1987, pp. 110–111]

In a similar vein, Winnicott himself describes how at times he makes interpretations "mainly to let the patient know the limits of my understanding" (Winnicott 1968, p. 219).

Both Alby's comments and Winnicott's "use" of interpretations to dispel omnipotent fantasies hint at Winnicott's wonderful capacity to adapt himself to the distinct needs of individual patients. It is precisely for this reason that there has been a certain misunderstanding about whether Winnicott actually engaged in "classical" analysis; he has been accused of substituting "holding" for "interpretation." There can be no doubt that Winnicott remained deeply suspicious of descriptions of analytic work that give credit to the interpretations for all that happens, especially for certain kinds of severely disturbed patients. He was far more attuned to the process that develops within the patient and the patient's capacity to make use of that process; although interpretive work is essential, more than just interpretation is involved in cure.

Still, from Winnicott's perspective, holding was not an alternative to interpretation in the sense of something the analyst does instead of analyzing. He
introduced the term *holding environment* as a metaphor for certain aspects of the
analytic situation and process *including* interpretation. The holding environment
provides a sense of safety and trust that depends upon the reliability of the
caretaker and the affective communication between caretaker and child. Since
reliability and affective communication express themselves in myriad ways, Winnicott was perfectly comfortable in believing that it in no way contradicted the
interpretive function. As he once noted:

> the analyst is holding the patient, and this often takes the form of
> conveying in words at the appropriate moment something that shows
> that the analyst knows and understands the deepest anxiety that is
> being experienced, or that is waiting to be experienced. [Winnicott
> 1979, p. 240]

Or, as one of his analysands confided:

> In my analysis most of the time he was quiet and in every way a
> "classical analyst." There were periods when I was more regressed when
> he responded to this state in me but not with any non-analytic
> interventions but with an understanding of my state of mind; and he
> was perhaps more silent even than usual, but made interpretations and
> comments which have remained with me for the rest of my life. His
> work with Margaret Little and Guntrip were obviously different from
> his work with me because their needs were different. As far as I am
> concerned I can only say he did not step outside the boundaries which
> I feel are necessary for ill patients and was always prepared to rethink
> and make discoveries which stemmed from his relationship with his
> patient rather than his knowledge of the theory.

From Winnicott's perspective, it is always a question of what the patient
needs and when and how the analyst offers what is offered. Like many other
analysts, he assumes there may be a long initial phase of treatment in which the
articulation of unconscious meaning of the patient's associations is not primary
(Ellman 1991). Similarly, during phases of regression to dependence, understanding
might go beyond the explication of unconscious wishes. At no point does Winnicott deny the crucial importance of the interpretive method. What he does caution
against, however, is what he calls the "making of interpretations" that, in his mind,
disrupts the "natural evolution of the transference." The analyst preoccupied with
"making" interpretations cannot be in a truly receptive frame of mind.

Furthermore, Winnicott believed that for certain individuals during certain phases of treatment, it is necessary for the analyst to adapt to their difficulties in appreciating the symbolic nature of transference. Transference, for Winnicott, is analogous to play in children. He is keenly attuned to the extent to which the patient is able to experience the illusion while recognizing that it is not fully real (Ellman 1991).

Winnicott's emphasis on the positive value of the illusory experience is at the root of what is perhaps the most common misreading of Winnicott's therapeutic stance. Especially among American practitioners, there is a tendency to equate Winnicott's use of the term *play* with a kind of jocularity, playfulness, or a playful mood (Bollas 1992). Although it is true that in many ways Winnicott gave permission to classical analysts to leave the cocoon of schizoid-like detachment and enter the therapeutic field in a more related and present way, he was neither advocating abandoning the seriousness of the endeavor nor denying the crucial significance of destructive fantasies. By playing, Winnicott did not mean foregoing interpretive work; he meant creating the psychic space necessary to formulate and use interpretations.

The analyst's interpretations cannot be used by the patient unless the patient is able to, in Winnicott's words, "place the analyst outside the area of subjective phenomenon" (Winnicott 1968, p. 219). This can only occur once the analyst has successfully "survived" the patient's destructive fantasies. The survival of the destroyed analyst means that this same analyst can be safely hated, repudiated, and rebelled against, all of which strengthens his or her being loved and relied upon. Conversely, Winnicott implies that unless one tolerates the ruthless side of one's character, it is impossible to have the full experience of the survival of the analyst. Trust is the confidence gained by the analyst's survival of the patient's destructiveness.

But where is the psychic space in which interpretations are formed and used? Much has been written about the relative importance of internal and external factors. Certainly, Winnicott's emphasis on "holding," the "facilitating environment," and "primary maternal preoccupation" have all contributed to a shift of attention—especially in the context of Klein's profound impact upon the British school—from the overall internal object to the role of the external object. But what is really crucial, from Winnicott's perspective, is precisely the interplay of the two. He turns our attention to the area of the intermediate and the success or failure to create it. Even interpretations, from Winnicott's perspective, emerge from neither the patient nor the analyst but from the movement of patient to analyst and analyst to patient (Bollas 1989).

That is why Winnicott, perhaps more than any other analyst, showed that for certain patients the only reality is the reality of that which is not there; their suffering is due to absence, to a gap, to a break in the continuity of what should have been. These are absences that lead to despair, not hope. Winnicott showed that the patient's subjective experience of the way environmental failures were repeated in the treatment was absolutely crucial. Countertransference, in this context, becomes a privileged instrument. The clinician is called upon to use his own reactions as keys not only to hidden meanings but to missing links of experience that are experienced as gaps (Green 1972).

Winnicott's capacity to look inward, to be in touch with his internal world, contributed to making him such an astonishing clinician. As Peter Rudnytsky commented: "Beneath his vitality and self-confidence, Winnicott must have had a tenaciously regressed ego of his own to tolerate his stressful work with patients" (Rudnytsky 1991, p. 140). Or, as Anne Clancier noted, he was "perhaps above all a man who allowed his unconscious to function, who knew how to identify with others at a deep level" (Clancier and Kalmanovitch 1987, p. 109). In his paper, "Hate in the Countertransference," Winnicott states quite explicitly that an analyst must be in touch with his or her own primitive nature. One cannot deny hate that really exists in oneself. He writes:

> If we are to become able to be the analysts of psychotic patients, we must have reached down to very primitive things in ourselves, and this is but another example of the fact that the answer to many obscure problems of psychoanalytic practice lies in further analysis of the analyst. [Winnicott 1947, p, 196]

It was precisely his ability to experience the ebb and flow of his own unconscious processes that also allowed Winnicott to respond genuinely and creatively to shared reality. As Marion Milner (1978) put it:

> Whatever it means to say that someone is a genius, I do wish to make clear that I believe Winnicott was on excellent terms with his primary process; it was an inner marriage to which there was very little impediment. [pp. 37–42]

This "inner marriage," however, was not without its external strains. It was probably this very same quality that led many who knew him to describe him as basically a loner and sometimes quite difficult (Grolnick 1990). He frequently gave the impression that he was asleep when he was listening, "waking up" only to ask a most pertinent question that seemed to come out of nowhere (Clancier and Kalmanovitch 1987). Serge Lebovici describes how during an International Congress of Psychoanalysis Winnicott chaired a session. Someone was reading a paper when he noticed that Winnicott had put his head down on his hands on the table, his eyes shut. When the speaker finished, Winnicott did not move. Lebovici remembers thinking at the time that Winnicott was dead. Then, suddenly, he sat up as if nothing at all had happened (Clancier and Kalmanovitch 1987).

To some, this undoubtedly appeared odd, if not downright eccentric. Evelyne Kestemberg, for example, met Winnicott in Stockholm in 1963. He appeared to her to have an "unconventional side" that sometimes seemed "strange." And she recalls her sense of fright watching him cross a street when nobody else would do so, feeling certain that he would certainly be run over. "I think the drivers saw that he was not looking," she writes, "for indeed he gave the impression that he was not looking, as if he were moving in a world of his own" (Clancier and Kalmanovitch 1987, p. 127). Was this a form of retreat? Withdrawal? Recourse to inner resources? Whatever the case, it was this "world of his own" that he brought to the clinical setting.

Winnicott's dialogue with his own inner processes seemed to express itself in the unique quality of his presence. Many who came in contact with him commented on his "poised somatic stillness" in one way or another (Khan 1975, p. xxxvi). Drawing on his experience as Winnicott's patient, for example, Khan wrote in the introduction to the French version of Winnicott's *Therapeutic Consultations* about

> the extraordinary tranquility emanating from that somatic presence, at once balanced and sparkling, that he possessed when he was sitting and "holding" the regressed patient in the clinical situation. Only those of us who have had the privilege to be his patients and were the object of his care can testify to his unique quality of attention, psychical as well as somatic. [Clancier and Kalmanovitch 1987, pp. 74–75]

Winnicott communicated powerfully with his patients because he knew how to speak with them about what felt most intimate in a way that did not come from outside the patient's own experience. This was Winnicott's corrective to certain excesses: the tendency of certain analysts to limit the patient's freedom of psychic movement by imposing interpretative matrices, and the stilted cerebral quality of some who claim to adhere to classical technique. We are dealing here with something more than analytic tact. Winnicott was exquisitely—some would say overly—concerned with the potential intrusiveness of the analyst. His way of working included presenting his ideas as expressions of his own subjectivity rather than his authority. This was the essence of his communicative genius: he regarded his own thoughts as subjective objects to be placed between the patient and himself rather than as official decodings of the patient's unconscious life (Bollas 1987).

The path Winnicott takes leads to the realm of preverbal affective communication. Just as individual affective development includes the mother's affects and her capacity to tolerate, contain, and respond to the baby's affective messages in a form that can be integrated by the infant's gradually developing sense of self, so does treatment include the unique affective climate of the analytic setting. It is not only the accuracy of the interpretation but the quality of the mutually lived experience that facilitates growth.

On the one hand, Winnicott assumed that everyone, child or adult, has a primary desire to be understood. He writes very little about "defenses" and a great deal about how patients guide therapists toward what they really need. Winnicott saw patients as more communicative than evasive, more collaborative than antagonistic. Playful self-revelation was far more curative, he believed, than "clever" interpretations.

At the same time, he theorized about an essentially isolated and noncommunicative core to the personality. This uncommunicative part of the personality is in no way pathological, however, since it strives to protect that which is most essential to the self. The task of the analyst is not to discover or uncover or decode this core, but to respect it.

In his therapeutic work, Winnicott knew how to tolerate and make clinical use of not-knowing. As one of his students observed, Winnicott's competence as a therapist included a "capacity to tolerate feeling ignorant or incompetent and a willingness to wait until something genuinely relevant and meaningful emerged" (Casement 1985, p. 9). Winnicott tended to work more from his body than from his mind. As he repeatedly acknowledged about himself: "I am not an intellectual and in fact I personally do my work very much from the body-ego" (Winnicott 1960a, p. 161). He challenged himself to put those bodily experiences into words. The process begins with muddle. This is not unlike the way the self comes into being according to Winnicott: from desultory formless activity reflected back. An infant, Winnicott claimed, gradually drifted from unintegrated to integrated states and back again. Winnicott had a unique capacity to tolerate and even enjoy both formless quiescence and the restive search for form. As he testified about himself in a lecture before students: "What you get out of me, you will have to pick out of chaos" (Grolnick and Barkin 1978, p. 37).

Marion Milner, in a memorial meeting of the British Institute of Psycho-analysis held after Winnicott's death, described this feature of his in vivid detail:

> Over the years, when we had a gap in time and we had arranged to meet and discuss some theoretical problem, he would open the door and then be all over the place, whistling, forgetting something, running upstairs, a general sort of clatter, so that I would be impatient for him to settle down. But, gradually, I came to see this as a necessary preliminary for the fiery flashes of intuition that would follow, when he did finally settle down. [Grolnick and Barkin 1978, p. 37]

Eventually, Winnicott was to elevate this personal characteristic into a principle of psychoanalytic technique: allowing for phases of "nonsense," when no thread of material should be analyzed because what is happening is the preliminary chaos that precedes the creative process. Muddle is not necessarily the expression of conflict, but the necessary formlessness out of which the self creates something real. It is precisely his receptivity to what Keats referred to as "uncertainties, Mysteries, doubts"—a receptivity uncontaminated by the need to flee into intellectual or philosophic systems—that is one of the hallmarks of Winnicott's clinical genius. He could remain content with half knowledge, which entails a provisional return to an "unintegrated" state. The unintegrated state is one in which the individual is able to flounder, to be without orientation, to exist without needing to either act or react (Winnicott 1958b).

Winnicott attempted to create in therapy a specialized atmosphere that would allow two people to be together without having to irritably reach after facts or meaning. "The person we are trying to help," he writes,

> needs a new experience in a specialized setting. The experience is one of a non-purposive state, as one might say a sort of ticking over of the unintegrated personality. I referred to this as formlessness. . . . In the relaxation that belongs to trust and to acceptance of the professional reliability of the therapeutic setting . . . there is room for the idea of unrelated thought sequences which the analyst will do well to accept as such, not assuming the existence of a significant thread. [Winnicott 1971c, pp. 64–65.]

Winnicott's technique obviously focused heavily on accepting unformed states and avoiding an intrusive attitude. He aimed to be as sensitive as possible to the patient's own spontaneous gestures and help the patient tolerate his inevitable failure to consistently do so. All this, of course, was rooted in his understanding of the purpose of the therapeutic encounter: to be a midwife to the natural developmental processes. From a different perspective, one could say that for Winnicott the real purpose of treatment was to prepare the individual for self-treatment. The patient develops the capacity to use the therapist and interpretations as objects that serve to establish the capacity to be alone. Initially, the patient learns to play in the presence of the therapist; eventually, play can proceed while the patient is alone, because the therapist is experienced as potentially present.

Self-cure, however, is not a flight into sanity; sanity, from Winnicott's point of view, could be as imprisoning as insanity. As he wrote once:

> There is . . . much sanity that has a symptomatic quality, being charged with fear or denial of madness, fear or denial of the innate capacity of every human being to become unintegrated, depersonalized, and to feel that the world is unreal. [Winnicott 1945, pp. 150]

Self-cure entails a strengthened ability to tolerate the constant dialectic between inside and outside, objective and subjective, sanity and insanity. What Winnicott wanted was not for his patients to feel sane, but for them to experience in a way that felt free; to feel real despite the demands of external reality, and to feel whole, while achieving a measure of insanity. As he claimed once, in saying a person is mad and that he has recovered,

> I am doing nothing worse than I would do in saying of myself that I was sane and that through analysis and self-analysis, I achieved a measure of insanity. Freud's flight to sanity could be something we psychoanalysts are trying to recover from. . . . [Winnicott 1964, pp. 483]

This volume offers the reader a taste of Winnicott's clinical work from three perspectives. Part I allows the reader to listen to Winnicott's own voice; it is composed of various examples of his clinical presentations demonstrating the breadth and depth of his work. It gathers together bits and pieces of Winnicott's work while aiming to give the reader a sense of him as an integrated whole. Like Winnicott, Part I covers a great deal of psychic territory: dreaming, communicating and not communicating, fear of breakdown, play, hate in the countertransference. It also covers a range of practical clinical concerns: varieties of psychotherapy, treatment of character disorders, the value of therapeutic consultations. Part I also provides examples of how Winnicott relates to various issues of technique: the use of interpretation, silences, the relationship of fantasy to body functioning. Bear in mind, however, that for Winnicott, activities such as the squiggle game are not really "techniques." The squiggle is not a readily adaptable format that can be employed by most clinicians; it is a mutual creation that is astonishingly effective only by virtue of Winnicott's conscious and unconscious associations.

A word of caution is in order: although Winnicott seems generally to have practiced what he preached, his clinical writings are somewhat of a failure. In fact, his most extensive and detailed clinical text, *Fragment of an Analysis*, of which only a brief excerpt is offered here, is probably his worst. The reason this is so is that the reader cannot get a sense of the passage of time, the hesitation, the silence as alive background, the exquisite timing of interventions, the bodily presence, the affective provision. Winnicott's interpretations tend to be too long and too wordy. It is evident that he frequently struggled unsuccessfully to inhibit his propensity to lecture. Winnicott admitted that he found it quite difficult to keep silent through sessions. To alleviate this problem, he would often write down premature interpretations or associations of his own on a piece of paper so as not to say them out loud.

Little of this, however, comes through in the majority of his clinical examples. Clare, his second wife, believed that this was because her husband was basically too impatient to devote more time to his clinical descriptions (Bollas 1992).

Whatever the reason, Winnicott's style of clinical communication—at both its best and its worst—is obviously difficult to pass on in writing outside of the shared experience. What his writing does convey is the brilliance and originality of his work.

Part II, "Remembering Winnicott," centers on personal recollections of Winnicott's clinical work. Although some of these sources have a sentimental gloss, they also convey a lot, both about the nature of Winnicott's clinical genius and about the potential problems inherent in his approach. It opens with an excerpt from an extensive interview given by Winnicott's wife, Clare, to Dr. Michael Neve in 1983, twelve years after her husband's death. This is followed by two tributes read at Winnicott's funeral—one by Masud Khan, the other by J. P. M. Tizard. Part II also includes personal reminiscences of a close follower and colleague of Winnicott, Marion Milner. Milner first trained as an industrial and educational psychologist before turning to psychoanalysis in the 1940s. She also painted professionally, exhibiting her work in the West End of London. Being the kind of person who tends to think in pictures, Milner offers the reader visual images of highlights of her personal contacts with Winnicott.

No account of Winnicott's clinical work would be complete without examples of his work from the perspective of patients whom he treated. Part II offers two. Margaret Little was in treatment with Winnicott from 1949 to 1955, and again in 1957. Little gives us an intimate picture of how Winnicott conducted her treatment, with its transference fluctuations and disorganizing regression. Little's vicarious and heartrending account demonstrates how the regression in the patient has a counterpart in the regression of the analyst.

Harry Guntrip first journeyed seven hours north to Edinburgh for double sessions with Fairbairn, and later seven hours south to London for sessions with Winnicott. His major difficulty—a pervasive background sense of unreality—was treated quite differently by the two analysts. It was with Winnicott that Guntrip felt most understood, especially when he reflected back to him how he felt alive by doing but was terrified of being. Guntrip believed that it was Winnicott's death that finally precipitated the dreams that cured his childhood amnesia. Glatzer and Evans (1977) have argued that Guntrip's treatment was actually a failure and that Winnicott reinforced his patient's narcissism instead of analyzing it. The reader is invited to judge for him-or herself whether or not Winnicott tended to become a "good" object rather than interpret his patient's wishes. Both the Little and Guntrip accounts show Winnicott selectively disclosing personal information to his patients. With Guntrip, Winnicott went so far as to tell him how much he enjoyed him as a patient. Guntrip's copious note-taking and involvement obviously made Winnicott feel good, and one cannot help but wonder about the countertransference implications of their relationship.

Part II also provides the reader with some examples of the profound effect Winnicott has had upon French psychoanalysts. Anne Clancier, a physician, psychoanalyst, and author of works on art and literature, interviews some of the leading figures of the psychoanalytic movement in France about the present effect that Winnicott has had on them. The interviewees include Jean-Marc Alby, professor, Department of Psychiatry and Medical Psychology, Faculté de Médecine Saint-Antoine, Paris; Evelyne Kestemberg, director of the Centre de Psychanalyse et Psychotherapie du XIII Arrondissement de Paris; Serge Lebovici, professor of child psychiatry, Université de Paris XIII; and Daniel Widlocher, professor of psychiatry, Université de Paris VI. Taken together, these interviews indicate that French psychoanalysts are both critical of and inspired by Winnicott's contribution.

"The ultimate compliment," Winnicott once averred, "is to be found and used." As the diverse sources in Part III demonstrate, Winnicott has fertilized many gardens. Clinicians are taking his ideas – play, absolute dependence, regression, transitional objects, potential space, holding environment, primary creativity – and using them in their own work. The section opens with Simon Grolnick's attempt to "imagine a fantasied Winnicott trying in one session to teach his method to an aspiring therapist." Grolnick's intention is to extract certain basic elements of Winnicott's clinical work and offer them as guiding principles. Grolnick's piece is followed by a series of articles that show how various clinicians are elaborating and transforming Winnicott's clinical ideas. Andre Green's article is an excerpt from his book On Private Madness, in which he pays tribute to Winnicott's notion of play in the analytic setting and elaborates upon it; Thomas Ogden extends Winnicott's notion of potential space to elaborate a theory of the psychopathology of the symbolic function; Philip Giovacchini utilizes Winnicott's ideas about dependence to understand a helpless patient who stresses her attempts to adapt to her milieu and to internalize helpful experiences; Renata Gaddini employs in her own clinical work Winnicott's ideas about regression and how facilitating regression can be a way to therapeutic progression; Arnold Modell discusses Winnicott's ideas about the holding environment in terms of both neurotic and narcissistic disorders.

As these pieces demonstrate, Winnicott is being found and created. He probably would have liked that.

Dodi Goldman, Ph. D.

REFERENCE

Bollas, C. (1987). The Shadow of the Object: Psychoanalysis of the Unthought Known. New York: Columbia University Press.

_____ (1989). *Forces of Destiny: Psychoanalysis and Human Idiom.* London: Free Association.

_____ (1992). Personal communication, October 23.

Casement, P. (1985). *Learning from the Patient.* New York: Guilford.

Clancier, A., and Kalmanovitch, J. (1987). *Winnicott and Paradox: From Birth to Creation.* London: Tavistock.

Davis, M., and Wallbridge, D. (1981). *Boundary and Space: An Introduction to the Work of D. W. Winnicott.* New York: Brunner/Mazel.

Ellman, S. (1991). *Freud's Technique Papers: A Contemporary Perspective.* Northvale, NJ: Jason Aronson.

Fromm, M. G. (1989). Winnicott's work in relation to classical psychoanalysis and ego psychology. In *The Facilitating Environment: Clinical Applications of Winnicott's Theory,* ed. M. G. Fromm and Bruce L. Smith. Madison, CT: International Universities Press.

Gillespie, W. H. (1971). A tribute read at Dr. Winnicott's funeral. *International Journal of Psycho-Analysis* 52:227.

Glatzer, H. T., and Evans, W. N. (1977). On Guntrip's analysis with Fairbairn and Winnicott. *International Journal of Psychoanalytic Psychotherapy* 6:81–98.

Green, A. (1972). *On Private Madness.* Madison, CT: International Universities Press.

Grolnick, S. (1990). *The Work and Play of Winnicott.* Northvale, NJ: Jason Aronson.

Grolnick, S., and Barkin, L. (1978). *Between Reality and Fantasy: Winnicott's Concepts of Transitional Objects and Phenomena.* Northvale, NJ: Jason Aronson.

Grosskurth, P. (1986). *Melanie Klein: Her World and Her Work.* New York: Alfred A. Knopf.

Guntrip, H. (1975). My experience of analysis with Fairbairn and Winnicott. *International Review of Psycho-Analysis* 2:155.

Khan, M. (1975). Introduction to D. W. Winnicott. In *Collected Papers: Through Paediatrics to Psycho-Analysis.* New York: Basic Books.

Little, M. L. (1990). *Psychotic Anxieties and Containment: A Personal Record of an Analysis with Winnicott..* Northvale, NJ: Jason Aronson.

Milner, M. (1972). For Dr. Winnicott Memorial Meeting, British Institute of Psycho-Analysis. January 19, 1972, London.

_____ (1978). D. W. Winnicott and the two-way journey. In *Between Reality and Fantasy: Winnicott's Concepts of Transitional Objects and Phenomena,* ed. S. Grolnick and L. Barkin. Northvale, NJ: Jason Aronson.

Phillips, A. (1988). *Winnicott.* Cambridge, MA: Harvard University Press.

Rees, K. (1991). Personal communication, September 23.

Riley, C. (1991). Personal communication, November 5.

Rodman, F. R. (1987). *The Spontaneous Gesture, Selected Letters of D. W. Winnicott.* Cambridge, MA: Harvard University Press.

Rudnytsky, P. L. (1991). *The Psychoanalytic Vocation: Rank, Winnicott, and the Legacy of Freud.* New Haven, CT: Yale University Press.

Trist, E. (1992). Personal communication, March 1.

Winnicott, D. W. (1941). The observation of infants in a set situation. In *Collected Papers: Through Paediatrics to Psycho-Analysis.* New York: Basic Books.

_____ (1942). Child department consultations. In *Collected Papers: Through Paediatrics to Psycho-Analysis.* New York: Basic Books.

_____ (1945). Primitive emotional development. In *Collected Papers: Through Paediatrics to Psycho-Analysis*. New York: Basic Books.

_____ (1947). Hate in the countertransference. In *Collected Papers: Through Paediatrics to Psycho-Analysis*. New York: Basic Books, 1975.

_____ (1948). Paediatrics and psychiatry. In *Collected Papers: Through Paediatrics to Psycho-Analysis*. New York: Basic Books, 1975.

_____ (1949). Birth memories, birth trauma, and anxiety. In *Collected Papers: Through Paediatrics to Psycho-Analysis*. New York: Basic Books.

_____ (1952). Psychoses and child care. In *Collected Papers: Through Paediatrics to Psycho-Analysis*. New York: Basic Books.

_____ (1957). The contribution of psycho-analysis to midwifery. In *The Family and Individual Development*. London: Routledge.

_____ (1958a). Child analysis in the latency period. In *The Maturational Processes and the Facilitating Environment*. London: Hogarth.

_____ (1958b). The capacity to be alone. In *The Maturational Processes and the Facilitating Environment*. London: Hogarth.

_____ (1960a). Counter-transference. In *The Maturational Processes and the Facilitating Environment*. London: Hogarth.

_____ (1960b). The theory of the parent–infant relationship. In *The Maturational Processes and the Facilitating Environment*. London: Hogarth.

_____ (1962). The aims of psycho-analytical treatment. In *The Maturational Processes and the Facilitating Environment*. London: Hogarth.

_____ (1963). Two notes on the use of silence. In *Psycho-Analytic Explorations*. Cambridge, MA: Harvard University Press.

_____ (1964). C. G. Jung, A review of memories, dreams, reflections. In *Psycho-Analytic Explorations*. Cambridge, MA: Harvard University Press, 1989.

_____ (1967). Postscript: D. W. W. on D. W. W. In *Psycho-Analytic Explorations*. Cambridge, MA: Harvard University Press.

_____ (1968). The use of an object and relating through identifications. In *Psycho-Analytic Explorations*. Cambridge, MA: Harvard University Press.

_____ (1970). On the basis for self in body. In *Psycho-Analytic Explorations*. Cambridge, MA: Harvard University Press.

_____ (1971a). *Therapeutic Consultations in Child Psychiatry*. New York: Basic Books.

_____ (1971b). The location of cultural experience. In *Playing and Reality*. New York: Penguin.

_____ (1971c). Playing: creative activity and the search for the self. In *Playing and Reality*. New York: Penguin.

_____ (1975). *Collected Papers: Through Paediatrics to Psycho-Analysis*. New York: Basic Books.

_____ (1977). *The Piggle: An Account of the Psychoanalytic Treatment of a Little Girl*. Madison, CT: International Universities Press.

_____ (1979). *The Maturational Processes and the Facilitating Environment*. London: Hogarth.

_____ (1984). *Deprivation and Delinquency*. New York: Routledge.

_____ (1989). *Psycho-Analytic Explorations*. Cambridge, MA: Harvard University Press.

Part I

LISTENING TO WINNICOTT

1

DREAMING, FANTASYING, AND LIVING

IN THIS CHAPTER I MAKE A FRESH ATTEMPT to show the subtle qualitative differences that exist between varieties of fantasying. I am looking particularly at what has been called fantasying and I use once more the material of a session in a treatment where the contrast between fantasying and dreaming was not only relevant but, I would say, central.[1]

The case I am using is that of a woman of middle age who in her analysis is gradually discovering the extent to which fantasying or something of the nature of daydreaming has disturbed her whole life. What has now become clear is that there is an essential difference for her between fantasying and the alternatives of dreaming, on the one hand, and of real living and relating to real objects, on the other. With unexpected clarity, dreaming and living have been seen to be of the same order, daydreaming being of another order. Dream fits into object-relating in the real world, and living in the real world fits into the dream-world in ways that are quite familiar, especially to psycho-analysts. By contrast, however, fantasying remains an isolated phenomenon, absorbing energy but not contributing-in either to dreaming or to living. To some extent fantasying has remained static over the whole of this patient's life, that is to say, dating from very early years, the pattern

---

1. For discussion of this theme from another angle see "The Manic Defence" (1935) in Winnicott (1958a).

being established by the time that she was two or three. It was in evidence at an even earlier date, and it probably started with a "cure" of thumb-sucking.

Another distinguishing feature between these two sets of phenomena is this, that whereas a great deal of dream and of feelings belonging to life are liable to be under repression, this is a different kind of thing from the inaccessibility of the fantasying. Inaccessibility of fantasying is associated with dissociation rather than with repression. Gradually, as this patient begins to become a whole person and begins to lose her rigidly organized dissociations, so she becomes aware[2] of the vital importance that fantasying has always had for her. At the same time the fantasying is changing into imagination related to dream and reality.

The qualitative differences can be extremely subtle and difficult to describe; nevertheless the big differences belong to the presence or the absence of a dissociated state. For instance, the patient is in my room having her treatment and a little bit of the sky is available for her to look at. It is evening. She says: "I am up on those pink clouds where I can walk." This, of course, might be an imaginative flight. It could be part of the way in which the imagination enriches life just as it could be material for dream. At the same time, for my patient this very thing can be something that belongs to a dissociated state, and it may not become conscious in the sense that there is never a whole person there to be aware of the two or more dissociated states that are present at any one time. The patient may sit in her room and while doing nothing at all except breathe she has (in her fantasy) painted a picture, or she has done an interesting piece of work in her job, or she has been for a country walk; but from the observer's point of view nothing whatever has happened. In fact, nothing is likely to happen because of the fact that in the dissociated state so much is happening. On the other hand, she may be sitting in her room thinking of tomorrow's job and making plans, or thinking about her holiday, and this may be an imaginative exploration of the world and of the place where dream and life are the same thing. In this way she swings from well to ill, and back again to well.

It will be observed that a time factor is operative which is different according to whether she is fantasying or imagining. In the fantasying, what happens happens immediately, except that it does not happen at all. These similar states are recognized as different in the analysis because of the fact that if the analyst looks for them he always has indications of the degree of dissociation that is present. Often the difference between the two examples cannot be discerned from a verbal description of what goes on in the patient's mind, and would be lost in a tape-recording of the work of the session.

This particular woman has rather exceptional talents or potential for various kinds of artistic self-expression and she knows enough about life and living and

---

2. She has a place from which to become aware.

about her potential to realize that in life terms she is missing the boat, and that she has always been missing the boat (at least, from near the beginning of her life). Inevitably she is a disappointment to herself and to all those relations and friends who feel hopeful about her. She feels when people are hopeful about her that they are expecting something of her or from her, and this brings her up against her essential inadequacy. All this is a matter for intense grief and resentment in the patient and there is plenty of evidence that without help she was in danger of suicide, which would simply have been the nearest that she could get to murder. If she gets near to murder she begins to protect her object so at that point she has the impulse to kill herself and in this way to end her difficulties by bringing about her own death and the cessation of the difficulties. Suicide brings no solution, only cessation of struggle.

There is an extremely complex etiology in any case like this but it is possible to say something brief about this patient's early childhood in a language which has some validity. It is true that a pattern was established in her early relationship to her mother, a relationship that too abruptly and too early became changed from very satisfactory to disillusionment and despair and the abandonment of hope in object-relating. There could also be a language for describing this same pattern in the little girl's relationship to her father. The father to some extent corrected where the mother had failed, and yet in the end he got caught up in the pattern that was becoming part of the child, so that he also failed essentially, especially as he thought of her as a potential woman and ignored the fact that she was potentially male.

The simplest way to describe the beginnings of this pattern in this patient is to think of her as a little girl with several older siblings, she being the youngest. These children were left to look after themselves a good deal, partly because they seemed to be able to enjoy themselves and to organize their own games and their own management with ever-increasing enrichment. This youngest child, however, found herself in a world that was already organized before she came into the nursery. She was very intelligent and she managed somehow or other to fit in. But she was never really very rewarding as a member of the group from her own or from the other children's point of view, because she could fit in only on a compliance basis. The games were unsatisfactory for her because she was simply struggling to play whatever role was assigned to her, and the others felt that something was lacking in the sense that she was not actively contributing-in. It is likely, however, that the older children were not aware that their sister was essentially absent. From the point of view of my patient, as we now discover, while she was playing the other people's games she was *all the time engaged in fantasying*. She really lived in this fantasying on the basis of a dissociated mental activity. This part of her which became thoroughly dissociated was never the whole of her, and over long periods her defense was to live here in this fantasying activity, and to watch herself playing the other children's games as if watching someone else in the nursery group.

By means of the dissociation, reinforced by a series of significant frustrations in which her attempts to be a whole person in her own right met with no success, she became a specialist in this one thing: being able to have a dissociated life while seeming to be playing with the other children in the nursery. The dissociation was never complete and the statement that I have made about the relationship between this child and the siblings was probably never entirely applicable, but there is enough truth in this kind of statement to enable a description to be usefully made in these terms.

As my patient grew older so she managed to construct a life in which nothing that was really happening was fully significant to her. Gradually she became one of the many who do not feel that they exist in their own right as whole human beings. All the time, without her knowing it, while she was at school and later at work, there was another life going on in terms of that part that was dissociated. Put the other way around, this meant that her life was dissociated from the main part of her, which was living in what became an organized sequence of fantasying.

If one were to trace this patient's life one could see the ways in which she attempted to bring together these two and other parts of her personality, but her attempts always had some kind of protest in them which brought a clash with society. All the time she had enough health to continue to give promise and to make her relations and her friends feel that she would make her mark, or at any rate that she would one day enjoy herself. To fulfill this promise was impossible, however, because (as she and I have gradually and painfully discovered) the main part of her existence was taking place when she was doing nothing whatever. Doing nothing whatever was perhaps disguised by certain activities which she and I came to refer to as thumb-sucking. Later versions of this took the form of compulsive smoking and various boring and obsessive games. These and other futile activities brought no joy. All they did was to fill the gap, and this gap was an essential state of doing nothing while she was doing everything. She became frightened during the analysis because she could see that this could very easily have led to her lying all her life in a bed in a mental hospital, incontinent, inactive and immobile, and yet in her mind keeping up a continuity of fantasying in which omnipotence was retained and wonderful things could be achieved in a dissociated state.[3]

As soon as this patient began to put something into practice, such as to paint or to read, she found the limitations that made her dissatisfied because she had let go of the omnipotence that she retained in the fantasying. This could be referred to in terms of the reality principle but it is more true, in the case of a patient like this, to

---

3. This is quite different from that "experience of omnipotence" which I have described as an essential process in the first experiences of the "me" and the "not-me" (cf. Winnicott 1962). The "experience of omnipotence" belongs essentially to dependence, whereas this omnipotence belongs to hopelessness about dependence.

speak of the dissociation that was a fact in her personality structure. Insofar as she was healthy and insofar as at certain times she acted like a whole person she was quite capable of dealing with the frustrations that belong to the reality principle. In the ill state, however, no capacity for this was needed because reality was not encountered.

Perhaps this patient's state could be illustrated by two of her dreams.

TWO DREAMS

1. She was in a room with many people and she knew that she was engaged to be married to a slob. She described a man of a kind that she would not in fact like. She turned to her neighbor and said: "That man is the father of my child." In this way, with my help, she informed herself at this late stage in her analysis that she has a child, and she was able to say that the child was about ten years old. In point of fact she has no child, yet she could see from this dream that she has had a child for many years and that the child is growing up. Incidentally this accounted for one of the early remarks she made in the session, which was to ask: "Tell me, do I dress too much like a child, considering that I am middle-aged?" In other words, she was very near to recognizing that she has to dress for this child as well as for her middle-aged self. She could tell me that the child was a girl.

2. There was a previous dream in a session a week earlier in which she felt intense resentment against her mother (to whom she is potentially devoted) because, as it came in the dream, her mother had deprived her daughter, that is herself, of her own children. She felt it was queer that she had dreamed in this way. She said: "The funny thing is that here I look as if I am wanting a child, whereas in my conscious thought I know that I only think of children as needing protection from being born." She added: "It is as if I have a sneaking feeling that some people do find life not too bad."

Naturally, as in every case, there is a great deal else that could be reported around these dreams which I omit because it would not necessarily throw light on the exact problem that I am examining.

The patient's dream about that man being the father of her child was given without any sense of conviction and without any link with feeling. It was only after the session had lasted an hour and a half that the patient began to reach to feeling. Before she went, at the end of two hours, she had experienced a wave of hate of her mother which had a new quality to it. It was much nearer to murder than to hate and also it felt to her that the hate was much nearer than it had previously been to a specific thing. She could now think that the slob, the father of her child, was put forward as a slob to disguise from her mother that it was her father, her mother's husband, who was the father of her child. This meant that she was very close to the feeling of being murdered by her mother. Here we were indeed dealing with dream and with life, and we were not lost in fantasying.

These two dreams are given to show how material that had formerly been locked in the fixity of fantasying was now becoming released for both dreaming and living, two phenomena that are in many respects the same. In this way the difference between daydreaming and dreaming (which is living) was gradually becoming clearer to the patient, and the patient was gradually becoming able to make the distinction clear to the analyst. It will be observed that creative playing is allied to dreaming and to living but essentially does *not* belong to fantasying. Thus significant differences begin to appear in the theory of the two sets of phenomena although it remains difficult to make a pronouncement or a diagnosis when an example is given.

The patient posed the question: "When I am walking up on that pink cloud, is that my imagination enriching life or is it this thing that you are calling fantasying which happens when I am doing nothing and which makes me feel that I do not exist?"

For me the work of this session had produced an important result. It had taught me that fantasying interferes with action and with life in the real or external world, but much more so it interferes with dream and with the personal or inner psychic reality, the living core of the individual personality.

It could be valuable to look at the subsequent two sessions in this patient's analysis.

The patient started with: "You were talking about the way in which fantasying interferes with dreaming. That night I woke at midnight and there I was hectically cutting out, planning, working on the pattern for a dress. I was all but doing it and was het-up. Is that dreaming or fantasying? I became aware of what it was all about but I was awake."

I found this question difficult because it seemed to be on the borderline in any attempt one might make to differentiate between fantasying and dreaming. There was psychosomatic involvement. I said to the patient: "We don't know, do we!" I said this simply because it was true.

We talked around the subject, how the fantasying is unconstructive and damaging to the patient and makes her feel ill. Certainly working herself up in this way restricts her from action. She talked about the way in which she often uses radio to hear talks rather than music, while playing patience. This experience seems to play into the dissociation almost as if it is making use of it and therefore giving her some degree of a sense that there might be an integration or a breakdown of the dissociation. I pointed this out to her and she gave me an example at the moment while I was talking. She said that while I was talking she was fiddling with the zip of her bag: why was it this end? how awkward it was to do up! She could feel that this dissociated activity was more important to her sitting there than listening to what I was saying. We both tried to make an attack on the subject in hand and to relate fantasying to dreaming. Suddenly she had a little insight and said that the meaning of this fantasying was: "So that's what *you* think." She had taken my interpretation of the dream and she had tried to make it foolish. There was evidently a dream which turned into this fantasying as she woke, and she wanted to make it quite clear to me that she was awake while fantasying. She said: "We need another word, which is neither dream nor fantasy." At this moment she reported that she had already "gone off to her job and to things that happened at work" and so here again while talking to me she had left me, and she felt dissociated as if she could not be in her skin. She remembered how she read the words of a poem but the words meant nothing. She made the remark that this kind of involvement of her body in the fantasying produces great tension, but since nothing is happening this makes her feel that she is a candidate for a coronary occlusion or for high blood pressure, or for gastric ulcers (which indeed she has had). How she longs to find something that will make her do things, to use every waking minute, to be able to say: "It is now and not tomorrow, tomorrow." One could say that she was noting the absence of psychosomatic climax.[4] The patient went on to say that she has been organizing the weekend as much as possible, but she is usually unable to distinguish between fantasying, which paralyzes action, and real planning, which has to do with looking forward to action. There is an enormous amount of distress because of the neglect of her immediate environment following the paralysis of action from which she suffers.

At a school concert the children sang "The skies will shine in splendor" exactly as she in school sang it forty-five years ago, and she was wondering whether some of the children would be like her, not knowing about the skies shining because eternally engaged in some form of fantasying.

We came round in the end to a discussion of this dream that she had reported at the beginning (cutting out a dress) which was experienced while she was awake and was a defense against dreaming: "But how is she to know?" Fantasying possesses her like an evil spirit. From here she went on to her great need to be able to possess herself and to be in possession and to be in control. Suddenly she became tremendously aware of the fact that this fantasying was not a dream and I could see from this that she had not been fully aware of this fact previously. It was like this: she woke, and there she was madly making a dress. It was like saying to me: "You think I can dream. Well, you are mistaken!" From here I was able to go to the dream

---

4. Another aspect of this type of experience I have discussed in terms of the capacity for ego orgasm (Winnicott 1958b).

equivalent, a dream of dressmaking. Perhaps for the first time I felt I could formulate the difference between dreaming and fantasying in the context of her therapy.

The fantasying is simply about making a dress. The dress has no symbolic value. A dog is a dog is a dog. In the dream, by contrast, as I was able to show with her help, the same thing would indeed have had symbolic meaning. We looked at this.

THE AREA OF FORMLESSNESS

The key word to be carried back into the dream was *formlessness*, which is what the material is like before it is patterned and cut and shaped and put together. In other words, in a dream this would be a comment on her own personality and self-establishment. In a dream it would only to some extent be about a dress. Moreover, the hope that would make her feel that something could be made out of the formlessness would then come from the confidence that she had in her analyst, who has to counteract all that she carries forward from her childhood. Her childhood environment seemed unable to allow her to be formless but must, as she felt it, pattern her and cut her out into shapes conceived by other people.[5]

At the very end of the session she had a moment of intense feeling associated with the idea that there had been no one (from her point of view) in her childhood who had understood that she had to begin in formlessness. As she reached recognition of this she became very angry indeed. If any therapeutic result came from this session it would be chiefly derived from her having arrived at this intense anger, anger that was about something, not mad, but with logical motivation.

At the next visit, another two-hour session, the patient reported to me that since the last visit she had done a very great deal. She was of course alarmed to have to report what I might take as implying progress. She felt that the key word was identity. A great deal of the first part of this long session was taken up with describing her activities, which included clearing up messes that had been left for months or even years, and also constructive work. Undoubtedly she had enjoyed a great deal of what she did. All the time, however, she was showing a great fear of loss of identity as if it might turn out that she had been so patterned, and that the whole thing was playing at being grown-up; or playing at making progress for the analyst's sake along the lines laid down by the analyst.

The day was hot and the patient was tired and she lay back in the chair and

---

5. This can be seen, then, in terms of compliance and a false self organization (cf. Winnicott 1960).

went to sleep. She had on a dress that she had been able to make wearable both for work and for coming to me. She slept for about ten minutes. When she woke she continued with her doubts about the validity of what she had actually done at home and even enjoyed. The important thing arising out of the sleep was that she felt it was a failure because she did not remember the dreams. It was as if she had gone to sleep in order to have a dream for the analysis. It was a relief to her when I pointed out that she went to sleep because she wanted to go to sleep. I said that dreaming is just something that happens when you are asleep. Now she felt that the sleep had done her a great deal of good. She wanted to go to sleep and when she woke up she felt much more real and somehow not remembering any dreams no longer mattered. She spoke about the way when your eyes go out of focus you know things are there but you don't quite see them, and how her mind is like that. It is out of focus. I said: "But in the dreaming that accompanies sleep the mind is out of focus because it is not focusing on anything unless coming round to the sort of dream that can be brought forward into waking life and reported." I had in mind the word formlessness from the last session, and I was applying it to generalized dream activity, as contrasted with dreaming.[6]

In the remainder of the session a great deal happened because the patient felt real and she was working at her problem with me her analyst. She gave a very good example of a tremendous lot happening all of a sudden in fantasying which was of the kind that paralyzes action. I took this now as the clue that she could give me towards the understanding of dream. The *fantasy* had to do with some people coming and taking over her flat. That is all. The *dream* that people came and took over her flat would have to do with her finding new possibilities in her own personality and also with the enjoyment of identifications with other people, including her parents. This is the opposite of feeling patterned and gives her a way of identifying without loss of identity. To support my interpretation I found a language which was suitable through knowing the patient's great interest in poetry. I said that fantasying was about a certain subject and it was a dead end. *It had no poetic value.* The corresponding dream, however, *had poetry in it,* that is to say, layer upon layer of meaning related to past, present, and future, and to inner and outer, and always fundamentally about herself. It is this poetry of the dream that is missing in her fantasying and in this way it is impossible for me to give meaningful interpretations about fantasying. I do not even try to use the material of fantasying that children in the latency period can supply in any quantity.

The patient went over the work that we had done with deeper recognition and understanding, especially feeling the symbolism in the dream which is absent in the limited area of fantasying.

---

6. One would expect a different EEG effect from these two extremes, according to which is dominant in any one phase.

She then made some excursions into imaginative planning of the future which seemed to give a prospect of future happiness that was different from the here-and-now fixity of any satisfaction that there can be in fantasying. All the time I needed to be extremely careful, and I pointed this out to her, lest I appeared to be pleased with her for all that she had done and the big change that had occurred in her; so easily she would have the feeling that she had fitted in and been patterned by me, and this would be followed by maximal protest and a return to the fixity of fantasying, playing patience and the other related routines.

Then a thought came to her and she said: "What was last time about?" (It is characteristic of this patient that she does not remember the previous session although often she is obviously affected by it, as in this case.) I had the word formlessness ready and from this she got back to the whole previous session and to the idea of the dress material before it was cut out and the feeling that nobody had ever recognized her need to start from formlessness. She repeated that she was tired today and I pointed out that this was something, not nothing. To some extent it is being in control: "I am tired, I am going to sleep." She had the same feeling in her car. She was tired but she did not go to sleep because she was driving. Here, however, she could go to sleep. Suddenly she saw a possibility of health and found it breath-taking. She used the words: "I might be able to be in charge of myself. To be in control, to use imagination with discretion."

There was one more thing to be done in this long session. She brought up the subject of playing patience, which she called a quagmire, and asked for help in regard to the understanding of it. Using what we had done together, I was able to say that patience is a form of fantasying, is a dead end, and cannot be used by me. If on the other hand she is telling me a dream—"I dreamt I was playing patience"— then I could use it, and indeed I could make an interpretation. I could say: "You are struggling with God or fate, sometimes winning and sometimes losing, the aim being to control the destinies of four royal families." She was able to follow on from this without help and her comment afterwards was: "I have been playing patience for hours in my empty room and the room really is empty because while I am playing patience I do not exist." Here again she said: "So I might become interested in me."

At the end she was reluctant to go, not as on the previous recent occasion because of sadness at leaving the only person she can discuss things with, but chiefly on this occasion because going home she might find herself less ill—that is to say, less rigidly fixed in a defense organization. Now, instead of being able to predict everything that will happen, she cannot any longer tell whether she will go home and do something she wanted to do or whether playing patience will possess her. It was clear that she had nostalgia for the certainty of the illness pattern and great anxiety about the uncertainty that goes with the freedom to choose.

It did seem to me at the end of this session that one could claim that the work of the previous session had had a profound effect. On the other hand, I was only too aware of the great danger of becoming confident or even pleased. The analyst's neutrality was needed here if anywhere in the whole treatment. In this kind of work we know that we are always starting again, and the less we expect the better.

REFERENCES

Winnicott, D. W. (1958a). *Collected Papers: Through Paediatrics to Psycho-Analysis*. London: Tavistock.

_____ (1958b). The capacity to be alone. In *The Maturational Processes and the Facilitating Environment*, pp. 29–36. London: Hogarth, 1965.

_____ (1960). Ego distortion in terms of true and false self. In *The Maturational Processes and the Facilitating Environment*, pp. 140–152. London: Hogarth, 1965.

_____ (1962). Ego integration in child development. In *The Maturational Processes and the Facilitating Environment*, pp. 56–63. London: Hogarth, 1965.

2

HATE IN THE
COUNTERTRANSFERENCE[1]

In THIS PAPER I WISH TO EXAMINE ONE aspect of the whole subject of ambivalence, namely, hate in the countertransference. I believe that the task of the analyst (call him a research analyst) who undertakes the analysis of a psychotic is seriously weighted by this phenomenon, and that analysis of psychotics becomes impossible unless the analyst's own hate is extremely well sorted-out and conscious. This is tantamount to saying that an analyst needs to be himself analyzed, but it also asserts that the analysis of a psychotic is irksome as compared with that of a neurotic, and inherently so.

Apart from psycho-analytic treatment, the management of a psychotic is bound to be irksome. From time to time I have made acutely critical remarks about the modern trends in psychiatry, with the too easy electric shocks and the too drastic leucotomies (Winnicott 1947, 1949). Because of these criticisms that I have expressed I would like to be foremost in recognition of the extreme difficulty inherent in the task of the psychiatrist, and of the mental nurse in particular. Insane patients must always be a heavy emotional burden on those who care for them. One can forgive those engaged in this work if they do awful things. This does not mean,

1. Based on a paper read to the British Psycho-Analytical Society on 5th February, 1947. *International Journal of Psycho-Analysis*, Vol. XXX, 1949.

however, that we have to accept whatever is done by psychiatrists and neuro-surgeons as sound according to principles of science.

Therefore although what follows is about psycho-analysis, it really has value to the psychiatrist, even to one whose work does not in any way take him into the analytic type of relationship to patients.

To help the general psychiatrist the psycho-analyst must not only study for him the primitive stages of the emotional development of the ill individual, but also must study the nature of the emotional burden which the psychiatrist bears in doing his work. What we as analysts call the countertransference needs to be understood by the psychiatrist too. However much he loves his patients he cannot avoid hating them and fearing them, and the better he knows this the less will hate and fear be the motives determining what he does to his patients.

One could classify countertransference phenomena thusly:

1. Abnormality in countertransference feelings, and set relationships and identifications that are under repression in the analyst. The comment on this is that the analyst needs more analysis, and we believe this is less of an issue among psycho-analysts than among psychotherapists in general.
2. The identifications and tendencies belonging to an analyst's personal experiences and personal development which provide the positive setting for his analytic work and make his work different in quality from that of any other analyst.
3. From these two I distinguish the truly objective countertransference, or if this is difficult, the analyst's love and hate in reaction to the actual personality and behavior of the patient, based on objective observation.

I suggest that if an analyst is to analyze psychotics or antisocials he must be able to be so thoroughly aware of the countertransference that he can sort out and study his *objective* reactions to the patient. These will include hate. Countertransference phenomena will at times be the important things in the analysis.

I wish to suggest that the patient can only appreciate in the analyst what he himself is capable of feeling. In the matter of motive: the *obsessional* will tend to be thinking of the analyst as doing his work in a futile obsessional way. A *hypo-manic* patient who is incapable of being depressed, except in a severe mood swing, and in whose emotional development the depressive position has not been securely won, who cannot feel guilt in a deep way, or a sense of concern or responsibility, is unable to see the analyst's work as an attempt on the part of the analyst to make reparation in respect of his own (the analyst's) guilt feelings. A *neurotic* patient tends to see the analyst as ambivalent towards the patient, and to expect the analyst to show a splitting of love and hate; this patient, when in luck, gets the love, because someone else is getting the analyst's hate. Would it not follow that if a *psychotic* is in a "coincident love-hate" state of feeling he experiences a deep conviction that the analyst is also only capable of the same crude and dangerous state of coincident love-hate relationship? Should the analyst show love, he will surely at the same moment kill the patient.

This coincidence of love and hate is something that characteristically recurs in the analysis of psychotics, giving rise to problems of management which can easily take the analyst beyond his resources. This coincidence of love and hate to which I am referring is something distinct from the aggressive component complicating the primitive love impulse, and implies that in the history of the patient there was an environmental failure at the time of the first object-finding instinctual impulses.

If the analyst is going to have crude feelings imputed to him he is best forewarned and so forearmed, for he must tolerate being placed in that position. Above all he must not deny hate that really exists in himself. Hate *that is justified* in the present setting has to be sorted out and kept in storage and available for eventual interpretation.

If we are to become able to be the analysts of psychotic patients we must have reached down to very primitive things in ourselves, and this is but another example of the fact that the answer to many obscure problems of psycho-analytic practice lies in further analysis of the analyst. (Psycho-analytic research is perhaps always to some extent an attempt on the part of an analyst to carry the work of his own analysis further than the point to which his own analyst could get him).

A main task of the analyst of any patient is to maintain objectivity in regard to all that the patient brings, and a special case of this is the analyst's need to be able to hate the patient objectively.

Are there not many situations in our ordinary analytic work in which the analyst's hate is justified? A patient of mine, a very bad obsessional, was almost loathsome to me for some years. I felt bad about this until the analysis turned a corner and the patient became lovable, and then I realized that his unlikeableness had been an active symptom, unconsciously determined. It was indeed a wonderful day for me (much later on) when I could actually tell the patient that I and his friends had felt repelled by him, but that he had been too ill for us to let him know. This was also an important day for him, a tremendous advance in his adjustment to reality.

In the ordinary analysis the analyst has no difficulty with the management of his own hate. This hate remains latent. The main thing, of course, is that through his own analysis he has become free from vast reservoirs of unconscious hate belonging to the past and to inner conflicts. There are other reasons why hate remains unexpressed and even unfelt as such:

Analysis is my chosen job, the way I feel I will best deal with my own guilt, the way I can express myself in a constructive way.

I get paid, or I am in training to gain a place in society by psycho-analytic work.
I am discovering things.

I get immediate rewards through identification with the patient, who is making
   progress, and I can see still greater rewards some way ahead, after the end of
   the treatment.

Moreover, as an analyst I have ways of expressing hate. Hate is expressed by the
   existence of the end of the "hour."

I think this is true even when there is no difficulty whatever, and when the patient
   is pleased to go. In many analyses these things can be taken for granted, so that
   they are scarcely mentioned, and the analytic work is done through verbal
   interpretation of the patient's emerging unconscious transference. The analyst
   takes over the role of one or other of the helpful figures of the patient's
   childhood. He cashes in on the success of those who did the dirty work when
   the patient was an infant.

These things are part of the description of ordinary psycho-analytic work,
which is mostly concerned with patients whose symptoms have a neurotic quality.

In the analysis of psychotics, however, quite a different type and degree of
strain is taken by the analyst, and it is precisely this different strain that I am trying
to describe.

Recently for a period of a few days I found I was doing bad work. I made
mistakes in respect of each one of my patients. The difficulty was in myself and it
was partly personal but chiefly associated with a climax that I had reached in my
relation to one particular psychotic (research) patient. The difficulty cleared up
when I had what is sometimes called a "healing" dream. (Incidentally I would add
that during my analysis and in the years since the end of my analysis I have had a
long series of these healing dreams which, although in many cases unpleasant, have
each one of them marked my arrival at a new stage in emotional development.)

On this particular occasion I was aware of the meaning of the dream as I woke
or even before I woke. The dream had two phases. In the first I was in the "gods" in
a theater and looking down on the people a long way below in the stalls. I felt severe
anxiety as if I might lose a limb. This was associated with the feeling I have had at
the top of the Eiffel Tower that if I put my hand over the edge it would fall off on
to the ground below. This would be ordinary castration anxiety.

In the next phase of the dream I was aware that the people in the stalls were
watching a play and I was now related through them to what was going on on the
stage. A new kind of anxiety now developed. What I knew was that I had no right
side of my body at all. This was not a castration dream. It was a sense of not having
that part of the body.

As I woke I was aware of having understood at a very deep level what was my
difficulty at that particular time. The first part of the dream represented the

ordinary anxieties that might develop in respect of unconscious fantasies of my neurotic patients. I would be in danger of losing my hand or my fingers if these patients should become interested in them. With this kind of anxiety I was familiar, and it was comparatively tolerable.

The second part of the dream, however, referred to my relation to the psychotic patient. This patient was requiring of me that I should have no relation to her body at all, not even an imaginative one; there was no body that she recognized as hers and if she existed at all she could only feel herself to be a mind. Any reference to her body produced paranoid anxieties, because to claim that she had a body was to persecute her. What she needed of me was that I should have only a mind speaking to her mind. At the culmination of my difficulties on the evening before the dream I had become irritated and had said that what she was needing of me was little better than hair-splitting. This had had a disastrous effect and it took many weeks for the analysis to recover from my lapse. The essential thing, however, was that I should understand my own anxiety and this was represented in the dream by the absence of the right side of my body when I tried to get into relation to the play that the people in the stalls were watching. This right side of my body was the side related to this particular patient and was therefore affected by her need to deny absolutely even an imaginative relationship of our bodies. This denial was producing in me this psychotic type of anxiety, much less tolerable than ordinary castration anxiety. Whatever other interpretations might be made in respect of this dream the result of my having dreamed it and remembered it was that I was able to take up this analysis again and even to heal the harm done to it by my irritability which had its origin in a reactive anxiety of a quality that was appropriate to my contact with a patient with no body.

The analyst must be prepared to bear strain without expecting the patient to know anything about what he is doing, perhaps over a long period of time. To do this he must be easily aware of his own fear and hate. He is in the position of the mother of an infant unborn or newly born. Eventually, he ought to be able to tell his patient what he has been through on the patient's behalf, but an analysis may never get as far as this. There may be too little good experience in the patient's past to work on. What if there be no satisfactory relationship of early infancy for the analyst to exploit in the transference?

There is a vast difference between those patients who have had satisfactory early experiences which can be discovered in the transference, and those whose very early experiences have been so deficient or distorted that the analyst has to be the first in the patient's life to supply certain environmental essentials. In the treatment of a patient of the latter kind all sorts of things in analytic technique become vitally important, things that can be taken for granted in the treatment of patients of the former type.

I asked a colleague whether he does analysis in the dark, and he said: "Why, no! Surely our job is to provide an ordinary environment: and the dark would be extraordinary." He was surprised at my question. He was orientated towards analysis of neurotics. But this provision and maintenance of an ordinary environment can be in itself a vitally important thing in the analysis of a psychotic, in fact it can be, at times, even more important than the verbal interpretations which also have to be given. For the neurotic the couch and warmth and comfort can be *symbolical* of the mother's love; for the psychotic it would be more true to say that these things *are* the analyst's physical expression of love. The couch *is* the analyst's lap or womb, and the warmth *is* the live warmth of the analyst's body. And so on.

There is, I hope, a progression in my statement of my subject. The analyst's hate is ordinarily latent and is easily kept so. In analysis of psychotics the analyst is under greater strain to keep his hate latent, and he can only do this by being thoroughly aware of it. I want to add that in certain stages of certain analyses the analyst's hate is actually sought by the patient, and what is then needed is hate that is objective. If the patient seeks objective or justified hate he must be able to reach it, else he cannot feel he can reach objective love.

It is perhaps relevant here to cite the case of the child of the broken home, or the child without parents. Such a child spends his time unconsciously looking for his parents. It is notoriously inadequate to take such a child into one's home and to love him. What happens is that after a while a child so adopted gains hope, and then he starts to test out the environment he has found, and to seek proof of his guardians' ability to hate objectively. It seems that he can believe in being loved only after reaching being hated.

During the second World War a boy of nine came to a hostel for evacuated children, sent from London not because of bombs but because of truancy. I hoped to give him some treatment during his stay in the hostel, but his symptom won and he ran away as he had always done from everywhere since the age of six when he first ran away from home. However, I had established contact with him in one interview in which I could see and interpret through a drawing of his that in running away he was unconsciously saving the inside of his home and preserving his mother from assault, as well as trying to get away from his own inner world, which was full of persecutors.

I was not very surprised when he turned up in the police station very near my home. This was one of the few police stations that did not know him intimately. My wife very generously took him in and kept him for three months, three months of hell. He was the most lovable and most maddening of children, often stark staring mad. But fortunately we knew what to expect. We dealt with the first phase by giving him complete freedom and a shilling whenever he went out. He had only to ring up and we fetched him from whatever police station had taken charge of him.

Soon the expected change-over occurred, the truancy symptom turned round, and the boy started dramatizing the assault on the inside. It was really a whole-time job for the two of us together, and when I was out the worst episodes took place.

Interpretation had to be made at any minute of day or night, and often the only solution in a crisis was to make the correct interpretation, as if the boy were in analysis. It was the correct interpretation that he valued above everything.

The important thing for the purpose of this paper is the way in which the evolution of the boy's personality engendered hate in me, and what I did about it.

Did I hit him? The answer is no, I never hit. But I should have had to have done so if I had not known all about my hate and if I had not let him know about it too. At crises I would take him by bodily strength, without anger or blame, and put him outside the front door, whatever the weather or the time of day or night. There was a special bell he could ring, and he knew that if he rang it he would be readmitted and no word said about the past. He used this bell as soon as he had recovered from his maniacal attack.

The important thing is that each time, just as I put him outside the door, I told him something; I said that what had happened had made me hate him. This was easy because it was so true.

I think these words were important from the point of view of his progress, but they were mainly important in enabling me to tolerate the situation without letting out, without losing my temper and without every now and again murdering him.

This boy's full story cannot be told here. He went to an Approved School. His deeply rooted relation to us has remained one of the few stable things in his life. This episode from ordinary life can be used to illustrate the general topic of hate justified in the present; this is to be distinguished from hate that is only justified in another setting but which is tapped by some action of a patient.

Out of all the complexity of the problem of hate and its roots I want to rescue one thing, because I believe it has an importance for the analyst of psychotic patients. I suggest that the mother hates the baby before the baby hates the mother, and before the baby can know his mother hates him.

Before developing this theme I want to refer to Freud. In *Instincts and Their Vicissitudes* (1915), where he says so much that is original and illuminating about hate, Freud says: "We might at a pinch say of an instinct that it loves the objects after which it strives for purposes of satisfaction, but to say that it hates an object strikes us as odd, so we become aware that the attitudes of love and hate cannot be said to characterize the relation of instincts to their objects, but are reserved for the relations of the ego as a whole to objects. . . ." This I feel is true and important. Does this not mean that the personality must be integrated before an infant can be said to hate? However early integration may be achieved—perhaps integration occurs earliest at the height of excitement or rage—there is a theoretical earlier stage in which whatever the infant does that hurts is not done in hate. I have used the term "ruthless love" in describing this stage. Is this acceptable? As the infant becomes able to feel to be a whole person, so does the word hate develop meaning as a description of a certain group of his feelings.

The mother, however, hates her infant from the word go. I believe Freud thought it possible that a mother may in certain circumstances have only love for her boy baby; but we may doubt this. We know about a mother's love and we appreciate its reality and power. Let me give some of the reasons why a mother hates her baby, even a boy:

The baby is not her own (mental) conception.

The baby is not the one of childhood play, father's child, brother's child, etc.

The baby is not magically produced.

The baby is a danger to her body in pregnancy and at birth.

The baby is an interference with her private life, a challenge to preoccupation.

To a greater or lesser extent a mother feels that her own mother demands a baby, so that her baby is produced to placate her mother.

The baby hurts her nipples even by suckling, which is at first a chewing activity.

He is ruthless, treats her as scum, an unpaid servant, a slave.

She has to love him, excretions and all, at any rate at the beginning, till he has doubts about himself.

He tries to hurt her, periodically bites her, all in love.

He shows disillusionment about her.

His excited love is cupboard love, so that having got what he wants he throws her away like orange peel.

The baby at first must dominate, he must be protected from coincidences, life must unfold at the baby's rate and all this needs his mother's continuous and detailed study. For instance, she must not be anxious when holding him, etc.

At first he does not know at all what she does or what she sacrifices for him. Especially he cannot allow for her hate.

He is suspicious, refuses her good food, and makes her doubt herself, but eats well with his aunt.

After an awful morning with him she goes out, and he smiles at a stranger, who says: "Isn't he sweet?"

If she fails him at the start she knows he will pay her out for ever.

He excites her but frustrates—she mustn't eat him or trade in sex with him.

I think that in the analysis of psychotics, and in the ultimate stages of the analysis, even of a normal person, the analyst must find himself in a position comparable to that of the mother of a new-born baby. When deeply regressed the patient cannot identify with the analyst or appreciate his point of view any more than the fetus or newly born infant can sympathize with the mother.

A mother has to be able to tolerate hating her baby without doing anything about it. She cannot express it to him. If, for fear of what she may do, she cannot hate appropriately when hurt by her child she must fall back on masochism, and I think it is this that gives rise to the false theory of a natural masochism in women. The most remarkable thing about a mother is her ability to be hurt so much by her baby and to hate so much without paying the child out, and her ability to wait for rewards that may or may not come at a later date. Perhaps she is helped by some of the nursery rhymes she sings, which her baby enjoys but fortunately does not understand?

"Rockabye Baby, on the tree top,
When the wind blows the cradle will rock,
When the bough breaks the cradle will fall,
Down will come baby, cradle and all."

I think of a mother (or father) playing with a small infant; the infant enjoying the play and not knowing that the parent is expressing hate in the words, perhaps in terms of birth symbolism. This is not a sentimental rhyme. Sentimentality is useless for parents, as it contains a denial of hate, and sentimentality in a mother is no good at all from the infant's point of view.

It seems to me doubtful whether a human child as he develops is capable of tolerating the full extent of his own hate in a sentimental environment. He needs hate to hate.

If this is true, a psychotic patient in analysis cannot be expected to tolerate his hate of the analyst unless the analyst can hate him.

If all this is accepted there remains for discussion the question of the interpretation of the analyst's hate to the patient. This is obviously a matter fraught with danger, and it needs the most careful timing. But I believe an analysis is incomplete if even towards the end it has not been possible for the analyst to tell the patient what he, the analyst, did unbeknown for the patient whilst he was ill, in the early stages. Until this interpretation is made the patient is kept to some extent in the position of infant – one who cannot understand what he owes to his mother.

An analyst has to display all the patience and tolerance and reliability of a mother devoted to her infant; has to recognize the patient's wishes as needs; has to put aside other interests in order to be available and to be punctual and objective; and has to seem to want to give what is really only given because of the patient's needs.

There may be a long initial period in which the analyst's point of view cannot be appreciated (even unconsciously) by the patient. Acknowledgement cannot be expected because, at the primitive root of the patient that is being looked for, there is no capacity for identification with the analyst; and certainly the patient cannot see that the analyst's hate is often engendered by the very things the patient does in his crude way of loving.

In the analysis (research analysis) or in ordinary management of the more psychotic type of patient, a great strain is put on the analyst (psychiatrist, mental nurse) and it is important to study the ways in which anxiety of psychotic quality and also hate are produced in those who work with severely ill psychiatric patients. Only in this way can there be any hope of the avoidance of therapy that is adapted to the needs of the therapist rather than to the needs of the patient.

REFERENCE

Winnicott, D. W. (1947). Physical therapy of mental disorder. *British Medical Journal* 1:68.
_____ (1949). Leucotomy. *British Medical Students' Journal* 3:2, 35.

3

COMMUNICATING AND
NOT COMMUNICATING[1]

Every point of thought is the centre of an intellectual world.
(Keats)

I HAVE STARTED WITH THIS OBSERVATION OF Keats because I know that my paper contains only one idea, a rather obvious idea at that, and I have used the opportunity for re-presenting my formulations of early stages in the emotional development of the human infant. First I shall describe object-relating and I only gradually get to the subject of communicating.

Starting from no fixed place I soon came, while preparing this paper for a foreign society, to staking a claim, to my surprise, to the right not to communicate. This was a protest from the core of me to the frightening fantasy of being infinitely exploited. In another language this would be the fantasy of being eaten or swallowed up. In the language of this paper it is *the fantasy of being found.* There is a considerable literature on the psycho-analytic patient's silences, but I shall not study or summarize this literature here and now. Also I am not attempting to deal comprehensively with the subject of communication, and in fact I shall allow myself considerable latitude in following my theme wherever it takes me. Eventually I shall allow a subsidiary theme, the study of opposites. First I find I need to restate some of my views on early object-relating.

---

1. Differing versions of this paper were given to the San Francisco Psychoanalytic Society, October 1962, and to the British Psycho-Analytical Society, May 1963.

OBJECT-RELATING

Looking directly at communication and the capacity to communicate one can see that this is closely bound up with relating to objects. Relating to objects is a complex phenomenon and the development of a capacity to relate to objects is by no means a matter simply of the maturational process. As always, *maturation* (in psychology) *requires and depends on the quality of the facilitating environment.* Where neither privation nor deprivation dominates the scene and where, therefore, the facilitating environment can be taken for granted in the theory of the earliest and most formative stages of human growth, there gradually develops in the individual a change in the nature of the object. The object *being at first a subjective phenomenon becomes an object objectively perceived.* This process takes time, and months and even years must pass before privations and deprivations can be accommodated by the individual without distortion of essential processes that are basic to object-relating.

At this early stage the facilitating environment is giving the infant the *experience of omnipotence;* by this I mean more than magical control, I mean the term to include the creative aspect of experience. Adaptation to the reality principle arises naturally out of the experience of omnipotence, within area, that is, of a relationship to subjective objects.

Margaret Ribble (1943), who enters this field, misses, I think, one important thing, which is the mother's identification with her infant (what I call the temporary state of Primary Maternal Preoccupation). She writes:

> The human infant in the first year of life should not have to meet frustration or privation, for these factors immediately cause exaggerated tension and stimulate latent defense activities. If the effects of such experiences are not skillfully counteracted, behavior disorders may result. For the baby, the pleasure principle must predominate, and what we can safely do is to bring balance into his functions and make them easy. Only after a considerable degree of maturity has been reached can we train an infant to adapt to what we as adults know as the reality principle.

She is referring to the matter of object-relating, or of id-satisfactions, but I think she could also subscribe to the more modern views on ego-relatedness.

The infant experiencing omnipotence under the aegis of the facilitating environment *creates and re-creates the object*, and the process gradually becomes built in, and gathers a memory backing.

Undoubtedly that which eventually becomes the intellect does affect the immature individual's capacity to make this very difficult transition from relating to subjective objects to relating to objects objectively perceived, and I have suggested that that which eventually gives results on intelligence testing does affect the individual's capacity to survive relative failures in the area of the adapting environment.

In health the infant creates what is in fact lying around waiting to be found. But in health *the object is created, not found.* This fascinating aspect of normal object-relating has been studied by me in various papers, including the one on "Transitional Objects and Transitional Phenomena" (1951). A good object is no good to the infant unless created by the infant. Shall I say, created out of need? Yet the object must be found in order to be created. This has to be accepted as a paradox, and not solved by a restatement that, by its cleverness, seems to eliminate the paradox.

There is another point that has importance if one considers the location of the object. The change of the object from "subjective" to "objectively perceived" is jogged along less effectually by satisfactions than by dissatisfactions. The satisfaction to be derived from a feed has less value in this respect of the establishment of object-relating than when the object is, so to speak, in the way. Instinct-gratification gives the infant a personal experience and *does but little to the position of the object*; I have had a case in which satisfactions eliminated the object for an adult schizoid patient, so that he could not lie on the couch, this reproducing for him the situation of the infantile satisfactions that eliminated external reality or the externality of objects. I have put this in another way, saying that the infant feels "fobbed off" by a satisfactory feed, and it can be found that a nursing mother's anxiety can be based on the fear that if the infant is not satisfied then the mother will be attacked and destroyed. After a feed the satisfied infant is not dangerous for a few hours, has lost object-cathexis.

Per contra, the infant's experienced aggression, that which belongs to muscle erotism, to movement, and to irresistible forces meeting immovable objects, this aggression, and the ideas bound up with it, lends itself to the process of placing the object, to placing the object separate from the self, insofar as the self has begun to emerge as an entity.

In the area of development that is prior to the achievement of fusion one must allow for the infant's behavior that is reactive to failures of the facilitating environment, or of the environment-mother, and this may look like aggression; actually it is distress.

In health, when the infant achieves fusion, the frustrating aspect of object behavior has value in educating the infant in respect of the existence of a not-me world. Adaptation failures have value *insofar as the infant can hate the object,* that is to say, can retain the idea of the object as potentially satisfying while recognizing its failure to behave satisfactorily. As I understand it, this is good psycho-analytic theory. What is often neglected in statements of this detail of theory is the immense development that takes place in the infant for fusion to be achieved, and for environmental failure therefore to play its positive part, enabling the infant to begin to know of a world that is repudiated. I deliberately do not say external.

There is an intermediate stage in healthy development in which the patient's most important experience in relation to the good or potentially satisfying object is the refusal of it. The refusal of it is part of the process of creating it. (This produces a truly formidable problem for the therapist in anorexia nervosa.)

Our patients teach us these things, and it is distressing to me that I must give these views as if they were my own. All analysts have this difficulty, and in a sense it is more difficult for an analyst to be original than for anyone else, because everything that we say truly has been taught us yesterday, apart from the fact that we listen to each other's papers and discuss matters privately. In our work, especially in working on the schizoid rather than the psycho-neurotic aspects of the personality, we do in fact wait, if we feel we know, until the patients tell us, and in doing so creatively make the interpretation we might have made; if we make the interpretation out of our own cleverness and experience then the patient must refuse it or destroy it. An anorexia patient is teaching me the substance of what I am saying now as I write it down.

THEORY OF COMMUNICATION

These matters, although I have stated them in terms of object-relating, do seem to affect the study of communication, because naturally there comes about a change in the purpose and in the means of communication *as the object changes over* from being subjective to being objectively perceived, insofar as the child gradually leaves the area of omnipotence as a living experience. Insofar as the object is subjective, *so far is it unnecessary for communication with it to be explicit.* Insofar as the object is objectively perceived, communication is either explicit or else dumb. Here then appear two new things, the individual's use and enjoyment of modes of communication, and the individual's non-communicating self, or the personal core of the self that is a true isolate.

A complication in this line of argument arises out of the fact that the infant develops two kinds of relationships at one and the same time—that to the environment-mother and that to the object, which becomes the object-mother. The environment-mother is human, and the object-mother is a thing, although it is also the mother or part of her.

Intercommunication between infant and environment-mother is undoubtedly subtle to a degree, and a study of this would involve us in a study of the mother as much as of the infant. I will only touch on this. Perhaps for the infant there is communication with the environment-mother, brought into evidence by the experience of her *unreliability*. The infant is shattered, and this may be taken by the mother as a communication if the mother can put herself in the infant's place, and if she can recognize the shattering in the infant's clinical state. When her *reliability* dominates the scene the infant could be said to communicate simply by going on being, and by going on developing according to personal processes of maturation, but this scarcely deserves the epithet communication.

Returning to object-relating: as the object becomes objectively perceived by the child so does it become meaningful for us to contrast communication with one of its opposites.

THE OBJECTIVELY PERCEIVED OBJECT

The objectively perceived object gradually becomes a person with part objects. Two opposites of communication are:

1. A simple not-communicating.
2. A not-communicating that is active or reactive.

It is easy to understand the first of these. Simple not-communicating is like resting. It is a state in its own right, and it passes over into communicating, and reappears as naturally. To study the second it is necessary to think in terms both of pathology and of health. I will take pathology first.

So far I have taken for granted the facilitating environment, nicely adjusted to need arising out of being and arising out of the processes of maturation. In the psycho-pathology that I need for my argument here the facilitation has failed in some respect and in some degree, and in the matter of object-relating the infant has developed a split. By one half of the split the infant relates to the presenting object, and for this purpose there develops what I have called a false or compliant self. By the other half of the split the infant relates to a subjective object, or to mere phenomena based on body experiences, these being scarcely influenced by an objectively perceived world. (Clinically do we not see this in autistic rocking movements, for instance; and in the abstract picture that is a cul-de-sac communication, and that has no general validity?)

In this way I am introducing the idea of a communication with subjective objects and at the same time the idea of an active non-communication with that which is objectively perceived by the infant. There seems to be no doubt that for all its futility from the observer's point of view, the cul-de-sac communication (communication with subjective objects) carries all the sense of real. *Per contra*, such communication with the world as occurs from the false self does not feel real; it is not a true communication because it does not involve the core of the self, that which could be called a true self.

Now, by studying the extreme case we reach the psycho-pathology of severe illness, infantile schizophrenia; what must be examined, however, is the pattern of all this insofar as it can be found in the more normal individual, the individual whose development was not distorted by gross failure of the facilitating environment, and in whom the maturational processes did have a chance.

It is easy to see that in the cases of slighter illness, in which there is some pathology and some health, there must be expected an active non-communication (clinical withdrawal) because of the fact that communication so easily becomes linked with some degree of false or compliant object-relating; silent or secret communication with subjective objects, carrying a sense of real, must periodically take over to restore balance.

I am postulating that in the healthy (mature, that is, in respect of the development of object-relating) person there is a need for something that corresponds to the state of the split person in whom one part of the split communicates silently with subjective objects. There is room for the idea that significant relating and communicating is silent.

Real health need not be described only in terms of the residues in healthy persons of what might have been illness-patterns. One should be able to make a positive statement of the healthy use of non-communication in the establishment of the feeling of real. It may be necessary in so doing to speak in terms of man's cultural life, which is the adult equivalent of the transitional phenomena of infancy and early childhood, and in which area communication is made without reference to the object's state of being either subjective or objectively perceived. It is my opinion that the psycho-analyst has no other language in which to refer to cultural phenomena. He can talk about the mental mechanisms of the artist but not about the experience of communication in art and religion unless he is willing to peddle in the intermediate area whose ancestor is the infant's transitional object.

In the artist of all kinds I think one can detect an inherent dilemma, which belongs to the co-existence of two trends, the urgent need to communicate and the still more urgent need not to be found. This might account for the fact that we cannot conceive of an artist's coming to the end of the task that occupies his whole nature.

In the early phases of emotional development in the human being, silent communicating concerns the subjective aspect of objects. This links, I suppose, with Freud's concept of psychic reality and of the unconscious that can never become conscious. I would add that there is a direct development, in health, from this silent communicating to the concept of inner experiences that Melanie Klein described so clearly. In the case descriptions of Melanie Klein certain aspects of a child's play, for instance, are shown to be "inside" experiences; that is to say, there has been a wholesale projection of a constellation from the child's inner psychic reality so that the room and the table and the toys are subjective objects, and the child and the analyst are both there in this sample of the child's inner world. What is outside the room is outside the child. This is familiar ground in psycho-analysis, although various analysts describe it in various ways. It is related to the concept of the "honeymoon period" at the beginning of an analysis, and to the special clarity of certain first hours. It is related to dependence in the transference. It also joins up with the work that I am doing myself on the full exploitation of first hours in the short treatments of children, especially antisocial children, for whom full-scale analysis is not available and not even always advisable.

But my object in this paper is not to become clinical but to get to a very early version of that which Melanie Klein referred to as "internal." At the beginning the word internal cannot be used in the Klein sense since the infant has not yet properly established an ego boundary and has not yet become master of the mental mechanisms of projection and introjection. At this early stage "inner" only means personal, and personal insofar as the individual is a person with a self in process of becoming evolved. The facilitating environment, or the mother's ego-support to the infant's immature ego, these are still essential parts of the child as a viable creature.

In thinking of the psychology of mysticism, it is usual to concentrate on the understanding of the mystic's withdrawal into a personal inner world of sophisti-cated introjects. Perhaps not enough attention has been paid to the mystic's retreat to a position in which he can communicate secretly with subjective objects and phenomena, the loss of contact with the world of shared reality being counterbal-anced by a gain in terms of feeling real.

> A woman patient dreamed: two women friends were customs officers at the place where the woman works. They were going through all the possessions of the patient and her colleagues with absurd care. She then drove a car, by accident, through a pane of glass.

There were details in the dream that showed that not only had these two women no right to be there doing this examining, but also they were making fools of themselves by their way of looking at everything. It became clear that the patient was mocking at these two women. They would not in fact get at the secret self. They stood for the mother who does not allow the child her secret. The patient said that in childhood (nine years) she had a stolen school book in which she collected poems and sayings, and she wrote in it "My private book." On the front page she wrote: "What a man thinketh in his heart, so is he." In fact her mother had asked her: "Where did you get this saying from?" This was bad because it meant that the mother must have read her book. It would have been all right if the mother had read the book but had said nothing.

Here is a picture of a child establishing a private self that is not communicating, and at the same time wanting to communicate and to be found. It is a sophisticated game of hide-and-seek in which *it is joy to be hidden but disaster not to be found.*

Another example that will not involve me in too deep or detailed a description comes from a diagnostic interview with a girl of seventeen. Her mother worries lest she become schizophrenic as this is a family trait, but at present it can be said that she is in the middle of all the doldrums and dilemmas that belong to adolescence.

Here is an extract from my report of the interview:

X. then went on to talk about the glorious irresponsibility of childhood. She said: "You see a cat and you are with it, it's a subject, not an object."

I said: "It's as if you were living in a world of subjective objects."

And she said: "That's a good way of putting it. That's why I write poetry. That's the sort of thing that's the foundation of poetry."

She added: "Of course it's only an idle theory of mine, but that's how it seems and this explains why it's men who write poetry more than girls. With girls so much gets caught up in looking after children or having babies and then the imaginative life and the irresponsibility goes over to the children."

We then spoke about bridges to be kept open between the imaginative life and everyday existence. She kept a diary when she was 12 and again at 14, each time apparently for a period of seven months.

She said: "Now I only write down things that I feel in poems; in poetry something crystallizes out,"—and we compared this with autobiography which she feels belongs to a later age.

She said: "There is an affinity between old age and childhood."

When she needs to form a bridge with childhood imagination it has to be crystallized out in a poem. She would get bored to write an autobiography. She does not publish her poems or even show them to anybody because although she is fond of each poem for a little while she soon loses interest in it. She has always been able to write poems more easily than her friends because of a technical ability which she seems to have naturally. But she is not interested in the question: are the poems really good? or not? that is to say: would other people think them good?

I suggest that in health there is a core to the personality that corresponds to the true self of the split personality; I suggest that this core never communicates with the world of perceived objects, and that the individual person knows that it must never be communicated with or be influenced by external reality. This is my main point, the point of thought which is the center of an intellectual world and of my paper. Although healthy persons communicate and enjoy communicating, the other fact is equally true, that *each individual is an isolate, permanently noncommunicating, permanently unknown, in fact unfound.*

In life and living this hard fact is softened by the sharing that belongs to the whole range of cultural experience. At the center of each person is an incommunicado element, and this is sacred and most worthy of preservation. Ignoring for the moment the still earlier and shattering experiences of failure of the environment-mother, I would say that the traumatic experiences that lead to the organization of primitive defenses belong to the threat to the isolated core, the threat of its being found, altered, communicated with. The defense consists in a further hiding of the secret self, even in the extreme to its projection and to its endless dissemination. Rape, and being eaten by cannibals, these are mere bagatelles as compared with the violation of the self's core, the alteration of the self's central elements by communication seeping through the defenses. For me this would be the sin against the self. We can understand the hatred people have of psycho-analysis which has penetrated a long way into the human personality, and which provides a threat to the human individual in his need to be secretly isolated. The question is: how to be isolated without having to be insulated?

What is the answer? Shall we stop trying to understand human beings? The answer might come from mothers who do not communicate with their infants except insofar as they are subjective objects. By the time mothers become objectively perceived their infants have become masters of various techniques for indirect communication, the most obvious of which is the use of language. There is this transitional period, however, which has specially interested me, in which transitional objects and phenomena have a place, and begin to establish for the infant the use of symbols.

I suggest that an important basis for ego development lies in this area of the individual's communicating with subjective phenomena, which alone gives the feeling of real.

In the best possible circumstances growth takes place and the child now possesses three lines of communication: communication that is *forever silent,* communication that is *explicit*, indirect and pleasurable, and this third or *intermediate* form of communication that slides out of playing into cultural experience of every kind.

Is silent communication related to the concept of primary narcissism?

In practice then there is something we must allow for in our work, the patient's non-communicating as a positive contribution. We must ask ourselves, does our technique allow for the patient to communicate that he or she is not communicating? For this to happen we as analysts must be ready for the signal: "I am not communicating," and be able to distinguish it from the distress signal associated with a failure of communication. There is a link here with the idea of being alone in the presence of someone, at first a natural event in child-life, and later on a matter of the acquisition of a capacity for withdrawal without loss of identification with that from which withdrawal has occurred. This appears as the capacity to concentrate on a task.

My main point has now been made, and I might stop here. Nevertheless I wish to consider what are the opposites of communication.

OPPOSITES

There are two opposites of communication, simple non-communication, and active non-communication. Put the other way round, communication may simply arise out of not-communication, as a natural transition, or communication may be a negation of silence, or a negation of an active or reactive not-communicating.

In the clear-cut psycho-neurotic case there is no difficulty because the whole analysis is done through the intermediary of verbalization. Both the patient and the analyst want this to be so. But it is only too easy for an analysis (where there is a hidden schizoid element in the patient's personality) to become an infinitely prolonged collusion of the analyst with the patient's negation of non-communication. Such an analysis becomes tedious because of its lack of result in spite of good work done. In such an analysis a period of silence may be the most positive contribution the patient can make, and the analyst is then involved in a waiting game. One can of course interpret movements and gestures and all sorts of behavioral details, but in the kind of case I have in mind the analyst had better wait.

More dangerous, however, is the state of affairs in an analysis in which the analyst is permitted by the patient to reach to the deepest layers of the analysand's personality because of his position as subjective object, or because of the dependence of the patient in the transference psychosis; here there is danger if the analyst interprets instead of waiting for the patient to creatively discover. It is only here, at the place when the analyst has not changed over from a subjective object to one that is objectively perceived, that psycho-analysis is dangerous, and the danger is one that can be avoided if we know how to behave ourselves. If we wait we become objectively perceived in the patient's own time, but if we fail to behave in a way that is facilitating the patient's analytic process (which is the equivalent of the infant's and the child's maturational process) we suddenly become not-me for the patient, and then we know too much, and we are dangerous because we are too nearly in communication with the central still and silent spot of the patient's ego-organization.

For this reason we find it convenient even in the case of a straightforward psycho-neurotic case to avoid contacts that are outside the analysis. In the case of the schizoid or borderline patient this matter of how we manage extra-transference contacts becomes very much a part of our work with the patient.

Here one could discuss the purpose of the analyst's interpreting. I have always felt that an important function of the interpretation is the establishment of the *limits* of the analyst's understanding.

INDIVIDUALS AS ISOLATES

I am putting forward and stressing the importance of the idea of the *permanent isolation of the individual* and claiming that at the core of the individual there is no communication with the not-me world either way. Here quietude is linked with stillness. This leads to the writings of those who have become recognized as the world's thinkers. Incidentally, I can refer to Michael Fordham's very interesting review of the concept of the Self as it has appeared in Jung's writings. Fordham writes: "The over-all fact remains that the primordial experience occurs in solitude." Naturally this that I am referring to appears in Wickes's *The Inner World of Man* (1938), but here it is not always certain that a distinction is always drawn between pathological withdrawal and healthy central self-communication (cf. Laing 1961).

Among psycho-analysts there may be many references to the idea of a "still, silent" center to the personality and to the idea of the primordial experience occurring in solitude, but analysts are not usually concerned with just this aspect of life. Among our immediate colleagues perhaps Ronald Laing is with most deliberation setting out to state the "making patent of the latent self" along with diffidence about disclosing oneself (cf. Laing 1961, p. 117).

This theme of the individual as an isolate has its importance in the study of infancy and of psychosis, but it also has importance in the study of adolescence. The boy and girl at puberty can be described in many ways, and one way concerns *the adolescent as an isolate*. This preservation of personal isolation is part of the search for identity, and for the establishment of a personal technique for communicating which does not lead to violation of the central self. This may be one reason why adolescents on the whole eschew psycho-analytic treatment, though they are interested in psycho-analytic theories. They feel that by psycho-analysis they will be raped, not sexually but spiritually. In practice the analyst can avoid confirming the adolescent's fears in this respect, but the analyst of an adolescent must expect to be tested out fully and must be prepared to use communication of indirect kind, and to recognize simple non-communication.

At adolescence when the individual is undergoing pubertal changes and is not quite ready to become one of the adult community there is a strengthening of the defenses against being found, that is to say being found before being there to be found. That which is truly personal and which feels real must be defended at all cost, and even if this means a temporary blindness to the value of compromise. Adolescents form aggregates rather than groups, and by looking alike they emphasize the essential loneliness of each individual. At least, this is how it seems to me.

With all this is bound up the crisis of identity. Wheelis, who has struggled with identity problems, states (1958) clearly and crudely the problem of the analyst's vocational choice, and links this with his loneliness and need for intimacy which, in analytic work, is doomed to lead nowhere. The analyst who seems to me to be most deeply involved in these matters is Erik Erikson. He discusses this theme in the epilogue of his book, *Young Man Luther* (1958), and he reaches to the phrase "Peace comes from the inner space" (i.e., not from outer space exploration and all that).

Before ending I wish to refer once more to the opposites that belong to negation. Melanie Klein used negation in the concept of the manic defense, in which depression that is a fact is negated. Bion (1962) referred to denials of certain kinds in his paper on thinking, and de Monchaux (1962) continued with the theme in her comment on Bion's paper.

If I take the idea of liveliness, I have to allow for at least two opposites, one being deadness, as in manic defense, and the other being a simple absence of liveliness. It is here that silence is equated with communication and stillness with movement. By using this idea I can get behind my rooted object to the theory of the Life and Death Instincts. I see that what I cannot accept is that Life has Death as its opposite, except clinically in the manic-depressive swing, and in the concept of the manic defense in which depression is negated and negatived. In the development of the individual infant living arises and establishes itself out of not-living, and being becomes a fact that replaces not-being, as communication arises out of silence. Death only becomes meaningful in the infant's living processes when hate has arrived, that is at a late date, far removed from the phenomena which we can use to build a theory of the roots of aggression.

For me therefore it is not valuable to join the word death with the word instinct, and less still is it valuable to refer to hate and anger by use of the words death instinct.

It is difficult to get at the roots of aggression, but we are not helped by the use of opposites such as life and death that do not mean anything at the stage of immaturity that is under consideration.

The other thing that I wish to tie on to the end of my paper is an altogether different opposite to aliveness or liveliness. This opposite is not operative in the majority of our cases. Usually the mother of an infant has live internal objects, and the infant fits into the mother's preconception of a *live* child. Normally the mother is not depressed or depressive. In certain cases, however, the mother's central internal object is dead at the critical time in her child's early infancy, and her mood is one of depression. Here the infant has to fit in with a role of *dead* object, or else has to be lively to counteract the mother's preconception with the idea of the child's deadness. Here the opposite to the liveliness of the infant is *an anti-life factor* derived from the mother's depression. The task of the infant in such a case is to be alive and to look alive and to communicate being alive; in fact this is the ultimate aim of such an individual, who is thus denied that which belongs to more fortunate infants, the enjoyment of what life and living may bring. To be alive is all. It is a constant struggle to get to the starting point and to keep there. No wonder there are those who make a special business of existing and who turn it into a religion. (I think that Ronald Laing's [1960, 1961] two books are attempting to state the predicament of this nature that many must contend with because of environmental abnormalities.) In healthy development the infant (theoretically) starts off (psychologically) without life and becomes lively simply because of being, in fact, alive.

As I have already said at an earlier stage, this being alive is the early communication of a healthy infant with the mother-figure, and it is as unselfconscious as can be. Liveliness that negates maternal depression is a communication designed to meet what is to be expected. The aliveness of the child whose mother is depressed is a communication of a reassuring nature, and it is unnatural and an intolerable handicap to the immature ego in its function of integrating and generally maturing according to inherited process.

You will have observed that I have brought the subject back to that of communication, but I do recognize that I have allowed myself a great deal of freedom in following trains of thought.

SUMMARY

I have tried to state the need that we have to recognize this aspect of health: the non-communicating central self, forever immune from the reality principle, and forever silent. Here communication is not non-verbal; it is, like the music of the spheres, absolutely personal. It belongs to being alive. And in health, it is out of this that communication naturally arises.

Explicit communication is pleasurable and it involves extremely interesting techniques, including that of language. The two extremes, explicit communication that is indirect, and silent or personal communication that feels real, each of these has its place, and in the intermediate cultural area there exists for many, but not for all, a mode of communication which is a most valuable compromise.

REFERENCES

Bion, W. (1962). The theory of thinking. International Journal of Psycho-Analysis 43:306–310.
de Monchaux, C. (1962). Thinking and negative hallucination. International Journal of Psycho-Analysis 43:311–314.
Erikson, E. (1958). Young Man Luther. London: Faber.
Laing, R. D. (1960). The Divided Self. London: Tavistock.
Ribble, M. (1943). The Rights of Infants. New York: Columbia University Press.
Wheelis, A. (1958). The Quest for Identity. New York: W. W. Norton.
Wickes, F. G. (1938). The Inner World of Man. New York: Farrar & Rinehart.
Winnicott, D. W. (1951). Transitional objects and transitional phenomena. Collected Papers: From Paediatrics through Psycho-Analysis. London: Tavistock.

4

FEAR OF BREAKDOWN[1]

PRELIMINARY STATEMENT

My clinical experiences have brought me recently to a new understanding, as I believe, of the meaning of a fear of breakdown.

It is my purpose here to state as simply as possible this which is new for me and which perhaps is new for others who work in psycho-therapy. Naturally, if what I say has truth in it, this will already have been dealt with by the world's poets, but the flashes of insight that come in poetry cannot absolve us from our painful task of getting step by step away from ignorance towards our goal. It is my opinion

---

1. This paper was published in the *International Review of Psycho-Analysis* (1974). The date of its composition is uncertain. There is some evidence that it was written as a lecture to be given at the Davidson Clinic in Edinburgh in 1963, but that another paper was given instead; it was around this time that Winnicott used the same material in the postscript to his paper "Classification" (1964), in *The Maturational Processes and the Facilitating Environment* (London: Hogarth Press; New York: International Universities Press, 1965). In the paper "The Psychology of Madness" (1965), Winnicott further addresses a difficulty that he encountered in the idea behind "Fear of Breakdown": namely, whether or not it is possible for a complete breakdown of defenses *to be experienced.* —ED.

that a study of this limited area leads to a restatement of several other problems that puzzle us as we fail to do as well clinically as we would wish to do, and I shall indicate at the end what extensions of the theory I propose for discussion.

INDIVIDUAL VARIATIONS

Fear of breakdown is a feature of significance in some of our patients, but not in others. From this observation, if it be a correct one, the conclusion can be drawn that fear of breakdown is related to the individual's past experience, and to environmental vagaries. At the same time there must be expected a common denominator of the same fear, indicating the existence of universal phenomena; these indeed make it possible for everyone to know empathetically what it feels like when one of our patients shows this fear in a big way. (The same can be said, indeed, of every detail of the insane person's insanity. We all know about it, although this particular detail may not be bothering us.)

EMERGENCE OF THE SYMPTOM

Not all our patients who have this fear complain of it at the outset of a treatment. Some do; but others have their defenses so well organized that it is only after a treatment has made considerable progress that the fear of breakdown comes to the fore as a dominating factor.

For instance, a patient may have various phobias and a complex organization for dealing with these phobias, so that dependence does not come quickly into the transference. At length dependence becomes a main feature, and then the analyst's mistakes and failures become direct causes of localized phobias and so of the outbreak of fear of breakdown.

MEANING OF "BREAKDOWN"

I have purposely used the term "breakdown" because it is rather vague and because it could mean various things. On the whole the word can be taken in this context to mean a failure of a defense organization. But immediately we ask: a defense against what? And this leads us to the deeper meaning of the term, since we need to use the word "breakdown" to describe the unthinkable state of affairs that underlies the defense organization.

It will be noted that whereas there is value in thinking that in the area of psycho-neurosis it is castration anxiety that lies behind the defenses, in the more psychotic phenomena that we are examining it is a breakdown of the establishment of the unit self that is indicated. The ego organizes defenses against breakdown of the ego-organization that is threatened. But the ego cannot organize against environmental failure insofar as dependence is a living fact.

In other words, we are examining a reversal of the individual's maturational process. This makes it necessary for me briefly to reformulate the early stages of emotional growth.

EMOTIONAL GROWTH, EARLY STAGES

The individual inherits a maturational process. This carries the individual along insofar as there exists a facilitating environment, and only in so far as this exists. The facilitating environment is itself a complex phenomenon and needs special study in its own right; the essential feature is that it has a kind of growth of its own, being adapted to the changing needs of the growing individual.

The individual proceeds from absolute dependence to relative dependence and towards independence. In health the development takes place at a pace that does not outstrip the development of complexity in the mental mechanisms, this being linked to neuro-physiological development.

The facilitating environment can be described as *holding*, developing into *handling*, to which is added *object-presenting*.

In such a facilitating environment the individual undergoes development which can be classified as *integrating*, to which is added *in-dwelling* (or *psycho-somatic collusion*) and then *object-relating*.

This is a gross over-simplification but it must suffice in this context.

It will be observed that in such a description forward movement in development corresponds closely with the threat of retrograde movement (and defenses against this threat) in schizophrenic illness.

ABSOLUTE DEPENDENCE

At the time of absolute dependence, with the mother supplying an auxiliary ego-function, it has to be remembered that the infant has not yet separated out the "not-me" from the "me"—this cannot happen apart from the establishment of "me."

PRIMITIVE AGONIES

From this chart it is possible to make a list of primitive agonies (anxiety is not a strong enough word here).
Here are a few:

1. A return to an unintegrated state. (Defense: disintegration.)
2. Falling forever. (Defense: self-holding.)
3. Loss of psycho-somatic collusion, failure of indwelling. (Defense: depersonalization.)
4. Loss of sense of real. (Defense: exploitation of primary narcissism, etc.)
5. Loss of capacity to relate to objects. (Defense: autistic states, relating only to self-phenomena.)

And so on.

PSYCHOTIC ILLNESS AS A DEFENSE

It is my intention to show here that what we see clinically is always a defense organization, even in the autism of childhood schizophrenia. The underlying agony is unthinkable.

It is wrong to think of psychotic illness as a breakdown, it is a defense organization relative to a primitive agony, and it is usually successful (except when the facilitating environment has been not deficient but tantalizing, perhaps the worst thing that can happen to a human baby).

STATEMENT OF MAIN THEME

I can now state my main contention, and it turns out to be very simple. I contend that clinical fear of breakdown is *the fear of a breakdown that has already been experienced*. It is a fear of the original agony which caused the defense organization which the patient displays as an illness syndrome.

This idea may or may not prove immediately useful to the clinician. We cannot hurry up our patients. Nevertheless we can hold up their progress because of genuinely not knowing; any little piece of our understanding may help us to keep up with a patient's needs.

There are moments, according to my experience, when a patient needs to be told that the breakdown, a fear of which destroys his or her life, *has already been*. It is a fact that is carried round hidden away in the unconscious. The unconscious here is not exactly the repressed unconscious of psycho-neurosis, nor is it the unconscious of Freud's formulation of the part of the psyche that is very close to neuro-physiological functioning. Nor is it the unconscious of Jung's which I would call: all those things that go on in underground caves, or (in other words) the world's mythology, in which there is collusion between the individual and the maternal inner psychic realities. In this special context the unconscious means that the ego integration is not able to encompass something. The ego is too immature to gather all the phenomena into the area of personal omnipotence.

It must be asked here: why does the patient go on being worried by this that belongs to the past? The answer must be that the original experience of primitive agony cannot get into the past tense unless the ego can first gather it into its own present time experience and into omnipotent control now (assuming the auxiliary ego-supporting function of the mother [analyst]).

In other words the patient must go on looking for the past detail which is *not yet experienced*. This search takes the form of a looking for this detail in the future.

Unless the therapist can work successfully on the basis that this detail is already a fact, the patient must go on fearing to find what is being compulsively looked for in the future.

On the other hand, if the patient is ready for some kind of acceptance of this queer kind of truth, that what is not yet experienced did nevertheless happen in the past, then the way is open for the agony to be experienced in the transference, in reaction to the analyst's failures and mistakes. These latter can be dealt with by the patient in doses that are not excessive, and the patient can account for each technical failure of the analyst as countertransference. In other words, gradually the patient gathers the original failure of the facilitating environment into the area of his or her omnipotence and the experience of omnipotence which belongs to the state of dependence (transference fact).

All this is very difficult, time-consuming and painful, but it at any rate is not futile. What is futile is the alternative, and it is this that must now be examined.

FUTILITY IN ANALYSIS

I must take for granted an understanding and acceptance of the analysis of psycho-neurosis. On the basis of this assumption I say that in cases I am discussing the analysis starts off well, the analysis goes with a swing; what is happening, however, is that the analyst and the patient are having a good time colluding in a psycho-neurotic analysis, when in fact the illness is psychotic.

Over and over again the analyzing couple are pleased with what they have done together. It was valid, it was clever, it was cosy because of the collusion. But each so-called advance ends in destruction. The patient breaks it up and says: So what? In fact the advance was not an advance; it was a new example of the analyst's playing the patient's game of postponing the main issue. And who can blame either the patient or the analyst? (Unless of course there can be an analyst who plays the psychotic fish on a very long psycho-neurotic line, and hopes thereby to avoid the final catch by some trick of fate, such as the death of one or other of the couple, or a failure of financial backing.)

We must assume that both patient and analyst really do wish to end the analysis, but alas, there is no end unless the bottom of the trough has been reached, unless *the thing feared has been experienced*. And indeed one way out is for the patient to have a breakdown (physical or mental) and this can work very well. However, the solution is not good enough if it does not include analytic understanding and insight on the part of the patient, and indeed, many of the patients I am referring to are valuable people who cannot afford to break down in the sense of going to a mental hospital.

The purpose of this paper is to draw attention to the possibility that the breakdown has already happened, near the beginning of the individual's life. The patient needs to "remember" this but it is not possible to remember something that has not yet happened, and this thing of the past has not happened yet because the patient was not there for it to happen to. The only way to "remember" in this case is for the patient to experience this past thing for the first time in the present, that is to say, in the transference. This past and future thing then becomes a matter of the here and now, and becomes experienced by the patient for the first time. This is the equivalent of remembering, and this outcome is the equivalent of the lifting of repression that occurs in the analysis of the psycho-neurotic patient (classical Freudian analysis).

FURTHER APPLICATIONS OF THIS THEORY

Fear of Death

Little alteration is needed to transfer the general thesis of fear of breakdown to a specific fear of death. This is perhaps a more common fear, and one that is absorbed in the religious teachings about an after-life, as if to deny the fact of death.

When fear of death is a significant symptom the promise of an after-life fails to give relief, and the reason is that the patient has a compulsion to look for death. Again, it is the death that happened but was not experienced that is sought.

When Keats was "half in love with easeful death" he was, according to my idea that I am putting forward here, longing for the ease that would come if he could "remember" having died; but to remember he must experience death now.

Most of my ideas are inspired by patients, to whom I acknowledge debt. It is to one of these that I owe the phrase "phenomenal death." What happened in the past was death as a phenomenon, but not as the sort of fact that we observe. Many men and women spend their lives wondering whether to find a solution by suicide, that is, sending the body to death which has already happened to the psyche. Suicide is no answer, however, but is a despair gesture. I now understand for the first time what my schizophrenic patient (who did kill herself) meant when she said: "All I ask you to do is to help me to commit suicide for the right reason instead of for the wrong reason." I did not succeed, and she killed herself in despair of finding the solution. Her aim (as I now see) was to get it stated by me that she died in early infancy. On this basis I think she and I could have enabled her to put off body death till old age took its toll.

Death, looked at in this way as something that happened to the patient but which the patient was not mature enough to experience, has the meaning of annihilation. It is like this, that a pattern developed in which the continuity of being was interrupted by the patient's infantile reactions to impingement, these being environmental factors that were allowed to impinge by failures of the facilitating environment. (In the case of this patient troubles started very early, for there was a premature awareness awakened before birth because of a maternal panic, and added to this the birth was complicated by undiagnosed placenta praevia.)

Emptiness

Again my patients show me that the concept of emptiness can be looked at through these same spectacles.

In some patients emptiness needs to be experienced, and this emptiness belongs to the past, to the time before the degree of maturity had made it possible for emptiness to be experienced.

To understand this it is necessary to think not of trauma but of nothing happening when something might profitably have happened.

It is easier for a patient to remember trauma than to remember nothing happening when it might have happened. At the time the patient did not know what might have happened, and so could not experience anything except to note that something might have been.

Example

A phase in a patient's treatment illustrates this. This young woman lay uselessly on the couch, and all she could do was to say: "Nothing is happening in this analysis!"

At the stage that I am describing the patient had supplied material of an indirect kind so that I could know that she was probably feeling something. I was able to say that she had been feeling feelings, and she had been experiencing these gradually fading, according to her pattern, a pattern which made her despair. The feelings were sexual and female. They did not show clinically.

Here in the transference was myself (nearly) being the cause now of her female sexuality fizzling out; when this was properly stated we had an example in the present of what had happened to her innumerable times. In her case (to simplify for the sake of description) there was a father who at first was scarcely ever present, and then when he came to her home when she was a little girl he did not want his daughter's female self, and had nothing to give by way of male stimulus.

Now, emptiness is a prerequisite for eagerness to gather in. Primary emptiness simply means: before starting to fill up. A considerable maturity is needed for this state to be meaningful.

Emptiness occurring in a treatment is a state that the patient is trying to experience, a past state that cannot be remembered except by being experienced for the first time now.

In practice the difficulty is that the patient fears the awfulness of emptiness, and in defense will organize a controlled emptiness by not eating or not learning, or else will ruthlessly fill up by a greediness which is compulsive and which feels mad. When the patient can reach to emptiness itself and tolerate this state because of dependence on the auxiliary ego of the analyst, then, taking in can start up as a pleasurable function; here can begin eating that is not a function dissociated (or split off) as part of the personality; also it is in this way that some of our patients who cannot learn can begin to learn pleasurably.

The basis of all learning (as well as of eating) is emptiness. But if emptiness was not experienced as such at the beginning, then it turns up as a state that is feared, yet compulsively sought after.

Non-Existence

The search for personal non-existence can be examined in the same way. It will be found that non-existence here is part of a defense. Personal existence is represented by the projection elements, and the person is making an attempt to project everything that could be personal. This can be a relatively sophisticated defense, and the aim is to avoid responsibility (at the depressive position) or to avoid persecution (at what I would call the stage of self-assertion [i.e., the stage of I AM with the inherent implication I REPUDIATE EVERYTHING THAT IS NOT ME]. It is convenient here to use in illustration the childhood game of "I'm the king of the castle—you're the dirty rascal").

In the religions this idea can appear in the concept of one-ness with God or with the Universe. It is possible to see this defense being negatived in existentialist writings and teachings, in which existing is made into a cult, in an attempt to counter the personal tendency towards a non-existence that is part of an organized defense.

There can be a positive element in all this, that is, an element that is not a defense. It can be said that *only out of non-existence can existence start*. It is surprising how early (even before birth, certainly during the birth process) awareness or a premature ego can be mobilized. But the individual cannot develop from an ego root if this is divorced from psycho-somatic experience and from primary narcissism. It is just here that begins the intellectualization of the ego-functions. It can be noted here that all this is a long distance in time prior to the establishment of anything that could usefully be called the self.

SUMMARY

I have attempted to show that fear of breakdown can be a fear of a past event that has not yet been experienced. The need to experience it is equivalent to a need to remember in terms of the analysis of psycho-neurotics.

This idea can be applied to other allied fears, and I have mentioned the fear of death and the search for emptiness.

5

FRAGMENT OF AN
ANALYSIS

TUESDAY, 8 FEBRUARY

The doorbell being out of order, he was kept waiting three minutes on the doorstep.

Patient: He reported having a formula for starting, and compared it with history-taking. Patients assume that you know more than you do.

Analyst: "I have to bear in mind that you may have been upset by the waiting." (Very unusual in the case of this patient.)

Patient: He went on with the description of how one gets stuck in history-taking between going into great detail or simply satisfying the patient, presumably pretending that one knows as much as one is expected to know. Somewhere in the middle of this he had a withdrawal. Recovering from the momentary withdrawal, he managed to report the fantasy belonging to the withdrawal, in which he was very annoyed with a surgeon who stopped midway in an operation. It was not so much that the surgeon was angry with the patient as that the patient was just out of luck; he was being operated on when the surgeon went on strike.

Analyst: I linked this with the reaction to the weekend following my acceptance of the dependence role. I brought in the bell failure, but this was relatively

49

unimportant; whereas the long breaks linked up directly with his statement at the end of the previous hour that I might not be able to stand his need for an extreme dependence, such as his living with me.

The effect of this interpretation was very marked; the analysis came alive and remained alive throughout the hour.

Patient: The patient spoke of his negativity, how it bores him and makes him depressed. It leaves him high and dry. When he gets sleepy he gets annoyed with himself. This negativity is a challenge. Sometimes speech is not worth the effort. He feels literally dried up. Sleep means lack of emotion. Nothing presents itself. He then described the contrast between his wife's attitude and his own. His wife feels things and cannot stand his own intellectual approach to everything and his absence of feelings. He began to discuss the word love, not its sexual aspect.

He then spoke about Jones' article in *The Observer*,[1] mentioning especially the child with the button and the way Jones linked this up with cannibalism.

I made no interpretation, knowing that he was coming the next day, and that the theme would reappear.

WEDNESDAY, 9 FEBRUARY

The patient came excited.

Patient: "I feel better." (Elation.) He reported having laughed with people. There was something new about all this. It was natural.

Analyst: I found that he could not remember what happened last time and I gave a summary. In giving this I was unable to remember the content of the withdrawal fantasy and said so. (It always helps this man if I am able to remind him of the material of the last hour.)

Patient: He said that this liberation brought about by his feeling better made him independent of his wife. He now had a bargaining weapon with her which he could use, although he felt no vindictiveness against her. He did not need to beg for sympathy any longer. It used to be nothing but himself, hopeless.

Analyst: I said that it seemed to have strengthened his whole personality, his getting a little bit nearer to cannibalism and to instincts.

Patient: He said that to make matters better he had had a discussion with a surgeon, very friendly, very satisfactory in result.

---

1. "The Dawn of Conscience" in the *The Observer* of 6 February 1955.

Analyst: Here I remembered his withdrawal fantasy and reminded him of it.

Patient: He continued that the surgeon had argued against the idea of an operation in regard to a certain treatment of a patient. The surgeon understood, but in a sense he had downed tools.

Pause.

Analyst: I interpreted that excitement was present but well under control because it brings its own anxieties.

Patient: He reported other minor incidents. "I can afford to be excited. A year ago the same things happened but as I could not afford to be excited they passed over me. I allowed an intellectual appreciation only. I could not afford to do without my depression. In fact I could not understand how anyone could get excited, and I had no conception of feeling competent. Now, because of the progress that seems to be maintained here in this treatment, I can let things go." *Pause.* "I do not want to talk about excitement."

Analyst: "The point of excitement is being excited."

Patient: "There is a risk involved. You look silly. People might laugh if you prattle." (This word belongs in the analysis to a phase of his early childhood in which it was said that he prattled before he became sullen and withdrawn.) "And then you are left holding the baby." (Meaning excitement.)

Pause.

Analyst: I made an interpretation joining together the prattling and the holding of the baby.[2]

Patient: "People despise adult prattling. I have always been serious-minded. Now I feel that I could prattle naturally outside the analysis. In the analysis I can only be serious even now or I can be excited about something. There is something different about excitement in its own right. The danger is that if you are excited you lose it. You have it taken away or undermined."

Analyst: "If you show excitement it gets bagged." (I might have interpreted the castration anxiety here but refrained.)

Patient: "Yes. You are light-hearted and then you become heavy if the excitement is claimed and considered to be attached to something. It is important to be fancy free, but this can only happen in the absence of a love relationship. I was thinking of this last night. The relationship to the girl is a fancy free affair. The relationship to my wife cannot be so."

Analyst: I reminded him that he was also talking about masturbation, and he developed the theme as he already was on the point of doing so.

Patient: "The advantage is that there is no risk taken; no social complications." He

---

2. For the concept of *holding* see Winnicott's (1960) "The Theory of the Parent–Infant Relationship" in *The Maturational Processes and the Facilitating Environment*, pp. 37–55. New York: International Universities Press, 1965.

was struck by the unexpected fact that when he was married the need continued, even though this jeopardized his potency.

At this point there were bell noises; a man was mending the bell. This caused an interruption, and the patient was surprised to find that he minded.

"It is usually the other way. You seem to be overworried when there are interruptions and I cannot see that they matter. Just now, however, with such intimate matters under discussion, I see for the first time the truth of what you have said about the setting of analysis and its importance."

Analyst: I linked this up with the theme of dependence.

THURSDAY, 10 FEBRUARY

Patient: He continued to report excitement, although this was at a low level compared with the elation.

Analyst: "It appears that you have lived most of your life at a level below par in regard to excitement, and now when you come even to ordinary excitability you feel conscious of it."

Patient: "Yes, I find I am able to be gay and lighthearted with less effort. I used to be able at times but it was always an act. Something happened today which made me realize, however, that caution is needed. There are still unanswered questions to do with work and family. I feel apprehensiveness and guilt at feeling well, and of course at having a secret affair. It would be dangerous to get too excited, that is to say, at the expense of the future. I cannot afford to ignore what remains to be done. But there is a difference. I can now look forward to a future. In the past it seemed that I had difficulties in the present with no solution, as well as no prospect for the future. There was no hope of living an ordinary life ever. My depression was something to do with looking for dependence. I could say that in the dependence and therefore in the depression I was claiming my birthright."

Analyst: "The hopelessness about the future and the present therefore turns out to be a hopelessness in the past which you did not know about. What you are looking for is your capacity to love, and, without our knowing all the details, we can say that some failure in your early life made you doubt your capacity to love."

Patient: After agreeing with all this, he said: "There is the task still to be done."

Analyst: I made a rather wide interpretation linking up the reality that belonged to his discovering his love of his daughter and reminding him that this followed tears at the cinema.

Patient: "I have always had an intellectual idea of pleasure associated with pain. Similarly I associate love with sadness. I told somebody this once. It was at a

Youth Club talk on sex. I said that there was an association between love and sadness, and I was forcibly rebuked and called sadistic."

Analyst: I remarked that nevertheless he knew that he was right and that the speaker was wrong.

Patient: "Perhaps she (the speaker) knew but she found it inconvenient to agree with this point in the setting."

Analyst: "There is no need for me to try to answer this because the answer is evolving in your analysis."

Patient: "I was not being sadistic, and this comment was therefore not true."

Analyst: Here I started making a rather more comprehensive interpretation, bringing in the word cannibalism which came from Ernest Jones' article in *The Observer.*

Patient: He filled out my remark by saying that he had always recognized that biting was important in love-making.

Analyst: In the comprehensive interpretation I spoke of this infancy situation which he had missed in some way and which he was needing me to provide in the analysis, speaking of the holding of a situation in time, so that the dependence phenomena could be tested in relation to the instinctual moments and ideas. I happened to say in illustration that an infant might have three nurses in the course of a day in an institution, thus presenting a difficulty in regard to reparation.[3]

Patient: He picked up the idea of my interpretation quickly and said: "In my case there seemed to be four, because of my four lives—hospital, home, analysis, and the girl. Everything depends on my being able to describe in the analysis what happens in the other phases." He then said: "But adversely what is happening is that this split in the total situation is giving me more to talk about. In any one of the four places I have a lot to say, whereas usually I feel exhausted if I say anything and have nothing more to say."

Analyst: I spoke first about his need to feel that he was contributing in this analysis and that if he has nothing to say he has often felt awkward and deficient. I said: "We are also talking about one of the origins of conversation in which each individual is integrating all the material of the split-off experiences by talking in one situation about another, there being in health a basic unified pattern."

Previously all he had been able to find were various examples of the original pattern which he was all the time seeking. Now in the analysis he had found the pattern and could benefit from being able to split it up.

---

3. Compare with Winnicott's (1963) "The Development of the Capacity for Concern" in *The Maturational Processes and the Facilitating Environment,* pp. 73–82. New York: International Universities Press, 1965.

Pause.

Patient: "There is a danger of going too far. One could get confused."

Analyst: At first I thought that he meant that my interpretation had been too complex. He was referring, however, to the innumerable odd things that he could bring into the analysis, and I was reminded of his having been noted for prattling until a certain age in early childhood when he changed over into being unable to talk except seriously.

Patient: He now told me about the fear of a hopeless jumble of bits and pieces, something that he called being too widely split. He chose to speak about the ward round that he does on Thursdays with Dr. X, especially as this always affects the Thursday evening session. I had never been told this fact before. Dr. X's round is never simple. It is always a series of challenges. He is full of ideas and demands. At present there is a new development in that the patient has innumerable ideas of his own and he now stands up to his chief, and they both enjoy the contact. There was also the matter of a rather difficult surgeon. He had written a history of a patient, and had received an amusing letter back thanking him for his very detailed and comprehensive report. This letter was praise, and it came just when the patient was in a mood to receive praise, perhaps for the first time for many years. He certainly welcomed it. Just now there seemed to be too much of everything. He became worried always when there were innumerable bits, and for this reason had developed a technique of generalizing and thereby simplifying issues.

Analyst: The alternative to an ordering of the material was getting lost in innumerable fragments. It would seem that the patient here was describing his growing ability to tolerate disintegration or unintegration.

Patient: He said that these ideas felt like too many children.

Analyst: My job as analyst was to help deal with these children and to sort them out and get some sort of order into the management of them. I pointed out that he was cluttered up with reparation capacity when he had not yet found the sadism that would indicate the use of the reparation phenomenon. The excitement in relation to me had only been indicated and had not appeared.

Patient: He then described the analytic situation as a difficult one for the excited patient. Analysts are well protected. They avoid violation by special mechanisms for protection. This was especially evident at the Institution, where patients and doctors do not meet except professionally, and appointments are arranged indirectly. The doctors also are having analysis. It is only possible to hurt them by actual physical violence. Once some men tried to break through and succeeded in annoying some of the doctors by deliberate rudeness and were rebuked. An analyst ought not to act that way. Or why do they? "There are two ideas," he added here. "One, I am annoyed that the analysts were not

immune to verbal trauma. At the same time I am annoyed at their invulner-
ability. You can only annoy an analyst by not turning up, but that's foolish."
Analyst: I said that he had omitted talking about not turning up (I ought to have
said playing at, but I left this out). It was as if he had told me a dream in which
he had not turned up, and we could now look into the meaning of this dream.
We could see that it contains sadism for him at the moment and that the
sadism leads us to cannibalism.

As an additional interpretation I said that, in joining together all the
different phases of his life, there was one which was the surgeon's praise. I had
been likened to the surgeon in the material of the previous hour, and it was
important to him that I should be able to see that I have praised him through
the surgeon.

Patient: His response to this was that he thought that I ought to be able to show
excitement along with his excitement. Why could I not be proud of his
achievement?

Analyst: I replied to this that I was indeed excited, although perhaps not as excited
as he would be since I was also not so much in despair during his despair
periods. I was in a position to see the thing as a whole.

Patient: He continued on the theme of the analyst's ability to be excited at progress
in patients and I said:

Analyst: "You can take it from me that I do this kind of work because I think it is the
most exciting thing a doctor can do, and it is certainly better from my point of
view when patients are doing well than when they are not."

6

INTERPRETATION IN
PSYCHO-ANALYSIS

I T IS IMPORTANT FROM TIME TO TIME to look at the basic principles of the psycho-analytic technique and to attempt to reassess the importance of the various elements that the classical technique comprises. It would be generally conceded that an important part of psycho-analytic technique is interpretation, and it is my purpose here to study once more this particular part of what we do.

The word "interpretation" implies that we are using words, and there is a further implication which is that material supplied by the patient is verbalized. In its simplest form there is the basic rule, which still has force, although many analysts never instruct their patients even on this detail. By this time, after more than half a century of psycho-analysis, patients know that they are expected to say what comes to their minds and not to withhold. It is also generally recognized now that a great deal of communication takes place from patient to analyst that is not verbalized.

This may have been noticed first in terms of the nuances of speech and the various ways in which speech certainly involved a great deal more than the meaning of the words used. Gradually analysts found themselves interpreting silences and movements and a whole host of behavioral details which were outside the realm of verbalization. Nevertheless there were always analysts who very much preferred to stick to the verbalized material offered by the patient. When this works it has obvious advantages in that the patient does not feel persecuted by the observer's eyes.

With a silent patient, a man of 25 years, I once interpreted the movement of his fingers as his hands lay clasped across his chest. He said to me: "If you start interpreting that sort of thing then I shall have to transfer that sort of activity to something else which does not show." In other words, he was pointing out to me that unless he had verbalized his communication it was not for me to make comment.

There is also the vast subject which can be explored of the analyst's communications that are not conveyed in direct verbalization or even in errors of verbalization. There is no need to develop this theme, because it is obvious, but it starts off with the analyst's tone of voice and the way in which, for instance, a moralistic attitude may or may not show in a statement which by itself could be said to be nothing more than an interpretation. Interpretative comments have been explored and have certainly been discussed at great length in innumerable supervisory hours. There is perhaps no need to make a further study along these lines at the present time.

The purpose of interpretation must include a feeling that the analyst has that a communication has been made which needs acknowledgment. This is perhaps the important part of an interpretation, but this very simple purpose is often hidden amongst a lot of other matters such as instruction in regard to the use of symbols. As an example of this one could take an interpretation like "the two white objects in the dream are breasts," etc., etc. As soon as the analyst has embarked on this kind of interpretation he has left solid ground and is now in a dangerous area where he is using his own ideas and these may be wrong from the point of view of the patient at the moment.

In the simplest form the analyst gives back to the patient what the patient has communicated. It may easily happen that the analyst feels that this is a futile occupation because if the patient has communicated something what is the point of saying it back except of course for the purpose of letting the patient know that what has been said has been heard and that the analyst is trying to get the meaning correctly.

Giving an interpretation back gives the patient opportunity to correct the misunderstandings. There are analysts who accept such corrections but there are also analysts who in their interpretative role assume a position which is almost unassailable so that if the patient attempts to make a correction the analyst tends rather to think in terms of the patient's resistance than in terms of the possibility that the communication has been wrongly or inadequately received.

Here one is already discussing varieties of psycho-analyst, of which there are many, and undoubtedly one of the tasks of being an analysand is to get to know what the analyst is like and what the analyst expects and what language the analyst talks and what kind of dreams the analyst can use, etc., etc. This is not entirely unnatural because it is rather like that with a child who has to get to know what kind of parents there are to be used as parents. Nevertheless in a discussion among analysts it would tend to be taken for granted that many patients are unable to make use of analysts who require the patient to do more than a certain amount of adapting; or to put it the other way round, to make use of analysts who are not able or willing to do more than a certain amount of adapting to the needs of the patient.

The principle that I am enunciating at this moment is that the analyst reflects back what the patient has communicated. This very simple statement about interpretation may be important by the very fact that it is simple and that it avoids the tremendous complications that arise when one thinks of all the possibilities that can be classified under the interpretative urge. If this very simple principle is enunciated it immediately needs elaboration. I suggest it needs elaboration of the following kind. In the limited area of today's transference the patient has an accurate knowledge of a detail or of a set of details. It is as if there is a dissociation belonging to the place that the analysis has reached today. It is helpful to remember that in this limited way or from this limited position the patient can be giving the analyst a sample of the truth; that is to say of something that is absolutely true for the patient, and that when the analyst gives this back the interpretation is received by the patient who has already emerged to some extent from this limited area or dissociated condition. In other words, the interpretation may even be given to the whole person, whereas the material for the interpretation was derived from only a part of the whole person. As a whole person the patient would not have been able to have given the material for the interpretation.

In this way the interpretations are part of a building up of insight. An important detail is that the interpretation has been given within a certain number of minutes or even seconds of the very insightful material presented. Certainly it is given in the same analytic hour. The right interpretation given tomorrow after a supervision is of no use because of this very powerful operation of a time factor. In other words, from a limited area the patient has insight and gives material for an interpretation. The analyst takes this information and gives it back to the patient and the patient that he gives it back to is now no longer in the area of insight in regard to this particular psycho-analytic element or constellation.

With this principle in mind it is possible to feel that the reflection back to the patient of what the patient has already said or conveyed is not a waste of time but it may indeed be the best thing that the analyst can do in the analysis of that patient on that particular day.

There is a certain amount of opposition to this way of looking at things because analysts enjoy exercising the skills that they have acquired and they have a very great deal that they can say about anything that turns up. For example, a rather silent patient tells the analyst, in response to a question, a good deal about one of his main interests, which has to do with shooting pigeons and the organization of this kind of sport. It is extremely tempting for the analyst at this point to use this material, which is more than he often gets in two or three weeks, and undoubtedly he could talk about the killing of all the unborn babies, the patient being an only child, and he could talk about the unconscious destructive fantasies in the mother, the patient's mother having been a depressive case and having committed suicide. What the analyst knew, however, was that the whole material came from a question and that it would not have come if the analyst had not invited the material, perhaps simply out of feeling that he was getting out of touch with the patient. The material therefore was not material for interpretation and the analyst had to hold back all that he could imagine in regard to the symbolic meaning of the activity which the patient was describing. After a while the analysis settled back into being a silent one and it is the patient's silence which contains the essential communication. The clues to this silence are only slowly emerging and there is nothing directly that this analyst can do to make the patient talk.

It need hardly be mentioned that often the patient produces material which the analyst can usefully interpret in another sense. It is as if the analyst can use the intellectual processes, both his own and those of the patient, to go ahead a little. The main thing is the reflection back to the patient of the material presented, perhaps a dream. Nevertheless the two together can play at using the dream for a deeper insight. There is great danger here because the interplay can be pleasurable and even exciting and can make both the patient and the analyst feel very gratified. Nevertheless there is only a certain distance that the analyst can safely take the patient beyond the place where the patient already is.

An example would be as follows: A patient gives a recurring dream, one which has dominated her life. She is starving and she is left with an orange, but she sees that the orange has been nibbled at by a rat. She has a rat phobia and the fact that the rat has touched the orange makes her unable to use the orange. The distress is extreme. It is a dream that she has been liable to all her life. Diagnostically she comes into the category of deprived child. The analyst need not do anything about this dream because the work has already been done in the dreaming and then in the remembering and in the reporting. The remembering and the reporting are results of work already done in the treatment and are of the nature of a bonus resulting from increased trust. The matter can be left there and the analyst can wait for more material to turn up. In this particular case that I am describing there was an external reason why the analyst could not afford to wait because there was not going to be an opportunity for further sessions. He therefore made the interpretation, thereby running the risk of spoiling the work that had already been done but also opening up the possibility that the patient might get further immediately. This is a matter of judgment and the analyst here felt that the degree of trust was such that he could proceed and even make a mistake. He said: The orange is the breast of the mother who was a good mother from your point of view but the mother that you lost. The rats represent both your attack on the breast and the breast's attack on you. The dream has to do with the fact that without help you are stuck because although you are still in touch with the original breast that seemed good you cannot make use of it unless you can be helped through the next stage in which you excitedly attack the breast to eat it as you would eat an orange.

It happened that in this case the patient was able to use this interpretation immediately, and she produced two examples; one of them illustrated her relationship to her mother before she lost her, and the other was a memory of the time of the actual losing of the mother. In this way the patient obtained emotional release and there was a marked clinical change for the better.

Any analyst can give innumerable examples of interpretations which patients were able to use and which took the patient further than they had reached when they were presenting the material specific to the session. Nevertheless this particular example highlights in a simple way the essential dynamics of the interpretation that goes beyond reflecting back the material presented.

It cannot be too strongly emphasized, however, in the teaching of students, that it is better to stick to the principle of the reflecting back of material presented rather than to go to the other extreme of clever interpretations which, even if accurate, may nevertheless take the patient further than the transference confidence allows, so that when the patient leaves the analyst the almost miraculous revelation that the interpretation represents suddenly becomes a threat because it is in touch with a stage of emotional development that the patient has not yet reached, at least as a total personality.

7

TWO NOTES ON THE USE

OF SILENCE

I

In this case I am not taking notes although I realize that my patient will one day wish that I had done so. I did make an attempt to keep notes in the early stages but I found that this interfered with my analysis of her by keeping the details over-emphasized in the conscious mind. In this way the unconscious or less conscious reaction became distorted.

Looking at the past two weeks I feel that a description might be valuable for reference at a later date and that the sort of things that happened illustrate the pattern of this analysis. Also the patient's reactions are less violent than they were at an earlier stage so that I can now even make mistakes or "blobs" as they are called in this treatment without a big risk that the patient will have a really serious reaction or seek another analyst.

The basis of the treatment at the present time is my silence. Last week I was absolutely silent the whole week except for a remark at the very beginning. This feels to the patient like something that she has achieved, getting me to be silent. There are many languages for describing this and one of them is that an interpretation is a male penis bursting across the field, the field being the breast with the infant unable to cope with the idea of a penis. The breast here is a field rather than an object for sucking or eating, and in the patient's associations it would be represented by a cushion rather than a source of food or of instinct gratification.

Last week was perhaps the most "successful" week in this respect of all weeks, and the patient was very appreciative of my playing this role, which she balances by a very close study that she is making of Henry James. In Henry James she finds a male analyst who deals in words and who has a very particular and comprehensive understanding but who is celibate.

This almost perfect week ended strangely. I had no idea of any trouble but on Monday the patient reported to me that what I had done at the end of the hour on Friday was very disturbing. In consequence all her old defenses had returned in moderate degree over the weekend. It appears that as she got up to go there was a sound as if paper were bring crinkled. On Monday she was able to talk about this and her reaction to it but not until she had found ways of complaining about me which were less delusional. From my point of view it is quite clear that my perfect behavior during the week is something that she cannot believe in and that at the end she had a delusion of some kind which indicated that I am extremely impatient in this role of not speaking. She says that by making me not speak she is turning me into a woman, castrating me, making me impotent, etc., etc., and she quite understands that I cannot stand this, and eventually she came to the idea that I am jealous of her when I give her what she needs because I never had it myself.

At another layer this noise meant to her that I had been masturbating, which was another evidence of my inability to stand doing nothing. The only reality basis for this delusion that I can discover would be that at the end of the hour I sometimes put my handkerchief in my pocket if I have had it in my hand. I am not sure, however, that anything at all took place which would form a reality basis for this delusion on this occasion.

On Monday I did say two things, and I said them not because I found it difficult to be silent but because I thought they ought to be said. She asked me to let her know what I was doing in the summer and next Christmas because of arrangements that had to be made, and she said that she thought she really wanted a reply. I meant to say: "I am not in a position to give you the answer that you require." What I said, however, was: "You want an answer here which I am not in a position to give." As I put it this way round she took it that I had rebuked her, telling her that she ought not to ask this sort of thing. Then again I made an interpretation when she said that she thought she might be able to stand just a little bit of an interpretation from me. I referred to a dream of the previous week and pointed out that a big solid object in amongst material which had to do with delicate tracery of one kind and another represented fact or external reality bursting in on fantasy. This is another version of the penis across the breast and of several other similar figures of speech. The trouble with this interpretation was that I was only repeating an interpretation that she had made herself. The patient now had two blobs which she could use and on the Tuesday she felt that she was in the same position that she had been in near the beginning of the analysis when she did not come back. She had studied my Ordinary Devoted Mother papers again and had underlined the relevant passages and she knew that I really do understand what she needs. "The only explanation can be," she said, "that you cannot do what you know is needed and that the whole thing is phony. The reason must be (she continued) that you can't stand being womanized or whatever silence means to you." And she had already stated that at the present time Henry James has all the male functioning and what she needs in the analysis is absolutely pure mothering. To meet this she is in the analytic session extremely regressed and dependent although able to function well most of the time in her work. Her private life at this stage is almost confined to very great activity in her own room and this includes reading and studying Henry James and his biography voraciously.

First of all I had to accept my position as someone who does not say anything. This was extremely difficult on Tuesday morning, not because I mind being silent but because I could see what was happening and there is nothing more difficult for an analyst to bear than the patient's delusional transference. The effect of this on me was that I got a tickling in the throat which, however, I was able to hide, and I recognized that if I had been able to speak three words the tickle would have gone. Not being able to talk has a curious effect in that it demands a listening which is different from my ordinary way of listening. To some extent I always listen with my throat, and my larynx follows the sounds that I hear in the world and particularly a voice of someone talking to me. This has always been characteristic of me and at one time was a serious symptom. After half an hour the patient said: "Now I feel quite different having said all that and I can stand your saying something; in fact I think I need it." The relief of this was great and I was quite clear that this was not because of my being silent; in fact I rather like it. The reason it was a relief to me was that I could then begin to do something about the patient's delusion, but of course I would not be able to do very much. In this sort of analysis it is essential to accept certain ideas about oneself which are untrue.

This permission to talk gave me a chance to interpret that the trouble was what happened at the end of Friday's session. This had very little basis in fact and it was easier for her to take the two blobs on Monday and talk about these as destroying the otherwise good analysis in which I am silent. I took a risk and said that the way I had put my information about the holiday did in fact make it look as if I was reproving her. Also there is not much point in making an interpretation which has already been made by the patient. These two things therefore had a reality basis as compared with which what happened at the end of Friday was tenuous and almost entirely dependent on her expectations. By the technique of silence I could have given conditions in which the patient herself would have solved the Friday problem. All she needed was time and opportunity without the "penis coming across the breast field." By this time the patient had almost returned to being able to believe in my silence as something that I could give because of her need. It has to be emphasized, however, that the patient retained a strong delusional idea that in fact I cannot stand being silent. Eventually she turned up with an interpretation of my inability to be silent in order to help me. This was that if I do something good for the patient I am jealous of the patient because nobody did that for me ever.

In the course of all this fortnight a very great deal has happened and I am quite confident about the technique of silence which I am very willing to employ except insofar as the patient cannot believe in it.

I do happen to know with a fair degree of certainty an interpretation which would be applicable to this whole phase. It is necessary, however, for me to wait for the patient to make this interpretation herself. As she has said: "With my history of an excitable father constantly breaking into whatever there was of mother-infant experience it is necessary for me to be able to reach the interpretations myself." It is of course compatible with this that there are moments when an interpretation is needed because of the fact that the patient needs something more than she has it in her to see. Nevertheless in this phase the patient is perfectly capable of reaching to the understanding which is needed and in fact has nearly reached this during the last week. I will make an attempt to state this interpretation:

The patient is at a very delicate point of transition from eating and being eaten, the latter being a talion reaction, and eating and being eaten in which this duality is simply an expression of the identification of infant and mother each with the other, or the lack of differentiation from the infant. The stage is represented in my writings which the patient has read in which a twelve-week infant feeds the mother with his finger while breast-feeding, and the patient has said that she feels like bringing me something to feed me with. I do, however, feel that she is trying to reach to the idea of being eaten by the mother and she feels that her own mother failed her in this area of experience. She did of course experience the fear of being eaten talionwise but the basis for this was lacking which is being eaten simply because whatever the infant feels the mother is also feeling.

II

Several problems are outstanding in a general way. Behind everything else is the problem that arises out of not speaking. I seldom make an interpretation and the analysis proceeds best on the basis of my saying nothing at all. This does, however, produce complications, because it becomes more and more evident that one of the purposes of interpreting is to establish the limits of the analyst's understanding. The basis for not interpreting and in fact not making any sound at all is the theoretical assumption that the analyst really does know what is going on. Probably up to the present I am able to say that I do know what is going on in this analysis and for this reason I continue with the policy of not speaking which is certainly what the patient asks of me. Within this framework there are two themes. More on the surface is the whole matter of triangular relationships as between whole people: the Oedipus complex, Electra, Cressida, etc. This theme started with "blond hair," etc., and it has included the idea of my being jealous of the patient's sexual relationship with men and also the idea of my wife being jealous of the patient in her relationship to me (umbrellas in stand, my wife might take her umbrella by mistake, etc.). There is a very great deal of material around this theme and there has been acting out which is very much part of the analysis. All this is altered by the fact of the other theme which could be called the theme of doom or fate. In this way everything of Oedipus nature is either inside or outside the doom area. The main statement about doom happened before the Easter holiday when the whole interpersonal problem was stated in terms of Greek mythology, so much so that I studied Bowra's *Sophoclean Tragedy* to be prepared for it. The operative phrase was "not a pawn of fate but an agent of fate." After the Easter holiday the same theme turned up in another language. "I have always been a part object." "For the first time I can say I am a very neurotic person; the accent is on the word person." Here the interpretation if it had been made would have been that a part object cannot experience omnipotence. The patient is not, however, prepared for being a whole person experiencing omnipotence and has not sufficient confidence in the facilitating environment to borrow strength from the maternal ego. Here comes the very well-behaved analyst who nevertheless cannot be trusted to be well behaved except negatively, i.e., not behaving badly.

The main interpretation which cannot be made because of the circumstances is that the infantile omnipotence which evidently the patient does not experience in her relationship with her mother has been projected wholesale on Greek mythology and now since the holiday onto ancient Irish history, Druids, the roots of Christianity in Ireland, the Irish cross which is in a circle. Restating this: for this patient with an insufficient experience of omnipotent living, the Oedipus complex and all triangular relationships and in fact all relationships are outside the projected omnipotence (part objects inter-related) or else they are doomed, caught up in fate, i.e., with the patient's infantile omnipotence projected wholesale.

8

PLAY IN THE ANALYTIC
SITUATION

I WISH TO DISCUSS SOME ASPECTS of play in adult analysis. In child analysis play is nearly always in evidence, but in adult analysis one expects to be able to leave play and to rely on dreams and hallucinations and fantasying.

Occasionally one hears of adult patients who are seen through a sticky patch by being given child-analysis toys which they manipulate over a phase and which enables the analyst to interpret in silent periods. What concerns me at the moment is not the introduction of play material into the analytic hour but the recognition of the importance of play in adult analysis, play being different from fantasy and dream.

An example was given me by a student in a supervision hour. The patient said, "I have just found a short-cut to analysis." In describing the short-cut he said he passed through the children's playground. The student quite rightly made the interpretation that the patient could see the value of play. As this patient has had violent episodes it is very important that in the analysis such things as a sense of humor should not be neglected, because the only hope that this man has of coming through his analysis without periods in which management will become necessary (as indeed it was at one time before the analysis started) is through his being able to play.

After the interpretation given by the student the patient leaned over and rearranged the mat and gave associations to this bit of play. In the circumstances it is understandable that the student neglected to continue on the subject of play and

69

became bogged down in the material of the free associations which indeed were important on their own account.

On one occasion a patient of mine came without having had coffee on the way and was in a dither about wanting coffee and feeling the whole hour would be wasted. I am sure that the management of this situation could be along two or more distinct lines. On this occasion I produced the coffee and we then saw what a tremendous difference there was between the patient's relationship to the coffee, the cup and saucer, the tray and sugar, and her relationship to the idea of wanting coffee from the dream that might have been there of having coffee given her by myself. It became a matter of play and an example of the introduction of play material into adult analysis.

Somewhere about this time another patient, a man, said to me "I have been meaning to let you know that I enjoy coming in and going out because it is playing. There is all the business about a routine and the avoidance of seeing other patients and so on." This was a surprising statement from a man who is unable to play and who comes because of an inability to keep his friendships as he can only talk in a ponderous manner and there is no play available. There was a reason why this man was able to make this observation and that was that in the previous sessions we had been dealing with play and the time had come in his analysis for me to let him see that instead of playing he was masturbating regularly, and the fantasying was locked up in the masturbation. This interpretation coming at the right moment began to free his playing and made him very conscious of his loneliness throughout childhood except when there were organized games. He had been unable to play because sharing the fantasy meant losing so much. A day or two later we came upon a game that he had never known about. We found that he had had an imaginary sister throughout his childhood of whom he was violently jealous, although in fact he was never jealous of either his older sister or his younger sister. This imaginary girl he found had represented his feminine self and had been practically a perfect individual and had had a close relationship with his father which he was unable to have through being a boy. In desperation he had tried dressing up as a girl a great deal during childhood but this had never been satisfactory because of the idealized girl that he always took with him and whom he hated and of course loved in a narcissistic way.

It has certainly been my practice to remember playing in adult analyses and often I have introduced pencil and paper and there have been play aspects, humorous interchanges, and so on, but it is only recently that I have recognized the very important differences between these play episodes and dreams and fantasying. One important thing is the obvious one that in play, although one has to drop a considerable amount which cannot be shared with the other person, there is a great deal to be gained from the overlap of other people's fantasy with one's own, so that there is a shared experience even if over a limited area of the total fantasying.

9

A POINT IN TECHNIQUE

I HAVE LEARNED RECENTLY TO ADOPT the following procedure in analytic practice.

When the fantasy that is represented in the transference material is revealed I ask myself: what and where is the accompanying orgastic bodily functioning? And, *per contra*, when in the analytic situation there is orgastic bodily functioning I ask myself: what fantasy material is the patient telling me about by this functioning?

When I come to expand this statement of a technical procedure I am at a loss to know where to start. I have put dots underneath the statement to represent the months which I hope anyone reading this will take to look into their own clinical behavior and to see how much they do and do not already act as I have come to do in this special respect.

Assuming that these months have passed, I now attempt to enlarge on this theme, which I must agree is neither original nor revolutionary.

A woman patient has a voice which is characteristic. When she works hard, at analysis for instance, she does a tremendous amount of work with her mouth and with her whole vocal apparatus. She talks loudly, and she has gradually become conscious of the fact that she enjoys the functioning of her speech department almost to a painful degree.

In the course of the analysis fantasy of all kinds has emerged accompanied by feeling of very great intensity.

One day, at a time when ideas of robbing and all sorts of hand actions of love, jealousy, hate and revenge were conscious, I wanted very badly to get her to see me half an hour before the arranged time. This I knew would suit her better, and also it made me able to avoid cutting short her hour owing to circumstances outside my control. I therefore risked going to look for her. I knew she would be dining in a certain restaurant, so I went there and attempted to speak to her.

She was eating, eating like a wild animal, and reading the newspaper. It was quite difficult to break through the invisible shell, and to get her to notice me.

The anxiety and rage roused by this action of mine were very great. I had found the hidden orgastic bodily functioning hidden from me in the analysis, but without which the fantasy material, though intensely felt, could never become quite real or personal. Gradually I came to understand that the clue could have been found all along in her voice, which was the part of her that was trying to be honest in spite of her general determination to keep apart (in her relationship to me) the fantasy and the bodily accompaniment.

Analysis along these lines produced material which made clear her thumb-sucking experiences (orgastic pleasure, defiance, guilt feelings, inhibition) and her hand masturbation which had been long inhibited and the idea repudiated.

10

VARIETIES OF
PSYCHOTHERAPY

Y OU WILL MORE OFTEN HEAR DISCUSSED varieties of illness than varieties of therapy. Naturally the two are interrelated, and I shall need to talk about illness first and therapy later.

I am a psychoanalyst, and you will not mind if I say that the basis of psychotherapy is the psychoanalytic training. This includes the personal analysis of the student analyst. Apart from such a training it is psychoanalytic theory and psychoanalytic metapsychology that influences all dynamic psychology, of whatever school.

There are, however, many varieties of psychotherapy, and these should depend for their existence not on the views of the practitioner but on the need of the patient or of the case. Let us say that where possible we advise psychoanalysis, but where this is not possible, or where there are arguments against, then an appropriate modification may be devised.

Of the many patients who come to me one way or another, only a very small percentage do in fact get psychoanalytic treatment, although I work at the center of the psychoanalytic world.

I could talk about the technical modifications that are called for when the patient is psychotic or borderline, but it is not this that I wish to discuss here.

My special interest here is in the way in which a trained analyst can do something other than analysis and do it usefully. This is important when, as is

73

usual, a limited amount of time is available for treatment. Often these other treatments can look better than the treatments that I personally feel have a more profound effect — i.e., psychoanalysis.

First let me say that one essential of psychotherapy is that no other treatment shall be mixed up with it. It is not possible to do the work if the idea of a possible shock therapy is looming large, as this alters the whole clinical picture. The patient either fears or secretly longs for the physical treatment (or both) and the psychotherapist never meets the patient's real personal problem.

On the other hand I must take for granted adequate physical care of the body. The next thing is, what is our aim? Do we wish to do as much as possible or as little? In psychoanalysis we ask ourselves: how much can we do? At the other extreme, in my hospital clinic, our motto is: how little need we do? This makes us always aware of the economic aspect of the case; also it makes us look for the central illness in a family, or for the social illness, so that we may avoid wasting our time and someone's money by giving treatments to the secondary characters in a family drama. There is nothing original in this, but you will perhaps like to hear a psychoanalyst say this since analysts are especially liable to get bogged down in long treatments in the course of which they may lose sight of an adverse external factor.

And then, how much of the patient's difficulties belong simply to the fact that no one has ever intelligently listened? I very quickly discovered as long as forty years ago that the taking of case-histories from mothers is in itself a psychotherapy if it be well done. Time must be allowed and a non-moralistic attitude naturally adopted, and when the mother has come to the end of saying what is in her mind, she may add: now I understand how the present symptoms fit into the whole pattern of the child's life in the family, and I can manage now, simply because you let me get at the whole story in my own way and in my own time. This is not only a matter that concerns parents who bring their children. Adults say this about themselves, and psychoanalysis could be said to be one long, very long, history-taking.

You know of course of the transference in psychoanalysis. In the psychoanalytic setting patients bring samples of their past and of their inner reality and expose them in the fantasy that belongs to their ever-changing relationship to the analyst. In this way the unconscious can gradually be made conscious. Once this process has started up and the unconscious co-operation of the patient has been gained, there is always much to be done; hence the length of the average treatment. It is interesting to examine the first interviews. If a psychoanalytic treatment is starting the analyst is careful not to be too clever at the beginning; and there is a good reason for this. The patient brings to the first interviews all his belief and all his suspicion. These extremes must be allowed to find real expression. If the analyst does too much at the beginning the patient either runs away or else, out of fear, develops a most splendid belief and becomes almost as if hypnotized.

Before I go further I must mention some other assumptions. There can be no reserved area in the patient. Psychotherapy does not prescribe for a patient's religion, his cultural interests or his private life, but a patient who keeps part of himself completely defended is avoiding the dependence that is inherent in the process. You will see that this dependence carries with it a corresponding thing in the therapist, a professional reliability which is even more important than the reliability of the doctor in ordinary medical practice. It is interesting that the Hippocratic oath which founded the medical practice recognized this with crude clarity.

Again, by the theory that underlies all our work a disorder that is not physically caused and that is therefore psychological represents a hitch in the individual's emotional development. Psychotherapy aims simply and solely at undoing the hitch, so that development may take place where formerly it could not take place.

In another though parallel language, psychological disorder is immaturity, immaturity of the emotional growth of the individual, and this growth includes the evolution of the individual's capacity to be related to people and to the environment generally.

In order to make myself clear I must give you a view of psychological disorder, of the categories of personal immaturity, even if this involves a gross simplification of a highly complex matter. I make three categories. The first of these brings to mind the term psycho-neurosis. Here are all the disorders of individuals who were well enough cared for in the early stages to be in a position, developmentally, to meet and to fail to some extent to contain the difficulties that are inherent in the full life, a life in which the individual rides and is not ridden by the instincts. I must include in with this the more "normal" varieties of depression.

The second of these categories brings to mind the word psychosis. Here something went wrong in the area of the very early details of infant nurture, the result being a disturbance of the basic structuring of the individual's personality. This basic fault, as Balint (*The Basic Fault*, 1968) has called it, may have produced an infantile or childhood psychosis, or difficulties at later stages may have exposed a fault in ego-structure which had passed unnoticed. Patients in this category were never healthy enough to become psycho-neurotic.

The third category I reserve for the in-betweens, those individuals who started well enough but whose environment failed them at some point, or repeatedly, or over a long period of time. These are children or adolescents or adults who could rightly claim: "all was well until . . . , and my personal life cannot be developed unless the environment acknowledges its debt to me," but of course it is not usual for the deprivation and the suffering it produced to be available to consciousness, so that instead of the words we find clinically an attitude, one which displays an antisocial tendency, and which may crystallize into delinquency and into recidivism.

For the moment, then, you are looking at psychological illness through the wrong end of three telescopes. Through one telescope you see reactive depression, which has to do with the destructive urges that accompany loving impulses in two-body relationships (basically, infant and mother) and also you see psychoneurosis, which has to do with ambivalence, that is to say co-existing love and hate, which belongs to triangular relationships (basically child and two parents), the relationship being experienced both heterosexually and homosexually, in varying proportions.

Through the second telescope you see the very early stages of emotional development becoming distorted by faulty infant care. I admit that some infants are more difficult to nurture than others are, but as we are not out to blame anyone we can ascribe the cause of illness here to a failure in nurture. What we see is a failure of the structuring of the personal self, and the capacity of the self for relating to objects that are of the environment. I would like to dig this rich seam with you but I must not do so.

Through this telescope we see the various failures which produce the clinical picture of schizophrenia, or which produce the psychotic under-currents that disturb the even flow of life of many of us who manage to get labelled normal, healthy, mature.

When we look at illness in this way we only see exaggerations of elements in our own selves, we do not see anything which would put psychiatrically ill people in a place apart. Hence the strain inherent in treating or in nursing ill people psychologically, rather than by drugs and by the so-called physical treatments.

The third telescope takes our attention away from the difficulties inherent in life to disturbances which have a different nature, for the deprived person is prevented from getting at his or her own inherent problems by a grudge, a justified claim for a mending of an almost remembered insult. We in this room are probably not in this category, not even slightly. Most of us can say of our parents: they made mistakes, they constantly frustrated us and it fell to their lot to introduce us to the Reality Principle, arch-enemy of spontaneity, creativity, and the sense of Real; BUT, they never really let us down. It is this being let down that constitutes the basis for the antisocial tendency, and however much we dislike our bicycles being stolen, or having to use the police to prevent violence, we do see, we understand, why this boy or that girl forces us to meet a challenge, whether by stealing or by destructiveness.

I have done as much as I can allow myself to do to build up a theoretical background for my brief description of some varieties of psychotherapy.

CATEGORY I (Psycho-neurosis)

If illness in this category needs treatment we would like to provide psychoanalysis, a professional setting of general reliability in which the repressed unconscious may become conscious. This is brought about as a result of the appearance in the "transference" of innumerable samples of the patient's personal conflicts. In a favorable case the defenses against anxiety that arises out of the instinctual life and its imaginative elaboration become less and less rigid, and more and more under the patient's deliberate control system.

CATEGORY II (Failure in Early Nurture)

Insofar as illness of this kind needs treatment, we need to provide opportunity for the patient to have experiences that properly belong to infancy under conditions of extreme dependence. We see that such conditions may be found apart from organized psychotherapy, for instance in friendship, in nursing care that may be provided on account of physical illness, in cultural experiences including for some those that are called religious. A family that continues to care for a child provides opportunities for regression to dependence even of a high order, and it is indeed a regular feature of family life, well embedded in a social milieu, this going on being available to re-establish and to emphasize elements of care that belong initially to infant care. You will agree that some children enjoy their families and their growing independence, while others continue to use their families psychotherapeutically.

Professional social work comes in here, as an attempt to give professionally the help which would be provided non-professionally by parents and by families and by social units. The social worker on the whole is not a psychotherapist in the sense described under patients in Category I. The social worker is a psychotherapist, however, in meeting Category II needs.

You will see that a great deal that a mother does with an infant could be called "holding." Not only is actual holding very important, and a delicate matter that can only be delicately done by the right people, but also much of infant nurture is an ever-widening interpretation of the word holding. Holding comes to include all physical management, insofar as it is done in adaptation to an infant's needs. Gradually a child values being let go, and this corresponds with the presentation to the child of the Reality Principle, which at first clashes with the Pleasure Principle (omnipotence abrogated). The family continues this holding, and society holds the family.

Casework might be described as the professionalized aspect of this normal function of parents and of local social units, a "holding" of persons and of situations, while growth tendencies are given a chance. These growth tendencies are present all the time in every individual, except where hopelessness (because of repeated environmental failure) has led to an organized withdrawal. The tendencies have been described in terms of integration, of the psyche coming to terms with the body, the one becoming linked with the other, of the development of a capacity for relating to objects. These processes go ahead unless blocked by failures of holding and of the meeting of the individual's creative impulses.

CATEGORY III (Deprivation)

Where patients are dominated by a *deprivation* area in their past history the treatment needs to be adapted to this fact. As persons they may be normal, neurotic, or psychotic. One can hardly see what is the personal pattern because whenever hope begins to become alive the boy or girl produces a symptom (stealing or being stolen from, destructiveness or being destroyed) which forces the environment to notice and to act. Action is usually punitive, but what the patient needs, of course, is a full acknowledgment and full payment. As I have said, this very often cannot be done because so much is unavailable to consciousness, but it is important that a serious digging done in the early stages of an antisocial career quite frequently does produce the clue and the solution. A study of delinquency should be started as a study of the antisocial in relatively normal children whose homes are intact, and here I find it frequently possible to track down the deprivation and the extreme suffering that resulted and which altered the whole course of the child's development. (I have published cases, and I can give other examples if there is time.)

The point here is that society is left with all the untreated and untreatable cases in which the antisocial tendency has built up into a stabilized delinquency. Here the need is for the provision of specialized environments, and these must be divided into two kinds:

1. those which hope to socialize the children they are holding, and
2. those which are merely designed to keep their children in order to preserve society from them until these boys and girls are too old to be detained, and until they go out into the world as adults who will repeatedly get into trouble. This latter kind of institution may run most smoothly when very strictly administered.

Can it be seen that it is very dangerous to base a system of child-care on the work done in homes for the maladjusted, and especially on the "successful" management of delinquents in detention centers?

On the basis of what I have said it is now perhaps possible to compare the three types of psychotherapy.

Naturally a practicing psychiatrist needs to be able to pass easily from one kind of therapy to another, and indeed to do all kinds at one and the same time if necessary, as need arises.

Illness of psychotic quality (Category II) demands of us that we organize a complex kind of "holding," including if necessary physical care. Here the professional therapist or nurse comes in when the patient's immediate environment fails to cope. As a friend of mine (the late John Rickman) said, "Insanity is not being able to find anyone to stand you," and here there are two factors, the degree of illness in the patient and the ability of the environment to tolerate the symptoms. In this way there are some in the world who are more ill than some of those who are in mental hospitals.

Psychotherapy of the kind I am referring to can look like friendship, but it is not friendship because the therapist is paid and only sees the patient for a limited period by appointment, and moreover only over a limited course of time, since the aim in every therapy is to arrive at a point at which the professional relationship ends because the patient's life and living takes over and the therapist passes on to the next job.

A therapist is like other professional people in that in his job his behavior is at a higher standard than it is in his private life. He is punctual, he adapts himself to his patient's needs and he does not live out his own frustrated urges in his contact with his patients.

It will be evident that patients who are very ill in this category do put a very great strain on the integrity of the therapist, since they do need human contact, and real feelings, and yet they need to place an absolute reliance on the relationship in which they are maximally dependent. The greatest difficulties come when there has been a seduction in the patient's childhood, in which case there must be experienced in the course of the treatment a delusion that the therapist is repeating seduction. Naturally, recovering depends on the undoing of this childhood seduction which brought the child prematurely to a real instead of an imaginary sexual life, and spoiled the child's prerequisite: unlimited play.

In therapy designed to deal with psycho-neurotic illness (Category I) the classical psychoanalytic setting devised by Freud can be easily attained, since the patient brings to the treatment a degree of belief and capacity to trust. With all this taken for granted the analyst has the opportunity to allow the transference to develop in its own way, and instead of the patient's delusions there come into the material of the analysis dreams, imagination, and ideas expressed in symbolic form which can be interpreted according to the process as it develops through the unconscious co-operation of the patient.

This is all I have time to say about the psychoanalytic technique, which can be learned, and which is difficult enough, but not as exhausting as therapy designed to meet psychotic disorder.

Psychotherapy designed to deal with an antisocial tendency in a patient only works, as I have said, if the patient is near the beginning of his or her antisocial career, before secondary gains and delinquent skills have become established. It is only in the early stages that the patient knows he (or she) is a patient, and actually feels a need to get to the roots of the disturbance. Where work is possible along these lines the doctor and the patient settle down to a sort of detective story, using any clues that may be available, including what is known of the past history of the case, and the work is done in a thin layer that is somewhere between the deeply buried unconscious and the conscious life and memory system of the patient.

This layer that is between the unconscious and the conscious is occupied in normal people by cultural pursuits, and the cultural life of the delinquent is notoriously thin, because there is no freedom in such a case except in a flight either to the unremembered dream or to reality. Any attempt to explore the intermediate area leads not to art or religion or playing, but to antisocial behavior that is compulsive and inherently unrewarding to the individual as well as hurtful to society.

11

THE PSYCHOTHERAPY OF CHARACTER DISORDERS

ALTHOUGH THE TITLE CHOSEN for this paper is "The Psychotherapy of Character Disorders," it is not possible to avoid a discussion of the meaning of the term *Character Disorder*. As Fenichel *(The Theory of Neurosis*, 1945) remarks,

> The question may be raised whether there is any analysis that is not "character analysis." All symptoms are the outcome of specific ego attitudes, which in analysis make their appearance as resistances and which have been developed during infantile conflicts. This is true. And to a certain degree, really, all analyses are character analyses.

And again,

> Character disorders do not form a nosological unit. The mechanisms at the basis of character disorder may be as different as the mechanisms at the basis of symptom neuroses. Thus a hysterical character will be more easily treated than a compulsive one, a compulsive one more easily than a narcissistic one.

It is clear that either the term is too wide to be useful, or else I shall need to use it in a special way. In the latter case I must indicate the use I shall make of the term in this paper.

First, there must be confusion unless it be recognized that the three terms: character, a good character, and a character disorder, bring to mind three very different phenomena, and it would be artificial to deal with all three at one and the same time, yet these three are interrelated.

Freud wrote that "a fairly reliable character" is one of the prerequisites for a successful analysis but we are considering *unreliability* in the personality, and Fenichel asks: can this unreliability be treated? He might have asked: what is its etiology?

When I look at character disorders I find I am looking at *whole persons.* There is in the term an implication of a degree of integration, itself a sign of psychiatric health.

The papers that have preceded mine have taught us much, and have strengthened me in the idea of character as something that belongs to integration. Character is a manifestation of successful integration, and a disorder of character is a distortion of the ego structure, integration being nevertheless maintained. It is perhaps good to remember that integration has a time factor. The child's character has formed on the basis of a steady developmental process, and in this respect the child has a past and a future.

It would seem to be valuable to use the term character disorder in description of a child's attempt to accommodate his or her own developmental abnormalities or deficiencies. Always we assume that the personality structure is able to withstand the strain of the abnormality. The child needs to come to terms with the personal pattern of anxiety or compulsion or mood or suspicion, etc., and also to relate this to the requirements and expectations of the immediate environment.

In my opinion the value of the term belongs specifically to a description of personality distortion that comes about *when the child needs to accommodate some degree of antisocial tendency.* This leads immediately to a statement of my use of this term.

I am using these words which enable us to focus our attention not so much on behavior as on those roots of misbehavior that extend over the whole area between normality and delinquency. The antisocial tendency can be examined in your own healthy child who at the age of two takes a coin from his mother's handbag.

The antisocial tendency always arises out of a *deprivation* and represents the child's claim to get back behind the deprivation to the state of affairs that obtained when all was well. I cannot develop this theme here, but this thing that I call the antisocial tendency must be mentioned because it is found regularly in the dissection of character disorder. The child in accommodating the antisocial tendency that is his or hers may hide it, may develop a reaction formation to it, such as becoming a prig, may develop a grievance and acquire a complaining character, may specialize in day-dreaming, lying, mild chronic masturbating activ-

ity, bed-wetting, compulsive thumb-sucking, thigh-rubbing, etc., or may periodically manifest the antisocial tendency (that is his or hers) in a *behavior disorder*. This
latter is always associated with hope, and it is either of the nature of stealing or of
aggressive activity and destruction. It is compulsive.

Character disorder, then, according to my way of looking at things, refers
most significantly to the distortion of the *intact* personality that results from the
antisocial elements in it. It is the antisocial element that determines society's
involvement. Society (the child's family and so on) must meet the challenge, and
must *like or dislike* the character and the character disorder.

Here then is the beginning of a description:

Character disorders are not schizophrenia. In character disorder there is hidden
   illness in the intact personality.
Character disorders in some way and to some degree actively involve society.

Character disorders may be divided according to:

Success or failure on the part of the individual in the attempt of the total personality to hide the illness element. Success here means that the personality,
   though impoverished, has become able to socialize the character distortion to
   find secondary gains or to fit in with a social custom.
Failure here means that the impoverishment of the personality carries along with it
   a failure in establishment of a relation to society as a whole, on account of the
   hidden illness element.

In fact, society plays its part in the determination of the fate of a person with
character disorder, and does this in various ways. For example:

Society tolerates individual illness to a degree.
Society tolerates failure of the individual to contribute-in.
Society tolerates or even enjoys distortions of the mode of the individual's
   contributing-in.

Or society meets the challenge of the antisocial tendency of an individual, and its
reaction is being motivated by:

1. Revenge.
2. The wish to socialize the individual.
3. Understanding and the application of understanding to prevention.

The individual with character disorder may suffer from:

1. Impoverishment of personality, sense of grievance, unreality, awareness of lack of serious purpose, etc.
2. Failure to socialize.

Here then is a basis for psychotherapy, because psychotherapy relates to individual *suffering* and need for help. But this suffering in character disorder only belongs to the early stages in the individual's illness; the secondary gains quickly take over, lessen the suffering, and interfere with the drive of the individual to seek help or to accept help offered.

It must be recognized that in respect of "success" (character disorder hidden and socialized) *psychotherapy makes the individual ill*, because illness lies between the defense and the individual's health. By contrast, in respect of "unsuccessful" hiding of character disorder, although there may be an initial drive in the individual to seek help at an early stage, because of society's reactions, this motive does not necessarily carry the patient through to the treatment of the deeper illness.

The clue to the treatment of character disorder is given by the part the environment plays in the case of *natural cure*. In the slight case the environment can "cure" because the cause was an environmental failure in the area of ego-support and protection at a stage of the individual's dependence. This explains why it is that children are regularly "cured" of incipient character disorder in the course of their own childhood development simply by making use of home life. Parents have a second and third chance to bring their children through, in spite of failures of management (mostly inevitable) in the earliest stages when the child is highly dependent. Family life is the place therefore that offers the best opportunity for investigation into the etiology of character disorder; and indeed it is in the family life, or its substitute, that the child's *character* is being built up in positive ways.

ETIOLOGY OF CHARACTER DISORDER

In considering the etiology of character disorder it is necessary to take for granted both the maturational process in the child, the conflict-free sphere of the ego (Hartmann), also forward movement with anxiety drive (Klein), and the function of the environment which facilitates the maturational processes. Environmental provision must be "good" enough if maturation is to become a fact in the case of any one child.

With this in mind, one can say that there are two extremes of distortion, and

that these relate to the stage of maturation of the individual at which environmental failure did actually overstrain the ego's capacity for organizing defenses:

At one extreme is the ego hiding *psycho-neurotic* symptom-formations (set up
    relative to anxiety belonging to the Oedipus complex). Here the hidden illness
    is a matter of conflict in the individual's personal unconscious.
At the other extreme is the ego hiding *psychotic* symptom-formations (splitting,
    dissociations, reality side-slipping, depersonalization, regression and omnipo-
    tent dependencies, etc.). Here the hidden illness is in the ego structure.

But the matter of society's essential involvement does not depend on the
answer to the question: is the hidden illness psycho-neurotic or psychotic? In fact,
in character disorder there is this other element, *the individual's* correct perception
at a time in early childhood that at first all was well, or well enough, and then that
all was not well. In other words, that there happened at a certain time, or over a
phase of development, an actual failure of ego-support that held up the individual's
emotional development. A reaction in the individual to this disturbance took the
place of simple growth. The maturational processes became dammed up because of
a failure of the facilitating environment.

This theory of the etiology of character disorder, if correct, leads to a new
statement of character disorder at its inception. The individual in this category
carries on with two separate burdens. One of these, of course, is the increasing
burden of a disturbed and in some respects stunted or postponed maturational
process. The other is the hope, a hope that never becomes quite extinguished, that
the environment may acknowledge and make up for the specific failure that did the
damage. In the vast majority of cases the parents or the family or guardians of the
child recognize the fact of the "let-down" (so often unavoidable) and by a period of
special management, spoiling, or what could be called mental nursing, they see the
child through to a recovery from the trauma.

When the family does not mend its failures the child goes forward with
certain handicaps, being engaged in

1. arranging to live a life in spite of emotional stunting, and
2. all the time liable to moments of hope, moments when it would seem to be
    possible to force the environment to effect a cure (hence: acting-out).

Between the clinical state of a child who has been hurt in the way that is being
described here and the resumption of that child's emotional development, and all
that that means in terms of socialization, there is this need to make society
acknowledge and repay. Behind a child's maladjustment is always a failure of the
environment to adjust to the child's absolute needs at a time of relative depen-

dence. (Such failure is initially a failure of nurture.) Then there can be added a failure of the family to heal the effects of such failures; and then there may be added the failure of society as it takes the family's place. Let it be emphasized that in this type of case the initial failure can be shown to have happened at a time at which the child's development had made it just possible for him or her to perceive the fact of the failure and to perceive the nature of the environment's maladjustment.

The child now displays an antisocial tendency, which (as I have said) in the stage before the development of secondary gains is always a manifestation of hope. This antisocial tendency is liable to show in two forms:

1. The staking of claims on people's time, concern, money, etc. (manifested by stealing).
2. The expectation of that degree of structural strength and organization and "comeback" that is essential if the child is to be able to rest, relax, disintegrate, feel secure (manifested by destruction which provokes strong management).

On the basis of this theory of the etiology of character disorder I can proceed to examine the matter of therapy.

INDICATIONS FOR THERAPY

Therapy of character disorder has three aims:

1. 1. A dissection down to the illness that is hidden and that appears in the character distortion. Preparatory to this may be a period in which the individual is invited to become a patient, to become ill instead of hiding illness.
2. To meet the antisocial tendency which, from the point of view of the therapist, is evidence of hope in the patient; to meet it as an S.O.S., a *cri de coeur*, a signal of distress.
3. Analysis that takes into consideration both the ego distortion and the patient's exploitation of his or her id-drives during attempts at self-cure.

The attempt to meet the patient's antisocial tendency has two aspects:

The allowance of the patient's claims to rights in terms of a person's love and reliability.
The provision of an ego-supportive structure that is relatively indestructible.

As this implies, the patient will from time to time be acting-out, and as long as this has a relation to the transference it can be managed and interpreted. The troubles in therapy come in relation to antisocial acting-out which is outside the total therapeutic machinery, that is to say, which involves society.

In regard to the treatment of hidden illness and of ego distortion, the need is for psychotherapy. But at the same time the antisocial tendency must be engaged, as and when it appears. The aim in this part of the treatment is to arrive at the original trauma. This has to be done in the course of the psychotherapy or, if psychotherapy is not available, in the course of the specialized management that is provided.

In this work the failures of the therapist or of those managing the child's life will be real and they can be shown to reproduce the original failures, in token form. These failures are real indeed, and especially so insofar as the patient is either regressed to the dependence of the appropriate age, or else remembering. The acknowledgment of the analyst's or guardian's failure enables the patient to become appropriately angry instead of traumatized. *The patient needs to reach back through the transference trauma to the state of affairs that obtained before the original trauma.* (In some cases there is a possibility of quick arrival at deprivation trauma in a first interview.) The reaction to the current failure only makes sense insofar as the current failure *is* the original environmental failure from the point of view of the child. Reproduction in the treatment of examples as they arise of the original environmental failure, along with the patient's experience of anger that is appropriate, frees the patient's maturational processes; and it must be remembered that the patient is in a dependent state and needing ego-support and environmental management (holding) in the treatment setting, and the next phase needs to be a period of emotional growth in which the character builds up positively and loses its distortions.

In a favorable case the acting-out that belongs to these cases is confined to the transference, or can be brought into the transference productively by interpretation of displacement, symbolism, and projection. At one extreme is the common "natural" cure that takes place in the child's family. At the other extreme are the severely disturbed patients whose acting-out may make treatment by interpretation impossible because the work gets interrupted by society's reactions to stealing or destructiveness.

In a moderately severe case the acting-out can be managed provided that the therapist understands its meaning and significance. It can be said that acting-out is the alternative to despair. Most of the time the patient is hopeless about correcting the original trauma and so lives in a state of relative depression or of dissociations that mask the chaotic state that is always threatening. When, however, the patient starts to make an object relationship, or to cathect a person, then there starts up an antisocial tendency, a compulsion either to lay claims (steal) or by destructive behavior to activate harsh or even vindictive management.

In every case, if psychotherapy is to be successful, the patient must be seen through one or many of these awkward phases of manifest antisocial behavior, and only too often it is just at these awkward points in the case that treatment is interrupted. The case is dropped not necessarily because the situation cannot be tolerated, but (as likely as not) because those in charge do not know that these acting-out phases are inherent, and that they can have a positive value.

In severe cases these phases in management or treatment present difficulties that are so great that the law (society) takes over, and at the same time psychotherapy goes into abeyance. Society's revenge takes the place of pity or sympathy, and the individual ceases to suffer and be a patient, and instead becomes a criminal with a delusion of persecution.

It is my intention to draw attention to *the positive element in character disorder*. Failure to achieve character disorder in the individual who is trying to accommodate some degree of antisocial tendency indicates a liability to psychotic breakdown. Character disorder indicates that the individual's ego structure can bind the energies that belong to the stunting of maturational processes and also the abnormalities in the interaction of the individual child and the family. Until secondary gains have become a feature the personality with character disorder is always liable to break down into paranoia, manic depression, psychosis or schizophrenia.

To sum up, a statement on the treatment of character disorder can start with the dictum that such a treatment is like that of any other psychological disorder, namely, psychoanalysis if it be available. There must follow the following considerations:

1. Psychoanalysis may succeed, but the analyst must expect to find *acting-out* in the transference, and must understand the significance of this acting-out, and be able to give it positive value.
2. The analysis may succeed but be difficult because the hidden illness has psychotic features, so that the patient must become ill (psychotic, schizoid) before starting to get better; and all the resources of the analyst will be needed to deal with the primitive defense mechanisms that will be a feature.
3. The analysis may be succeeding, but as acting-out is not confined to the transference relationship the patient is removed from the analyst's reach because of society's reaction to the patient's antisocial tendency or because of the operation of the law. There is room for great variation here, owing to the variability of society's reaction, ranging from crude revenge to an expression of society's willingness to give the patient a chance to make late socialization.

4. In many cases incipient character disorder is treated and treated successfully in the child's home, by a phase or by phases of special management
(spoiling) or by especially *personal* care or strict control by a person who
loves the child. An extension of this is the treatment of incipient or early
character disorder without psychotherapy by management in groups
designed to give what the child's own family cannot give in the way of
special management.

5. By the time the patient comes to treatment there may already be a fixed
antisocial tendency manifest, and a hardened attitude in the patient
fostered by secondary gains, in which case the question of psychoanalysis
does not arise. Then the aim is to provide firm management by understanding persons, and to provide this as a *treatment* in advance of its being
provided as a *corrective* by court order. Personal psychotherapy can be
added if it is available.

Finally,

6. The character disorder case may present as a court case, with society's
reaction represented by the probation order, or by committal to an
approved school or a penal institution.

It can happen that early committal by a court proves to be a *positive* element
in the patient's socialization. This corresponds again to the natural cure that
commonly takes place in the patient's family; society's reaction has been, for the
patient, a practical demonstration of its "love," that is of its willingness to "hold" the
patient's unintegrated self, and to meet aggression with firmness (to limit the effects
of maniacal episodes) and to meet hatred with hatred, appropriate and under
control. This last is the best that some deprived children will ever get by way of
satisfactory management, and many restless antisocial deprived children change
from ineducable to educable in the strict regime of a remand home. The danger
here is that because restless antisocial children thrive in an atmosphere of dicta-
torship this may breed dictators, and may even make educationalists think that an
atmosphere of strict discipline, with every minute of the child's day filled, is good
educational treatment for normal children, which it is not.

GIRLS

Broadly speaking, all this applies equally to boys and girls. At the stage of
adolescence, however, the nature of the character disorder is necessarily different in
the two sexes. For example, at adolescence girls tend to show their antisocial
tendency by prostitution, and one of the hazards of acting-out is the production of

illegitimate babies. In prostitution there are secondary gains. One is that girls find they contribute-in to society by being prostitutes, whereas they cannot contribute-in by any other means. They find many lonely men, who want a relationship rather than sex, and who are ready to pay for it. Also, these girls, essentially lonely, achieve contacts with others of their kind. The treatment of adolescent antisocial girls who have started to experience the secondary gains of the prostitute presents *insuperable difficulties*. Perhaps the idea of treatment does not make sense in this context. In many cases it is already too late. It is best to give up all attempts to cure prostitution, and instead to concentrate on giving these girls food and shelter and opportunity for keeping healthy and clean.

CLINICAL ILLUSTRATIONS

A Common Type of Case

A boy in later latency (first seen at ten years) was having psychoanalytic treatment from me. His restlessness and liability to outbreaks of rage started from a very early date, soon after his birth and long before he was weaned at eight months. His mother was a neurotic person and all her life more or less depressed. He was a thief and given to aggressive outbursts. His analysis was going well, and in the course of a year of daily sessions much straightforward analytic work was accomplished. He became very excited, however, as his relationship to me developed significance, and he climbed out on to the clinic roof and flooded out the clinic and made so much noise that the treatment had to stop. Sometimes there was danger to me; he also broke into my car outside the clinic and drove off in bottom gear by using the self-starter, thus obviating the need for a car key. At the same time he started stealing again and being aggressive outside the treatment setting, and he was sent by the Juvenile Court to an approved school just at a time when the treatment by psychoanalysis was in full spate. Perhaps if I had been much stronger than he I might have managed this phase, and so have had opportunity to complete the analysis. As it was I had to give up.

   (This boy did moderately well. He became a lorry driver, which suited his restlessness. He had kept his job fourteen years at the time of the follow-up. He married and had three children. His wife divorced him, after which he kept in touch with his mother, from whom the details of the follow-up were obtained.)

Three Favorable Cases

A boy of eight started stealing. He had suffered a relative deprivation (in his own good home setting) when he was two, at the time his mother conceived, and became pathologically anxious. The parents had managed to meet this boy's special needs and had almost succeeded in effecting a natural cure of his condition. I helped them in this long task by giving them some understanding of what they were doing. In one therapeutic consultation when the boy was eight it was possible for me to get this boy into feeling-contact with his deprivation, and he reached back to an object relationship to the good mother of his infancy. Along with this the stealing ceased.

A girl of eight years came to me because of stealing. She had suffered a relative deprivation in her own good home at the age of 4–5 years. In one psychotherapeutic consultation she reached back to her early infantile contact with a good mother, and at the same time her stealing disappeared. She was also wetting and messing and this minor manifestation of the antisocial tendency persisted for some time.

A boy of thirteen years, at a public school a long way from his good home, was stealing in a big way, also slashing sheets and upsetting the school by getting boys into trouble and by leaving obscene notes in lavatories, etc. In a therapeutic consultation he was able to let me know that he had been through a period of intolerable strain at the age of six when he went away to boarding school. I was able to arrange for this boy (middle child of three) to be allowed a period of "mental nursing" in his own home. He used this for a regressive phase, and then went to day school. Later he went to a boarding school in the neighborhood of his home. His antisocial symptoms ceased abruptly after his one interview with me and follow-up shows that he has done well. He has now passed through a university, and is establishing himself as a man. Of this case it is particularly true to say that the patient brought with him the understanding of his case, and what he needed was for the facts to be acknowledged and for an attempt to be made to mend, in token form, the environmental failure.

Comment

In these three cases in which help could be given when secondary gains had not become a feature the general attitude of myself as psychiatrist enabled the child in each case to state a specific area of relative deprivation, and the fact that this was accepted as real and true enabled the child to reach back over the gap and make anew a relationship with good objects that had been blocked.

A Case on the Borderline between Character Disorder and Psychosis

A boy has been under my care over a period of years. I have only seen him once, and most of my contacts have been with the mother at times of crisis. Many have tried to give direct help to the boy, who is now twenty, but he quickly becomes uncooperative.

This boy has a high I.Q. and all those whom he has allowed to teach him have said that he could be exceptionally brilliant as an actor, a poet, an artist, a musician, etc. He has not stayed long at any one school but by self-tuition has kept well ahead of his peers, and he did this in early adolescence by coaching his friends in their school-work, then keeping in touch.

In the latency period he was hospitalized and diagnosed schizophrenic. In hospital he undertook the "treatment" of the other boys, and he never accepted his position as a patient. Eventually he ran away and had a long period without schooling. He would lie in bed listening to lugubrious music, or lock himself into the house so that no one could get to him. He constantly threatened suicide, chiefly in relation to violent love affairs. Periodically he would organize a party, and this would go on indefinitely, and damage was sometimes done to property.

This boy lived with his mother in a small flat and he kept her constantly in a state of worry, and there was never any possibility of an outcome since he would not go away, he would not go to school or to hospital, and he was clever enough to do exactly as he wanted to do, and he never became criminal, and so kept out of the jurisdiction of the law.

At various times I helped the mother by putting her in touch with the police, the probation service, and other social services, and when eventually he said he would go to a certain grammar school I "pulled strings" to enable him to do this. He was found to be well ahead of his age group, and the masters gave him great encouragement because of his brilliance. But he left school before time, and obtained a scholarship for a good college of acting. At this point he decided that he had the wrong-shaped nose, and eventually he persuaded his mother to pay a plastic surgeon to alter it from retroussé to straight. Then he found other reasons why he could not go forward to any success, and yet he gave no one any opportunity to help him. This continues, and at present he is in the observation ward of a mental hospital, but he will find a way of leaving this and will settle in at home once more.

This boy has an early history that gives the clue to the antisocial part of his character disorder. In fact he was the result of a partnership that foundered soon after its unhappy start, and the father soon after separating from the mother himself became a paranoid casualty. This marriage followed immediately after a tragedy, and was doomed to failure because the boy's mother had not yet recovered from the loss of her much-loved fiancé whom, as she felt, was killed by the carelessness of this man whom she married and who became the father of the boy.

This boy could have been helped at an early age, perhaps six, when he was first seen by a psychiatrist. He could then have led the psychiatrist to the material of his relative deprivation, and he could then have been told about his mother's personal problem, and the reason for the ambivalence in her relationship to him. But instead the boy was placed in a hospital ward, and from this time on he hardened into a case of character disorder, becoming a person who compulsively tantalizes his mother and his teachers and his friends.

I have not attempted to describe a case treated by psychoanalysis in this series of short case-descriptions.

Cases treated by management alone are innumerable and include all those children who when deprived in one way or another are adopted, or fostered out, or placed in small homes that are run as therapeutic institutions and on personal lines. It would be giving a false impression to describe one case in this category. It is indeed necessary to draw attention to the fact that incipient character disorder is being treated successfully all the time, especially in the home, in social groups of all kinds, and quite apart from psychotherapy.

Nevertheless, it is intensive work with the few cases that throws light on the problem of character disorder as of other types of psychological disorders, and it is work of the psychoanalytic groups in various countries that has laid the basis for a theoretical statement and has begun to explain to the specialized therapeutic groups what it is that is being done in such groups that so often succeeds in the prevention or treatment of character disorder.

12

THE VALUE OF THE

THERAPEUTIC

CONSULTATION[1]

THERE IS AN ASPECT OF APPLIED psycho-analysis which has come to interest me more and more in the past two decades. This is the exploitation of the first interview, or the first few interviews.

First I must make it abundantly clear that what I am describing is not psycho-analysis. If starting an analysis I do not adopt the procedure described here. Nevertheless I hold the view that in order to prepare himself to do this work the therapist should make himself thoroughly familiar with the classical psycho-analytic technique, and should carry through to the bitter end a number of analyses conducted on a basis of daily sessions, continued over the years. Only in this way does the analyst learn what has to be learned from the patients, and only in this way does the analyst master the technique of withholding interpretations that have validity without immediate or urgent relevance.

I would not say that a full-scale analysis is always better for the patient than a psychotherapeutic interview. Treatment by psycho-analysis often leaves the symptomatology untouched for a period of time during which social repercussions may infinitely complicate the issue; moreover, treatment may necessitate the child's removal from a good-enough home to a strange setting and this again is a

1. Published in *Foundations of Child Psychiatry*, ed. Emanuel Miller (London: Pergamon Press, 1965).

complication that were better avoided. In other words, there are cases in which a quick symptomatic change is preferable to a psycho-analytic cure even though one would prefer the latter.

Apart from this, there is a vast clinical demand for psychotherapy that is not related in any way to the supply of psycho-analysts, and therefore if there is a type of case that can be helped by one or three visits to a psycho-analyst this vastly extends the social value of the analyst and helps to justify his needing to do full-scale analyses in order to learn his craft.

It is well known that the first interview in an analysis can contain material that will come forward for analysis for months and even years. Students are advised to make careful notes of first interviews, notes which can be used at all later stages and which make possible a reconstruction of the analysis in terms of the discovery of deeper and more subtle meaning in events and free associations given in the first session.

That which I am calling the psychotherapeutic interview makes the fullest possible use of this relatively undefended material. There is real danger in this work, yet there is danger of doing nothing at all, and the risks come from the therapist's timidity or ignorance rather than from the patient's feeling of having been tricked.

The psychotherapist at this the stage of the first interview is a subjective object. Often a child will dream of the psychiatrist *the night before* the day of the interview, so that in fact the psychiatrist is fitting into the patient's preconceived notion. In another language, the patient brings to the situation a certain measure of belief or of the capacity to believe in a helping or understanding person. Also he brings a measure of suspicion. The therapist cashes in on what the patient brings and acts up to the limit of the chance that this affords. The patient goes away without having made an objective perception of the therapist, and a second visit will be needed to get the therapist objectified and shorn of magic.

There is a difference, then, between this technique and that of psycho-analysis in that whereas in the latter the transference neurosis gradually unfolds itself and is used for interpreting, in the psychotherapeutic interview there is a fore-ordained role for the therapist, based on the patient's pattern of expectation. The difficulty often is for the therapist to do as well as he could find himself allowed to do. Many patients do indeed expect to be basically understood immediately, and it might be said that we either fit in with this or else we work on the basis of "psycho-analysis or nothing." Of course we cannot understand immediately unless we are briefed, and in the first interview the patient is often willing and indeed eager to brief the therapist, giving all that is needed for the deep significant interpretation.

It often happens that we find a child has given all to the psychologist who is performing an intelligence test, and the fact that the material presented has not led to understanding (this not being included in the psychologist's aims) has proved traumatic to the child, leading to a strengthening of suspicion and an unwillingness to give the appropriate clues. This especially applies in Thematic Apperception Tests in which the patient has reached to unexpected ideas, fears, states. For this reason I have always seen my patients first, referring them to the psychologist where necessary, after I have come to grips with the case by doing something significant in the first interview or first few interviews.

I would say that it is a common thing for patients to go away from a first interview disillusioned and unwilling to make a further attempt to seek psychiatric help, because of the failure of the consultant to use the material presented. It is comparatively rare for a patient to be hurt by wrong interpretations made in a genuine attempt to use what is presented, the mistakes in omissions being due to the limits that belong to all human endeavor. I learned this from my psychotic patients (borderline schizophrenics) who are remarkably tolerant of an analyst's limitations of understanding, though they may be at the same time extremely intolerant of irregularities in the analyst's behavior (his unreliability, an uneven performance, display through reassurance of unconscious hate, bad taste, etc.).

TECHNIQUE

In order to make the most of a first interview the therapist needs to be very careful not to complicate the situation. All sorts of things need to be said and done which simply belong to the fact that the therapist is human and is not sitting on a professional high-horse and is nevertheless aware of the sacredness of the occasion. This is true regardless of the age of the patient.

A little girl, 2½ years old, saw me five times. She demanded that she should see someone to ask about a fear which her parents could not understand, and when she got some help from me she insisted on making further use of me until she had resolved her problem. Each time she gathered herself together for the interview and after it she emerged in a relaxed state. The fifth time, for instance, she came up (by train journey) curled up on her father's lap, sucking her thumb or her father's finger. She was very tense right up to her arrival at my door, and on entry she immediately went into my room and took up her position on the floor among the toys. After this interview she (now 3 years old) was in a happy state as usual. She was interested in everything she could see on the way home by train. In the afternoon she was playing constructively and with great satisfaction. In the evening she made one remark that was appropriate to the work of the session.

This was like a child's reaction to some analytic sessions but there was, in a sense, more at stake, because of the distance of the child's home from my room, which she actually talked about in the session.

A boy of 6, with a relatively low I.Q., the backwardness being secondary to an infantile psychosis, came to his first and only interview in a state of apprehension. The mother wrote: "He naturally wanted to know where we were going and we had to give him a definite answer because of his experience at 4 when he had his tonsils out. I didn't quite know what to say, so I mentioned something about learning at school and his sometimes annoying habit of finger-sucking. Anyway he mentioned after the interview with you that you hadn't asked him about this. He seemed to feel that I had misled him slightly. . . . When he asked again why we had gone to visit you and not taken our other boys I replied that you were a friend and that we thought he would enjoy meeting you, and we had only taken him as he was our biggest boy. He was contented with this answer. On that morning he had been very anxious to go straight to you and not waste time on proposed shopping."

This boy made significant use of his interview, and came away "delighted," and he was jealous of his parents when they came to see me a few weeks later.

It is good to be able to prepare the parents beforehand, perhaps by phone, that it will probably be best for the child to be seen first. The fact is that the parent may have to be neglected on this first occasion. It is the patient's right to be the patient, and if the parent cannot cooperate in this arrangement then one needs to consider whether in fact the ill person may not be the parent rather than the child. If it is the parent who is the patient, then the parent should be seen first, in which case it may be best to do nothing with the child, so as to avoid raising hopes that cannot be met.

It is axiomatic that if a proper professional setting is provided the patient, that is the child (or adult) who is in distress, will bring the distress into the interview in some form or other. The motivation is very deeply determined. Perhaps it is suspicion that is shown, or too great a trust, or trust is soon established and confidences soon follow. Whatever happens it is the happening that is significant.

A boy of 8 had a very rich interview with me; we had worked hard and I had been able to give help on the basis of the clues provided. At the second interview nothing happened at all. I allowed the boy his full hour, and all I said was: "I don't know what is going on but I do know that you have reason to be in control of me. Last time you helped me to help you; this time I can do nothing." So we parted. That evening this boy casually told his mother while he was in the bath that a man had tried to assault him in the park; the mother said: "Did you tell Dr. Winnicott?" and he said: "No!" in a surprised way, as if he could not have imagined this to be an important thing to do. He had in fact told me in a better way, by being suspicious of me and by having me in his control. I saw him next day as an emergency case, and he gave me another richly rewarding interview, reporting the incident and his own imaginative homosexual yearnings, based on a relative father-deprivation.

The point in all this was the boy's communication through making nothing happen, and my acceptance of this as a communication.

There is no clear-cut technical instruction to be given to the therapist, since he must be free to adopt any technique that is appropriate to the case. The main principle is that a human setting is provided and while the therapist is free to be himself he does not distort the course of events by doing things or not doing things because of his own anxiety or guilt, or his own need to have a success. It is the patient's picnic, and even the weather is the patient's weather. The end of the interview belongs to the patient too, except where there is no structure to the interview because of a lack of structure in the patient's personality or in the patient's relating to objects, in which case this lack of structuring is itself communicated.

A student attempting to study my personal technique would need to study the way that I behaved in a long series of cases, and it would be found that what I did in each example belonged to that particular case.

I hope that the only set feature that will be observed after a broad examination of my cases will be a freedom on my part to use my knowledge and experience to meet the particular patient's need as displayed in the one session that is being described.

One more observation: it is necessary to do this work in a wider setting in which there is opportunity for a case to slip over into another kind of child psychiatry category. There is no need for any case to fail (except where one lacks the necessary understanding, in which event there is no need for self-criticism). If the psychotherapeutic interview should prove inadequate even under the slogan: "How little need we do in this case?" then a more complex mechanism can be set in motion. The case can become one of those that need the full child psychiatry system of management.

It is wise, however, not to think in terms of *psycho-analysis* for the cases in which the psychotherapeutic consultation with its limited objective does not succeed; better, if psycho-analysis is likely to be a practical proposition to work from the start on the basis that psycho-analysis will be instigated. The reason for this is that a high-powered use of the first interview tends to make the initial stages of a classical analysis difficult, especially if the analysis is to be done by someone else, other than the initial consultant who went deep quickly in the first interview when attempting to make a diagnosis.

SUMMARY

1. A diagnostic interview must of necessity be a therapeutic one, since one of the main criteria for diagnosis is the response that indicates the degree of rigidity or relative lack of rigidity of the defense organization. The overall clinical picture may be deceptive without this additional key to the assessment of the patient's personality.

2. A human setting is provided, and into this setting the patient brings and displays the immediate strain and stress.

3. The psychiatrist is a subjective object, and the use that is made of the interview represents the patient's capacity to believe in significant persons, that is if the psychiatrist does not interfere with the pattern of the interview.

4. The psychiatrist needs to have training and experience based on long treatments, in which the work is done on the transference material as it gradually evolves, and which allows for the patient's objective perception of the analyst.

5. In this work interpretation is reserved for the significant moment, and then the analyst gives as much understanding as it is in his power to give. The fact that the patient has produced the material specifically for interpretation gives the therapist confidence that interpretation is needed and that it is more dangerous not to interpret than to interpret. The danger is that the patient will feel confirmed in the belief that no one understands and that no one wants to understand.

6. This is not "wild" interpreting; though even wild interpreting may convey the idea of a wish to understand.

A girl of 10 said to me: "It doesn't matter if some of the things you say are wrong because I know which are wrong and which are right." A little later on in the treatment she said to me: "I shouldn't go on guessing if I were you," implying that she could tolerate my not knowing.

13

THE SQUIGGLE GAME

IN MY CHILD PSYCHIATRY PRACTICE I HAVE found that a special place has to be given for a first interview. Gradually I have developed a technique for fully exploiting first interview material. To distinguish this work from psychotherapy and from psycho-analysis I use the term "psychotherapeutic consultation." It is a diagnostic interview, based on the theory that no diagnosis can be made in psychiatry except over the test of therapy.

The basis for this specialized work is the theory that a patient–child or adult– will bring to the first interview a certain amount of capacity to *believe* in getting help and to trust the one who offers help. What is needed from the helper is a strictly professional setting in which the patient is free to explore the exceptional opportunity that the consultation provides for communication. The patient's communication with the psychiatrist will have reference to the specific emotional tendencies which have a current form and which have roots that go back into the past or deep into the structure of the patient's personality and of his personal inner reality.

In this work the consultant or specialist does not need to be clever so much as to be able to provide a natural and freely moving human relationship within the professional setting while the patient gradually *surprises* himself by the production of ideas and feelings that have not been previously integrated into the total personality. Perhaps the main work done is of the nature of integration, made possible by the reliance on the human but professional relationship–a form of "holding."

Although opportunities do occur for interpretative comment, these can be kept to a minimum or, in fact, can be excluded deliberately. In this way, suitably selected consultants can do this work while in process of learning how to do psychotherapy that includes verbalized interpretation. The rewards of this work are great because the consultant is able to learn in this way from the patient, and it is necessary for the consultant to be ready to learn rather than to be eager to pounce on the material with interpretations. In selection of consultants, as in selection of psychotherapists in general, those who are eager to pounce on the material by interpreting should be reckoned to be temperamentally unsuitable for psychotherapeutic practice, and this is particularly true of suitability to carry out therapeutic consultations.

In doing this work, which I call "therapeutic consultation," with a child (or adult for that matter) it is necessary to be able to use the limited time profitably and to have techniques ready—however flexible these may be. It has to be assumed that in many of these cases what is not done during this consultation will not be done at all. The first consultation may be re-duplicated, but if the child needs to see the consultant several times, then the case already is changing over into one in which the team work of the clinic is becoming necessary and quite possibly the child will need to be handed over for treatment in long-term psychotherapy.

It is interesting that the cases that do not need to go over into casework or psychotherapy are relatively common. This is partly due to the fact that the majority of children do have good-enough homes and schooling, although they may at times present acute clinical problems. A little help given to an individual child can often lead to better relationships all around; the family and the school are waiting to do the rest of the treatment.

In regard to any technique that the consultant must be prepared to use, the basis is playing. Elsewhere (1971a) I have made the statement that in my opinion psychotherapy either is performed in the overlap of the two areas of playing (that of the patient and that of the therapist), or else the treatment must be directed towards enabling the child to become able to play—that is to say, to have reason to trust the environmental provision. It has to be assumed that the therapist can play, and can enjoy playing.

One useful technique has been called the Squiggle Game, which is simply one method for making contact with a child patient. It is a game any two people can play, but usually in social life the game quickly ceases to have meaning. The reason this game can have value for the psychotherapeutic consultation is that the consultant uses the results according to his knowledge of what the child would like to communicate. It is the way the material, produced in the act of playing, is used that keeps the child interested.

The method can easily be learned, and it has the advantage that it greatly facilitates the taking of notes. If a boy or girl communicates by talking or by recounting dreams, then note-taking is a truly formidable problem, and it must be remembered that I am not referring to those few cases that we treat by prolonged psychotherapy, but to the many that come for consultation. Each one of them hopes for more than a diagnosis – each hopes for a need to be met, even if help can only be given in regard to one detail or in one area of the vast extent of the personality.

Nevertheless I have hesitated to describe this technique, which I have used a great deal over a number of years, not only because it is a natural game that any two people might play, but also, if I begin to describe what I do, then someone will be likely to begin to rewrite what I describe as if it were a set technique with rules and regulations. Then the whole value of the procedure would be lost. If I describe what I do there is a very real danger that others will take it and form it into something that corresponds to a Thematic Apperception Test. The difference between this and a T.A.T. is firstly that it is not a test, and secondly that the consultant contributes from his own ingenuity almost as much as the child does. Naturally, the consultant's contribution drops out, because it is the child, not the consultant, who is communicating distress.

The fact that the consultant freely plays his own part in the exchange of drawings certainly has a great importance for the success of the technique; such a procedure does not make the patient feel inferior in any way as, for instance, a patient feels when being examined by a doctor in respect of physical health, or, often, when being given a psychological test (especially a personality test).

At a suitable moment after the arrival of the patient, usually after asking the parent to go to the waiting room, I say to the child: "Let's play something. I know what I would like to play and I'll show you." I have a table between the child and myself, with paper and two pencils. First I take some of the paper and tear the sheets in half, giving the impression that what we are doing is not frantically important, and then I begin to explain. I say: "This game that I like playing has no rules. I just take my pencil and go like that . . . ," and I probably screw up my eyes and do a squiggle blind. I go on with my explanation and say: "You show me if that looks like anything to you or if you can make it into anything, and afterwards you do the same for me and I will see if I can make something of yours."

This is all there is by way of technique, and it has to be emphasized that I am absolutely flexible even at this very early stage, so that if the child wishes to draw or to talk or to play with toys or to make music or to romp, I feel free to fit in with the child's wishes. Often a boy will want to play what he calls a "points game"; that is to say, something that can be won or lost. Nevertheless, in a high proportion of first-interview cases the child fits in sufficiently long with my wishes and with what I like playing for some progress to be made. Soon the rewards begin to come in, so that the game continues. Often in an hour we have done twenty to thirty drawings together, and gradually the significance of these composite drawings has become deeper and deeper, and is felt by the child to be a part of communication of significance.

It is interesting to note, regarding the squiggles themselves, that

1. I am better at them than the children are, and the children are usually better than I am at drawing.
2. They contain an impulsive movement.
3. They are mad, unless done by a sane person. For this reason some children find them frightening.
4. They are incontinent, except that they accept limitations, so some children feel them to be naughty. This is allied to the subject of *form and content*. The size and shape of the paper is a factor.
5. There is an integration in each squiggle that comes from the integration that is part of me; this is not, I believe, a typically obsessional integration, which would contain the element of *denial of chaos*.
6. Often the result of a squiggle is satisfactory in itself. It is then like a "found object," for instance a stone or piece of old wood that a sculptor may find and set up as a kind of expression, without needing work. This appeals to lazy boys and girls, and throws light on the meaning of laziness. Any work done spoils what starts off as an idealized object. It may be felt by an artist that the paper or the canvas is too beautiful, it must not be spoiled. Potentially, it *is* a masterpiece. In psycho-analytic theory we have the concept of the dream screen (Lewin 1948), a place into or onto which a dream might be dreamed.[3]

All this is linked to the very early stage of maximal dependence when the infant self is unformed. The ego is very weak, unless (as usually happens) the mother's ego gives ego-support. The infant starts off living with the mother's ego which she lends by her sensitive adaptation to her infant's needs.

It must be understood that no two cases are alike, and I would be highly suspicious if two cases resembled each other, because I would think then that I was planting something out of some need of my own. The description of only one case must be deceptive, and a student of this technique would certainly need to go through a score of cases in order to see that, in fact, no two cases *are* alike.

REFERENCE

Lewin, B. (1948). Inferences from the dream screen. *International Journal of Psycho-Analysis* 29:224–231.
Winnicott, D. W. (1971). Playing: creative activity and the search for the self. In *Playing and Reality*, pp. 62–75. New York: Basic Books.

Part II

REMEMBERING WINNICOTT

14

CLARE WINNICOTT: INTERVIEW WITH DR. MICHAEL NEVE

CW: I think the difference between D.W.W. and a great many other psychoanalysts—in fact, almost everybody—is that he came at psychoanalysis from pediatrics. From a study of normal families who are ill, with ill children, but seeing—He saw 60,000 cases in his clinics, in his three clinics, by the time he retired. He'd seen 60,000 mothers with children, parents with children. He ran three clinics.

And he studied, he studied the whole family, always took the whole family into account, because he just couldn't do it just with the child. He made very quick contact *with* the child, but it was the family structure that he tried to support in his clinical work. Very much so. So that he got experience of normality, normal families—*poor*, poverty stricken—he worked in the East End and Paddington Green, which are both *very* poor areas.

But he would go and visit the families if he felt like it. Go out and visit them. Often did. Round, round about Paddington Green. And I think this experience of normal family-working and how it can work he brought in with him to psychoanalysis. And it comes with a positive—it comes with something positive. It comes at psychoanalysis from health, rather than from illness, pathology. It doesn't get at it from pathology.

He discovers pathology as he goes along. And he was, he had no illusions about pathology and the, you know, the serious illnesses and the effect of serious illness on people. In fact, I'd often be surprised that he'd pick up—you know, from a contact with somebody—When we left them he'd say, "Well now, I wonder how long he's been on drugs." Or whatever. And I thought, "My goodness, you know, he doesn't miss a thing really." He had very, very acute powers of observation—about everything.

MN: But take the Freudian death instinct and so on. He doesn't seem to—

CW: He doesn't believe in it. He's written about that. I don't know if you know. He doesn't go along with it at all. He thinks death is a *disaster*, which you have to put up with, because you're human. No, he didn't like the idea of death at all.

MN: What about loneliness? He talked wonderfully about, as we know, the capacity to *be alone*. What's the difference between being alone and being lonely?

CW: Being lonely is you're—you feel incomplete. You're missing somebody. There's a bit of depression and pathology in it perhaps. Not necessarily. Yes, perhaps to some extent.

　　The capacity to be alone is an achievement of good experiences—enough good experiences to keep your own inner world good. Loneliness is being without your good object in a sense. Being alone with the bad, you know, you *are* alone then. There's a great deal of difference. Mrs. Klein, of course, wrote on loneliness. Soon after he'd written his paper. And they're very different papers.

　　But I think for him loneliness has got depression—illness perhaps—and the capacity to be alone has got health in it.

MN: What about waiting?

CW: Waiting for the patient, you're talking about? Waiting for the patient to—?

MN: Well, something—he says something very interesting about just waiting.

CW: For development to happen?

MN: Yes.

CW: For things to happen?

MN: Yes. Or a child waiting for the meal, knowing the meal will come. Learning that the meal will be coming and waiting, as against demanding or screaming or whatever.

CW: Yes.

MN: That seems very—

CW: I think that does—Yes, he does make that in fact an important issue. That the child builds up—When his intellectual powers are developing, he knows the sound means there's something happening, and can rationalize and can wait. For a *certain* length of time. You can keep the good thing going for a certain length of time. If it's over that edge, then there's disaster.

　　But this is very much according to age and stage of development and, yes, emotional development—according to emotional development. I mean, how far have you gotten in the waiting game? And that's really according to how you've experienced it. If you've not been left waiting too long, till the thing snapped. Then it's very hard to mend it again. It's like being brought out tight and then the elastic snapped and can't be put together. And there *are* stages when it's gone too far.

But he—I mean, timing for him was tremendously important in all developmental processes. The right time for the right thing, you know. And that people *have* got a time and a rhythm in their own, in themselves, which he would work to free or let develop.

MN: One thing that seems quite, sort of, strangely different from Freud is the stuff on infantile sexuality. I mean, he doesn't seem to think that sexuality is absolutely primary in infantile development, but comes when other cognitive capacities or whatever have matured. Is that right?

CW: Yes.

MN: Because that seems quite an important difference, doesn't it—?

CW: Yes.

MN: From classic Freudian theory?

CW: Yes. In a way, Freud, of course, pioneered all that, didn't he? So Donald could take it for granted. I mean, he knew about it. He didn't have to *discover* it. Freud did. So perhaps that's why Freud—the emphasis is there. But I think he thought it would happen. There was no *denying* it. This happened. It had to be dealt with by parents.

It would be *discussed* with parents. He had many of these sexual problems always. He would use it in his *work* with children. I should think it comes into *Therapeutic Consultations*. And it does with *The Piggle*, definitely. But I think if it wasn't for him the land—it *hadn't* got the importance that it had for Freud.

Or the *central position* let's say. It isn't importance. It's important, all right. But it had a central importance for Freud, did it not? I mean, Freud developed his other theories around this one, quite a lot. But I think Donald could take it for granted, and it worked in with—it was a part of a deep developmental process. He believed *deeply* in the developmental process. There was *always* a drive towards health—biological, biologically backed drive towards health. And that includes mental health. That was his conviction.

MN: Which might be Darwinian. Or—did he read Piaget?

CW: Yes, but not . . . well. Not well. *That was very—yes, I think Darwinian.* But that started him off on this.

Another thing I'm—I'm jumping a bit. There was another person who influenced him a great deal during his medical training . . . was Lord Horder. He was then Dr. Thomas Horder, training medical students. Now, he was attached to Tommy Horder at some points. And it was Horder who said to

him, "Listen to your patient. Don't you go in with your wonderful knowledge
and apply it all. Just listen. They'll tell you quite a lot of things. You'll learn a
lot if you listen."

   And Horder practiced this himself. And he watched Horder work. And
he cottoned on immediately to this, and found how fascinating it was to hear
people talk about themselves! Now, this is very unusual in medical practice.

MN: To listen to the patient?

CW: Very much so. [MN laughs] It *really* is. I mean [CW laughs], I don't know.
You're the history of medicine, but I'm, I'm a very experienced patient.
Anyhow it was said to me the other day, "Well, we didn't believe you when
you said this—that if you stopped taking these pills, your temperature would
go up. We didn't believe you."

   I said, "I know you didn't. But there it is. I was right."

MN: So that the analyst is not lording it over the patient, as it were [CW makes
sounds of agreement], in Winnicott's scheme.

CW: He would very much feel that. It's what we can do together.

15

MASUD KHAN AND J. P. M. TIZARD: OBITUARIES FOR DONALD W. WINNICOTT

BRIDGING PEDIATRICS AND PSYCHOANALYSIS

Dr. Donald Winnicott died suddenly at his home on Monday, 25 January, at the age of 74. With his death, the living tradition of one man's sustained clinical dedication, across some 50 years, to the care and facilitation of children and adults to psychic health and maturity, changes into a rich heritage and responsibility for his colleagues and co-workers.

Dr. Winnicott started his long psychotherapeutic odyssey as an Assistant Physician at the Paddington Green Children's Hospital in 1923, where he worked for 40 years. It was in this setting of intensive pediatric involvement with infants and mothers that he gradually carved his specific therapeutic sensibility. In the early 30s he turned to psychoanalysis to supplement and enlarge his clinical experience and skills. He was analyzed by the late James Strachey, and later by Mrs. Riviere. He became a qualified psycho-analyst in the mid-30s, and from then onwards, with indefatigable energy and devotion, he tried to assimilate his clinical experience as a pediatrician to his insights into psychic functioning that accrued from psychoanalytic work. His published works, particularly *Collected Papers: Through Paediatrics to Psycho-Analysis* (1958) and *The Maturational Processes and the Facilitating Environment* (1965), give a clear account of his researches and theoretical innovations.

Winnicott was a solitary, willful and extremely modest, non-factional theo-retician and clinician. Gradually over the decades, the impact of his researches has permeated in all the neighboring disciplines, from pediatrics and psychoanalysis to social work and education. He was a true revolutionary in his clinical outlook and thinking, but a revolutionary without a dogmatic evangelical program.

At the beginning of this century, Freud had established the ubiquity of the role of unconscious instinctual wishes and conflicts in the development of the human individual. Freud had also invented a therapeutic setting and process which he named psychoanalysis, where these conflicts could be discovered, explored and resolved. The emphasis was on knowing and insight. Winnicott, from his deep involvement with infants and their caretaking mothers, took the next logical step and enlarged the scope of the psychotherapeutic task to include the realization and meeting the need of the patient as a person. His clinical work developed on two parallel and reciprocal lines. He evolved a Squiggle Game for therapeutic consul-tations with children, and his researches in this area are shortly to be published in his book, *Therapeutic Consultations in Child Psychiatry* (Hogarth). Alongside, Win-nicott had the courage as well as the tenacity to allow the adult ill person maximal scope for moments of regression, when necessary, in the clinical setting, and to hold and meet this regression patiently and vigilantly towards its resolution into the finding and becoming of his own true self by the patient as a person. His researches in this area have had a momentous impact on the whole character of the therapeutic undertaking by analysts regarding their patients. Winnicott, un-daunted by the criticisms and misgivings of his colleagues, whose opinion he always respected and was equally unhindered by, compelled the analytic clinicians to respect the need in the patient as the true guide to the predicament of the patient as a person. Naturally, his work involved him with very ill persons, and there were inevitable casualties and failures. Winnicott modeled his clinical orientation to the patient largely on an "ordinary devoted mother's" holding care of her infant.

The very simplicity of this undertaking involves arduous devotion and knowledge because it entails responding to the patient's need as it arises in the clinical situation. One can best sum up Winnicott's clinical achievement in the verse of Ezra Pound:

"Here error is all in the not done, all in the diffidence that faltered."

It is this therapeutic diffidence that Winnicott transcended by providing maximum clinical coverage to the extreme vulnerability of the ill person at the point of need. There was also an extraordinary sagacity in Winnicott that enabled him to help normal persons to discover their hidden areas of immaturity towards a fuller realization of their potential in lived day to day life.

Winnicott's was a long and distinguished career. He became Fellow of the

Royal College of Physicians in 1944; was a Fellow of the British Psychological Society; served two terms as President of the British Psycho-Analytical Society; was President of the Paediatric Section of the Royal Society of Medicine, and was awarded the James Spence Medal for Paediatrics in 1968. He had been for over 25 years on the training staff of the Institute of Psycho-Analysis, and had lectured to various organizations and institutes all over the world. Everyone who came into contact with him was not only enriched but enlarged by the experience. He had a unique talent for engendering fruition of the innate potential of those he encountered. With his death, psychoanalysis has lost one of its truly creative, courageous and self-critical thinkers.

Winnicott married for the second time, in 1951, Clare Britton, who survives him.

M. Masud R. Khan

It would be wrong to say that Donald Winnicott was a many-sided man: in reality he was a man of many depths and there is so much to be said about him at any level that it is difficult to know which aspects of his life and work and personality to select.

I was greatly touched and honored when Mrs. Winnicott asked me to speak[1] about him. My qualifications for doing so are twofold and neither is unique. Firstly, I am a pediatrician, and pediatrics was Donald Winnicott's primary discipline within medicine, and secondly, in the words of Ben Jonson about his friend William Shakespeare, "I loved the man, and do honour his memory, on this side idolatry, as much as any."

I first got to know Donald Winnicott 22 years ago when I became a physician at the Paddington Green Children's Hospital. I went there with a poor opinion of the general usefulness of child psychiatry but I soon found that however difficult and damaging a child's past and present circumstances the situation was always changed for the better once Dr. Winnicott became involved. At first I attributed this to his obvious high intelligence, his intuitive powers and the fact that he was "good with children"; but while all these attributions were correct, I later realized – and I am sure he would have liked me to say so – that his success also owed much to his professional discipline and his training as a psychoanalyst. Donald Winnicott had the most astonishing powers with children. To say that he understood children would to me sound false and vaguely patronizing; it was rather that children understood him and that he was at one with them. He used to allow some of his younger colleagues at Paddington Green to be present while he interviewed a child. The presence of others would be regarded by most doctors as prohibitively disturbing, but the fact was that within a few minutes of a child entering his

---

1. A tribute read at Dr. Winnicott's funeral.

consulting room both the child and Dr. Winnicott were oblivious of the presence of anyone else. A good example of his acceptance by and communication with children is what happened when he was about to visit a Danish family for the second time after an interval of a few years. The children remembered his playing with them very well and were delighted at the prospect of again meeting an Englishman who could speak Danish. When their father said that Dr. Winnicott could not speak a word of their difficult language his children simply did not believe him.

It is impossible to estimate the extent of Donald Winnicott's influence on British pediatrics. I believe it to have been enormous, but its full extent will probably not be realized for many years. The way in which he influenced a generation of pediatricians younger than himself and *their* students was not by doctrinal teaching but by revealing to us the possibilities for teaching ourselves about the personalities of others. The key to this self-education was a profound respect for other people. This quality was obvious in Donald Winnicott and it is, of course, the hallmark of morality. His ideas were on the whole rejected by his contemporaries in pediatrics and I am afraid that he suffered a real, though unintended, persecution at their hands. A great artist is one who changes the tastes not of his own generation—for that is impossible—but of the next. A great man of ideas likewise changes the way in which the next generation thinks. Mozart was considered by most of his contemporaries to be revolutionary and difficult to grasp—and I am quoting a contemporary source.

Donald Winnicott was a great physician and, I believe, a philosopher of great importance, but I shall remember him best as a conversationalist. He was the diametrical opposite of a bore. A bore is somebody who is dull and also insensitive to his hearer's feelings. Donald had the liveliest wit and was acutely sensitive to his hearers.

To those who are unsympathetic, he could be shy and uncommunicative, but to those who appreciated him he was a sparkling talker. There was no aspect of life—morals, art or politics—which he did not illuminate with a new truth, just as a great artist makes one see a familiar object in a new light and with new meaning. He was sensitive not only to the feelings of individual hearers but also to the feelings of an audience. He was a brilliant lecturer and a masterly exponent of what one might call the banana skin theory of laughter—the briefly anticipated disaster which does not take place—and in evoking this kind of laughter he had a comedian's sense of timing.

One is peculiarly blessed if in the course of a lifetime one can get to know well someone who seems to have the truth in him, that is to say profound wisdom with never a trace of pretense. Donald was such a man. It was an endearing aspect of his character that he could afford to acknowledge his own weaknesses, normal human attributes which most of us cannot admit possessing. He was given to a little self-dramatization; he had a certain vanity in the sense of wanting to be loved and admired; he was easily hurt; and while he was far too courageous a man to fear death, he couldn't be reconciled to the idea of extinction. But it is of his enormous zest for life which I like to think and one particular aspect of it was his never-ending curiosity and wish to learn, an example of which he put to me within a few hours of his death.

How lucky we were to know him; but in a sense how lucky was he to know us! I wonder if any of you have ever known a man or woman who had so many truly devoted friends? And in no respect was he luckier than in his wife, Clare. I am sure he was right in supposing that without her he would have died twenty years ago; and she not only gave him the happiest years of his life, but years which were also the most productive and the most influential.

A true and vivid remembrance of Donald Winnicott will only last the lifetimes of those who knew him, but I like to think that those who remember us for a brief period of time will do so more kindly because of Donald Winnicott's influence on us.

J. P. M. Tizard

16

MARION MILNER: D. W. WINNICOTT AND THE TWO-WAY JOURNEY

O FTEN, WHEN I TALKED TO PEOPLE about D. W. Winnicott they would say, "Oh, but of course, he was a genius." I do not know what makes a genius. All I know is that I must take as my text for this paper something he once said to his students just before a lecture: "What you get out of me, you will have to pick out of chaos."

I want to describe the highlights of my contacts with him in matters of theory. I find this particularly hard to do, because I am one of those people who Freud reminded us exist, people who think in pictures. So what I want to say about Winnicott must center around certain visual images.

One night in 1957, driving through France, I saw a crowd in the marketplace of a little town, all gathered around an arc lamp where a trapeze had been set up by traveling acrobats. The star performers were there, in spotless white, doing wonderful turns and handstands on the bar. Below them was a little clown in a grey floppy coat too big for him, just fooling around while the others did their displays. Occasionally he made a fruitless attempt to jump up and reach the bar. Then, suddenly, he made a great leap and there he was, whirling around on the bar, all his clothes flying out, like a huge Catherine wheel, to roars of delight from the crowd.

This is my image of Winnicott. Often over the years when we had a gap of time and arranged to meet to discuss some theoretical problem, he would open the door, and there he would be, all over the place, whistling, forgetting something, running upstairs, making a general clatter, so that I would become impatient for him to settle down. Gradually, I came to see this as a necessary preliminary to those fiery flashes of his intuition that would always follow. He has actually written about the logic of this in one of his papers, where he talks of the necessity, when doing an analysis, of recognizing and allowing for phases of nonsense, when no thread ought to be searched for in the patient's material because what is going on is preliminary chaos, the first phase of the creative process.

After the whirling clown on the bar comes another image, an actual Catherine wheel firework, nailed to a tree and lit by a small boy, in the still dark of the countryside. The wheel at first splutters and misfires, then gets going as a fizzing, fiery ring of light, sending off sparks into the darkness around. I always have an image of the dark disk at the center whenever I read in his writings about the unknowable core of the self.

My third image, woven into my thoughts for this chapter, is part of a shared joke we had. During the war I had shown him a cartoon from the New Yorker. It was of two hippopotamuses, their heads emerging from the water, and one saying to the other, "I thought it was Thursday." It was typical of him that he never forgot this joke. After all these years, I see how it fits in with a dominant preoccupation of mine—the threshhold of consciousness, the surface of the water as the place of submergence or emergence.

And from this picture of the water's surface I come to one of his images, that is, the quotation from Tagore that he put at the head of his paper "The Location of Cultural Experience" (Winnicott 1971b): "On the sea-shore of endless worlds children play." I too have had this line at the back of my mind, ever since I first read it in 1915. Winnicott said that, for him, the aphorism aided speculation upon the question, if play is neither inside nor outside, where is it? For me it stirred thoughts of the coming and going of the tides, the rhythmic daily submergence and smoothing out of this place where children play.

Later in this paper about the place of cultural experience he uses another image that we both had in common—only I had completely forgotten about it. He is talking about how the baby comes to be able to make use of the symbol of union and can begin to allow for and benefit from separation, a separation that is not a separation, but a form of union; and here he refers to a drawing that I had made, long ago in the thirties, showing the interplay of the edges of two jugs. He says the drawing conveyed to him the tremendous significance there can be in the interplay of edges.

I too found myself using this same drawing as a visual symbol for his concept of potential space. And it still has many overtones for me, since a patient of mine used it constantly, in the more abstract form of two overlapping circles which become two faces and then oscillate between being two and being one.

So much for the images. Now for the actuality.

I first saw Winnicott when he was giving a public lecture in the late thirties, talking about his work with mothers and babies and the famous spatula game. He told how he would leave a spatula on the table in front of the mother and baby, well within the baby's reach. Then he simply watched what the baby did with the spatula, watched for variations in the normal pattern of reaching for it, grabbing it, giving it a good suck and then chucking it away. He told how, out of this very simple experimental situation, he could work out, according to the observed blocks in the various stages, a diagnosis of the problems between the mother and the baby. As he talked, I was captivated by the mixture in him of deep seriousness and his love of little jokes, that is, the play aspect of his character, if one thinks of true play as transcending the opposites of serious and nonserious.

It was after this lecture that I began to attend his clinic as an observer, and I well remember the pleasure he took in this spatula game. I feel it was the neatness that satisfied both the artist and the scientist in the man, the formal qualities so simple and clear, providing a structure within which he made his observations. And this same feeling for aesthetic form continued in his therapeutic use with children of what he called the squiggle game. In fact, as described in his book on the subject (1971c) he used these games to structure the therapeutic consultations. Each account of those drawing sessions with the child exemplifies as well his beautiful concept of potential space—an essentially pictorial concept, although he defines it as "what happens between two people when there is trust and reliability." Thus there is also the way the account of each session organizes time. Time stretches back, not only through the child's lifetime, but also through Winnicott's own years of psychoanalytic practice, so that he has at his fingertips the tools of psychoanalytic concepts, though using them here in a different setting.

Then there is what I have gained from his concept of the holding environment. I will not say much about this, for I have already given it extensive form in my book about a patient's drawings, having even embodied the idea in my title: *The Hands of the Living God* (Milner 1969). The phrase is in fact taken from a poem by D. H. Lawrence, a poem in which Lawrence describes the ghastly feelings of terror at falling forever when contact with the inner holding environment is lost.

I would in addition like to say something about Winnicott's comment, in his paper on play (1971a), on my 1952 paper on the play of a boy patient. Near the beginning of his paper Winnicott points out that I have related playing to concentration in adults, and that he has done the same thing. A little later he quotes my remark about "moments when the original poet in us created the world for us perhaps forgotten . . . because they were too much like visitations of the gods" (Milner 1952). His quoting this reminded me that one of the jumping-off places for my paper had been a growing preoccupation with certain moments in the boy's play, moments which seemed to both express and be accompanied by a special kind of concentration, moments actually symbolized, it seemed to me, by his continual play with lighted candles and fires in the dark, as well as by explicit play concerning visitations of the gods. All this seems to me now to link up with what Winnicott came to call "creative apperception," the coloring of external reality in a new way, a way that can give a feeling of great significance and can in fact, as he claims, make life feel worth living, even in the face of much instinct deprivation.

I realized too that this starting point for that paper of mine had also been the starting point for the first book I ever wrote, a book based on a diary I kept in 1926, about the sudden moments when one's whole perception of the world changes — changes that happen, sometimes apparently out of the blue, but sometimes as the result of a deliberate shift of attention, one that makes the whole world seem newly created. Although when I became an analyst I tried to fit these experiences into such psychoanalytic concepts as manic defenses against depression and so on, these ideas did not seem quite adequate to account for the phenomena. But then I found Winnicott making the distinction between the vicissitudes of instinct and what happens in creativity, which for him was the same as creative playing. This seemed to offer a more useful approach. Not that I found his way of putting his ideas about creativity entirely easy: sometimes he seemed to be talking about a way of looking at the world, sometimes about a way of doing something deliberately, and sometimes about simply enjoying a bodily activity, breathing, for instance, that just happens. I asked myself: In what sense are these all creative? Certainly they are different, as he says, from the making of anything, such as a house or a meal or a picture, though all these may include what he is talking about. Then I happened upon a statement that helped me clarify the problem. It was Martin Buber's remark about "productivity versus immediacy of the lived life." He was referring to what he called the dominant delusion of our time, that creativity (meaning, I supposed, *artistic* creativity) is the criterion of human worth. Buber went on to say that "the potentiality of form also accompanies every experience that befalls the nonartistic man and is given an issue as often as he lifts an image out of the stream of perception and inserts it into his memory as something single, definite and meaningful in itself" (Buber 1969). This phrase — lifting an image out of the stream of perception — clearly related to Winnicott's comment, "What you get out of me you must pick out of chaos." Thus one gets the idea of creativeness as not simply perceiving, but as deliberately relating ourselves to our perceiving. It is perceiving that has an "I AM" element in it. And this brings me to Winnicott's use of the word *self*.

First, what does he say about the way self comes into being? He claims that the sense of self comes only from desultory formless activity or rudimentary play, and then only if reflected back; he adds that it is only in being creative that one discovers oneself. I have a difficulty here. I can understand him when he claims that the sense of self comes on the basis of the unintegrated state, but when he adds that this state is by definition not observable or communicable, I begin to wonder. Not communicable, yes. Not observable, I am not so sure. I think of the dark still center of the whirling Catherine wheel and feel fairly certain that it can, in the right setting, be related to by the conscious ego discovering that it can turn in upon itself, make contact with the core of its own being, and find there a renewal, a rebirth. In fact isn't Winnicott himself referring to this when he speaks of "quietude linked with stillness"? This reminds me of T. S. Eliot's "still point of the turning world" or "words after speech reach into silence."

Linked to this question of the discovery of the self is surely the discovery of one's own body. So the question arises, What is the relation of the sense of being, which Winnicott says must precede the finding of the self, to the awareness of one's own body? I think there is a hint about this when he speaks of the "summation or reverberation of experiences of relaxation in conditions of trust based on experience." For me this phrase stirs echoes throughout years of observation of how deliberate bodily relaxation brings with it, if one can wait for it, a reverberation from inside, something spreading in waves, something that brings an intense feeling of response from that bit of the outer world that is at the same time also oneself: one's own body. Here is what I think he means when he speaks of enjoying one's own breathing as an example of creativity.

As for his statements concerning the first toy, which he says we do not challenge as to its coming from inside or from outside (Winnicott 1953), these serve as a bridge for me, particularly to the special cultural field of religion. When I encounter, in a book entitled *The God I Want* (Williams 1967), the idea that to discover God as myself is also to discover Him as other than myself, when I read that receiving implies otherness and that at the same time what we receive is our own, I am reminded of the creative paradox so dear to Winnicott. And when he speaks of the transitional object as the symbol of a journey, it seems really to be a two-way journey: both to the finding of the objective reality of the object and to the finding of the objective reality of the subject—the I AM.

There was, as well as this word *creativity* and all its implications, another term that, since the late forties, had given me a lot of uneasiness, like a shoe beginning to feel too tight. The term was *primary process*. I had been taught that this was a form of archaic thinking that had to be outgrown. But slowly, over the years, *primary process* seems to have changed its meaning, so that it is now seen, certainly by some writers, as part of the integrating function of the ego: that is, it serves to join up experiences and assimilate them into the ego, in order to preserve the ego's wholeness. As such it is not something to be grown out of, but, rather, is complementary to secondary process functioning and as necessary to it as male and female are to each other. It is this primary process that enables one to accept paradox and contradiction, something that secondary process does not like at all, being itself bound by logic, which rejects contradiction. Although Winnicott hardly ever uses the term, I feel that given this new meaning, the concept of primary process is implicit in all of his work and integral to his idea of what it means to be healthy.

So what the hippopotamus joke means to me now is this: One must not try to make the hippo live only on land, because it is, by nature, incurably amphibious. And whatever it means to say that someone is a genius, I do wish to make clear that I believe Winnicott was on excellent terms with his primary process; it was an inner marriage to which there was very little impediment.

REFERENCES

Buber, M. (1969). The Healthy Personality. Ed. Hung-min Chiang and A. Maslow. London: Van Nostrand, Reinhold.

Milner, M. (1969). The Hands of the Living God. London: Hogarth.

_____ (1952). Aspects of symbolism in comprehension of the not-self. International Journal of Psycho-Analysis 33:181–195.

_____ (1969). The Hands of the Living God. London: Hogarth.

Williams, I. H. A., (1967). The God I Want. Ed. J. Mitchell. London: Constable.

Winnicott, D. W. (1953). Transitional objects and transitional phenomena. In Collected Papers: Through Paediatrics to Psycho-Analysis. New York: Basic Books, 1958.

_____ (1971a). Playing: a theoretical statement. In Playing and Reality. New York: Basic Books.

_____ (1971b). The location of cultural experience. In Playing and Reality. New York: Basic Books.

_____ (1971c). Therapeutic Consultations in Child Psychiatry. New York: Basic Books.

17

MARGARET LITTLE:
PSYCHOTHERAPY
WITH D. W. W.

So, THIRTEEN YEARS AFTER FIRST SEEKING psychiatric help, and now aged 48, I came to D. W. I cannot give as clear, coherent, or detailed an account of the time with him as I could wish. I can only recount some of the things that happened.

My previous acquaintance with him had been slight. The first scientific meeting of the British Psycho-Analytical Society that I attended was on a noisy evening with bombs dropping every few minutes and people ducking as each crash came. In the middle of the discussion someone I later came to know as D. W. stood up and said, "I should like to point out that there is an air raid going on," and sat down. No notice was taken, and the meeting went on as before!

I heard him speak at other meetings and read papers. Then, at the end of the evening in 1945 when I read my membership paper, "The Wanderer: Some Notes on a Paranoid Patient," which he had not discussed, he came and asked if I would take a child patient. I was very pleased to be asked, but regretfully said No. I had recently finished analysis with a child, for training (in child analysis) which I never completed. It had aroused enormous anxiety and I felt badly about the way I had ended. I was in turmoil about this, about my father's death and the circumstances surrounding it, and could not consider dealing with another child just then, but I left it open for the future.

I heard him read his papers "Reparation in Respect of Mother's Organized

Defence against Depression" (Winnicott 1948) and "Birth Memories, Birth Trauma, and Anxiety" (Winnicott 1949) and felt that this was someone who could really help me.

The preliminary interview with him was short, perhaps fifteen minutes. At no time did he take a formal history of any kind, but feeling his way, built up gradually his understanding of what was troubling me and of my "heart's need" (George Eliot, *Mill on the Floss*). I made my sexual affair an excuse for not pursuing the analysis; he accepted this but said that he would keep the vacancy open for the time being and I could take it up later if I wished. It was not long before I went back to him, as I found the sexual relationship difficult.

The first session brought a repetition of the terror. I lay curled up tight, completely hidden under the blanket, unable to move or speak. D. W. was silent until the end of the hour, when he said only, "I don't *know*, but I have the feeling that you are shutting me out for some reason." This brought relief, for he could admit not knowing, and could allow contradiction if it came. Much later I realized that I had been shutting myself in, taking up the smallest possible amount of space and being as unobtrusive as I could, hiding in the womb, but not safe even there.

In one early session with D. W. I felt in utter despair of ever getting him to understand anything. I wandered round his room trying to find a way. I contemplated throwing myself out of the window, but felt that he would stop me. Then I thought of throwing out all his books, but finally I attacked and smashed a large vase filled with white lilac, and trampled on it. In a flash he was gone from the room, but he came back just before the end of the hour. Finding me clearing up the mess he said, "I might have expected you to do that [clear up? or smash?] but later." Next day an exact replica had replaced the vase and the lilac, and a few days later he explained that I had destroyed something that he valued. Neither of us ever referred to it again, which seems odd to me now, but I think that if it had happened later on he would probably have reacted differently. As it was, it felt as useless as my struggles with Miss Sharpe or my mother, and I forgot it until recently. Many years later, long after termination, when asking for advice about a very disturbed patient who hurt me knowingly and repeatedly, I spoke of having hurt him. He agreed that I had, but added that it had been "useful."

Some weeks after this, throughout a whole session I was seized with recurring spasms of terror. Again and again I felt a tension begin to build up in my whole body, reach a climax, and subside, only to come again a few seconds later. I grabbed his hands and clung tightly till the spasms passed. He said at the end that he thought I was reliving the experience of being born; he held my head for a few minutes, saying that immediately after birth an infant's head could ache and feel heavy for a time. All this seemed to fit, for it was birth *into a relationship*, via my spontaneous movement, which was accepted by him (Little and Flarsheim 1964). Those spasms never came again, and only rarely that degree of fear.

He soon found that for the first half of every session nothing happened. I could not talk until I found a "settled" state, undisturbed by any impingement such as being asked to say what I was thinking, etc. It was as if I had to take into myself the silence and the stillness that he provided. This was in such contrast with the disturbances of childhood, my mother's anxiety-driven state, and the general hostility from which I had always felt the need to retreat to find quietness. From then he extended the length of the sessions to an hour and a half, at the same fee, until nearly the end of the analysis.

Here I feel it is appropriate to speak of the two things about which there has been most misunderstanding—holding and regression to dependence. D. W. used the word holding both metaphorically and literally. Metaphorically he was holding the situation, giving support, keeping contact on every level with whatever was going on, in and around the patient and in the relationship to him.

Literally, through many long hours he held my two hands clasped between his, almost like an umbilical cord, while I lay, often hidden beneath the blanket, silent, inert, withdrawn, in panic, rage, or tears, asleep and sometimes dreaming. Sometimes he would become drowsy, fall asleep, and wake with a jerk, to which I would react with anger, terrified and feeling as if I had been hit. He has himself described such sessions (Winnicott 1970). He must have suffered much boredom and exhaustion in these hours, and sometimes even pain in his hands. We could speak of it later.

"Holding," of which "management" was always a part, meant taking full responsibility, supplying whatever ego strength a patient could not find in himself, and withdrawing it gradually as the patient could take over on his own. In other words, providing the "facilitating environment" (Winnicott 1965), where it was safe to be.

Only rarely did holding mean literally restraining or controlling. He was compassionate, but consistently firm, sometimes to the point of ruthlessness where he felt it necessary for the safety of his patient. Short of bodily intervention he could "forbid" action. This was powerfully effective, for although it might be disobeyed it could not be unnoticed, because it had been said and also because in the context of a delusional transference (Little 1957) it became automatically the patient's own prohibition, and then joined up with some element of sanity (Little 1959). It worked on both conscious and unconscious levels.

Sometimes the holding had to be delegated, handing over a dependent patient temporarily to someone else so that he could get rest, or a holiday, but always keeping in close touch.

During one of his holidays he arranged, without my knowing, for a friend of mine to invite me to join her and two others in Switzerland: later, when he feared that I might kill myself while he was away, he arranged for hospitalization. (I will come to this again.)

At one time I was liable to rush out of his room in a fury and drive away dangerously. He took charge of my car keys until the end of the session, and then allowed me to lie quietly alone in another room, till I could be safe. He emphasized the need to "come back" (Winnicott 1954) from the deep regression to ordinary life, for "regression to dependence" means regression to dependence for life itself — to the level of infancy, and sometimes even to prenatal life.

All of this, of course, was built up on his wide knowledge and understanding of children of all ages, and of parents, recognizing the need for support and for someone *to be there*, to take responsibility. His always growing capacity for empathy, being in touch with id, ego, and superego, in people of all sorts and all ages, including himself, understanding body language in all its forms, was an essential part of him. He did not defend against his own feelings but could allow their full range and, on occasion, expression. Without sentimentality he was able to feel about, with, and for his patient, entering into and sharing an experience in such a way that emotion that had had to be dammed up could be set free.

I told him of an early remembered loss. I had found a friend, "A.," at school, someone who had chosen me to be *her* friend. She had made me free of her home, her nursery, her Nanny, and her toys. One day after a holiday she wasn't there, and then for many days she was "ill"; and then she was "dead." I had been "unkind" and "selfish" in not writing to her. I "couldn't have cared," or I "would have written." He found himself in tears — for me — and I could cry about it as I had never done before, and mourn my loss.

"Why do you always cry silently?" he asked. I told him I had learned that early. Once, crying with toothache at the end of a long day which had been trying for everyone, I was told, "Do stop crying, darling, you make everybody else miserable," and next morning, when the abscess had burst in the night and the pain was gone, "You see, it was all a fuss about nothing." And often, "Cheer up, darling! You'll soon be dead."

This made him very angry. "I really *hate* your mother," he said. He was "shocked" when I told him how till the age of 10 and over I had to "rest" every afternoon in a darkened room with no toy or book, and was shamed when I had gnawed the candle by my bed until it had a waist and I could get small fragments of wax that I could chew and squeeze and mold.

I found D. W. essentially a truthful person, to whom "good manners" were important; he had respect for the individual, whether patient or colleague, though he could be outspoken in criticism. To demand "associations" or to push an "interpretation" would be "bad manners," as well as being useless. He was as honest as anyone could be, responding to observations and answering questions truthfully unless there was a need to protect another person, but it was essential to *know* when his answer was not wholly true, and why.

He would answer questions directly, taking them at face value, and only then considering (always with himself, often with the patient) why was it asked? Why then? And what was the unconscious anxiety behind it?

I was allowed to work at my own pace, and he adapted himself to it. Only when some circumstances—usually unforeseen and external—made it necessary would he put on pressure. This was very important for me. It allowed me to be myself, to have a pace that was my own, whereas at an early time I had been alternately pushed and held back, so that neither the pace nor the inconsistencies were mine.

The timing of the full regression could not be mine alone: it depended to a large extent on his case load. He spoke of patients having to "queue up" sometimes to go into such a state, one waiting until another had worked through it and no longer needed him in that way. But it was mine insofar as it could not be until I was ready.

He gave very few interpretations, and those only when I had already reached the point where the matter could become conscious. Then of course the interpretation would ring true. He was not "infallible," but often spoke tentatively, or speculated: "I think perhaps . . . ," "I wonder if . . . ," or "It seems as if. . . ." This let me taste or feel what he said, and be free to accept or reject it. Interpretations were not given as if I had access to symbolic function where I had not.

One day his secretary told me that he was not well and would be a little late for my session. He came, looking *grey* and very ill, saying he had laryngitis. I said, "You haven't got laryngitis, you've got a coronary. Go *home*." He insisted that it was laryngitis, but he couldn't carry on; he rang me that evening and said, "You were right, it *is* a coronary." This meant quite a long break, which was very painful, but at last I was *allowed* to know the truth: *I* could be right, and I could trust my own perceptions. It was a landmark, and he knew it.

He had said of me a little earlier, "Yes, you *are* ill, but there's plenty of mental health there too." I began to react with anxiety, and he added, "But that's for later on, the important thing now is the illness," having recognized my fear that he would deny or lose sight of it. Later he described me as being "like a person suffering from multiple sclerosis whose brain was involved."

This was a very true picture of my "borderline" state, and of my transference to him (Little 1964a), for the lesions in multiple sclerosis are scattered, and cerebral involvement brings patchy mental disturbance; and there were, as I knew, "patches" of illness and of health. They also reflected my mother's state, as he spoke of her. "Your mother is unpredictable, chaotic, and she organizes chaos around her" (see Winnicott 1961). "She's like a Jack-in-a-box, all over the place." This had indeed been my earliest environment from which I could not separate myself despite my father's stability and reliability, for her chaos affected him too. D. W. later commented that I would probably have been all right if I had been removed early to the care of a stable foster-mother. (I should perhaps emphasize here that despite my difficulties I did not give an appearance of "abnormality." I had attended school, passed exams, even won scholarships; I had qualified in medicine, run a successful general practice, and trained and qualified as a psychoanalyst. Also, except for three periods each of about eight weeks, plus holidays, I worked continuously as an analyst, throughout my analysis with D. W.)

A note about my family is needed; otherwise much of what I say is difficult to believe or understand. I am surprised to find how little I actually told D. W. about it *in words*, yet his comment about my mother was like a revelation (not an analytic "interpretation"). It made it possible and allowable for me to understand much of what I already knew, things I had observed or been told.

My mother's childhood, in Australia, was *horrific*, with an alcoholic and unstable father and a loving but dominating, meddlesome and unpredictable mother, to whom my grandfather was unfaithful. Two older brothers, one of whom my mother adored, both teased and petted, frightened and bullied her. A younger brother was born blind, and at the age of 5, she was made responsible for looking after him when another child was born. Nearby were the frightening worlds of the convict settlement from which my grandfather drew his labor force, the cannibal Aborigines, and the Bush where children were often lost, and seldom found.

My mother had to be brave, amusing, and clever. Her father too teased, petted, and bullied her, and finally disowned both her and his blind son. She learned to dance for him and kick over the brandy bottle "accidentally," also to defend her mother in parental quarrels. This is not the place for all the details that I know, but she told me shortly before her death that she "could only live at all by turning everything into a game" (see Searles 1959). The wonder is that she *did* live at all, to marry my father who was as devoted to her as she to him. That was never in doubt, though they teased each other and their children often quite sadistically. Her idea of sex was "an unpleasant duty that a woman owed her husband"; childbirth was sheer horror, warded off by padding her body so that her pregnancy could not be perceived, and avoiding labor (which would inevitably be fatal) by "not thinking about it" until this became impossible. Being afraid was "cowardice," "contemptible."

My father was by no means a nonentity. He was a mathematician, who gave up prospects of a university career and became instead a schoolmaster, to pay his college fees (unpaid through his father's bankruptcy). He was stable, warm, and companionable, but all his relationships and outgoing activities (yachting, golf, etc.) were systematically destroyed by my mother; only solitary pursuits or those involving his family were tolerated, and he became irritable and short-tempered. He was overconscientious, inhibited, and shy with women, and undemonstrative with his children. The only woman he was ever known to speak to was my mother; it was love at first sight and for life, and he could seldom stand up to her.

Small wonder then that all their children were disturbed in some degree. She expressed her fear that each one would "turn out badly." My elder sister, Ruth, brilliant intellectually, developed a savage superego and considerable moral courage and power of endurance. She became a legend in her lifetime, and a saint; sadly, for her, "This life would not be worth living if there were not to be a better life hereafter." My younger sister, Cecily, became ill immediately after my parents emigrated to Australia (always the Promised Land) in 1934, and died (aged 28) almost before they got there. (They stayed only four years.) My two brothers—uni-ovular twins ten years younger than I, born prematurely after a near-fatal pregnancy, to a mother aged 42 who already had three children—are both alive and they have had their difficulties.

To Ruth I was "an irritant," and I must have been a threat to her supremacy, for I was sickly both as a baby and later, needing and getting a lot of attention, probably owing to congenital hiatus hernia together with celiac condition (both genetic), which have troubled me all my life, neither being diagnosed until my late sixties. (Before that, of course, my complaints were "fuss," or "imagination" and later "psychogenic," but always something that I "should control."

My mother did her level best to be a good wife and mother, sometimes successfully, but anxiety made her a compulsive meddler, possessive and always interfering in other people's concerns and relationships. She was a highly intelligent and gifted person, warm and loving, but in a wholly uncoordinated way, being tragically damaged. The only predictable thing was that she would be unpredictable; one had to live with it and find ways of dealing with it. The only play possible—whether with toys, balls, or words, etc.—had to be hers; it was often good, but any play of my own would either be stopped or taken over. Spontaneity, "idea, impulse, action . . . all one . . . together, knowing what to do" (Sacks 1985) was aborted. Her own mother, the benevolent tyrant, was never far away, and not always so benevolent.

My blind uncle was almost the only person I could ever talk to. He was a scholar, widely read, musical, and very independent. When he married I lost all contact with him and became deeply depressed and physically ill.

During my analysis with D. W. I went through three periods of serious depression during which I was unable to work. I had long been aware of spells of depression lasting about ten days, at intervals of about three months, quite apart from any known loss, which I had never understood. And there had been two incapacitating depressions that followed losses that I knew.

Early in the analysis, after a severe attack of gastroenteritis (which I recognized later was a flare-up of the celiac condition), I went on feeling very ill and exhausted physically and deeply depressed. I was not able to go for my sessions. D. W. came to me at home—five, six, and sometimes seven days a week for ninety minutes each day for about three months. During most of those sessions I simply lay there, crying, held by him. He put no pressure on me, listened to my complaints and showed that he recognized my distress and could bear with it. As I recovered physically the depression gradually lifted, and I was able to work again.

Psyche and soma for him were not separable, they were "body and spirit which deep down are interdependent aspects of the same reality" (van der Post 1982). He was always concerned for my physical state; he kept stethoscope, sphygmomanometer, and clinical thermometer handy, and used them. He would advise me to see my G.P. or a consultant if necessary, but he would also take my word for my own condition. Once, when I had a mild bronchitis, he questioned whether I should not go to my G.P., but I told him, "I'm not ill. I'm unhappy." And that was enough.

The time from the autumn of 1950 to the spring of 1952 was a particularly painful one for me. I had come back from my summer holiday with an appointment fixed to see D. W. again, but found that he had had a second, though less severe, coronary, which again meant a long break.

Then, I was asked to be assistant to the Business Secretary of both the British Psycho-Analytical Society and the Institute of Psycho-Analysis, taking two years to prepare to take over. After attending only three meetings of the Board and Council I knew I did not want this, but the next week my predecessor died suddenly, and I was left with it. I was "the obvious person" to succeed her, and the pressure on me to undertake it was so great that I could not refuse.

This was when the move from Gloucester Place to Mansfield House was being planned and carried out. I was by far the most junior member of the Board and Council of which D. W., as Training Secretary, was a member. I disagreed with much that was decided, and I came to detest the job and everything to do with it. I tried to convey that a *trained* Secretary was needed. I felt guilty, futile, and inadequate and wanted to resign, and I became ill again. Although it was a great relief when at last, in May 1952, I was replaced, and soon a trained Company Secretary was appointed, the guilt and depression persisted, especially as I found that there was now no place for me to take part in the training scheme, whereas at the time of Miss Sharpe's death I had already been invited to do so. (In fact, D. W. told me that he had intervened to forestall it because I was "too ill.") Also, in 1951, following publication of my paper "Counter-transference and the Patient's Response to it," I had been invited to go to Topeka as a training analyst but had had to refuse as I was deeply involved in my analysis.

At the same time as my unhappiness about all this I was in great anxiety about D. W., who was himself depressed after his coronary. It was like a childhood year, when I was in difficulties at school due to a mistake about my age, and simultaneously in anxiety at home on account of my mother's pregnancy. I don't think we spoke of his depression at all, but I was aware of it (as with Miss Sharpe) from his altered appearance and manner, for every analysand is sensitive to what is going on in his analyst.

I was always afraid that he would have a third coronary and die, which would have been fatal for me. One day when I went for my session I waited to be told that he was ready for me. Several times I asked the receptionist, "Is he still not here?"

Finally, after forty-five minutes, I went to his room expecting to find him ill or dead and found he had fallen asleep on the couch and not heard the bell! So I was saved, and again I was allowed to know, and to follow my own impulse. But my depression continued, and at the lowest time I could not sleep at night until I had phoned D. W. ringing repeatedly until he answered.

I learned afterward that both his second coronary and his depression came about through his distress about the question of breaking up his first marriage—a decision which he did not take lightly. Eventually he told me of his divorce and coming remarriage, lest I should hear of it elsewhere or read of it in the press. I found it difficult, especially as my own love affair was finally falling apart. I was very jealous, and some oedipal material could be worked through, though it remained as an isolated patch that had to be joined up later.

My sessions went on as before, but now at his new home. The analysis seemed unending, and I blamed him for my failures. But then, in the summer (1952), for the first time in my life, I *exploded* at my mother, at some piece of her jibing and "clever" nonsense. I told her exactly what I felt: that she was being unkind and ridiculous, that she had had no business to marry or have children, and a great deal more in the same strain, quite regardless of any effect on her.

D. W.'s comment was, "You've owed it to yourself for a long time." It was an important spontaneous self-assertion that had never been possible before, and although I did not see her again until she was dying, two years later, I have never regretted it.

His holiday and mine came. I went to the far north of Scotland, to wild country where I walked by myself. My mother wrote making an outrageous demand; my "explosion" was ignored and made useless, her possession of me reasserted. I *stomped* furiously up a steep, slippery, and remote mountain path in a thick mist. Next day, still raging, I slipped on wet grass outside my hotel, fell, and broke my ankle. (Had this happened the previous day I might well have lain all night before being found.) I was taken to hospital and cared for; my leg was put up in a light plaster over a gutter splint. My postcard to D. W. telling him of the accident brought a telegram in reply, and a letter.

The Medical Superintendent of the hospital was most helpful. He spoke of the depression that follows sudden loss of mobility, having experienced it himself as a young man, when he had polio.

At the end of a fortnight I was beginning to get about and was discharged. But then came the difficulty of getting home. My car and other things were sixty miles away in one direction, my home six hundred in the other! Fortunately, two friends I had made in the hotel came to my rescue, one dispatched the car to me, the other invited me to stay in her home, which was on my way, until I could arrange my own journey and the car transport.

By the time I reached home the plaster was loose and had to be replaced. The new cast was heavy and unwieldy with a rocker badly placed under the heel, so once more my mobility was greatly restricted and walking precarious.

When I saw D. W. again six weeks later, so many things had happened that I was confused and had lost all contact with what had triggered off the accident and so never told him about it. He assumed that it belonged wholly to the transference, to do with his holiday (cf. Miss Sharpe's reaction to my mourning), also that it was a serious suicidal attempt. I might have protested, but the fresh loss of mobility had renewed the depression, and I suppose there was unconscious guilt about my verbal attack on my mother, my refusal of her demand, and the physical attack I had surely wanted to make but had turned against myself.

I find I have no recollection of the content of the next year's work in the analysis, so I think I must have projected the confusion, etc., and D. W. must have taken it over (Searles 1959), otherwise it is difficult to understand what followed, in particular why the hospitalization and regression that had already happened consequent on the accident were apparently not used as fully as they might have been.

As I understand it now something *had* to be broken—to free me from my mother's hold and to destroy finally the pattern of repetition. Two childhood memories belong here. One is of her gripping both my wrists, and saying emphatically. "You *must* control *yourself!*" But in fact *she* was controlling *me*.

The second is of being ill with pneumonia—part of an early "breakdown" (aged 5) brought about by massive sudden changes including a move to a new house, where my father was in charge of school boarders; overnight there were nineteen boys, to none of whom I was allowed to speak. At the same time there was a change of kindergarten. I had not liked the first one, but I detested the second, where I was teased by a boy older and bigger than myself. (A year earlier Cecily had appeared overnight, and I was moved to share a room with Ruth, who teased and frightened me.)

At the new kindergarten sexual identity was confused. In a singing game of "Birds in a Nest" the "father bird" was a little boy with long fair curls like my own, dressed in a frock, and with permanently running nose (uncontrolled). But he was a "boy," and I a "girl," so I couldn't have been the "father bird." ("Men and boys have short hair and wear trousers; women and girls have long hair and wear skirts," I had been told!)

Now, suddenly ill with very high fever and delirium, I was moved to my mother's bedroom and my father moved out. The content of the delirium has never been recalled as such, but I think it must have been concerned with these questions of freedom to be myself and of sexual identity.

My mother's account is that I clung to her night and day and would not let her go. D. W.'s understanding was that "She would not let you die"—which was true (as I learned later) but now I would say: "She would not let me *choose* whether to live or die." I *had* to live, for her.

So, when she reasserted her hold on me after my "explosion," something had to break and it was my own ankle.

I was tied by the leg again on my return from Scotland. The confusion then was a repetition of the delirium in which I could not distinguish between my mother and myself and literally did not know what "myself" was. Being in this confusion meant that I could not make clear to D. W. what it was about, or what had happened to precipitate it, any more than I had been able to make my mother understand the earlier confusion (or to stop vomiting). Then, I had only been able to be ill and threaten to die. D. W. too could not let me choose whether to live or die, and he did not realize that I had already made my choice unconsciously, in falling where I did.

So when the next summer holiday lay ahead, D. W. told me that he wanted me to go into hospital as a voluntary patient, "to make sure that I did not commit suicide." I went for him, wildly; I think I hit him, though I am not certain. He caught my wrists and held me, and was not hurt. Eventually I agreed, on condition that he would ensure that I was not given electro-shock, that I could have a private room, that I could discharge myself if I wished (make my own choice), and that he would take me there himself and bring me back—all of which he agreed and carried out. He made it clear that he would also keep in touch with the hospital.

We went on the day after the International Congress in London (1953) ended. On the station platform he found that I was clinging to the edge of his raincoat, terrified. He took my arm in his, and when we arrived he said, "You're being very brave," and added something about "innate creativeness," which I did not understand and do not remember, but later found had been important as relating to spontaneity.

He was distressed that the Medical Superintendent had gone on holiday, not having told him this before. The Deputy was a hard man, antagonistic to analysis and not too pleased to be given extensive notes and an absolute ban on ECT!

At first when D. W. had left me I felt protected, but after a few days forlorn and abandoned. I was confused and slightly disorientated. (I made notes from day to day of those five weeks, which I still have.) For ten days I kept to my room, weepy and afraid, but to my surprise I began to write poetry.

Then, one morning I asked and was promised to be left alone and undisturbed. One after another, no less than eight people came, and when the eighth, a ward maid, was on the floor by my bed I spanked her bottom. Immediately the Deputy-Superintendent came. I felt he threatened me; there were "other ways of treating mental illness besides analysis which were sometimes necessary." I reminded him of the ban on ECT. By the evening I was full up with anger. I let fly at my supper tray; I hurled the reading lamp and anything I could find across the room in an orgy of smashing. I was promptly secluded for the night, and all night long was paranoid, seeing the nurses who came as "devils." But I had clung to two things that later proved to be "transitional objects" (Little 1950), a handkerchief that D. W. had given me and a soft blue woolly scarf that I had liked and bought. In the morning I was moved to an open room in a locked ward, and the ward Sister came. Later, bathed and fed and cared for like an infant, I was settled in the room where I stayed for the rest of the time.

In my sessions with D. W. there had been "token" infant care; he always opened the door to me himself, each session wound up with coffee and biscuits, he saw to it that I was warm and comfortable, and provided tissues, etc. But here was the full "regression to dependence," an extension of what he had given me; and he kept in constant touch with the hospital and sent me postcards letting me know where he was.

The hospital care was total and interference minimal; everything was provided and no demand made. I spent the time sleeping, reading, writing, and painting, sometimes on the walls of my room, playing, in fact. I wandered in the garden and roamed the streets; when it rained a ward orderly would fetch me in with umbrella and waterproof. When my feet were blistered the Sister dressed them and told me, "You should have telephoned for a car to fetch you."

There might be distress or disturbance going on round me but the place went on *being*, and holding and looking after me, calm and apparently unperturbed. (Nothing could have been more different in that way from my early environment. I recalled a day in 1944 when Ruth and I were both visiting our parents; there was no time when all four of us were sitting down together for as long as five minutes, for something had always to be fetched or done. It couldn't have been quite so bad earlier, but then I would have been less well able to cope with it than I was now.)

Something had again been broken (plates, lamp, etc.) but not *me*, and I was now in what had become my real "nursery," where it was *safe* not to control myself. The boundaries were wide and flexible. It was psychically an extension of D. W.'s consulting-room where, earlier, I had smashed his vase. I could now make clear to *myself* my choice between life and death ("To be . . . or . . . not to be"—*Hamlet*, III. i, *pace* Winnicott 1971b). His putting me in hospital was a repetition of his reaction to that earlier smashing, but this time the contact was not broken as it had been then, when he left me alone with the wreckage I had made.

It was only much later that I realized that the wreckage *itself* was a creation, for destruction and creation are inseparable—you can't paint a picture without destroying a white canvas and tubes of paint (and everything has ambivalency), "for there is nothing lives but something dies, and nothing dies but something lives" (Thompson 1924), and "love involves destruction" (Winnicott 1963).

Though there were plenty of things I didn't like in the hospital, overall it was kind and cozy, and at times even fun. One day I painted a sea, and added suddenly a huge monster's head emerging, with flaming eyes and fierce jaws. It was pinned up, and the occupational therapist stood looking at it with his back to me. I said, "A nice piece of schizophrenic art, what?" He shot out of the room and down the corridor, and the Sister came in chuckling, "What *have* you done to poor Mr. Y?" she said. "He looked as if the devil was after him!" And we laughed together, not at him, but at my painting. Spontaneity was restored, and even welcomed.

But I couldn't have accepted living so for long. That I had to be there at all depressed me further, and one day seeing a bit of rope in the garden I thought again of suicide. All at once I realized that it would be no real solution, only a victory for the crazy world I had struggled against all my life and too often complied with (Winnicott 1963), and a really mad act. I never considered it again, and I came back from the regression to ordinary life (Winnicott 1954).

I started work about a fortnight after going home. My analysis had begun to move toward termination. There was plenty to tell D. W. about the time in hospital, working through the experience, talking over the content of my paintings and poems, telling of my play and my fantasies much as a child would tell its mother. I still sat up half the night painting wild pictures and writing melancholy poems. D. W. would look at them and comment. He was not critical or judgmental though he would say what he *felt*, and it was some time before I realized that his disliking a picture didn't mean I should destroy it. It had a value simply as a creation, for him as well as for me.

At some point in this terminal phase D. W. gave me one particularly important interpretation that had the same quality of "revelation" as had, earlier, his observation about my mother's "chaos." He told me that such fear of annihilation as I felt belonged to "annihilation" that had already happened: I *had been* annihilated psychically, but had in fact survived bodily, and was now emotionally reliving the past experience. It was some time before I could assimilate this and use it (Winnicott 1968). Even now I tend to forget it in times of stress, but as soon as I recall that interpretation the anxiety is relieved. ("Dread is only memory in the future tense"—Elizabeth Ayrton, *Day Eight*; and "Survival is the twin brother of annihilation"—Churchill, speech in 1941.)

It was true that I had been annihilated, before I even existed. I was not a person in my own right, only an appendage of someone else: introduced, "This is my daughter"; known as, "Ruth's sister"; one of three Margarets in my class and two M. Littles in the school. My second name, Isabel, was useless too: "It's always I, I, I," I was told, and in trying to get rid of the self-centeredness I discarded the initial, and have only used it lately to distinguish myself from another psychiatrist of the same name!

By now the character of the sessions had largely changed, for so much grief and pain and anger had been worked through that play, the ground of creativeness (Winnicott 1971a), could take its place and the relationship born years before could develop. There are analysts who apparently believe that every session *ought* to be painful, but while D. W. was fully aware that analysis could only work for someone who really suffered, he believed in the value of a relationship that could also be encouraging and enjoyable. Quite a lot of the play through which I now grew psychically *could* have been like my mother's: jokes, stories, and nonsense (I once asked him why he had chosen to join the Navy rather than Army or Airforce: The uniform suited his blue eyes better!), bits of gossip, information, and serious discussion about analysis. But these things were not used to defend against anxiety, to ward off anger or excitement, or to deflect pain or unhappiness by making me laugh. They were not forced on me, I could have them or not as *I* wished. Being *human* was the all-important thing and play an essential part of human life at any age.

D. W. could let me see something of the demands that such an analysis as mine made on him, demands that he was willing to meet, and not only on condition that the analysis should succeed: standing anxiety, guilt, pain and grief, uncertainty and helplessness, standing what couldn't *be* stood. There was no defense against paradox or ambivalence, whether in a patient or in himself. He told me of one patient who for many months had threatened suicide seriously enough for him to arrange hospitalization. The suicide happened, unnecessarily and for the wrong reason as he felt, because his instructions had been ignored. He had gone through a long period of anxiety before it, and guilt because he hated the patient for making him suffer (Winnicott 1947). He wanted to scream, "For God's sake, get on and *do* it." When it did happen, there were fresh guilt and helplessness (he should have been able to prevent it), fury with those who had failed to carry out his instructions, and finally a deep sense of loss of someone about whom he cared intensely and in whom he had invested so much feeling.

All the same, he made it clear that total self-sacrifice was just not on. If he did not care for himself, providing for his own needs, bodily and emotional, he would be no use to anyone, including himself. Hence the importance of his marriage, holidays, music, friends, etc. I came to see changes in him, growth and development, alterations in his way of working: intangible things perceived only after they had happened. I once spoke of regretting that I had not come to him earlier: he answered that he could not have done my analysis earlier.

His letting me share something of this made it safe for me; it increased my own sense of being valued and therefore valuable, and so my ability to value myself could build up. I became aware that the D. W. whom I knew was different from the D. W. known to anyone else, even though others might know some of the same aspects of him. I "created" him imaginatively for myself, and this because they and I were different, however much we might all *seem* alike; it gave them their values and reality. Above all, D. W. became a real living person with whom I had a relationship born years earlier and no longer based only on transference.

Other relationships followed with colleagues and friends. Early in 1954 my mother died; I had not seen her or Ruth since my "explosion," and now some relationship with Ruth became possible for the first time. I was finding pleasure and satisfaction in my work and elsewhere, especially in painting and in my garden, which seemed to be my only positive tie with my mother.

We began to cut down both the length and frequency of the sessions, and to increase the fee at my insistence, and in the summer of 1955 I agreed to finish. Once again I became involved sexually, and unsuccessfully, for again it was an oedipal situation. I went back to D. W. for help and he saw me once a week for about eighteen months, at the end of which he told me plainly that it was time I took over my own responsibilities and got on with my life – "be yourself," but now for *me*, not for him.

REFERENCES

Little, M. (1945). The wanderer: notes on a paranoid patient. In *Transference Neurosis and Transference Psychosis: Toward Basic Unity*, pp. 3–31. New York: Jason Aronson, 1981.

———— (1951). Countertransference and the patient's response to it. In *Transference Neurosis and Transference Psychosis: Toward Basic Unity*, pp. 33–50. New York: Jason Aronson, 1981.

———— (1957). On delusional transference (transference psychosis). In *Transference Neurosis and Transference Psychosis: Toward a Basic Unity*, pp. 81–91. New York: Jason Aronson, 1981.

———— (1959). On basic unity. In *Transference Neurosis and Transference Psychosis: Toward a Basic Unity*, pp. 109–125. New York: Jason Aronson, 1981.

Little, M., and Flarsheim, A. (1964). Toward mental health: early mothering care. In *Transference Neurosis and Transference Psychosis: Toward a Basic Unity*, pp. 167–181. New York: Jason Aronson, 1981.

Sacks, O. (1985). *A Leg to Stand on*. London: Duckworth.

Searles, H. F. (1959). The effort to drive the other person crazy – an element in the etiology and psychotherapy of schizophrenia. In *Collected Papers on Schizophrenia and Related Subjects*, pp. 254–283. London: Hogarth, 1965.

Thompson, F. (1924). "Ode to the Setting Sun." In *Collected Poetry*. London: Burns, Oates and Washbourne.

van der Post, L. (1982). *Yet Being Someone Other*. London: Hogarth.

Winnicott, D. W. (1947). Hate in the countertransference. In *Collected Papers: Through Paediatrics to Psycho-analysis*, pp. 194–203. London: Hogarth, 1975.

———— (1948). Reparation in respect of mother's organized defence against depression. In *Collected Papers: Through Paediatrics to Psycho-Analysis*, pp. 91–96. London: Hogarth, 1975.

———— (1949). Birth memories, birth trauma, and anxiety. In *Collected Papers: Through Paediatrics to Psycho-Analysis*, pp. 174–193. London: Hogarth, 1975.

———— (1954). Withdrawal and regression. In *Collected Papers: Through Paediatrics to Psycho-Analysis*, pp. 255–261. London: Hogarth, 1975.

———— (1961). The effects of psychotic parents on the emotional development of the child. *British Journal of Psychiatric Social Work* 6:12–20.

———— (1963). Morals and education. In *The Maturational Processes and the Facilitating Environment*, pp. 93–105. London: Hogarth, 1965.

———— (1965). *The Maturational Processes and the Facilitating Environment: Studies in the Theory of Emotional Development*. London: Hogarth.

———— (1968). The use of an object and relating through identifications. In *Playing and Reality*, pp. 101–111. London: Tavistock, 1971.

———— (1970). The mother–infant experience of mutuality. In *Parenthood*, ed. J. Anthony and T. Benedek, pp. 245–256. New York: Little, Brown and Company.

———— (1971a). Creativity and its origins. In *Playing and Reality*, pp. 76–100. London: Tavistock.

———— (1971b). *Playing and Reality*. London: Tavistock.

18

HARRY GUNTRIP: MY EXPERIENCE OF ANALYSIS WITH FAIRBAIRN AND WINNICOTT: How Complete a Result Does Psycho-Analytic Therapy Achieve?

IT DOES NOT SEEM TO ME USEFUL to attempt a purely theoretical answer to the question forming the subtitle. Theory does not seem to me to be the major concern. It is a useful servant but a bad master, liable to produce orthodox defenders of every variety of the faith. We ought always to sit light to theory and be on the look-out for ways of improving it in the light of therapeutic practice. It is therapeutic practice that is the real heart of the matter. In the last resort good therapists are born not trained, and they make the best use of training. Maybe the question "How complete a result can psycho-analytic therapy produce?" raises the question "How complete a result did our own training analysis produce?" Analysts are advised to be open to post-analytic improvements, so presumably we do not expect "an analysis" to do a "total" once for all job. We must know about post-analytic developments if we are to assess the actual results of the primary analysis. We cannot deal with this question purely on the basis of our patients' records. They must be incomplete for the primary analysis and non-existent afterwards. As this question had unexpected and urgent relevance in my case, I was compelled to grapple with it; so I shall risk offering an account of my own analysis with Fairbairn and Winnicott, and its after-effects: especially as this is the only way I can present a realistic picture of what I take to be the relationship between the respective contributions of these two outstanding analysts, and what I owe to them.

The question "How complete a result is possible?" had compelling importance for me because it is bound up with an unusual factor; a total amnesia for a severe trauma at the age of three and a half years, over the death of a younger brother. Two analyses failed to break through that amnesia, but it was resolved unexpectedly after they had ended, certainly only because of what they had achieved in "softening up" the major repression. I hope this may have both a theoretical and a human interest. The long quest for a solution to that problem has been too introverted an interest to be wholly welcomed, but I had no option, could not ignore it, and so turned it into a vocation through which I might help others. Both Fairbairn and Winnicott thought that but for that trauma, I might not have become a psychotherapist. Fairbairn once said: "I can't think what could motivate any of us to become psychotherapists, if we hadn't got problems of our own." He was no super-optimist and once said to me: "The basic pattern of personality once fixed in early childhood can't be altered. Emotion can be drained out of the old patterns by new experience, but water can always flow again in the old dried up water courses." You cannot give anyone a different history. On another occasion he said: "You can go on analyzing forever and get nowhere. It's the personal relation that is therapeutic. Science has no values except scientific values, the schizoid values of the investigator who stands outside of life and watches. It is purely instrumental, useful for a time but then you have to get back to living." That was his view of the "mirror analyst," a non-relating observer simply interpreting. Thus he held that psychoanalytic interpretation is not therapeutic *per se*, but only as it expresses a personal relationship of genuine understanding. My own view is that science is not necessarily schizoid, but is really practically motivated, and often becomes schizoid because it offers such an obvious retreat for schizoid intellectuals. There is no place for this in psychotherapy of any kind.

I already held the view that psychoanalytic therapy is not a purely theoretical but a truly understanding personal relationship, and had published it in my first book before I had heard of Fairbairn; after reading his papers in 1949, I went to him because we stood philosophically on the same ground and no actual intellectual disagreements would interfere with the analysis. But the capacity for forming a relationship does not depend solely on our theory. Not everyone has the same facility for forming personal relationships, and we can all form a relationship more easily with some people than with others. The unpredictable factor of "natural fit" enters in. Thus, in spite of his conviction Fairbairn did not have the same capacity for natural, spontaneous "personal relating" that Winnicott had. With me he was more of a "technical interpreter" than he thought he was, or than I expected: but that needs qualification. I went to him in the 1950s when he was past the peak of his creative powers of the 1940s, and his health was slowly failing. He told me that in the 1930s and 1940s he had treated a number of schizophrenic and regressed patients with success. That lay behind his "theoretical revision" in the 1940s. He felt he had made a mistake in publishing his theory before the clinical evidence. From

1927 to 1935 he was psychiatrist at The University Psychological Clinic for Children, and did a lot of work for the N.S.P.C.C. One cannot be impersonal with children. He asked one child whose mother thrashed her cruelly: "Would you like me to find you a new kind Mummy?" She said: "No. I want my own Mummy," showing the intensity of the libidinal tie to the bad object. The devil you know is better than the devil you do not, and better than no devil at all. Out of such experience with psychotic, regressed and child patients, his theoretical revision grew, based on the *quality* of parent–child relations, rather than the *stages* of biological growth, a "personality-theory" not an impersonal "energy-control theory." He summed it up in saying that "the cause of trouble is that parents somehow fail to get it across to the child that he is loved for his own sake, as a person in his own right." By the 1950s when I was with him, he wisely declined to take the strains of severely regressing patients. To my surprise I found him gradually falling back on the "classical analyst" with an "interpretative technique," when I felt I needed to regress to the level of that severe infancy trauma.

Stephen Morse (1972), in his study of "structure" in the writings of Winnicott and Balint, concluded that they discovered new data but did not develop structural theory in a way that could explain them; which, however, he felt could be done by what he called the "Fairbairn–Guntrip metaphor." Having had the benefit of analysis with both these outstanding analysts, I feel the position is somewhat more complex than that. The relation between Fairbairn and Winnicott is both theoretically important and very intriguing. Superficially they were quite unlike each other in type of mind and method of working, which prevented their knowing how basically close they were in the end. Both had deep roots in classic Freudian theory and therapy, and both outgrew it in their own different ways. Fairbairn saw that intellectually more clearly than Winnicott. Yet in the 1950s Fairbairn was more orthodox in clinical practice than Winnicott. I had just over 1,000 sessions with Fairbairn in the 1950s and just over 150 with Winnicott in the 1960s. For my own benefit I kept detailed records of every session with both of them, and all their correspondence. Winnicott said, "I've never had anyone who could tell me so exactly what I said last time." Morse's article suggested a restudy of those records last year, and I was intrigued to find the light they cast on why my *two analyses failed to resolve my amnesia for that trauma at three and a half years, and yet each in different ways prepared for its resolution as a post-analytic development.* I had to ask afresh, "What is the analytic therapeutic process?"

In general I found Fairbairn becoming more *orthodox in practice* than in theory while Winnicott was more *revolutionary in practice* than in theory. They were complementary opposites. Sutherland in his obituary notice (1965) wrote:

> Fairbairn had a slightly formal air about him – notably aristocratic, but in talking to him I found he was not at all formal or remote. Art and religion were for him profound expressions of man's needs, for which he

felt a deep respect, but his interests revealed his rather unusual conservatism.

I found him formal in sessions, the intellectually precise interpreting analyst, but after sessions we discussed theory and he would unbend, and I found the human Fairbairn as we talked face to face. Realistically, he was my understanding good father after sessions, and in sessions in the transference he was my dominating bad mother imposing exact interpretations. After his experimental creative 1940s, I feel his conservatism slowly pushed through into his work in the 1950s. The shock of his wife's sudden death in 1952 created obvious domestic problems. Early in the 1950s he had the first attack of viral influenza, and these became more virulent as the decade advanced. For two years after his wife's death he worked hard on his fine paper "Observations on the Nature of Hysterical States" (Fairbairn 1954) which finalized his original thinking. He clarified his views on "psycho-analysis and science" in two papers (Fairbairn 1952b, 1955). But there was a subtle change in his next paper, "Considerations arising out of the Schreber case" (Fairbairn 1956). Here he fell back from his "ego and object relations" psychology, explaining everything as due to "primal scene" libidinal excitations and fears. Finally, in his last paper, "On the nature and aims of psycho-analytical treatment" (Fairbairn 1958) his entire emphasis was on the "internal closed system" of broadly oedipal analysis, not in terms of instincts, but of internalized libidinized and antilibidinized bad-object relations. I went to him to break through the amnesia for that trauma of my brother's death, to whatever lay behind it in the infancy period. There, I felt, lay the cause of my vague background experiences of schizoid isolation and unreality, and I knew that they had to do with my earliest relations with mother, though only because of information she had given me.

After brother Percy's death I entered on four years of active battle with mother to force her "to relate," and then gave it up and grew away from her. I will call that, for convenience, the oedipal internalized bad-object relations period: it filled my dreams, but repeatedly sudden, clear schizoid experiences would erupt into this, and Fairbairn steadily interpreted them as "withdrawal" in the sense of "escapes" from internalized bad-object relations. He repeatedly brought me back to oedipal three-person libidinal and anti-libidinal conflicts in my "inner world," Kleinian "object splits" and Fairbairnian "ego splits" in the sense of oedipal libidinal excitations. In 1956 I wrote to ask him to say exactly what he thought about the Oedipus complex, and he replied: "The Oedipus complex is central for therapy but not for theory." I replied that I could not accept that: for me theory *was* the theory of *therapy*, and what was true for one must be true for both. I developed a double resistance to him consciously, partly feeling he was my bad mother forcing her views on me, and partly openly disagreeing with him on genuine grounds. I began to insist that my real problem was not the bad relationships of the post-Percy period, but mother's basic "failure to relate at all" right from the start. I said that I felt oedipal analysis kept me marking time on the same spot, making me use bad relations as better than none at all, keeping them operative in my inner world as *a defense against the deeper schizoid problem*. He saw that as a defensive character trait of "withdrawness" (Fairbairn 1952a, chap.1). I felt it as a problem in its own right, not just a defense against his closed-system "internal world of bad-object relations."

But my oedipal analysis with Fairbairn was not a waste of time. Defenses have to be analyzed and it brought home to me that I had actually repressed the trauma of Percy's death and all that lay behind it, by building over it a complex experience of sustained struggle in bad-object relations with mother, which in turn I had also to repress. It was the basis of my spate of dreams, and intermittent production of conversion symptoms. Fairbairn for long insisted that it was the *real core* of my psycho-pathology. He was certainly wrong, but it did have to be radically analyzed to open the way to the deeper depths. That happened. Steadily regressive and negative schizoid phenomena thrust into the material I brought to him, and at last he began to accept in theory what he no longer had the health to cope with in practice. He generously accepted my concept of a "regressed ego" split off from his "libidinal ego" and giving up as hopeless the struggle to get a response from mother. When I published that idea, Winnicott wrote to ask: "Is your Regressed Ego withdrawn or repressed?" I replied; "Both. First withdrawn and then kept repressed." Fairbairn wrote to say:

> This is your own idea, not mine, original, and it explains what I have never been able to account for in my theory, Regression. Your emphasis on ego-weakness yields better therapeutic results than interpretation in terms of libidinal and anti-libidinal tensions.

When in 1960 I wrote "Ego-weakness, the Hard Core of the Problem of Psychotherapy" he wrote to say: "If I could write now, that is what I would write about." I knew my theory was broadly right for it conceptualized what I could not yet get analyzed. With I think great courage, he accepted that.

I shall complete my account of Fairbairn as analyst and man by illustrating the difference in "human type" between him and Winnicott, a factor that plays a big part in therapy. The set-up of the consulting room itself creates an atmosphere which has meaning. Fairbairn lived in the country and saw patients in the old Fairbairn family house in Edinburgh. I entered a large drawing room as waiting room, furnished with beautiful valuable antiques, and proceeded to the study as consulting room, also large with a big antique bookcase filling most of one wall. Fairbairn sat behind a large flat-topped desk, I used to think "in state" in a high-backed plush-covered armchair. The patient's couch had its head to the front of the desk. At times I thought he could reach over the desk and hit me on the head. It struck me as odd for an analyst who did not believe in the "mirror-analyst" theory. Not for a long time did I realize that I had "chosen" that couch position, and there was a small settee at the side of his desk at which I could sit if I wished, and ultimately I did. That this imposing situation at once had an unconscious transference meaning for me became clear in a dream in the first month. I must explain that my father had been a Methodist Local Preacher of outstanding eloquence as a public speaker, and from 1885 built up and led a Mission Hall which grew into a Church which still exists. In all my years of dreaming he never appeared as other than a supportive figure *vis-à-vis* mother, and in actual fact she *never* lost her temper in his presence. I wanted Fairbairn in transference as the protective father, helping me to stand up to my aggressive mother, but unconsciously I felt otherwise, for I dreamed:

> I was in father's Mission Hall. Fairbairn was on the platform but he had mother's hard face. I lay passive on a couch on the floor of the Hall, with the couch head to the front of the platform. He came down and said: "Do you know the door is open?" I said: "I didn't leave it open," and was pleased I had stood up to him. He went back to the platform.

It was a thinly disguised version of his consulting room set-up, and showed that I wanted him to be my supportive father, but that wish was overpowered by a clear negative transference from my severe dominating mother. That remained by and large Fairbairn's transference role "in sessions." He interpreted it as the "one up and the other down" bad parent–child "see-saw" relation. It can only be altered by turning the tables. I found that very illuminating, containing all the ingredients of unmet needs, smothered rage, inhibited spontaneity. It was the dominant transference relationship in sessions. After sessions Fairbairn could unbend in our theory and therapy discussion, the good human father.

This negative transference in sessions was, I feel, fostered by his *very intellectually precise interpretations*. Once he interpreted: "Something forecloses on the active process in the course of its development." I would have said: "Your mother squashed your naturally active self." But he accurately analyzed my emotional struggle to force mother to mother me after Percy died, and showed how I had internalized it. That had to be done first, but he held it to be the central oedipal problem, and could not accept till it was too late, that this masked a far deeper and more serious problem. Later Winnicott twice remarked: "You show no signs of ever having had an Oedipus complex." My family pattern was not oedipal. It was always the same in dreams and is shown by the most striking one of them.

> I was being besieged and was sitting in a room discussing it with father. It was mother who was besieging me and I said to him: "You know I'll never give in

to her. It doesn't matter what happens. I'll never surrender." He said, "Yes. I know that. I'll go and tell her" and he went and said to her, "You'd better give it up. You'll never make him submit," and she did give up.

Fairbairn's persistence in oedipal interpretations I could not accept as final cast him in the role of the dominating mother. It came to our ears that Winnicott and Hoffer thought my adherence to his theory was due to its not allowing him to analyze my aggression in the transference. But they didn't see me knock over his pedestal ashtray, and kick his glass door-stopper, "accidentally" of course, and we know what that means in sessions, as he was not slow to point out. They did not see me once strew some of his books out of that huge bookcase over the floor, symbolic of "tearing a response out of mother," and then putting them back tidily to make reparation à la Melanie Klein. But after sessions we could discuss and I could find the natural warm-hearted human being behind the exact interpreting analyst.

I can best make this clear by comparison with Winnicott. His consulting room was simple, restful in colors and furniture, unostentatious, carefully planned, so Mrs. Winnicott told me, by both of them, to make the patient feel at ease. I would knock and walk in, and presently Winnicott would stroll in with a cup of tea in his hand and a cheery "Hallo," and sit on a small wooden chair by the couch. I would sit on the couch sideways or lie down as I felt inclined, and change position freely according to how I felt or what I was saying. Always at the end, as I departed he held out his hand for a friendly handshake. As I was finally leaving Fairbairn after the last session, I suddenly realized that in all that long period we had never once shaken hands, and he was letting me leave without that friendly gesture. I put out my hand and at once he took it, and I suddenly saw a few tears trickle down his face. *I saw the warm heart of this man with a fine mind and a shy nature.* He invited my wife and me to tea whenever we visited her mother in Perthshire.

To make the ending of my analysis with Fairbairn meaningful, I must give a brief sketch of my family history. My mother was an over-burdened "little mother" before she married, the eldest daughter of 11 children and saw four siblings die. Her mother was a feather-brained beauty queen, who left my mother to manage everything even as a schoolgirl. She ran away from home at the age of twelve because she was so unhappy, but was brought back. Her best characteristic was her strong sense of duty and responsibility to her widowed mother and three younger siblings, which impressed my father when they all joined his Mission Hall. They married in 1898 but he did not know that she had had her fill of mothering babies and did not want any more. In my teens she occasionally became confidential and told me the salient facts of family history, including that she breast-fed me because she believed it would prevent another pregnancy; she refused to breast-feed Percy and he died, after which she refused further intimacy. My father was the youngest son of a High-Church and high Tory family, the politically left-wing and religiously

Nonconformist rebel; an anti-imperialist who nearly lost his position in the City by refusing to sign his firm's pro-Boer War petition. That passing anxiety gave my mother the chance to wean me suddenly and start a business of her own. We moved when I was one year old. She chose a bad site and lost money steadily for seven years, though everything was more than retrieved by the next move. *That first seven years of my life, six of them at the first shop, was the grossly disturbed period for me.* I was left to the care of an invalid aunt who lived with us. Percy was born when I was two years old and died when I was three and a half. Mother told me father said he would have lived if she had breast-fed him, and she got angry. It was a disturbed time. In her old age, living in our home, she would say some revealing things. "I ought never to have married and had children. Nature did not make me to be a wife and mother, but a business woman," and "I don't think I ever understood children. I could never be bothered with them."

She told me that at three and a half years I walked into a room and saw Percy lying naked and dead on her lap. I rushed up and grabbed him and said: "Don't let him go. You'll never get him back!" She sent me out of the room and I fell mysteriously ill and was thought to be dying. Her doctor said: "He's dying of grief for his brother. If your mother wit can't save him, I can't," so she took me to a maternal aunt who had a family, and there I recovered. Both Fairbairn and Winnicott thought I would have died if she had not sent me away from herself. All memory of that was totally repressed. The amnesia held through all the rest of my life and two analyses, till I was 70, three years ago. But it remained alive in me, to be triggered off unrecognized by widely spaced analogous events. At the age of 26, at the University, I formed a good friendship with a fellow student who was a brother figure to me. When he left and I went home on vacation to mother, I fell ill of a mysterious exhaustion illness which disappeared immediately I left home and returned to College. I had no idea that it was equivalent to that aunt's family. In 1938, aged 37, I became minister of a highly organized Church in Leeds, with a Sunday afternoon meeting of 1,000 men, an evening congregation of 800, and well organized educational, social and recreational activities. It was too large for one minister and I had a colleague who became another Percy-substitute. He left as war clouds loomed up. Again I suddenly fell ill of the same mysterious exhaustion illness. It was put down to overwork, but by then I was psychoanalytically knowledgeable, had studied classical theory under Flugel, knew the stock literature, had an uncompleted M.A. thesis under supervision of Professor John Macmurray, seeking to translate Freud's psychobiology, or rather clinical data, into terms of "personal relations" philosophy, and had studied my own dreams for two years. So I was alerted when this illness brought a big dream.

I went down into a tomb and saw a man buried alive. He tried to get out but I threatened him with illness, locked him in and got away quick.

Next morning I was better. For the first time I recognized the re-eruption of my illness after Percy's death, and saw that I lived permanently over the top of its repression. I knew then I could not rest till that problem was solved.

I was drawn into war-time emergency psychotherapy by the Leeds Professor of Medicine, appointed to a lectureship in the Medical School, and went on studying my own dreams. I recently re-read the record and found I had only made forced text-bookish oedipal interpretations. Of more importance was that three dominant types of dream stood out: (1) a savage woman attacking me, (2) a quiet, firm, friendly father-figure supporting me, and (3) a mysterious death-threat dream, the clearest example based on the memory of mother taking me at the age of six into the bedroom of my invalid aunt, thought to be dying of rheumatic fever, lying white and silent. In one dream:

> I was working downstairs at my desk and suddenly an invisible band of ectoplasm tying me to a dying invalid upstairs was pulling me steadily out of the room. I knew I would be absorbed into her. I fought and suddenly the band snapped and I knew I was free.

I knew enough to guess that the memory of my dying aunt was a screen memory for the repressed dead Percy, which still exercised on me an unconscious pull out of life into collapse and apparent dying. I knew that somehow sometime I must get an analysis. In 1946 Professor Dicks appointed me as the first staff member of the new Department of Psychiatry, and said that with my views I must read Fairbairn. I did so and at the end of 1949 I sought analysis with him.

For the first few years, his broadly oedipal analysis of my "internalized bad-object relations" world did correspond to an actual period of my childhood. After Percy's death and my return home, from the age of three and a half to five, I fought to coerce mother into mothering me by repeated petty psychosomatic ills, tummy-aches, heat spots, loss of appetite, constipation and dramatic, sudden high temperatures, for which she would make me a tent-bed on the kitchen couch and be in and out from the shop to see me. She told me the doctor said: "I'll never come to that child again. He frightens the life out of me with these sudden high temperatures and next morning he's perfectly well." But it was all to no purpose. Around five years I changed tactics. A new bigger school gave me more independence, and mother said: "You began not to do what I told you." She would fly into violent rages and beat me, from about the time I was five to the age of seven. When canes got broken I was sent to buy a new one. At the age of seven I went to a still larger school and steadily developed a life of my own outside the home. We moved when I was eight to another shop where mother's business was an outstanding success. She became less depressed, gave me all the money I needed for hobbies and outdoor activities, scouting, sport, and gradually I forgot not quite all the memories of the first seven bad years. It was all the fears, rages, guilts, psychosomatic transient symptoms, disturbed dreams, venting the conflicts of those years from three and a half to seven, that Fairbairn's analysis dealt with. In mother's old age she said: "When your father and Aunt Mary died and I was alone, I tried keeping a dog but I had to give it up. I couldn't stop beating it." It's what happened to me. No wonder I had an inner world of internalized libidinally excited bad-object relations, and I owe much to Fairbairn's radical analysis of it.

But after the first three or four years I became convinced that this was keeping me marking time in a sadomasochistic inner world of *bad-object relations* with mother, as a defense against quite different problems of the period before Percy's death. This deeper material kept pushing through. The crunch came in December 1957 when my old friend, whose departure from College caused the first eruption of that Percy-illness in 1927, suddenly died. For the third time exhaustion seized me. I kept going enough to work and travel to Edinburgh for analysis, feeling I would now get to the bottom of it. Then, just as I felt some progress was being made, Fairbairn fell ill with a serious viral influenza of which he nearly died, and was off work six months. I had to reinstate repression, but at once began to "intellectualize" the problem I could not work through with him in person. It was not pure intellectualization by deliberate thinking. Spontaneous insights kept welling up at all sorts of times, and I jotted them down as they flowed with compelling intensity. Out of all that I wrote three papers; they became the basis of my book *Schizoid Phenomena, Object-Relations and The Self* (1968): "Ego-weakness, the Core of the Problem of Psycho-therapy" written in 1960 (chapter 6), "The Schizoid Problem, Regression and the Struggle to Preserve an Ego" (chapter 2) written in 1961, and "The Manic-depressive Problem in the Light of the Schizoid Process" (chapter 5) written in 1962. In two years they took me right beyond Fairbairn's halting point. He generously accepted this as a valid and necessary extension of his theory.

When he returned to work in 1959, I discussed my friend's death and Fairbairn's illness and he made a crucial interpretation: "I think since my illness I am no longer your good father or bad mother, but your brother dying on you." I suddenly saw the analytical situation in an extraordinary light, and wrote him a letter which I still have, but did not send. I knew it would put a bigger strain on him than he could stand in his precarious health. I suddenly saw that I could never solve my problem *with* an analyst. I wrote: "I am in a dilemma. I have got to end my analysis to get a chance to finish it, but then I do not have you to help me with it." Once Fairbairn had become my brother in transference, *losing him* either by ending analysis myself, or by staying with him till he died, would represent the death of Percy, and I would be left with a full scale eruption of that traumatic event, and no one to help me with it. Could Fairbairn have helped me with that in transference analysis? Not in his frail state of health and I phased out my analysis in that year.

I have much cause to be grateful to him for staying with me, in his increasingly weak state of health, till I had reached that critical insight. The driving force behind my theory writing in 1959–1962 was the reactivation of the Percy-trauma, causing a compelling spate of spontaneous ideas. I could contain it and use it for constructive research, partly because I was giving Fairbairn up gradually, partly because he accepted the validity of my ideas, and partly because I had resolved to seek analysis with Winnicott before Fairbairn died.

Fairbairn first introduced me to Winnicott in 1954 by asking him to send me a copy of his paper: "Regression Within the Psycho-Analytical Set-Up" (in Winnicott 1958). He sent it and, rather to my surprise, a letter saying: "I do invite you to look into the matter of your relation to Freud, so that you may have your own relation and not Fairbairn's. He spoils his good work by wanting to knock down Freud." We exchanged three long letters on each side. I stated that my relation to Freud had been settled years before I had heard of Fairbairn, when studying under Flugel at University College, London. I rejected Freud's psychobiology of instincts, but saw the great importance of his discoveries in psychopathology. Regarding that correspondence I now find I anticipated Morse's (1972) conclusion almost in his words, 18 years earlier: that Winnicott's "true self" has no place in Freud's theory. It could only be found in the id, but that is impossible because the id is only impersonal energy. In fact I felt that Winnicott had left Freud as far behind in therapy as Fairbairn had done in theory. In 1961 I sent him a copy of my book *Personality Structure and Human Interaction* (Guntrip 1961) and he replied that he had already purchased a copy. I was reading his papers as they were published, as also was Fairbairn who described him as "clinically brilliant." By 1962 I had no doubt that he was the only man I could turn to for further help. I was by then only free to visit London once a month for a couple of sessions, but the analysis I had had made it easier to profit by that. From 1962 to 1968 I had 150 sessions and their value was out of all proportion to their number. Winnicott said he was surprised that so much could be worked through in such widely spaced sessions, due I think in the first place to all the preliminary clearing that had been done by Fairbairn and to the fact that I could keep the analysis alive between visits; but most of all to *Winnicott's profound intuitive insights into the very infancy period I so needed to get down to.* He enabled me to reach extraordinarily clear evidence that my mother had almost certainly had an initial period of natural maternalism with me as her first baby, for perhaps a couple of months, before her personality problems robbed me of that "good mother." I had quite forgotten that letter I did not send to Fairbairn about the dilemma of not being able either to end analysis or go on with it, once my analyst became Percy in the transference. Ending it would be equivalent to Percy dying and I would have no one to help me with the aftermath. If I did not end it, I would be using my analyst to prevent the eruption of the trauma and so get no help with it, and risk his dying on me. My amnesia for that early trauma was not broken through with Winnicott either. Only recently have I realized that in fact, unwittingly, he altered the whole nature of the problem by enabling me to reach right back to *an ultimate good mother, and to find her recreated in him in the transference.* I discovered later that he had put me in a position to face what was a double trauma of both Percy's death and mother's failing me.

As I reread my records I am astonished at the rapidity with which he went to the heart of the matter. At the first session I mentioned the amnesia for the trauma of Percy's death, and felt I had had a radical analysis with Fairbairn of the "internalized bad-object defense" I had built up against that, but we had not got down to what I felt was my basic problem, not the actively bad-object mother of later childhood, *but the earlier mother who failed to relate at all.* Near the end of the session he said: "I've nothing particular to say yet, but if I don't say something, you may begin to feel I'm not here." At the second session he said:

> You know about me but I'm not a person to you yet. You may go away feeling alone and that I'm not real. You must have had an earlier illness before Percy was born, and felt mother left you to look after yourself. You accepted Percy as your infant self that needed looking after. When he died, you had nothing and collapsed.

That was a perfect object relations interpretation, but from Winnicott, not Fairbairn. Much later I said that I occasionally felt a "static, unchanging, lifeless state somewhere deep in me, feeling I can't move." Winnicott said:

> If 100% of you felt like that, you probably couldn't move and someone would have to wake you. After Percy died, you collapsed bewildered, but managed to salvage enough of yourself to go on living, very energetically, and put the rest in a cocoon, repressed, unconscious.

I wish there were time to illustrate his penetrating insight in more detail, but I must give another example. I said that people often commented on my ceaseless activity and energy, and that in sessions I did not like gaps of silence and at times talked hard. Fairbairn interpreted that I was trying to take the analysis out of his hands and do his job; steal father's penis, oedipal rivalry. Winnicott threw a dramatic new light on this talking hard. He said:

> Your problem is that that illness of collapse was never resolved. You had to keep yourself alive in spite of it. You can't take your ongoing being for granted. You have to work hard to keep yourself in existence. You're afraid to stop acting, talking or keeping awake. You feel you might die in a gap like Percy, because if you stop acting mother can't do

anything. She couldn't save Percy or you. You're bound to fear I can't keep you alive, so you link up monthly sessions for me by your records. No gaps. You can't feel that you are a going concern to me, because mother couldn't save you. You know about "being active" but not about "just growing, just breathing" while you sleep, without your having to do anything about it.

I began to be able to allow for some silences, and once, feeling a bit anxious, I was relieved to hear Winnicott move. I said nothing, but with uncanny intuition he said:

You began to feel afraid I'd abandoned you. You feel silence is abandonment. The gap is not you forgetting mother, but mother forgetting you, and now you've relived it with me. You're finding an earlier trauma which you might never recover without the help of the Percy trauma repeating it. You have to remember mother abandoning you by transference on to me.

I can hardly convey the powerful impression it made on me to find Winnicott coming right into the emptiness of my "object relations situation" in infancy with a non-relating mother.

Right at the end of my analysis I had a sudden return of hard talking in session. This time he made a different and extraordinary statement. He said:

It's like you giving birth to a baby with my help. You gave me half an hour of concentrated talk, rich in content. I felt strained in listening and holding the situation for you. You had to know that I could stand your talking hard at me and my not being destroyed. I had to stand it while you were in labor being creative, not destructive, producing something rich in content. You are talking about "object relating," "using the object" and finding you don't destroy it. I couldn't have made that interpretation five years ago.

Later he gave his paper on "The Use of an Object" (in Winnicott 1971) in America and met, not surprisingly I think, with much criticism. Only an exceptional man could have reached that kind of insight. He became a good breast mother to my infant self in my deep unconscious, at the point where my actual mother had lost her maternalism and could not stand me as a live baby any more. It was not then apparent, as it later became to me, that he had transformed my whole understanding of the trauma of Percy's death, particularly when he added:

You too have a good breast. You've always been able to give more than take. I'm good for you but you're good for me. Doing your analysis is almost the most reassuring thing that happens to me. The chap before you makes me feel I'm no good at all. You don't have to be good for me. I don't need it and can cope without it, but in fact you are good for me.

Here at last I had a mother who could value her child, so that I could cope with what was to come. It hardly seems worth mentioning that the only point at which I felt I disagreed with Winnicott was when he talked occasionally about "getting at your primitive sadism, the baby's ruthlessness and cruelty, your aggression," in a way that suggested not my angry fight to extract a response from my cold mother, but Freud's and Klein's "instinct theory," the id, innate aggression. For I knew he rejected the "death instinct" and had moved far beyond Freud when I went to him. He once said to me: "We differ from Freud. He was for curing symptoms. We are concerned with living persons, whole living and loving." By 1967 he wrote, and gave me a copy of his paper, "The Location of Cultural Experience" (in Winnicott 1971), in which he said: "I see that I am in the territory of Fairbairn: "object-seeking" as opposed to "satisfaction-seeking.' " I felt then that Winnicott and Fairbairn had joined forces to neutralize my earliest traumatic years.

I must complete this account with the one thing I could not foresee. Winnicott becoming the good mother, freeing me to be alive and creative, transformed the significance of Percy's death in a way that was to enable me to resolve that trauma, and my dilemma about how to end my analysis. Winnicott, relating to me in my deep unconscious, enabled me to stand seeing that it was not just the loss of Percy, but being left alone with the mother who could not keep me alive, that caused my collapse into apparent dying. But thanks to his profound intuitive insight, I was not now alone with a non-relating mother. I last saw him in July 1969. In February 1970 I was told medically that I was seriously overworked, and if I did not retire "Nature would make me." I must have felt unconsciously that that was a threat that "Mother Nature" would at last crush my active self. Every time I rested I found myself under a compulsion to go back to the past, in the form of rehearsing the details of my ministerial "brother-figure's" leaving in 1938, and my reacting with an exhaustion illness. I soon saw that this was significant and it led on to an urge to write up my whole life-story, as if I had to find out all that had happened to me. By October I developed pneumonia and spent five weeks in hospital. The consultant said: "Relax. You're too overactive." I still did not realize that I was fighting against an unconscious compulsive regression. I had never linked the idea of "retirement" with the deep fear of losing my battle with mother to keep my active self alive, in the end. After a slow winter recuperation, I heard in the New Year 1971 that Winnicott had a flu attack. Presently I inquired of Masud Khan how Winnicott was, and he replied that he was about again and liked to hear from his friends, so I dropped him a line. A little later the phone rang, and the familiar voice said: "Hallo. Thanks for your letter" and we chatted a bit. About two weeks later the phone rang again and *his secretary told me he had passed away. That very night I had a startling dream. I saw my mother,* black, immobilized, staring fixedly into space, *totally ignoring me* as I stood at one side staring at her and feeling myself frozen into immobility: the first time I had ever seen her in a dream like that. Before she had always been attacking me. My first thought was: "I've lost Winnicott and am left alone with mother, sunk in depression, ignoring me. That's how I felt when Percy died." I thought I must have taken the loss of Winnicott as a repetition of the Percy trauma. Only recently have I become quite clear that it was not that at all. I did not dream of mother like that when my college friend died or my ministerial colleague left. Then I felt ill, as after Percy's death. This time it was quite different. That dream started a compelling dream-sequence which went on night after night, taking me back in chronological order through every house I had lived in, in Leeds, Ipswich, College, the second Dulwich shop, and finally the first shop and house of the bad first seven years. Family figures, my wife, daughter, Aunt Mary, father and mother kept recurring; father always supportive, mother always hostile, but no sign of Percy. I was trying to stay in the post-Percy period of battles with mother. Then after some two months two dreams at last broke that amnesia for Percy's life and death. I was astonished to see myself in a dream clearly aged about three, recognizably me, holding a pram in which was my brother aged about a year old. I was strained, looking anxiously over to the left at mother, to see if she would take any notice of us. But she was staring fixedly into the distance, ignoring us, as in the first dream of that series. The next night the dream was even more startling.

> I was standing with another man, the double of myself, both reaching out to get hold of a dead object. Suddenly the other man collapsed in a heap. Immediately the dream changed to a lighted room, where I saw Percy again. I knew it was him, sitting on the lap of a woman who had no face, arms or breasts. She was merely a lap to sit on, not a person. He looked deeply depressed, with the corners of his mouth turned down, and I was trying to make him smile.

I had recovered in that dream the memory of collapsing when I saw him as a dead object and reached out to grab him. But I had done more. I had actually gone back in both dreams to the earlier time before he died, to see the "faceless" depersonalized mother, and the black depressed mother, who totally failed to relate to both of us. Winnicott had said: "You accepted Percy as your infant self that needed looking after. When he died, you had nothing and collapsed." Why did I dream of "collapsing" first, and then of going back to look after Percy? My feeling is that my collapse was my first reaction of terrified hopelessness at the shock of finding Percy dead on mother's lap, but in that aunt's family I quickly seized the chance of staying alive by finding others to live for.

That dream series made me bring out and restudy all my analysis records, till I realized that, though Winnicott's death had reminded me of Percy's, the situation was entirely different. That process of compelling regression had not started with Winnicott's death, but with the threat of "retirement" as if mother would undermine me at last. I did not dream of Winnicott's death, but of Percy's death and mother's total failure to relate to us. What better dream-evidence could one have of Winnicott's view that "There is no such thing as a baby": i.e., there must be a "mother and baby," and what better evidence for Fairbairn's view that the basic psychic reality is the "personal object relation"? What gave me strength in my deep unconscious to face again that basic trauma? It must have been because Winnicott was not, and could not be, dead for me, nor certainly for many others. I have never felt that my father was dead, but in a deep way alive in me, enabling me to resist mother's later active paralyzing inhibiting influence. Now Winnicott had come into living relation with precisely that earlier lost part of me that fell ill because mother failed me. *He has taken her place and made it possible and safe to remember her in an actual dream-reliving of her paralyzing schizoid aloofness.* Slowly that became a firm conviction growing in me, and I recovered from the volcanic upheaval of that autonomously regressing compelling dream-series, feeling that I had at last reaped the gains I had sought in analysis over some twenty years. After all the detailed memories, dreams, symptoms of traumatic events, people and specific emotional tensions had been worked through, one thing remained: *the quality of the over-all atmosphere of the personal relations that made up our family life in those first seven years.* It lingers as a mood of sadness for my mother who was so damaged in childhood that she could neither be, nor enable me to be, our "true selves." I cannot have a different set of memories. But that is offset by my discovery in analysis of how deeply my father became a secure mental possession in me, supporting my struggle to find and be my "true self," and by Fairbairn's resolving my negative transference of my dominating mother on to him, till he became another good father who had faith in me, and finally by Winnicott entering into the emptiness left by my non-relating mother, so that I could experience the security of being my self. I must add that without my wife's understanding and support I could not have had those analyses or reached this result. What is psychoanalytic psychotherapy? It is, as I see it, the provision of a reliable and understanding human relationship of a kind that makes contact with the deeply repressed traumatized child in a way that enables one to become steadily more able to live, in the security of a new real relationship, with the traumatic legacy of the earliest formative years, as it seeps through or erupts into consciousness.

Psychoanalytic therapy is not like a "technique" of the experimental sciences, an objective "thing-in-itself" working automatically. It is a process of interaction, a function of two variables, the personalities of two people working together towards free spontaneous growth. The analyst grows as well as the analysand. There must be something wrong if an analyst is static when he deals with such dynamic personal experiences. For me, Fairbairn built as a person on what my father did for me, and as an analyst enabled me to discover in great detail how my battles for independence of mother from three and a half to seven years had grown into my personality make-up. Without that I could have deteriorated in old age into as awkward a person as my mother. Winnicott, a totally different type of personality, understood and filled the emptiness my mother left in the first three and a half years. I needed them both and had the supreme good fortune to find both. Their very differences have been a stimulus to different sides of my make-up. Fairbairn's ideas were "exact logical concepts" which clarified issues. Winnicott's ideas were "imaginative hypotheses" that challenged one to explore further. As examples, compare Fairbairn's concepts of the libidinal, antilibidinal and central egos as a theory of endopsychic structure, with Winnicott's "true and false selves" as intuitive insights into the confused psychic reality of actual persons. Perhaps no single analyst can do all that an analysand needs, and we must be content to let patients make as much use of us as they can. We dare not pose as omniscient and omnipotent because we have a theory. Also Fairbairn once said: "You get out of analysis what you put into it," and I think that is true for both analyst and analysand. I would think that the development of clear conscious insight represents having taken full possession of the gains already made emotionally, putting one in a position to risk further emotional strains to make more emotional growth. It represents not just conscious understanding but a strengthening of the inner core of "selfhood" and capacity for "relating." So far as psychopathological material is concerned, dreaming expresses our endopsychic structure. It is a way of experiencing on the fringes of consciousness, our internalized conflicts, our memories of struggles originally in our outer world and then as memories and fantasies of conflicts that have become our inner reality, to keep "object relations" alive, even if only "bad-object relations," because we need them to retain possession of our "ego." It was my experience that the deeper that final spate of dreams delved into my unconscious, the more dreaming slowly faded out and was replaced by "waking up in a mood." I found I was not fantasying or thinking but simply feeling, consciously in the grip of a state of mind that I began to realize I had been in consciously long ago, and had been in unconsciously deep down ever since: a dull mechanical lifeless mood, no interest in anything, silent, shut in to myself, going through routine motions with a sense of loss of all meaning in existence. I experienced this for a number of consecutive mornings till I began to find that it was fading out into a normal interest in life: which after all seems to be what one would expect.

There is a natural order peculiar to each individual and determined by his history, in which (1) problems can become conscious and (2) interpretations can be relevant and mutative. We cannot decide that but only watch the course of the individual's development. Finally, on the difficult question of the sources of theory, it seems that our theory must be rooted in our psychopathology. That was implied in Freud's courageous self-analysis at a time when all was obscure. The idea that we could think out a theory of the structure and functioning of the personality without its having any relation to the structure and functioning of our own personality should be a self-evident impossibility. If our theory is too rigid, it is likely to conceptualize our ego defenses. If it is flexible and progressive it is possible for it to conceptualize our ongoing growth processes, and throw light on others' problems and on therapeutic possibilities. Balint's "basic fault" and Winnicott's "incommunicado core," since they regard these phenomena as universal, must be their ways of "intuitively sensing" their own basic reality, and therefore other people's. By contrast with Fairbairn's exactly intellectually defined theoretical constructs which state logically progressive developments in existing theory, they open the way to profounder exploration of the infancy period, where, whatever a baby's genetic endowment, the mother's ability or failure to "relate" is the *sine qua non* of psychic health for the infant. To find a good parent at the start is the basis of psychic health. In its lack, to find a genuine "good object" in one's analyst is both a transference experience and a real life experience. In analysis as in real life, all relationships have a subtly dual nature. All through life we take into ourselves both good and bad figures who either strengthen or disturb us, and it is the same in psychoanalytic therapy: it is the meeting and interacting of two real people in all its complex possibilities.

REFERENCES

Fairbairn, W. R. D. (1952a). *Psychoanalytic Studies of the Personality*. London: Tavistock.
_____ (1952b). Theoretical and experimental aspects of psycho-analysis. *British Journal of Medical Psychology*. 25:122–127.
_____ (1954). Observations of the nature of hysterical states. *British Journal of Medical Psychology*. 27:106–125.
_____ (1955). Observations in defence of the object-relations theory of the personality. *British Journal of Medical Psychology*. 28:144–156.
_____ (1956). Considerations arising out of the Schreber case. *British Journal of Medical Psychology*. 29:113–127.
_____ (1958). On the nature and aims of psychoanalytical treatment. *International Journal of Psycho-Analysis*. 39:374–385.
Guntrip, H. (1960). Ego-weakness, the hard core of the problem of psychotherapy. In *Schizoid Phenomena, Object-Relations and the Self*. London: Hogarth, 1968.
_____ (1961). *Personality Structure and Human Interaction*. London: Hogarth.
_____ (1968). *Schizoid Phenomena, Object-Relations and the Self*. London: Hogarth.

Morse, S. J. (1972). Structure and reconstruction: a critical comparison of Michael Balint and D. W. Winnicott. *International Journal of Psycho-Analysis.* 53:487–500.

Sutherland, J. (1965). Obituary. W. R. D. Fairbairn. *International Journal of Psycho-Analysis.* 46:245–247.

Winnicott, D. W. (1958). *Collected Papers. Through Paediatrics to Psycho-Analysis.* London: Tavistock.

———— (1971). *Playing and Reality.* London: Tavistock.

19

JEAN-MARC ALBY: BEING ENGLISH AND A PSYCHOANALYST (INTERVIEW)

Jean-Marc Alby: My first meeting with Winnicott took place at an International Congress of Psychoanalysis at Copenhagen. In a small group, Winnicott was recounting, with all his vitality and veracity, his consultation with a Finnish boy whom he had been asked to see during a tour of Finland. This child, who had been hospitalized in the orthopedic department of a children's hospital, presented certain symptoms of a vague kind, including messing, headaches, and abdominal pains. There was no urgent symptom to justify recourse to a psychotherapist.

He spoke no English and Winnicott did not know Finnish. Winnicott picked up a sheet of paper and began to scribble: a relationship was then established with the child, who began to project his own personality, dreams, and anxieties into the drawing. In this way Winnicott was able to assess the child's difficulties.

Later, during Anglo-French psychoanalytical meetings, I realized, paradoxically through Michael and Enid Balint, how important Winnicott was: Winnicott had been a pediatrician, Balint's father a doctor. I was able to identify with them in this medical connection; intellectual complicity with Winnicott is often marked by interlinked paths.

Anne Clancier: Were you already interested in pediatrics and child psychoanalysis?

J-MA: Yes, I had already been involved with pediatrics and child psychiatry. One thing sticks out in my memory: as an intern at a pediatric consultation I saw pediatricians take the hand of an infant and gently hold it. It is one of the gestures that reading Winnicott reminds me of all the time: the physical contact, the informal relationship between this bundle of flesh, the mother, and the pediatrician—I was very moved by that.

AC: Yes, pediatricians often have intuitions about infants' needs. I remember how in the 1930s, long before psychoanalysts had advocated physical and emotional contacts with babies, Dr. Lere Boullet, in his hospital pediatrics department asked both externs and interns to take the babies out for walks into the hospital courtyards, saying: "Can't you see those children are bored. You must look after them, take them out for walks." Some of the students laughed. But that pediatrician was right, because those children, deprived of contact with their mothers during their hospitalization and separated from them, perhaps for the first time, needed those contacts. It helped them to cure their somatic disturbances.

J-MA: Yes, I feel completely on Winnicott's side on this—like when he allows us to share in his observation of a child in a "set situation." From the theoretical point of view, what interests me—and where I found him most helpful—is his concept of the transitional object and the field of illusion. When he speaks of the false self, however, I find him much more difficult to follow.

AC: You mentioned Balint in relation to Winnicott. Do you think the Hungarian school played a role in the formation of Winnicott's thinking?

J-MA: One may well think of Ferenczi and his active technique. When Winnicott speaks about the value of the body, of breathing, of relaxation, of being and at the way of being in one's body, he raises the question of the self that is or is not in the body at certain times. The body and the self link him to Ferenczi and to Balint. On this matter, I would mention the psychoanalyst's "presence," as Sacha Nacht did, when we remember that Winnicott, when with a very "regressed" patient, a borderline case, always had a glass of water nearby, in case she felt she needed it.

I would like to talk to you about the touchstone of every therapeutic relationship: the counter-transference. In teaching, in the groups, in the case studies, does one not aim at helping the future psychiatrist, the doctor, to become aware of his counter-attitude?

To return to his work with children, what greatly impressed me in Winnicott, in his assessments, was the way he took into account the child's infirmities in his development and his relationships with the environment. This testified very much to Winnicott the pediatrician.

On the subject of the environment, he might have been accused of naivety; in fact, Winnicott was far from being naive. He certainly knew what a good-enough environment was, he knew what people were, how profoundly ambivalent they were. He reminded me very much of a character I am very fond of, Father Brown, the priest-detective hero of G.K. Chesterton, who, like Graham Greene, was very fond of detective stories. While appearing to be utterly innocent, Father Brown solves the most complicated riddles. His innocence is only apparent and is used by the character as a weapon. He has a sense of human understanding; he is self-effacing, a believer in grace, an order beyond situations and conflicts: his power lay in that "naive" certainty. Chesterton's idealist and religious convictions won through. His conception of human relations reminded me strongly of Winnicott.

AC: When you describe this individual, one might imagine him to be some kind of idealist, but perhaps above all he was someone who allowed his unconscious to function, who knew how to identify with others at a deep level. These are indispensable qualities for a psychoanalyst and ones that Winnicott possessed to the highest degree.

What do you think of the transitional object, of the transitional area, particularly where creativity is concerned? Isn't it very important in clinical medicine, because, after all, one often sees patients who, when things get better, are capable of creative activity?

J-MA: Winnicott is right: there is something of the order of illusion in all psychical reality, but why attach so much importance to this field of illusion? It is a rather too Platonic conception for my taste.

AC: It is true that he uses the word illusion in order to be able to say dis-illusion and dis-illusionment. The field of illusion is a creative field because, at a given moment, it makes it possible to move to a domain which is that of the mother who knows, because she is good enough, at what moment to frustrate the infant and to force him to confront opposition thanks to her aggressive movement.

J-MA: You are quite right to remind me of Winnicott's concern for the dynamics of development. Before him, Freud had denounced that same illusion in *Mass Psychology and the Analysis of the Ego*, since every feeling of love was essentially illusion. This brings us to the question of the reality of the sense of self. Is it not all mere reflexion? Is there a living reality?

AC: Winnicott speaks of the incommunicable kernel, that is to an say, the silent kernel of the personality that is not necessarily an illusion, but incommunicable.

J-MA: That is a useful notion.

AC: One might refer here to Freud's view of what might be included under the heading of illusions, religion, for example, and art. When he speaks of art he seems to be saying that it is a good illusion—doesn't this amount to saying that in creation one rediscovers good internal objects and gives them to others, thus rediscovering communication with them? It belongs to the order of love, it is libidinal.

J-MA: Analysts tend too often to interpret everything in terms of defense: Winnicott dealt severely with this will to reduce. Furthermore we may have doubts as to our capacity to intervene in the preoedipal period, which is experienced in an ineffable manner, perhaps re-experienced during analysis in the same way, without any possible interpretation, whereas what concerns the oedipal conflict may be elaborated more easily in verbal terms, the "as if." You will find an echo of these themes in Reik, in the place he gives to intuition: interpretation counts for less than the capacity for identification.

In Winnicott, the absence of systematization and the pragmatism are closely bound up, for me, with the English mentality. It reminds me of Locke. In his *Treatise on Education*, you will find the same mentality: absence of systematization, pragmatism, a sense of fantasy. Someone else who would be in good company with Winnicott is Lewis Carroll.

AC: Yes, there is even a point in common on a biographical level between Lewis Carroll and Winnicott: both were the only boy in a family surrounded by several sisters.

J-MA: But there is also the playful use of nonsense.

AC: Yes, and one finds Shakespeare, who, in poetic formulas, gives us dazzling insights into the human psyche.

J-MA: I have also been very susceptible to an attitude in Winnicott that I might dare to call "goodness." But, since that might be misunderstood, let us call it openness to others, a profound availability to others' needs.

AC: Might one not say receptiveness, empathy? One should also remember his capacity to give or receive criticism, while preserving a respect for the other person, and his tolerance. We know that when there were tensions in the British psychoanalytic world, between the groups that had formed around Anna Freud and Melanie Klein, Winnicott belonged to the "middle group" and acted as conciliator. As he said, he took from each side those theoretical elements that suited him, which he considered useful in his clinical practice.

J-MA: I liked his modesty, too; he did not believe himself to be omnipotent with his patients. He did not ask of them what they were not capable of giving. Thus he did not expect mothers to be very good or even good, but simply good enough; he sustained those who had difficulties with their children, telling them to do at least what they could, whereas Freud said that whatever mothers do it will be bad in any case.

A very important point, common to Winnicott and Balint, is their conviction that the patient "cures his doctor."

To end, I would like to draw attention to Winnicott's love of paradox, which is suggested in the title of your book. Winnicott loved to be paradoxical, in the manner of many English thinkers, if one includes in it a sense of humour and respect for others.

20

EVELYNE KESTEMBERG:
A YEAST FOR THOUGHT
(INTERVIEW)

Evelyne Kestemberg: I must have met Winnicott in London in the 1950s. At first I took him to be one of those original Englishmen, attractive by their eccentricity, but not very serious. Later I heard him give a lecture to the Société Psych-analytique de Paris; he talked about a very difficult patient who had led him to develop his conception of the *as if* personality and the way of treating that personality. I think he also talked to us on that day about the capacity to be alone with someone.

Anne Clancier: That seems to me to be one of his most important articles.

EK: It's quite crucial. You know that my present practice is very taken up with psychotics, and I believe that the capacity to be alone with someone is the most operational, the most heuristic concept, one of those that have served me most in understanding patients.

Talking to us about a woman in her fifties, a psychotic, Winnicott showed us how, in the impossibility of doing anything, he had realized that she needed to be silent with him and that when she spoke, she developed an "as if" personality. That's all I remember of that lecture, but, as you see, it is something of fundamental importance to me. At the time, Winnicott was received with a great deal of reserve. It was said that he was eccentric, that he had an inadequate knowledge of psychoanalysis, and his brilliant clinical intuition was misunderstood. Winnicott began to be quoted only in the last years of his life and at first by child psychoanalysts.

Then I met Winnicott at various conferences. In late 1960, I gave a lecture on the character neuroses to the British Psycho-Analytical Society. As almost always Winnicott gave the impression that he was asleep when he was listening, and then he asked me the most pertinent question that one could possibly ask on what I had said and on the point that was certainly the most controversial. Later, I met him at Stockholm in 1963. He had such an unconventional side to him that he sometimes seemed strange, odd: to my great fright, I have seen him cross a street when nobody else would do so and felt sure that he would be run over – he wasn't. I think the drivers saw that he was not looking, for indeed he gave the impression that he was not looking, as if he were moving in a world of his own.

AC: Could we say that it was a kind of retreat?

EK: Not a pathological retreat, in the sense of withdrawal. I would say that it is a kind of recourse to some inner resources.

AC: A word has to be found for it. I was thinking of retreat, in the sense that people go on a retreat.

EK: One had the impression that he distanced himself in that way from whatever might distract him. He withdrew into himself with total contempt for the outside world.

AC: When, later, he was ill, it was perhaps thanks to that characteristic that he was able to struggle against the disease and emerge once again alive after an attack, in the way that some of my colleagues have described it to me.

EK: Yes, probably. I believe that he had auto-erotic capacities of a quite remarkable kind. Paradoxical, no doubt, given social conformism, but certainly without any sense of guilt.

AC: His wife, Clare Winnicott, tells how he played all the time. And that when they were together they seemed to be playing.

EK: I believe it was thanks to that that he was able to invent the squiggle.

AC: Mrs. Winnicott describes how he had a cupboard full of squiggles. It was his game.

EK: Yes. It was that quite remarkable auto-erotic capacity that also seemed to run throughout his work.

AC: What was also remarkable about it was that it was without guilt, whereas many of us hide from it.

EK: And I would say without perversion, without perverseness.

AC: Without perversion, or shame.

EK: Which is very rare.

AC: One sometimes meets that with the English, who are capable of being both terribly conformist and very original.

EK: Yes, he had that very English side to him.

AC: The Lewis Carroll side.

EK: Yes, absolutely, without the terrorizing side; it was as if Winnicott had found a sort of grace in living.

AC: Which concepts interest you most in Winnicott?

EK: I have been interested above all, following Winnicott, yet at the same time keeping my distance, in the transitional object and his conception of the self.

It was by setting out from Winnicott's view, but in a different way, that we described the self. Winnicott was a sort of yeast that enabled us to elaborate a concept that is not the same as his, but which owes it something.

AC: After Winnicott's seminars, I gave a seminar on the self and we studied your report to the Congrès des Langues Romanes on genetic psychoanalysis. I had the impression that Winnicott had been very important for you.

EK: I don't know whether we already referred to Winnicott in our work, but at the time Winnicott was criticized for describing the self on the basis of a false self. It may be that the notion of false self is clearer in his work than that of the self.

I believe that we owe a great deal to Winnicott in the elaboration of ideas on the self. The idea of the transitional object was a sort of yeast for our own elaboration. Of course, it ended up as something different, since we now think that the self is the first psychical configuration that functions within the ego, but with a certain specificity, but which perhaps gives rise not to specific representations but to specific feelings, which are not to be confused with what belongs to the object. The self is, I believe, the element of the object in auto-eroticism, that is to say, in narcissism, but without the object being recognized as distinct. The hallucinatory satisfaction of desire may be the first manifestation of the psychical functioning at the same time as the first manifestation of the self, before the ego is the agency that envelops self and object. Perhaps it is a pre-ego, but one that is not to be confused with the ego that continues to function at the level of auto-eroticism and is more or less bound up with or separated from the object. It is at a deeper level, not necessarily more archaic, but deeper. This is something that Winnicott stresses.

AC: That is interesting. It seems to me that, like Winnicott, you use a paradoxical mode of thought. Saying that it is not what is archaic that is deepest certainly looks like a paradox.

EK: I believe that our clinical work forces that conclusion upon us. If one sees a varied range of patients—neurotics, psychotics, adolescents, children—one is certainly forced to acknowledge that the most archaic is not necessarily the deepest, and vice versa.

I owe a great deal to Winnicott at the level of auto-eroticism. This is something fundamental, which he had laid great stress on. But I believe, unlike him, that the transitional object is already an elaboration, that it is an encounter between the projection of auto-eroticism and the cathection of the object, and therefore already an elaboration of the object and of the self in an encounter. I believe, for example, that schizophrenics have no transitional object.

AC: You have more experience than I in this field, but I would not be surprised if that were the case.

EK: I am quite definite on the matter. Relentless masturbation, for example, has nothing to do with the auto-erotic use of the transitional object.

AC: Winnicott says – another paradox – that the transitional object is neither outside nor inside. What do you think?

EK: It's a notion that I find very sympathetic. I have made a distinction between the organization of the fetishistic relationship, the object as fetish and the transitional object. The transitional object is neither outside nor inside, in the sense that it is based on a thing-object which represents the internal object, but at the same time, one on which the subject projects himself. Therefore it is an object that is not experienced as an external object, since it is a projection of the subject and related to the object. It is different from what I call the fetishistic relationship, since, as we have seen in therapy, for example, the animated object must acquire the quality of being unanimated in order to remain permanent and to be a guarantee of narcissism. The transitional object, on the other hand, is more complex, more subtle, and certainly less archaic, and it has a ludic dimension, a quality of specific pleasure that is absent from the fetishistic relationship. I used Winnicott a great deal, not necessarily to follow in his footsteps but as a yeast to my own thought. I mean that he has always given me a great deal to think about.

AC: I like your formula, for it seems to correspond perfectly to the impression that I have had in studying Winnicott.

EK: Yes, he raises lots of things. He raises the question of auto-eroticism and interior play.

AC: One always gets something out of him. Winnicott makes one invent.

There is another interesting concept, but one that is difficult to define, namely the difference between "fantasy" and "fantasying." It might be said that between fantasy . . . and . . .

EK: And daydreaming (rêvasserie).

AC: Ah! I was looking for the word. Daydreaming is very good, because it's like a machine ticking over without a load.

EK: Yes, I think daydreaming is to fantasy what a photograph is to life. Daydreaming is sterile, repetitive. It lacks the dimension of fantasy creation. It's a kind of desiccation of a fantasy into a narrative, shaped, but in a shape that's not very creative. It's like certain literary or musical works. You might say it's like the work of Brücke as compared with that of Beethoven. It's well turned, but a bit boring, a bit desiccated.

Adolescents are very well aware of this because they experience their daydreams as something gloomy and one might almost say tiring. When one has worked a great deal with adolescents, one becomes very aware of the distinction they draw between their daydreams and their "dreams," in the sense of projects. Having dreams in that sense is something that moves forward, whereas daydreaming is something closed, something that catches you in its toils, something that swirls around you like fog. It's like a grey, drizzly day. Dreaming about the future, on the other hand, may be stormy, but at least there is movement.

AC: Isn't there pleasure in daydreaming though?

EK: Yes, there is pleasure, but it's a gloomy sort of pleasure, like the pleasure derived from mechanical masturbation, in which the eroticism is repressed and thwarted. Adolescents are well aware of the difference. Thus one sometimes sees them suddenly come to life, there's a light in their eyes, but they need some object or project to reanimate them.

AC: Maybe it's as if they no longer had any contact with an object in the relationship.

EK: They lose it—it's a degraded, rather dehiscent object.

AC: Do you think there is any connection there with anality?

EK: It isn't "anchored" to it, as you might say, but it may be connected to a certain level of anality. It's a sort of emotional evasion, not putrid, but without smell or savor.

AC: Are you interested in the squiggles?

EK: Yes, they interest me a great deal, but as far as Winnicott's book, *Therapeutic Consultations*, is concerned, I had many reservations and was even very negative in my attitude to it. I think that if one took it as a method, it would be catastrophic. Indeed, you need Winnicott's own genius and creativity to make it work. If one tried to imitate it, it would be transmitted magic, a mere conjuring trick: whereas it must be nourished by all Winnicott's intuitive genius. He had extraordinary capacities and very long, very deep experience behind him.

AC: Do you use Winnicott's books in your teaching?

EK: There was a Winnicott fashion that did no good at all. It was, I believe, a way of not reading Freud. Winnicott, however, knew Freud's work very well—and Melanie Klein's—and he accommodated them both in his own way. He plundered them to make his own honey. In my teaching I don't often quote authors, because I don't always have the lectures in my head, but I believe I often have Winnicott in my head, whether to agree with him or not.

There was a time when people were using such notions as transitional space quite wrongly. It didn't do Winnicott any good. If one becomes the prisoner of a conceptualization, one goes right against his way of thinking.

What is important is that one should work out one's own ideas. Anyway, that is my understanding of Winnicott — it doesn't have to be valid for anyone else.

I'd like to say a word about illusion. A great deal has been said about illusion, in relation to parents and children, but I would like to say something about it in relation to the treatment of psychotics. It is something quite fundamental in that area. If one spends one's time treating psychotics, one has to have a degree of illusion to emerge from repetition, but not too much to enclose the patient in an illusory environment and to reduce their psychical mode of functioning to ours. I use this a great deal in the teaching I do on the psychotherapy of psychotics. One needs enough illusion to believe that one will overcome repetition and alter the psychical economy, and as long as the economy is not altered, one remains in an area in which the translation of contents produces wrong meanings. The patients are enclosed in our understanding, one takes their place, and in fact one is rejecting them. One is not allowing them to develop according to their own rhythm. Winnicott's intuition was to grasp the rhythm of each of the individuals he dealt with, though he didn't put it in these terms. I am putting it in Freud's terms. Freud wrote something quite crucial about rhythm and I find it extremely valuable, both in the direct observation of mother–child relationships and in the case of psychotics. It is the "counter-time" or counter-rhythm that is most harmful to the child's psychical organizations.

Lastly, there is certainly much more in Winnicott's work than I have derived from it — I've simply been saying a few things about what it has meant to me.

21

SERGE LEBOVICI:
AN INIMITABLE GENIUS
(INTERVIEW)

Serge Lebovici: I met Winnicott immediately after the war. With René Diatkine, I took part in a conference organized by the International Association of Mental Health. It must have been in 1946. We sat in on Winnicott's consultations at Paddington Green Hospital. We were very struck by his methods. He stayed with a family and a child for ten minutes, for example, then he went to join another family, jumping over the seats. As we listened to him, it seemed to us that he was clearly a man inspired. We had been impressed by the quality of contact that he had with families and children and the great air of freedom about him. I believe that this freedom can be most dangerous when Winnicott's zealous followers try to imitate him.

I then saw Winnicott again during the Annual Days of Child Psychoanalysis, in 1949, I think, at the Hôpital des Enfants Malades. Each year we invited a foreign colleague: later we had Melanie Klein, but Winnicott was the first to be asked. Now Augusta Bonnard, a pupil of Anna Freud's, a famous old lady of the time, because she had written an article on the treatment of a child carried out through the mother, had also been invited. She had not been told that Winnicott would also be there. It didn't occur to me to tell her because it was not a secret. But when she saw him in the room, she cried: "Oh! There's the murderer." That gives some idea of how Winnicott was regarded at the time by Anna Freud's pupils. I'm not saying that this is how Augusta Bonnard actually regarded Winnicott, but certainly some of her pupils did.

From then on I remained on very good terms with Winnicott and I would like to talk to you about two occasions that impressed me. Once, during an International Congress of Psychoanalysis, he chaired a session. Someone was reading a paper. I then saw Winnicott put his head down on his hands on the table, his eyes shut. When the speaker had finished, he didn't move—I thought he had died. I was horrified. For what seemed like an interminable time, he didn't move. Then, suddenly, he sat up as if nothing had happened. Quite obviously, he hadn't been asleep. I wondered what he was showing by that: interest, a sort of withdrawal into himself? The last time I saw him, I was very moved after the event because I felt that at the time he was drawing away a little from the land of the living: it was at the European Congress of Child Psychology at Wiesbaden. At a conference in Rome I was particularly struck by how much he seemed to be in love with his wife; what she told me did not seem in any way exaggerated, when she spoke of the way he danced with her at conference receptions. And I saw him at the Institut de Psychanalyse, where he was a guest of Sacha Nacht and me, saying how delighted he was to be in Paris, to drink champagne, etc. He was a man who loved life and knew how to live.

On the scientific level, I think Winnicott is a model of the transition from medicine to psychoanalysis, with no intermediary stage in psychiatry. He was initially a pediatrician, then a child psychiatrist, but without really going through psychiatry. He left out the less good part of that discipline. It's not that I am anti-psychiatry, but I think he cut out the least good part of psychiatry by trusting that narrow nosography. With hindsight one sees the extent to which he was a precursor.

For example, what we are now discovering about the life of the infant shows that he had already made some remarkable observations. We didn't believe in them at the time, but what I saw recently (on a videotape during a conference) concerning infants shows how right Winnicott was.

One of the most fascinating parts of his work concerns the mother–infant relationship. The nature of this relationship for Winnicott does not conform to psychoanalytic tradition. His postulate on the set-up of infant and maternal care is the fundamental premise of his theories and his qualities of observation as a pediatrician played a large part in this, as did the type of dazzling intuition that was his.

It has happened to me, too, in therapeutic consultations with children, to feel things as he did, what he calls "the sacred moments." It's marvellous, but there is no method in it. Many people work out fixed schemata for all consultations of this type, but they are quite inapplicable if one lacks the capacity to use them.

Anne Clancier: Capacity and long experience.

SL: Yes, one has to be able to identify with every little baby—not everybody can do that. I think he is right when he says that the holding environment is never expressible in analysis. I think one can say the kind of things he says, have intuitions like his, only if one experiences the relationship at a very deep level.

Take, for example, a child having sleep disturbances. Yesterday I saw a video of the first observation I'd done on sleep disturbances. As I was led to see the child again four years later, I looked again at the tape and showed it to my colleagues. I realized that I had said something like Winnicott might had said. The mother had said: "I never loved anyone as I loved that baby," but she had not asked that baby to love her. I said to her: "When you look at him, you don't let him look at you straight in the eyes; he hasn't been able to make a mother of you." In the end, I think we worked with various interpretations of the catastrophe that had taken place. The whole problem of reconstruction was there: these disasters, which cannot be expressed, which can be expressed only in analysis, must be taken into account and elaborated. Everything Winnicott said on this matter is wonderful. Some people criticize him for these interventions. "This isn't analysis," they say. Up to a point, it isn't analysis, but at least he is always an analyst.

Thus in his last, posthumously published book, *The Piggle*, Winnicott recounts how he was sitting next to the two-year-old girl and said to her: "You're afraid of the greedy Winnicott baby, the baby born out of Piggle and who is very fond of Piggle and wants to eat her." The little girl then went out to look for her father, sat on his knees and, pointing to the Winnicott baby said, "I'm shy"; then, "I'm a baby, too." She put her head down as if she was emerging head first from between her father's legs. Winnicott then said to her, "I want to be the only baby"; then, in a different voice, "Do you have to be angry?" Piggle said "Yes" and she went on playing, adding, "I want to be the baby too." What she did, therefore, was to mime a birth. Winnicott went on playing in front of the father the role of the greedy baby. That is typical of Winnicott's intuition and of his capacity to play not only with the infant, but also in the presence of the father and mother.

AC: Would you like to say something about other important points in Winnicott's work?

SL: Yes, I'd like to say a word about holding, about the depressive position, and the self.

The notion of a mother and infant set-up and that of holding seem to me to be impregnable on the level of the theory of development. The union between the child and maternal care is the tool that I am using at present most often to make people who are not analysts feel and understand what psycho-analytic theory is. Thus when I have to deal with problems concerning the child and his mother with first-year students, I talk about Winnicott. The word holding is very telling. When I speak of the mother and the child, of the mother in an almost psychotic state after the child's birth, of the sated and angry child, everything goes very well, that is to say, it makes sense, it's assimilable for people who are fairly attentive.

It's the same in the case of the depressive position.

When we come to the notions of the self and the transitional object, a lot of nonsense is talked. They are notions that don't fit into psychoanalytic theory, are still very phenomenological. I don't see the need to refer to the object relation in that case. But nevertheless it is true that there is an area of culture and idealization, of religion and creativity, where the metaphor of the transitional object extended to creativity makes sense. Nevertheless, in a coherent theory of the object relation, I don't see the need for it, especially as there might be a confusion between it and fetishism.

Another excellent formula is Winnicott's notion that the child must be capable of playing alone in his mother's presence.

As for the self, I think there is something true about it at the developmental level, though it may be a source of confusion, because the word self has different connotations from one country or author to another. But if one defines the self as a continuous experience of maternal care, as Winnicott does, it is an indispensable notion, and I don't think one can understand narcissistic neuroses without reference to it.

The false self often leads to regrettable confusion. Thus the self is confused with "as if" personalities. It is not the same thing at all. The notion of "as if" is interesting in clinical work, but the self is a metapsychological notion. Winnicott says that we all to a greater or lesser degree have a false self and that the self cannot be seen.

I find that this reference to what cannot be seen or heard, and will never be seen or heard, may be the most prophetic thing in Winnicott's theories. I think it deserves to be studied much more seriously and has been the victim of a fashion.

I would like to go back to some rather anecdotal details that seem to me to be interesting for those who like Winnicott. For a long time Winnicott found it difficult to get accepted, even in England, yet the last time I was in London for a conference on child psychoanalysis, Anna Freud, who took part in the conference, seemed much more tolerant to Winnicott than she used to be. The fact that he was for a time Dean of the British Psycho-Analytical Society certainly went some way to altering his colleagues' attitude.

I've just remembered that the last time I met Winnicott was at the funeral of a British colleague, Joffe; I was representing the International Psychoanalytical Society. Winnicott delivered the funeral oration; it was shortly before his own death.

AC: I, too, met him shortly before his death. It was at the inauguration of the statue of Freud. He was standing next to me while the speeches were being made: it was very cold and his cheeks and lips were blue. I knew he had a bad heart and I was afraid throughout the ceremony that he might die at any moment. He survived it however.

SL: Yes, he even got better, because at Joffe's funeral he made an excellent speech in the columbarium—it was very clear and very English in style.

To conclude, I would say that one should not try to imitate Winnicott, as many have done, because it is not enough to apply certain formulas to have his intuition and clinical experience. He himself possessed these qualities to the utmost degree. One might say that Winnicott was an inimitable genius.

22

DANIEL WIDLÖCHER:
FREEDOM OF THOUGHT
(INTERVIEW)

Daniel Widlöcher: I first knew Winnicott through his article on intermediate space, which had been translated and published in the *Revue Française de Psychanalyse*; later, I got to know his work better. Two of his contributions interested me particularly. First, his work on the general theory of development, on the relationship between the mother and the child, on the facilitating environment. The *International Journal of Psychoanalysis* asked me to write an article on Winnicott's book, *The Maturational Processes and the Facilitating Environment*. I wrote an enthusiastic review, while criticizing certain aspects of Winnicott's work. Winnicott replied to me and showed interest in the analysis that I had done.

The second pole of interest was for me the squiggle game, for I had been very struck by what Winnicott proposed. Since I was myself working a great deal on children's drawing, I was often scandalized by the way psychoanalytic interpretations were imposed on drawings that were highly constructed, very elaborated, very secondary, in the sense of secondary processes, and on which hypotheses and interpretations were built rather as on tea leaves at the bottom of a cup. What I admired a great deal in Winnicott was the way in which he induced an atmosphere of formal regression, of fantasy activity in the child— that is to say, the activity of scribbling, the child's graffiti, was not a production, but a gesture almost like a dream, in which the child's imagination was given full rein. I found that very positive in counterbalancing a sort of rigidity with which drawings were treated by the French, as a document to be deciphered, rather like a dream text.

At that time, I had the good fortune to meet Winnicott at a conference. He was then invited to France by a colleague, Granoff, who ran a children's center at Nanterre. Winnicott had been asked to communicate with families and children, through the squiggle game, and I invited him to take part in this group. Winnicott was impressed at the idea of doing drawings for French children, Parisian children, while he claimed that he did not speak French at all, which was not quite true, but he was so worried that he asked someone in the room to act as interpreter. This was how I had the privilege of attending a squiggle game with Winnicott.

A small boy was waiting in the waiting room, without being in any way prepared for this contact, and he suddenly found himself sitting next to this old Englishman who purred and miaowed like a cat, in order to make contact with the child almost without using French. I translated nothing, I was there in case there might be some problem to be resolved, I was quite passive, quite outside the relationship. It is obvious that the contact that was made, the child's delight, the closeness of the child to this man who did not speak his language and who was supposed not to understand it, the way in which the child formulated things concerning his fantasy life, his memories, in so short a time and in such astonishing intimacy, obviously convinced me of what I had first read in the books and articles. For me it was a most instructive encounter, one that later led me to develop—I won't go as far as to say the squiggle game—but any contact with a child that makes him begin to dream with the adult and not to remain frozen in a rigid attitude, as one sees so often in consultations, even in psychotherapy. That for me really was a turning-point in my life.

Anne Clancier: I had the same impression when, in London, I saw Winnicott practice the squiggle game, but it struck me as even more extraordinary that he was able to do it with a child who didn't speak the same language.

DW: Yes, he was with a little fellow who had an extraordinary Parisian accent and who was no doubt wondering what he was doing there with this white-haired Englishman.

AC: Your phrase "the child starts to dream with the adult" seems an excellent one to me and highly significant of what could take place with Winnicott.

DW: Before, I was a bit reticent about Winnicott's theories. It seemed to me that their clinical richness was not always linked to theoretical rigor; in particular the concept of intermediate or transitional space bothered me rather by its empirical, very intuitive aspect.

Later, I was bothered, too, by Winnicott's success, by the reception accorded to any article he happened to publish at the time, by a Winnicott fashion that was then spreading. Nevertheless, I believe that it did have the merit of providing a sort of justification of emotion, the affect, the affective participation in the therapist's relationship with his patient. In short, it counterbalanced a rather intellectualist formalism that was particularly common at the time. Winnicott served as an antidote. He was certainly one of the best agents of the influence of the British school on French psychoanalysis, not only in terms of psychoanalytical theory, but also on French psychoanalytical practice. Winnicott brought a great deal, especially to young psychoanalysts, by making them aware of the dimensions that a rather cold or academic theory would not enable them to perceive.

Although subsequently I have distanced myself to some extent from Winnicott's positions, I do share with him that concern to take into account in treatment mobilizing emotional charges and the need to induce an atmosphere of regression. Indeed I insisted in my report to the Barcelona Conference on the value of a communication that is not only a communication of information.

It cannot be said that Winnicott provides an original overall theory in relation to psychoanalytical theory and indeed I cannot see why he should do so—and he certainly never made such a claim. I simply mistrusted a certain enthusiasm for Winnicott that struck me sometimes as rather disturbing.

AC: Perhaps one might situate Winnicott in relation to Melanie Klein. It seems to me that Klein is more of a theoretician, whereas Winnicott provides the raw material, interesting, even valuable as it is, but leaves us to erect the building. So Melanie Klein and Winnicott respond better to analysts of different temperaments, but Winnicott is particularly appreciated by those who are fond above all of clinical practice and who lay particular stress on intuition.

DW: I agree and I would say that certain Kleinians in Europe and in England have a fairly rigid theory, whereas in France they seem to be much more subtle.

At the risk of generalizing too much, I would say that there are two categories of psychoanalytic works, those that provide theories, metapsychological concepts in the formalized, that is to say, highly rational language of science, and those that contribute what might be called, depending on the case, psychoanalytic poetry or psychoanalytic fiction. What I am saying here is not at all intended to be pejorative: I just want to stress that there are works that offer the reader not so much a knowledge of theory and hypothesis as an aid to thinking analytically while reading the book.

AC: One might say that this allows the functioning of imaginative thought.

DW: Yes, for example, I have had people on the couch saying things like: "I admire Winnicott, because when I read him I feel a bit more like a psychoanalyst." You may regard that as good or bad; good because it may help certain patients to develop their capacity for thought, their psychoanalytic mind, but bad because people who have great difficulties in being analysts, when they are unable to find pleasure in their analytical thinking when it is tied up with their practice, sometimes compensate for that by their reading. What is left to them is only fiction . . . that is why I spoke of psychoanalytic fiction.

AC: It might be said that, in France, there were two opposite tendencies at a certain time. There were the psychoanalysts who needed to cling to language, to a sort of formalism, and who found their support in the work of Lacan, and those who, on the contrary, gave precedence to the therapeutic relationship, the affect, and therefore to Winnicott's works.

DW: Yes, that was also my impression at a certain time.

AC: You spoke of your interest in the squiggle game. It always seemed to me when I watched Winnicott that there was a sort of creation when he practiced this game with a child. Don't you think there was something of the artist in Winnicott? You have worked a great deal on art and written about children's drawing, on painting, especially on the work of the painter Segantini; don't you think that to analyze art in a productive way one has to be something of a Winnicottian?

DW: Yes, Winnicott was much more interested in the creative act and in the mental operations that made it possible than in the meaning of the thing created, as psychoanalysts had previously been. Winnicott has enabled others after him to transpose into other areas what he felt to be very important in the analytical situation. The risk is that some people have been able to interpret Winnicott's works as an authorization of a kind of spontaneism, whereas in him there was a very profound knowledge of psychoanalytic technique and practice.

AC: Yes, I have often heard, in seminars, Winnicott's words quoted by people who wanted to criticize him. Torn out of context and distorted, they lost the meaning that they had in Winnicott's work. So one must always keep very close to his text if one is to avoid misunderstanding what he meant or what he was trying to do in his analyses.

What other aspects of Winnicott's work have been of particular interest to you?

DW: On the question of transitional space, which we mentioned earlier, I am no longer entirely in agreement with this concept. I believe much more in the creation of a common space between two people who begin to function on the same level and in the same register, and who create a common dream space, rather than relating that to the concept of an object that is not quite the "me," but which is not yet the "not-me" either. It may be useful to represent a particular moment in the child's development and to find some trace of it in the adult, but I don't believe that it is necessary to make it the foundation of interpersonal relationships. I think that would be excessive.

On the other hand, I have found the concept of the false self extremely important, particularly in understanding certain mechanisms in infantile psychosis. There clinical experience completely confirms Winnicott's hypothesis. An excessive use has been made of the false self and nowadays one finds people calling any defensive armature the false self. I don't think Winnicott can be blamed for this excessive use, for from what I know of his text on the false self his use of the concept seems very precise; the term refers to a particular mode of response to dissociation but does not seem to me to justify generalizations.

AC: Winnicott said that we all have a certain false self within us. Perhaps it's what others have called the social ego.

DW: Yes, we all have aspects that are not very linked to our libidinal dynamics and which nevertheless function. Winnicott's concepts being both intuitive and very concrete, and not very articulated theoretically, it is easier to reduce them to some banal use than others: it's the risk one runs with Winnicott.

AC: Has Winnicott's work had any consequences as far as your clinical practice is concerned?

DW: Winnicott certainly helped me to internalize a greater freedom of action and thought with children. I haven't practiced child psychotherapy for some years, but in the early 1960s this led me to a very different kind of practice with children. With adults, Winnicott's influence may have led me, not in the direction of a freedom of action, but of a freedom of thought. By that I mean that I allowed myself in a way a certain emotional warmth and a recognition that this was something fundamental. What Winnicott has to say about holding in the analytical situation—which does not mean attitudes of support or reassurance—is fundamental. Too often, I think, people have confused an emotional atmosphere with directive interventions.

It should be said that, as a psychoanalyst, Winnicott did have interventions of this type, but he was dealing with serious cases, borderline cases, for which it was absolutely necessary to have technical innovations, and a great freedom of approach. That has been very important, because at a time when analysts began to treat serious, fairly atypical cases, Winnicott was beginning to work out a theorization adapted to these problems.

I have the impression that I use Winnicott less now, but I don't at all think that this relates to any decline in Winnicott's work.

AC: After a temporary fashion, Winnicott will assume his true place.

A lot is talked now about Bion. How do you situate Bion in relation to Winnicott?

DW: Bion is almost the opposite of Winnicott. There is in him a certain hyperformalism in the return to neologism that is sometimes very off-putting, because one has to absorb a lot of definitions before one can come to grips with his thought. However, there is also a fairly poetic style in Bion. At present I am fairly influenced by Bion, because it seems that one needs a sort of general conceptualization of the analytical situation, for example of the notion of the analyst's thought as being directly influenced by the analysand's thought. From this point of view, Bion's ideas are parallel with those of Winnicott. However, they come from very different horizons, since Bion began with group studies, whereas Winnicott doesn't seem to have any interest in groups. He was even rather contemptuous of group techniques.

I would also draw a parallel between Winnicott and Balint, because they had similar situations. On the historical level of psychoanalytical thought, they were for a time the two great thinkers of the British "middle group."

AC: It is worth noting that they both had a psychiatric training; Balint was in general practice as a physician and Winnicott a pediatrician. That probably played a role.

Has your position on children's drawing altered?

DW: No, it is still the same, but I find Winnicott's ideas comforting: the squiggle game, the comparison between the act of graphic elaboration and the dream, regression, I find all that very sympathetic.

To conclude, I would like to stress once again the freedom of thought that Winnicott helps one to acquire.

Part III

USING WINNICOTT

23

SIMON GROLNICK: HOW TO DO WINNICOTTIAN THERAPY

Achapter on technique does not belong in a book on Winnicott. The concept of technique implies a rigor, the adherence to a body of certain rules, and an attempt to achieve a perfection of execution. It implies training as opposed to liberal, open education. How can we mix a Winnicottian emphasis on creativity, having the freedom to make mistakes, with technique? We can't. Yet we, his followers, or those who want to use some of what he had to offer, can, and must, think out what the artist Winnicott did in terms of technique and guidelines (we can do away with rules here).

Imagine a fantasied Winnicott trying in one session to teach his method to an aspiring therapist, really an absurdity. Perhaps this is the way to approach the problem of a chapter on Winnicottian technique. This fantasied Winnicott would show the student his office. It would have chairs, a couch, a floor, ceiling, walls, decorations, drapes, or shades. But to Winnicott it is a setting, a potential space. Perhaps another way of putting it is to see it as a theater or stage upon which the drama of psychotherapy or psychoanalysis is played out. Winnicott would say the patient could be on the couch, in the chair, pacing the room, or even lying or sitting on the floor. What is happening between the two people takes precedence over the method one is using. Of course, for analysis, the couch is best. There are reasons for this that will be discussed later.

The student therapist might be told to keep his or her psychoanalytic knowledge in back of his or her mind. A model of development, even the images of a mother and a baby, or a toddler, or a child may come closer to the surface. The therapist might try to let him- or herself oscillate between feeling merged with and separate from the patient (the patient as subjective object versus the patient as objectively perceived).

The therapist must know what's going on, where the patient is on the developmental and diagnostic scale. But the therapist must get in touch with the patient. But not too fast—slowly, slowly as Winnicott advises. Don't impinge on fragile boundaries or carefully hidden away, frightened authentic selves within your patients.

Perhaps Winnicott might say:

Therapist, even with all this responsibility, relax. After all, you are only a facilitator, not prime mover. You can't (and shouldn't) be perfect. You have to make mistakes, which, when worked out between you and the patient, help toward creating the deepest change. You can be angry at the patient. If you never are, go for help!

Don't let yourself be destroyed or demoralized by patients who are trying to foster their own development when they attack or deprecate you.

Relax; it's only therapy—but it's real at the same time, and patients suffer unthinkable anxieties. So do you—or so you did. Try to get in touch with them. Any of us can go crazy. You are the patient's equal, but at the same time, you are the steady, concerned, earnest thinking and feeling professional, flappable sometimes, but essentially unshakable.

You should be able to enjoy this work—because so much of it is play. Hard play in the beginning, but, hopefully if things go well, lighter and more symbolic play later on. Oh, by the way, don't try to show the patient how smart you are, you are good enough. Acting like a smart aleck won't help. And sometimes it is necessary to keep quiet and leave the patient alone, and not insist that every little thing means something (even though deep down you think it does).

Maybe there are too many instructions already. Take what I say with a grain of salt, and go out there and try it. Let me know what happens (we can make that into supervision if you want).

Now my one-lesson Winnicott fantasy must come to earth. Maybe it isn't a fantasy but an illusion, in Winnicott's sense of that word. If a therapist is an original therapist, that is, he or she was held well, handled well, presented to the world in a well-timed manner, and forced to deal with the disillusionments life always offers (unless we are too protected); if a therapist's capacity to be in touch with his or her soma hasn't been discouraged; if a therapist's innate creativity hasn't been squelched by various trainers, ranging from parents to psychotherapy supervisors;

if a therapist is blessed by having navigated the world of development optimally, then perhaps one lesson in how to do therapy would work. Most of us have to struggle, learn from the creative process of trial and error, and learn from the working out of failures with the patient. Learning from reading Winnicott, or this chapter, helps, but doing therapy is the best supervisor (even though for a good while a supervisor is good to have). Winnicott's guidelines and, above all, his permissions (it's okay to play, it's okay not to analyze everything, it's okay to hate your patient, etc.) do provide a facilitating setting for the therapist that is analogous to the setting the therapist provides for the patient.

An important guiding image, alluded to above, is that of the mother and baby. Read in Winnicott "mother" and replace her with "therapist." Read "baby" and replace it with "patient." It works, most of the time. To the extent that the therapist has diagnosed the therapeutic field as a developmental one, and to the extent that he or she conceptualizes the therapeutic situation as a new developmental stage (Loewald 1960), when they don't know what to do, they can think out the maternal situation and use it as a model. Of course babies and patients are different. But there are baby stages in patients (and in therapists) that must be dealt with in not the same, but in an analogous manner. An experiential as well as a cognitive understanding of development can facilitate the therapist's facilitation of a patient's development when that development has hit a snag due to environmental failure or mix-up (Balint 1968). Beware, however; this model may not work for the psychoneurotic patient where development was able to proceed well, the intrapsychic world is well peopled and well integrated, and where the creative symbolic processes have built those semiotic nuisances we call neurotic symptoms and inhibitions. Sigmund Freud, Anna Freud, and the ego psychologists are better teachers where conflict and advanced rather than primitive defense mechanisms prevail and earlier stages of development are used defensively. However, in the author's clinical experience, he has rarely treated a patient who has not had some developmental difficulty and some experience with the unthinkable and annihilation anxieties that didn't need tending to at some point in the therapy or analysis. As Winnicott noted, the well-equipped therapist can move back and forth between both developmental levels and diagnostic entities. He, and this chapter, are geared more to patients who have suffered deeply from the woes coming from vicissitudes of the developmental process, where internalization and object and self constancy have not set in adequately and where the integration of the psyche and the soma have not occurred optimally.

FIELDS OF PERSONS AND DRAMA

To move more toward the specific, let me allude to some of the qualities of the Winnicottian therapeutic field. As it is an object relations oriented field, it is personified. Internal and external objects, transitions between them, constant and inconstant objects are the images that lead to understanding and toward interpretation. As Friedman (1988) has suggested, contemporary patients are assaulting therapists with primitive defenses, anxieties, rages, and raw thrusts of eros; that is, therapists are seeing and treating more borderline, narcissistic, and psychotic patients. A personified, simpler (than orthodox) theory seems to be more attractive and of more assistance to the therapist. Such a theory helps to provide a relatively experience-close system to hold onto to help face the onslaught of the patient's primitivity. In a more specifically Winnicottian object relations field, when the time is right and the patient ready, the personifications and the persons can play and interplay. It is this play, and setting up the playground when the patient is not ready, that tries to further the missed developmental play, and interplay, that led to the developmental difficulty in the first place. In sum, the particular level of play that is called for by the patient's needs (nursery presymbolic play, or symbolic play) is facilitated by a personified theory that cries out for a setting or stage to be built for it (Grolnick 1984, Loewald 1975, McDougall 1982, Winnicott 1971a). The theater is improvisational, but as in good improvisational theater, there are overlying meta guidelines and outer limits. There must be a rationale, a reason, in a sense a plot or series of plots, to carry the action along. So according to this model, the therapist is a vitally involved, modernist creative player on a basically developmental stage. This is not acting or performing in its pejorative sense. But it is the use of the theater's essential ingredient of illusion that brings the qualities of creative involvement, the capacity for a make-believe transference, and the ability to be real and not real (human and professional) at the same time.

A theatrical model brings along with it one of the essential characteristics of the creative, that of ambiguity (Adler 1989). Aesthetic ambiguity (Empson 1930) has long been recognized as a necessary but not sufficient ingredient of art. Even though the art of therapy and analysis has been always acknowledged, the more scientific models (Hook 1959), such as the experimental and the observational models, have tended to squeeze ambiguity out of the consultation room. It was not unusual for supervisors and teachers to advise that we shouldn't make an interpretation until we were sure it was correct, and when we were, to deliver it in a forthright, declarative manner. Hardly an ambiguous field! In fact, this technique and the concept of the exact interpretation that informed it are just what Winnicott considered to be the indoctrination of (and impingement upon) the patient. Recently Adler (1989) has written of the dangers of "pathological certainty" within a field of psychoanalysis that is characterized by its essential ambiguity. Adler sees this field as compatible with Winnicott's concepts of transitional phenomena, transitional objects, illusion, and play. The advantages of the personalized nursery and theatrical models that Winnicott provides us are that ambiguity, openness, and creativity are seen as essential ingredients of the therapeutic process, rather than attributes that have to be forced into models that have a more positivistic flavor. Thus Winnicott's good enough, less than perfect alternation of gratification and frustration has its ambiguous dimension that allows the therapeutic field to be developmentally sound, yet provide an opportunity to utilize a creative, playing, open milieu that reaches into the patient's inner creative self, rather than providing a pedantic, indoctrinating schoolroom that can only help to perpetuate the false self of the patient and, very possibly, the grandiosity of the therapist.

SUCCEEDING BY FAILING

Before Winnicott, analyses and therapies were either successes or failures, or sometimes they were middling. Then Winnicott said in 1955:

> There builds up an ability of the patient to use the analyst's limited successes in adaptation, so that the ego of the patient becomes able to begin to recall the original failures, all of which were recorded, kept ready. These failures had a disruptive effect at the time, and a treatment of the kind I am describing has gone a long way when the patient is able to take an example of original failure and be angry about it. Only when the patient reaches this point, however, can there be the beginning of reality testing. . . .
>
> The way this change comes about from the experience of anger is a matter that interests me in a special way, as it is at this point in my work that I found myself surprised. The patient makes use of the analyst's failures. [p. 298]

Winnicott goes on to elaborate:

> Others may be surprised, as I was, to find that while a gross mistake may do but little harm, a very small error of judgement may produce a big effect. The clue is that the analyst's failure is being used and must be treated as *past* failure, one that the patient can perceive and encompass, and be angry about now. The analyst needs to be able to make use of his failures in terms of their meaning for the patient, and he must if possible account for each failure even if this means a study of his unconscious countertransference. [p. 298]

It should be stressed that Winnicott did not mean planned failures or mistakes. These would lead to an artificial analytic field that could only perpetuate rather than relieve the pressure of these buried caches of previous developmental failures. The therapist can rest assured that empathic and technical errors will come in the natural course of events. It is here that Winnicott differentiates himself from other psychoanalytic innovators who advocated various manipulations of the transference, such as Alexander's advice that the analyst *act* in a manner opposite to that of the original parents. Again, when developmental work is needed, Winnicott advocates setting up a good enough analytic environment, which includes the building of a potential play space in which the successes and failures of both parties can be experienced, worked through, and played through.

There is a similarity between Winnicott's use of failure with Kohut's (1971) way of allowing a buildup of a narcissistic transference and then awaiting analyst's empathic failures, which are to be worked out with the patient in an experiential and a cognitive manner. Actually, there is not much difference between Winnicott and the concept that Kohut termed "transmuting internalization." This is the structure-building goal of both Winnicottian and Kohutian therapy. Perhaps the most important difference is timing. Winnicott seems to advocate working with failures earlier in the treatment than Kohut, who required a gradually unfolding, ultimately intense narcissistic transference to occur before failures are negotiated with the patient. There is also an implication in Kohut's work that the analyst should attempt to supply as much of a reflective, empathic, mistake-free environment as possible before allowing natural errors of empathy to occur. I wouldn't be surprised if Winnicott might see Kohut's first phase of analysis as a kind of unnaturalness that might not do the trick in his good enough terms. Of course, Winnicott always implied that a holding environment did have to be established before the patient could tolerate the disappointments, frustrations, regressions, and rages that can indwell the working out of the analyst's errors, but his process didn't seem to take the length of time of Kohut's carefully developed narcissistic transference. Perhaps one of the important differences here could also be accounted for by the fact that Kohut worked primarily with narcissistic character disorders, whereas Winnicott's patients were frequently borderline or psychotic. Also, it could be said that Winnicott was beginning to erode the concept of the exact interpretation and to turn failure into success years before Kohut brought his self psychology upon the psychoanalytic scene.

Several years ago I saw a male patient in his late twenties who complained of mild to moderate depression, a certain lack of goal direction, and a chronic sense of feeling empty. He had been in a long intensive psychoanalytic psychotherapy that seemed to have been pitched primarily at the oedipal level of development. This seemed justifiable, as the patient did have a neurotic diagnosis, and his major trauma occurred during the oedipal period when his father became ill. The therapy had been helpful, but the symptoms with which the patient presented tended to reemerge after the first treatment ended. The patient wanted to enter psychoanalysis because he felt that his difficulty must have had even deeper and earlier determinants than he had been made aware of during his psychotherapy.

One day toward the end of his first year of analysis, we were having what seemed to be an ordinary session. I had been up late the night before and was also developing the early symptoms of a viral illness. I fell asleep and dozed off for what was probably a few seconds. The patient at first started to talk through my little nap, but then gathered up the courage to confront me by asking whether the change in my breathing pattern was due to having fallen asleep. While my first tendency was to defend myself and give myself a chance to develop a strategy by asking the patient to associate to what he heard and felt, I decided to own up to the accusation and tell him about my missing sleep the night before and the feeling that I was coming down with something. After a moment of hesitation, he burst out crying. Once he could contain himself, he said that he was sure I would not tell him the truth and would try, as I had been tempted, to protect myself. He described his tears as those of gratefulness and closeness with me. He went on associating to the incident. Both of his parents had always tried to cover up their personal failures in a myriad of ways. It made him feel that he had to be perfect in order to gain their love. It was clear that the part of him that could have faults had to be buried and received no validation from his parents. He felt I had touched an area that had not been reached in his intensive psychotherapy. His first therapist did not acknowledge mistakes.

This rather significant failure on my part, my response to it and the patient's response to my response, became the focus of analytic work for some time. It became clearer than had been suggested during the earlier part of the year that the patient suffered from a true and false self disturbance and that there had been all too little validation of his authenticity during his early years. That issue was to become a crucial one in his analysis.

THE ACKNOWLEDGMENT OF FAILURE

This shows one way in which the therapist's failures as far as the patient is concerned, when dealt with in realistic yet tactful ways, can be turned around to further the therapeutic process. Winnicott tended to avoid the issue of whether and to what degree the therapist should acknowledge a failure. In his paper "Hate in the Countertransference" (1947), Winnicott emphasized the importance of the analyst acknowledging his or her capacity to hate the patient. Instances of hatred, according to Winnicott, occurred during every therapy or analysis. This hatred of the patient is universal, and during the everyday process of treatment, it is "latent," as he called it (dismissing a patient summarily, even though tactfully at a session's end, is a way the analyst's hatred is structured into the therapeutic situation). The therapist's hatred is both characterized by and paralleled by the mother's inevitable hatred of her baby, hatred that is, in both instances, handleable by the respective parties in the setting of a good enough holding environment. Winnicott (1947), in one of his most important contributions, stresses that it is necessary for the baby or the patient to experience hatred from the parent or the therapist in order to hate. He points out, "It seems to me doubtful whether a human child as he develops is capable of tolerating the full extent of his own hate in a sentimental environment. He needs hate to hate." (This sentence should do away with the unthinking claims that Winnicott was essentially a "momist.") He cites the nursery song "Rockabye Baby" to show the built-in outlets for aggression in motherhood.

   Looking at the childhood model, it is easy to picture the mother, and father, sitting around with their adult offspring and their recent or not so recent mates, and reminiscing about how much ambivalence there had been during the tribulations of parenting. In good enough families the ex-children muse and generally forgive, and learn something. They are then a little more prepared to carry the process on into the next generation. Perhaps it is the model that led Winnicott to write this within his seismic paper on hate in the countertransference. Speaking of the analyst, he said, "Eventually, he ought to be able to tell his patient what he has been through on the patient's behalf, but an analysis may never get as far as this" (p. 198). He also wrote, "The analyst must be prepared to bear strain without expecting the patient to know anything about what he is doing, perhaps over a long period of time" (p. 198). While not meeting this issue in any detail, in another of his revolutionary papers, "The Use of an Object and Relating through Identifications" (1971c), very close to the end of his career and life, he wrote again of the analyst's failures: "Even this failure may have value if both analyst and patient acknowledge the failure."

   My patient would not have been able to experience the recreation of a failure unless I had validated his feeling that I had, if only momentarily, left him. If it had been an instance of a more direct personal aggression on my part against him, the same principle would hold. Winnicott wrote of the analyst's inner acknowledgment of his or her aggression against the patient at a time when he had not fully declared his independence from classical and Kleinian theory. He was also working on two important developmental and therapeutic issues, validation of the self by the object and the ability to internalize object usage through the interplay of therapist and patient aggression. These two developmental lines are inextricably interwoven. If Winnicott had continued his explorations, he would have had to acknowledge even more of his own aggression toward the patient by a more explicit permission to the student therapist to spell out therapist aggression when the setting is solid enough to handle it, and in a manner in which what is told to the patient is only that which is necessary for the occasion. Personal confessions beyond the need to validate the patient's aggressive impulses and implicitly reassure the patient that the analyst can tolerate his or her own aggression would only be an indulgence and an abuse, and not developmental usage of the patient.

HOLDING, HANDLING, AND OBJECT-RELATING

Winnicott's developmental lines of holding, handling, and object-relating can be applied to the therapy situation. Classically oriented therapists have done this intuitively by depending on their empathic capacities and their diagnostic impressions of the patient. However, there is a distinct advantage for the therapist when he or she knowingly applies this line to patients who require developmental "fixing" and who cannot become engaged in a meaningful, affective treatment relationship without first feeling well established and trusting in a stable, supporting, reliable setting.

Holding comes first. Winnicott (1962) saw that the issues involved were "in terms of motor and sensory elements. This would acquire a tendency towards a sense of existing." For Winnicott, the main task of holding the patient enables the infant to form a sense of continuity, *going-on-being*, as he put it so aptly. "All this tends towards the establishment of a unit self, but it cannot be over-emphasized that what happens at this very early stage depends on the ego-coverage given by the mother of the infant–mother coupling" (p. 60). The Winnicottian language and word linkage says something to the therapist. It is the therapist's job to find the metaphorical equivalence of the mother's basically nonverbal physical holding. This is a task of translation, from the nonverbal to the verbal. Winnicott referred to the issue in "Hate in the Countertransference" (1947): "For the neurotic the couch and warmth and comfort can be *symbolical* of the mother's love; for the psychotic it would be more true to say that these things *are* the analyst's physical expression of love. The couch *is* the analyst's lap or womb, and the warmth is the live warmth of the analyst's body. And so on" (p. 199). Simply stated and conceptualized, but profound in its implications! Winnicott is of course referring to the developmental hierarchy of symbol formation. In out-patient treatment it is rare that the patient is so psychotic that the issue of physical holding comes into the mind of the caretaker–therapist. This work is more necessary during hospital care,

194 In One's Bones

where basic, "primitive" use of the symbolically equated (Grolnick and Lengyel 1978, Segal 1957) environment can be done. It is the work that was so admired by Winnicott, described by Madame Sechehaye in *Symbolic Realization* (1951). Sechehaye presented her food-refusing, psychotic young woman with pieces of apples, which were equated by the patient with the breast. The therapist did this while holding the patient and literally associating the breast and the apple pieces by their physical proximity. As the patient began to improve, the apples became "abstracted" into applesauce, which was eaten by the patient at a distance from the therapist. And words gradually became the substitutes for thing-apples.

In the out-patient situation, the sicker patients are usually not at a symbolic equation, symbiotic level, but more in keeping with that of presymbolic, transitional object and phenomena. In this sense the predominant transference is toward the therapist and the setting as a transitional object provision. So with the words of the therapist (Weich 1978). Studies have not been done, but it is likely that when the therapist is tuned into the right developmental station, his or her words would tend to have more textural, "thing," concrete qualities, and would deemphasize the discursive, presentational (rather than representational) aspect of language (Langer 1942). Presumably this therapist language would be more body language and imagistic to meet the patient's sensory motor and sensory tonic needs as well as his or her presymbolic needs. Hopefully the patient who is able to progress developmentally will build a fuller sense of and actuality of integration and continuity, the base for future self-evocable self and object constancy.

Handling is Winnicott's term for the more advanced phase of physical interaction with the infant. This is the time of the gestural interplay that feels good to both parties. The environment is still necessary, for the patient's self-evocation is still in the future. This mixture of physical interaction and meaning in a setting of a good enough object relationship helps personalize the infant and develop what Winnicott termed the state of the "psyche indwelling in the soma" (Winnicott 1960, p. 45). Winnicott uses the word *psyche* on purpose. He attempted to define it in his important paper "Mind and Its Relation to the Psyche-soma" (1949):

I suppose that the word psyche here means the *imaginative elaboration of somatic parts, feelings and functions*, that is, of physical aliveness. We know that this imaginative elaboration is dependent on the existence and the healthy functioning of the brain, especially certain parts of it. The psyche is not, however, felt by the individual to be localized in the brain, or indeed to be localized anywhere. [p. 244]

Winnicott sees this stage of handling as an opportunity for the caretaker, whether parent or therapist, to establish this psychosomatic base that is *"felt by the individual* to form the core for the imaginative self." A lack of an integration between the psyche and the soma could lead to a predisposition to psychosomatic illness and acting out behavior. Clearly with such disorders or patients with tendencies in this direction, the therapist is challenged by the need to meet with language and nonverbal gestural communication the needs of his or her therapeutic partner.

This handling phase merges seamlessly with object relating. It is here where Winnicott's concept of primary creativity comes into the picture. This phase essentially involves a parallel to the time when the infant waits for the mother to present a thing or a manipulation when the infant is ready for it to be there, creating the illusion that the infant created it (primary creativity). In his paper on ego integration Winnicott (1962) wrote, "In this way the baby comes to feel confident in being able to create objects and to create the actual world. The mother gives the baby a brief period in which omnipotence is a matter of experience" (p. 62).

How does this apply to the therapist? One way of looking at it is that psychosomatic play moves more into the early symbolic arena, actually the protosymbolic (Werner and Kaplan 1963). The therapist's words and acts become involved in the transitional process, enabling the patient to feel that he can create an object world that is not just projective or an extension of himself, but in part, the real world. (Gradually the object presenting therapist lends him- or herself to the patient's aggressions at both these objects and the presenter, thereby helping this created world to have an externality, a reality that can be used.) It is here that the therapist's creative capacities are most challenged. This is probably the same area that once was referred to within the classical analytic ethos as interpreting just a bit ahead of where the patient was, when the meaning was on the tip of the tongue of the patient's preconscious. But the difference here is that the therapist can use more than a discursive interpretation. Images, phrases, words even will do. And the setting and atmosphere must be one in which there is a partnership of play; when a meaning or word appears, the playing couple is not so dominated by one part, and it sometimes becomes unclear as to who set up a specific meaning or word. Thus, through the medium of optimal object presenting, the child is gradually induced into object relating.

A clinical example elucidates Winnicott's important developmental sequence.

Some years ago I treated a man in his early twenties. He can be called the Gardener, as his garden was virtually, or really, his whole life. He was short, slight, a little bit vacant in his eyes, and he spoke quietly and somewhat deliberately, without spontaneity. It turned out that his mother had insisted that he go to a psychiatrist because she had been concerned that after he returned from his job as a manager in a retail store, he spent all his time preoccupied with or working in his garden. He had no friends, had never dated, and showed no signs of being at all concerned about his mother's concerns. His mother especially, but also his father and other members of his family, frequently tried to pry him away from his beloved garden, but to no avail. He only felt more and more devoted to and concerned for its welfare. It turns out that the inspiration for the creation of what was a rather formal garden was the well-kept yet luxuriant garden of a woman whose house was along the route he walked every day from the bus stop to his own home. One day, while passing, he was so taken by the beauty of her garden that he resolved to duplicate it on his own property. It took several years, but he achieved an exact, almost mirror model of the other garden. At this point it became necessary to devote all his spare time to the maintenance of the garden. He treasured every hedge and every bud. He watched the buds for hours on end, and could almost see them grow into beautiful flowers. The Gardener especially esteemed his roses. In the evenings he would watch from his bedroom window, which overlooked the garden. If any of the neighborhood children or teenagers would disturb a hedge, or even a branch, during their episodes of horseplay, he would become extremely disturbed and rush down to chase them away. He would mourn over the loss of a carefully nurtured shrub, or even a twig.

The Gardener was willing to see me, at least manifestly, because he was afraid of his mother. There had been hints that she would destroy the garden unless he eventually began to move out into the "real" world. If the garden was no longer there, he would have no reason to live. Clearly his first transference to me was displaced from his mother. I was seen as her hired hand, someone who would eventually tread on his Elysian fields and destroy his paradise.

Fortunately for both of us, I had already become interested in Winnicott's concept of transitional object, and was able to see the garden as illusional, not delusional, and that it was serving as a transitional object that was bordering onto the fetishistic side of the spectrum. I knew I would have to respect the boundaries of his garden and of his ego, and that I would have to protect him from and differentiate myself from his angry and quite confounded mother. As the garden held him, it was necessary for me to hold simultaneously both him and his garden.

How was this done? By a combination of omission and commission. What was left out was any attempt to interpret the meaning, particularly the defensive or drive meaning, of my patient's use of the garden. As far as I was concerned, the garden was his entire life (even though it wasn't), and the adaptive and developmental illusion had to be maintained. For months we talked about his garden. I like gardening (to a degree) and think that if I had not, the shared illusion wouldn't have worked. I used whatever I knew and had felt about gardens and the plants they are peopled by. The Gardener and I shared our experiences and feelings about the mystery of how a bud becomes a flower, about the pain that occurs when the elements or careless humans harm any aspect of the symmetry of a garden, and about how there is something both thrilling and romantic about a rose and its fragrance that transcends other flowers. He taught me a lot about gardening and, surprisingly, I was able to inform him of a few things about which he hadn't been aware. In a sense, we talked of the birds, the bees, and the flowers, without talking about them. The symbol, or again, the protosymbol, was lived in without the disruptive and separating effects or bringing in the referent. We were talking of his love life and its vicissitudes. Love and the sharing of one's body with someone else is dangerous. It could break your limbs and your very self. He was frightened about castration and separation trauma. That was the symbolic meaning. But these symbols were only bits floating in a sea of presymbolic dangers and defenses. His garden was a transitional place in which and about which he could rest, gird himself, (fore) play, and practice a possible ultimate actual love life. Presumably his mother's hired hand surprised him by turning out to be with him and willing to be part of him and, because of my gardening sensibilities and knowledge, part of his garden. I was endowed with a transitional object significance that, before his therapy, had been exclusively invested in the garden. Even though his garden, the real one, was very much up front in reality, internally it had been hidden away deep inside of him. In the beginning the Gardener only humored me. It was only when enough time had been spent together in the garden that he allowed me to see this secret part of himself. This schizoid young man actually harbored deeply romantic emotions and desires to love and be loved. These desires could only be played out within the safe and comforting confines of his created garden, which had been constructed in the mirror image of the neighborhood woman's garden that he saw as an ideal. The garden had to be constructed from scratch to have had meaning. The woman had presented him with the images of the garden when he was ready to use them.

One may very well accuse me of building my own fantasy gardens of psychological plenty. Why was my stance toward the garden, which I would never have had the time or motivation to create myself, any different than, say, Alexander's manipulation of the transference? Wasn't I lying to the Gardener, deceiving him, and really contributing to his false self formation? No, but it is important to share some of the experience; it is crucial for an understanding of what Winnicottian therapy is. This patient's need for illusion and the need *not* to interpret defense, drive, and superego components of his symptomatology for some time were quite marked. But the principle can apply to many patients with various psychological developmental disorders.

My justification for the authenticity of the use of my "gardening self" is that the core of it felt natural. To some extent I had been there. Isn't it the essence of illusion that there is a core of reality around which it is built? This differentiates it from fantasy and delusion. The therapeutic arena is a theater, a place where illusions are allowed to become psychologically real. In the beginning the patient and I were only skirting his garden. He was suspicious that I was a "spy in the house of love," as Anaïs Nin put it, and I was somewhat clumsily trying to enter into his experience enough to both *feel* and *be* authentic. But gradually a process began to develop between us and in the potential play space between us that allowed us to come closer and closer to each other's experience. He began to trust me more. And my counterpart experience was that I trusted him more. He became less of a pathological misfit and more of a romantic figure, even an artist. As he started to pick this up, he felt better about himself and safer to allow me further and further into his garden.

As this happened, my alter ego, alter gardener, role could relax a little, and to an extent he let me be myself. I could be more of the therapist, and I began slowly to express an interest in his past, an out-of-the-garden aspect of his life. He could begin to do this because he felt more secure with an ally, and he was starting to experience me more as a human being than as an inanimate object. What came out was most interesting.

His father had a hobby that involved the use of bundles of brightly colored wires. The patient was told that when he was an infant he had taken a piece of this wire as his security object. Then, when he was 4 or 5, his father built him a little go-cart that was constructed of wood and wire. He became attached to this cart for some time, and when it needed repair, his father would fix it for him. It became clear that the difficult relationship with his mother offered little solace and steadiness, and that he utilized his father and the objects he provided as developmental stabilizers.

The pattern continued into his adolescence. I was surprised when he revealed that he had become a scholar of bridges. A local suspension bridge with its delicate-looking yet strong vertical wires intrigued him. He went into the city's architectural archives to search out the original plans. In the back of his mind he was thinking of an article or even a book that he could write about the bridge. He would walk the bridge and savor its structural and architectural beauties.

During this phase of the therapy, which was always supported by journeys back to the garden, I felt we had moved from a holding to a handling level. We were having the equivalence of a gestural and action dialogue together. As with the holding phase, there was no attempt to interpret the symbolic, defensive, drive, or superego implications of this interesting developmental line that was emerging. It was material that I felt I had to contain, and contain myself from uttering any disrupting, clever interpretations. It was enough that he was aware we had moved into a new level of our relationship. The narrative continuity and the joint trip into the past deepened our experience together and provided an arena in which we could interchange ideas and clarify and share the various points in his life when he was affectively alive and, in a real sense, able to be in love, albeit the objects of his love had been first inanimate objects and then animate members of his beloved garden. By allowing a reexperiencing of his transitional worlds, I believed that a certain amount of loosening of development was occurring, allowing a furthering of both object relations and symbolization.

The tangible by-products of this process came in the form of his reports of a young woman he had met on a bus. At first they began to talk politely, then more conversationally. He did discuss his garden and found that it involved an interest that she shared. This new development (in both senses of the word) was another (pleasant) surprise to me. I had avoided, with difficulty at times, urging him to begin socializing. It seemed to emerge from him, and he felt it to be a change of his own making.

The Gardener's transformation continued as he began to report feelings of affection for the young woman. As might be expected, there was a concomitant but gradual waning of his preoccupation with his garden. The terms of endearment used for the roses and peonies were beginning to be applied to the young woman whom he started to date. The story was headed toward a happy ending when, after a number of months of seeing his partner and gradually having his first sexual experiences (without intercourse), of "neglecting" his garden, he announced that he was going to be engaged. This took place, and soon the two young people were married. They were able to successfully perform intercourse. The patient decided to stop his treatment at that point. Since it was only once-a-week psychotherapy, and a cognitive understanding in depth did not seem to be a real possibility at that time, we suspended our visits together after a reasonable period of termination. He never recontacted me, but later on I did hear that he had divorced after two years of marriage. Apparently there had been no reversion back to his garden.

A case seen so infrequently with limited follow-up is always difficult to evaluate. However, it is safe to say that there had been a developmental advance of a significant nature. The patient seemed to have had the developmental capacity to progress, within certain circumscribed limits, from Winnicott's phase of holding to handling to object relating. While there was a cognitive, insight element to the treatment, most of it was conducted with the insight in my head, not his. Without the psychoanalytic object relational understanding I had accumulated for some years, I could have easily become an antidevelopmental figure, forcing him more and more into his transitional-fetishistic world.

While this therapy is not ideal to illustrate Winnicottian therapy, it could be said that Winnicott's influence and ideas pervaded the interaction we had. The patient's regression to a kind of transitional object, protosymbolic level in his relationship to his garden, through the facilitating medium of the therapeutic alliance, allowed him to move closer to the truly object relational and the symbolic. That this was not a full move in those directions is clear. If circumstances had allowed, a longer and more frequent contact might have been more successful. But meaningful work had been done. If the patient's true self, his transitional object needs, his developmental timing, his protosymbolic use of language, and his need for a period of "going-on-being" had not been taken into account, the treatment would have floundered.

GOING IT (ALMOST) ALONE

One of Winnicott's most important contributions was his work on the capacity to be alone. This developmental line, which so involves our capacity to be reasonably mature adults, seems to have already been built into the therapeutic situation, even going back to Freud. In many ways the classical analytic situation consists of one person (the patient) working, free associating, playing (in a Winnicottian sense) on the couch in the presence of someone (the analyst) who sits behind the couch. How close this is to Winnicott's description of the baby's playing along but being supervised by a (hopefully) empathic caretaker who stays in the wings, available to move in when the contemporary capacity to go it alone is all used up and needs refueling! Clearly an analogy can be drawn between that developmental progression and some of the things that happen when a therapy works.

Although Freud obviously did not read Winnicott, speculatively he may have been tuned in to the same unconscious developmental issues. He placed himself so close, so very close, to the patient, but at the same time so far (out of sight). The patient led and talked freely, and the analyst was supposed to intervene only when the patient needed an assist to reach a degree of insight. I suspect that when there are developmental issues present in the patient in addition to conflictual ones, the analyst or therapist—as the case may be or calls for—consciously or unconsciously titrates his or her interventions in keeping with the patient's developmental abilities at the time, the capacity to be alone being one of these. The interpretations, or clarifications, or questions, may have, aside from their cognitive, symbolic meanings, the function of the analyst touching base when it seems appropriate to break the silence and provide a bridge. This intuitive, caretaking ability works also in the therapist's personal life, in raising children, in spouse relationships, in friendships.

Winnicott wrote about another aspect of this when he referred to the holding value of interpretations in an ego psychological paper he wrote somewhat early on, in the chapter "The Concept of Health Using Instinct Theory," included in *Human Nature* (Winnicott 1988):

> It can be noted here that the analysis of psychosis of schizoid type is essentially different from the analysis of psycho-neurosis, because the former requires of the analyst a toleration of actual regression to tolerate ideas and feelings (love, hate, ambivalence, etc.) and an understanding of processes, and also a wish to show understanding by appropriate exposition of language (interpretation of what the patient is just ready to allow to consciousness). A correct and well-timed interpretation in an analytic treatment gives a sense of being held physically that is more real (to the non-psychotic) than if a real holding or nursing had taken place. Understanding goes deeper and by understanding, shown by the use of language, the analyst holds physically in the past, that is, at the time of the need to be held, when love meant physical care and adaptation. [p. 61]

This is a statement that Winnicott respected the differences between treatment of the neurotic and of the more deeply disturbed. But characteristically he understood the similarities. Here Winnicott implies to the therapist that technique is adjusted to the developmental level of the patient and the limits of the therapist's understanding. When nonverbal needs must be met, too many words and too much meaning can preclude understanding. When higher-level, developmental internalizations have taken place in a good enough manner, the holding operation moves to the verbal, symbolic level. Whereas drive psychologists might have commented on this issue in their way by saying, "A good interpretation is a good feed," Winnicott would say it is a good *hold*. The important point is not to get caught in the dualistic trap of thinking that it is only the cognitive aspect of interpretation (with some affect thrown in) that changes the patient. This same thinking would claim that any theoretical or technical concept that includes the nonverbal and developmental is merely a "corrective emotional experience." In therapy and in life (which is more than therapy!), developmental progression occurs optimally when meaning and affect are as seamless as possible. When parents interpret the world to their offspring, if they do it with absent or inappropriate affect, the child is given disparate messages that don't fit immediately or ultimately insofar as development is concerned. The child is forced to imitate the limited communication or hide away his or her true communicative self deep within the psyche. It is self-evident that a developmentally tuned therapy or analysis must take these factors into account when there was affective-cognitive dissonance the first time around.

SQUIGGLING WITH ADULTS

Winnicott used his squiggle technique primarily in his time-limited consultations with children. He used it as a combined projective and therapeutic technique. Diagnosis and interpretations were overlapping and interwoven. But isn't this the way it is with modern theories of perception and meaning? Our observations and formulation of the world are inextricably involved in constructed interpretations of the symbolic meaning of what we see. And when two people are pursuing a developmental task together, the construction of the world (which allows recon-structions to be made later on) is a joint enterprise involving a feedback commu-nicative system. So when Winnicott began to use his squiggle technique, he wasn't really superimposing an artificial technique onto day-to-day experience. He merely epitomized that day-to-day experience in a simple exercise that enabled him to engage in "simply one way of getting into contact with the child" (Winnicott 1971b, p. 3).

A longer quote from Winnicott's introduction to *Therapeutic Consultations in Child Psychiatry* (Winnicott 1971b) should help to show the reader how he felt about and used the squiggle game:

> There is nothing original of course about the squiggle game and it would not be right for somebody to learn how to use the squiggle game and then to feel equipped to do what I call a therapeutic consultation. The squiggle game is simply one way of getting into contact with a child. What happens in the game and in the whole interview depends on the use made of the child's experience, including the material that presents itself. In order to use the mutual experience one must have in one's bones a theory of the emotional development of the child and of the relationship of the child to the environmental factors. In my case described here an artificial link is made between the squiggle and the psychotherapeutic consultation, and this arises out of the fact that from the drawings of the child and of the child and myself one can find one way of making the case come alive. It is almost as if the child, through

the drawings, is alongside me, and to some extent taking part in describing the case, so that the reports of what the child and the therapist said tend to ring true. [p. 3]

A little further on Winnicott wrote that he gradually began to realize that in these consultations he was in the role of the "subjective object, which rarely outlasts the first or first few interviews," but "the doctor has great opportunity for being in touch with the child"(p. 4).

The squiggle game can be thought of as a metaphor describing the essence of what is going on in Winnicottian therapy when it is working the way it works best. Winnicott is a subjective object to the patient, and the patient is a subjective object to Winnicott. In the quote above, Winnicott uses the phrase "as if," implying his conviction that a potential space between two subjective objects is set up in his kind of therapy (with his kinds of patients) and that it is probably only when this milieu exists that his contributions to psychodynamic technique can thrive.

Winnicott never directly advised a squiggling technique for adults. For the most part he kept it reined into the limiting boundaries of the therapeutic consultation with the child. However, he always implied that it could be applicable to adults. Squiggling, bilateral mutual play, is at another realm of discourse than standard free associative technique. Squiggling verbally, interplaying the words and images of the therapist to construct a meaning between them immediately smacks of the impure, that is, the patient's responses are contaminated directly by the associations of the therapist. What kind of science is this? That's a hard one to answer—if the theoretician, or the reader, has a hard science view of the psycho-analytic situation, then the innovation may not do. However, with a more relativistic, hermeneutic, and dialogic view of treatment, squiggling might just be helpful. One could argue, after all, that the patient is so closely tuned to the person of and the expectations of the therapist that his associations are by definition always contaminated by the very presence of the influential therapist. So it could be claimed that there is an implied squiggling effect built into the very nature of psychoanalytic and psychotherapy situations. Why not make it explicit, and be able to take advantage of the benefits of the squiggling technique? What are these advantages? We can go back to the previous Winnicott quote, "The doctor has a great opportunity for being in touch with the child [substitute adult]." There are patients who cannot tolerate the deprivation involved in the classical technique of the plentiful patient free association and the rare therapist response. How many patients have called me in my capacity as a referral source for my hospital department and specifically asked, even begged, to have a therapist who will be active, who will provide feedback, who will be there! This kind of patient is better served by an interactive technique that insinuates itself into the derivatives of earlier developmental phases when reality was being constructed by both the parent and child. A relationship of a mature, internalized nature is not taken for granted, but *built* instead. To the extent that mutual meanings, understandings, and interpretations can arise from the treatment situation, the patient is provided with an externalized method of building a symbolic world that can ultimately be internalized. If this internalization does occur, presumably the therapist half of the squiggling becomes unnecessary.

Susan Deri (1984) wrote about the adult version of squiggling toward the very end of the last chapter of her book *Symbolism and Creativity*. The chapter is entitled "Fostering Good Symbolization." Referring to the need for what she termed "obsessive intellectualizers" to have a squiggling kind of experience, she wrote:

> Obsessive intellectualizers are in particular need of learning how to "play" freely and creatively within and outside of analysis. What they do not need is an impersonal, silent analyst who occasionally mutters "knowing" interpretations. This stance plays into their all-too-willing readiness to fill the role of "good patient." [p. 340]

A little later on she wrote:

> The patient's communicative and form-creative potential should be fostered by every intervention the analyst makes. Informative statements offered in a professional voice will not serve this aim. Only if interpretations are not "given" (in the sense of "pronounced"), but casually tossed into the patient's play space, i.e., into the transitional space between the patient and analyst, only then can the patient pick up the offered material and weld it with his or her own inner content into a newly created gestalt. Put slightly differently: When the analyst's ideas are unobtrusively thrown into the patient's transitional play space, these ideas can lie around until the patient is ready to "find" them and blend them with his or her wishes and fantasies into a new, very personal ("treasured") possession. [p. 341]

In a footnote to this passage, Deri saw this process on a more abstract level as similar to Piaget's ideas of how new ideas are assimilated into new schema formation. Deri emphasized how the developmental use of Winnicott's potential space can foster the acquisition of higher levels of symbolization. She understood the need for some patients to be able to externalize early levels of more primitive, protosymbolic forms into a jointly built potential space in order to ultimately reach higher, more autonomous levels of symbolic functioning. While she stressed the obsessive intellectualizer, her comments apply to a wider range of "presymbolic disorders," which includes patients with significant developmental difficulty as well as many, or possibly most, borderline patients.

By now the reader must be crying out for a clearer way of understanding what might be called the dialogic squiggle. Deri was on target when she wrote of an interpretation "not being 'given' [in the sense of pronounced], but actually tossed into the patient's play space." When I am "squiggling" with adult patients, I feel that the patient and I are involved in a light form of Ping-Pong. Most of it consists of visual images that are evoked in each "partner," although these may be words or phrases that do not necessarily evoke strong visual images. The joint enterprise results in what is not too different from Freud's well-known comparison of the dream with the rebus, where the whole is constructed of combinations of visual and verbal images. Again, the difference between this and a more classical technique is that here the therapist decides that the patient needs another half and there is more to be gained from bringing in the "contaminant" of the therapist's projections than leaving the patient to his or her own devices. This occurs when the creative act of free associating is not possible and only occasional interpretive responses from the therapist do defiance to the patient's partially internalized object constancy.

A clinical example will help.

A while back I saw a woman in her early sixties who came to treatment for the first time after finding herself crying profusely during a Schubert lieder concert. The flow seemed to arise out of nowhere. She could only recall that it began during the last song of the cycle, "The Organ Grinder." She related the story and imagery of the song. The scene is winter and the wind is blowing. An old man dressed virtually in rags is playing his barrel organ in the street, surrounded by laughing children and barking dogs who are nipping at his feet. For no conscious reason the image evoked a profound sadness and its accompanying tears.

During the next few weeks the patient's story began to unfold. She was a book editor who thrived on reading and music. A long marriage to a dominating, apparently paranoid lawyer had produced no children. In fact, she maintained that all during her childbearing years they had not talked about having children. He never led, and she never asked. She related how an early difficult sexual encounter initiated her husband's refusal to have intercourse or engage in affectionate behavior of any kind. In public they were an ideal couple, attending parties and cultural functions. But at night he would lie in the bed with his back to her and she would have to be content with touching his back or arm. It became clear that she was a cyclothymic, passive, and masochistic woman who had developed a kind of folie à deux with her paranoid husband. Apparently it took a gradual accumulation of repressed rage and mourning plus the external stimulus of the lieder to bring her affects to the surface. Dialogue had broken down years before, and clearly had never been established in her original family.

In fact, it could be said that she was a master of monologue. After she told me her basic story in response to my questions, she filled the twice-weekly therapy sessions with ceaseless anecdotal accounts of her work life and her day-to-day experiences and frustrations. She seemed content to use me as a container and a holder, so great was her frustration and deprivation. When I thought the relationship was well established, I began to engage her in a kind of banter and wordplay that she was quite good at and enjoyed. She was a master of the verbal pun and used her wide cultural knowledge to "play" with me during these what might be called sessions in a rather sophisticated kindergarten. The foundations of a dialogue were being established. I began to feel that interpretive work was more of a possibility. In the beginning it had only served to break the continuity of our relationship and interfere with the holding environment she needed to provide a bridge from her pathological relationship to our therapeutic alliance. But I felt we had moved up the developmental scale in both our basic relationship and communication.

One session she alluded to her relationship with her husband with hints of an increasing sense of frustration and annoyance. I reminded her of the image of the organ grinder that had been so important in her decision to enter into an alternative interpersonal world, that of therapy. She countered my reminder by attending to the strength of the image of the barking dogs. She called them hounds. Francis Thompson's poem "The Hound of Heaven" came to my mind, and I told her that, in a bit of an ironic tone. She said that as soon as I said "Hound of Heaven," she saw the image of Cerberus, the three-headed dog who guarded the gates of Hades. She was then able to carry it alone. She had been living in a hell with her husband. Standing guard, like a dog, in fact, she was treated like a dog, at his master's feet. She asked how could she have done it all those years? She began to feel she understood how the deep sadness was able to arise during the concert. She saw how she was the beggar, looking for crumbs from her withholding and biting, sadistic husband. It was a breakthrough, not to deep layers of the unconscious, but a look behind the crumbling of some of the walls of denial that had character-ized her life.

Sessions like this gave the patient the sense she had arrived at the knowledge herself, that it hadn't been superimposed on her by a dominating, moralistic therapist who would have been another version of her husband. But clearly, some of the work (or play) had been contributed by me. A more traditional therapy would have relied on her too much, a holding environment might not have been established, and the absence of a safe and secure environment for dialogic playing would not have allowed the kind of mutually arrived at meaning that was ultimately able to win out over her long-standing blindness. It could be argued that other techniques and theoretical orientations could have accomplished the same task. However, all too often this kind of patient is thought of as "untreatable" and that "therapeutic" maneuvers too early could intensify primitive defenses rather than help the patient to give them up.

Another clinical example might also be illustrative.

A bright and talented female teacher had a long history of early developmental traumata and resultant sadomasochistic fantasies. In one session she described one of these embarrassing fantasies, part of which consisted of a pair of lips facing a pair of vaginal labia, within a rather sinister setting. Almost immediately, I translated her image into my own, a Norman Rockwell *Saturday Evening Post* painting of an adolescent couple in a candy store, facing each other while sipping soda from two straws placed in the same glass. My image led her back to images from her past that involved a paternal aunt with whom she had a close relationship, quite in contrast with the stormy times she had with her often cruel, unempathic, and "gaslighting" mother. She recalled the close feelings she had when she played simple card games with her aunt. And she cried. The interaction between us had helped her to begin to see the sadomasochistic fantasies in a better perspective, not as shameful parts of herself but as products of a very difficult time during her early years. As with the first patient, the "squiggling" helped her construct a new meaning that she began to carry on herself with her own associations.

The question "What went on in these two instances?" must be asked at this point. How much were my "lightly tossed out" images, the Hound of Heaven and the Norman Rockwell cover, principally countertransferential projections and how much were they empathic responses to the patient's imagery and fantasies? No definite answer to this question is possible. The principle that therapist imagery and fantasies can tell us something about what is happening in the patient's psyche has been established in both the ego psychological (Arlow 1969) and Kleinian (Segal 1975) camps (in the latter in the form of projective identification). The radical nature of the squiggling technique is that it involves the sharing of reactive imagery in order to foster the associative and symbol building capacities. This technique has more advantages than disadvantages. An important example of a disadvantage is the danger of leading the patient—certainly a real danger. It is here that the therapist's own training and treatment come in, at least insofar as they offer the possibility of more perception than projection. However, even with optimal and long treatment and training, we are still symbolic animals; therapist meaning must have to intermingle with patient meaning. Since Ping-Pong is a fast game, there isn't much time for the therapist's ego-observing faculties to look over his or her intuitive-empathic response—for a moment, perhaps, but hardly more. It is here that the nature and qualities of the relationship come in. If it is one of hard-earned mutual trust and ease, the patient can serve as a co-guardian against the danger of having a pure projection inflicted on him or her. When the therapist's response is way off, the patient can, and often will, spell this right out, or, in his or her own way, drop it. If there is enough of the patient in the therapist's repsonse, if the therapist–patient milieu is right, then the patient can take up and use the therapist's contribution. Of course, this whole process involves a Winnicottian democratiza-tion of the therapy process that embodies his having analogized the "analyzing couple" to the "nursing couple." But so be it. There are problems with democracy, but most of us prefer it to totalitarianism.

WINNICOTTIAN CHILD THERAPY AND ANALYSIS

In a book that is primarily devoted to a Winnicottian view of adult therapy and analysis, the treatment of children, which he did so much of, has been given short shrift. However, with Winnicott, adult and child therapy were never very far apart.

The principal point is that there are some basic differences (as well as overlappings) between the use of play in Winnicottian child therapy and what we could call Anna Freudian, or certainly Kleinian treatment. It might be easiest to take Klein as the most extreme example. Klein (1932) used play as a substitute for the free association of adults. It was seen as a *means* of discovering the derivatives of unconscious symbolism. For Winnicott, when development was still possible, play was therapy in itself. It could be said that his play was situated somewhere between being and doing, between meaning and development, and, certainly, between reality and fantasy (Grolnick et al. 1978). When therapy is working optimally, these "betweens" become seamless, and the sharing of meaning, or the interpretive aspect of therapy, and playing a developmental partner become inseparable. By using play as such a central structure in his theoretical and technical contributions, Winnicott began to substitute the importance of bringing development and insight together in contrast to the more classical psychoanalytic emphasis on the combining of insight and affect. It is implied that playing must have its affective side in order to be playing.

Of course, this use of play as therapy is directly involved in Winnicott's way of doing adult therapy and analysis. However, the play enters the therapy session as more metaphoric and imagistic. Whereas any psychoanalytically oriented ther-apist would agree that in treatment at the symbolic level, affect and insight must go together, bringing in playing helps to counter the dualistic tendencies in psychoanalytic theorizing and technique.

Although children and adults are generally at different levels of development, it is clear from our patients and from ourselves how much overlap there is. Winnicott deeply believed that development proceeded throughout life, as did the possibility of creative living. Play, therefore, is a necessary part of living and therapy in both adults and children.

A "how to do it" stance both applies to and does not apply to Winnicott. I have been caught between the Scylla and Charybdis of telling the reader what to do, and presenting both Winnicott and myself as facilitators rather than dictators. But the "natural," talented therapist is a rare entity. The Winnicott literature should serve as a facilitator and "permitter" to allow the natural talent of the therapist to emerge. But this aspect of learning how to do Winnicottian therapy stirs up my superego concerns, some of them stemming from my own classical psychoanalytic training.

There is much about Winnicott that is reminiscent of the existential philosophers and psychologists. Ticho (1974) showed how the ideas of Martin Buber and Winnicott are similar, neither of whom having been directly aware of the works of the other. Buber's concepts of I-thou versus I-it and "seeming" experience are very close to Winnicott's true and false self concept. To both, to a significant degree the self is constituted by the other. One can mine such existential phenomenologists as Merleau-Ponty (1968) for similar compatibilities. The awareness of the existential aspects of Winnicott's ideas is a cause of concern among some psychoanalysts. The '50s – under the influence of the works of Sartre, Binswinger, May, and others – produced an existential analysis and therapy that was highly interpersonal, action oriented, intuitive, and anti-intellectual. While it took into account ideas beyond awareness, Sartre's (1953) unconscious was more like the Freudian preconscious. But Winnicott had a background of orthodox psychoanalytic training; a belief in classical analysis for the psychoneurotic patient; a developmental, historical perspective; a concept of internal, unconscious object relations; conscious and unconscious primitive affects; and even a continued utilization of the drive concept. The danger exists that his existential side will lead to an interpersonal, watered-down version of psychoanalysis. However, it is necessary to remember that in order even to get close to what Winnicott brought to his patients, a rather extensive knowledge of psychoanalytic theory and history and one's own personal therapy or analysis are essential. In other words, a Freudian informed knowledge of the basics of psychoanalysis and developmental theory, years of practicing and being supervised, along with the acquisition of a deep understanding of Winnicott's sometimes complex ideas, should help to ensure that therapy based on them will not degenerate either into wild analysis or nonanalysis, and will allow them to promote an important new addition to psychoanalytic theory and technique.

REFERENCES

Adler, G. (1989). Transitional phenomena, projective identification, and the essential ambiguity of the psychoanalytic situation. *Psychoanalytic Quarterly* 58:81–104.

Arlow, J. (1969). Unconscious fantasy and disturbances of conscious experience. *Psychoanalytic Quarterly* 38:28–51.

Balint, M. (1968). *The Basic Fault: Therapeutic Aspects of Regression.* New York: Brunner/Mazel.

Deri, S. (1984). *Symbolization and Creativity.* New York: International Universities Press.

Empson, W. (1930). *Seven Types of Ambiguity.* 3rd ed. Norfolk, VA: New Directions, 1953.

Friedman, L. (1988). The clinical popularity of object relations concepts. *Psychoanalytic Quarterly* 57:667–691.

Grolnick, S. (1984). Play, myth, theater and psychoanalysis. *Psychoanalytic Review* 71:247–262.

Grolnick, S., Barkin, L., in collaboration with Muensterberger, W., eds. (1978). *Between Reality and Fantasy: Transitional Objects and Phenomena.* Northvale, NJ: Jason Aronson.

Grolnick, S., and Lengyel, A. (1978). Etruscan burial symbols and the transitional process. In *Between Reality and Fantasy: Transitional Objects and Phenomena,* ed. S. Grolnick, L. Barkin, in collaboration with W. Muensterberger, pp. 381–410. Northvale, NJ: Jason Aronson.

Hook, S., ed. (1959). *Psychoanalysis, Scientific Method and Philosophy.* New York: New York University Press.

Klein, M. (1932). *The Psycho-analysis of Children.* New York: Grove, 1960.

Kohut, H. (1971). *The Analysis of the Self.* New York: International Universities Press.

Langer, S. (1942). *Philosophy in a New Key.* Cambridge, MA: Harvard University Press, 1973.

Loewald, H. (1960). On the therapeutic action of psychoanalysis. *International Journal of Psycho-Analysis* 58:463–472.

———— (1975). Psychoanalysis as an art and the fantasy character of the psychoanalytic situation. *Journal of the American Psycho-analytic Association* 23:227–299.

McDougall, J. (1982). *Theaters of the Mind.* New York: Basic Books, 1985.

Merleau-Ponty, M. (1968). *The Visible and the Invisible.* Evanston, IL: Northwestern University Press.

Sartre, J-P. (1953). *Existential Psychoanalysis.* Chicago: Henry Regnery.

Sechehaye, M. (1951). *Symbolic Realization: A New Method of Pyschotherapy Applied to a Case of Schizophrenia.* Trans. B. Wursten and H. Wursten. New York: International Universities Press.

Segal. H. (1957). Notes on symbol formation. *International Journal of Psycho-Analysis* 38:391–397.

———— (1975). *Introduction to the Work of Melanie Klein.* London: Hogarth.

Ticho, E. (1974). Donald W. Winnicott, Martin Buber and the theory of personal relationships. *Psychiatry* 37:240–253.

Weich, M. (1978). Transitional language. In *Between Reality and Fantasy: Transitional Objects and Phenomena,* ed. S. Grolnick, L. Barkin, in collaboration with W. Muensterberger, pp. 413–423. Northvale, NJ: Jason Aronson.

Werner, H., and Kaplan, B. (1963). *Symbol Formation.* New York: Wiley.

Winnicott, D. W. (1947). Hate in the countertransference. In *Collected Papers: Through Paediatrics to Psycho-Analysi*, pp. 194-203. New York: Basic Books.

_____ (1949). Mind and its relation to the psyche-soma. In *Collected Papers: Through Paediatrics to Psycho-Analysis*, pp. 243-254. New York: Basic Books, 1958.

_____ (1955). Clinical varieties of transference. In *Collected Papers: Through Paediatrics to Psycho-Analysis*, pp. 295-299. New York: Basic Books, 1958.

_____ (1960). The theory of the parent–infant relationship. In *The Maturational Processes and the Facilitating Environment*, pp. 37-55. New York: International Universities Press, 1965.

_____ (1962). Ego integration in child development. In *The Maturational Processes and the Facilitating Environment*, pp. 56-63. New York: International Universities Press, 1965.

_____ (1971a). Dreaming, fantasying and living. In *Playing and Reality*, pp. 26-37. New York: Basic Books.

_____ (1971b). *Therapeutic Consultations in Child Psychiatry*. New York: Basic Books.

_____ (1971c). The use of an object and relating through identifications. In *Playing and Reality*, pp. 86-94. New York: Basic Books.

_____ (1988). The concept of health using instinct theory. In *Human Nature*, pp. 51-64. New York: Schocken.

24

ANDRÉ GREEN: ANALYTIC PLAY AND ITS RELATIONSHIP TO THE OBJECT

A GREAT CREATIVE THINKER–AND such Winnicott undoubtedly was, perhaps the greatest of the contemporary analytic epoch–provides endless proof of his gifts, I ought to say even of his genius, throughout his life's work. But often it is during the final stage of his career, struggling it may be against the threat of a fast-approaching death, that he rises to his full stature. I was deeply impressed by feelings of this kind while reading *Playing and Reality* (1971b). I should like here to pay tribute to this book, elaborating in my own way what I brought away from it.

Winnicott's name will always be associated with the idea of the transitional object and transitional phenomena, of potential space, of playing and illusion. What has progressively emerged from his initial description of the transitional object–which was constantly being enriched as the years went by–is that Winnicott, in a series of observations which seemed harmless and unassuming enough, had in fact delineated a conceptual field of the highest importance, whose definition was based at one and the same time on child observation and the analytic situation. We must get one thing straight: in his case the observation of the child did not, as one might think, take priority over the observation of the analytic situation. On the contrary: it was because Winnicott was first analyzed, and then went on to become an analyst himself, that he was able, in looking at children, to notice what had been escaping everyone's attention. For we cannot say that the discovery of the transitional object brought to light some recondite and obscure reality. Freud once said that he had done nothing but discover the obvious. The same could be said of Winnicott. The least observant of mothers has always known that her child likes to fall asleep with his teddy bear, or while fondling a bit of cloth or a corner of his blanket. But before Winnicott no one had understood the importance of this, just as no one before Freud had ever been struck by the significance there might be in an eighteen-month-old's game, played during his mother's absence, of throwing away from him and then pulling back again a reel of cotton. Here too it had to be a psychoanalyst, the very first one, who could observe this spectacle with new eyes.

Thus, analytic experience seems to have been the determining factor in the formation of Winnicott's concepts, as it was in those of Freud. Nor is it by accident that it should be Winnicott and his students Khan, Milner, and Little who have provided us with the most fertile reflections on the *analytic setting*.

[Earlier] I proposed the hypothesis that the analytic situation is characterized by the fact that each of its two partners produces a double of himself. What the analysand communicates is an analogue, a double of his affective and bodily experience; what the analyst communicates is a double of the effect produced on his own bodily, affective, and intellectual experience by the patient's communication. Thus the communication *between* analysand and analyst is an object made up of two parts, one constituted by the double of the analysand, the other by the double of the analyst. What is called the "therapeutic alliance" or "working alliance," which I prefer to call the *analytic association*, is, in my belief, founded on the possibility of creating an *analytic object* formed by these two halves. This corresponds precisely to the etymological definition, in Robert's *Dictionary*, of a symbol: "an object cut in two, constituting a sign of recognition when its bearers can put together the two separate pieces." In my opinion this is what occurs in the analytic setting. The analytic object is neither internal (to the analysand or to the analyst), nor external (to either the one or the other), but is situated *between* the two. So it corresponds exactly to Winnicott's definition of the transitional object and to its location in the intermediate area of *potential space*, the space of "overlap" demarcated by the analytic setting. When a patient terminates his analysis, it is not only that he has "internalized" the analytic interplay, but also that he can take away with him the potential space in order to reconstitute it in the outside world, through cultural experience, through sublimation and, more generally, through the possibility of pairings or (let us rather say) of coupling.

The analytic situation differs from the game of chess (to which Freud was fond of comparing it) in that it is *the analyst who determines the rules of the game*, as Viderman (1970) has rightly observed. In case of disagreement, arbitration is possible only if (in a juridical sense) the rules of law are contravened; but the law governing analysis remains in the hands of the analyst, who exercises both legislative and executive power. These rules which are laid down before the game begins confer a considerable advantage upon the analyst (1) because he has already been analyzed and (2) because usually he has already conducted other analyses. All equality between the two parties is abolished.

But this spatial account of the game needs to be complemented by a temporal one. In analysis it is *always* the analysand who makes the first move. No analysis is conceivable in which, after the statement of the fundamental rule, the analyst speaks first. The analyst can only respond to the first move, which is always played by the patient and only when he decides on it. Similarly, it is always the analysand who makes the last move in the final farewell, the analyst taking leave of his patient only in answer to this farewell (although it may be only temporary).

This structure, which invokes the notion of the double, must also make room for the absent. The absent one in analysis is none other than the analyst's own analyst[1] – which goes to show that analysis always proceeds across generations. As I said before, even if it is his first analysis, the analyst has already been analyzed. In the analytic interplay, the absent, metaphorically represented by the analyst's analyst is connected with two other modes of absence: that of past reality, inaccessible as such both to analyst and to analysand, and that of an equally inaccessible present reality. The analyst cannot get to *know* his patient's real life; he can only imagine it. And likewise the analysand can never know the analyst's life; he too can only imagine it. Both are reduced to approximations. Even as the analytic process unfolds, each partner communicates, through verbalization, only a part of his life experience. Here we get back to Winnicott's concept of the silent self and a memorable sentence comes to mind: "each individual is an isolate, permanently non-communicating, permanently unknown, in fact unfound" (1963a). From this springs the importance of the capacity to be alone (in the presence of the mother or of the analyst) and its consequence: the analyst is always having to navigate between the risk of separation anxiety and that of anxiety concerning his intrusiveness.

Winnicott has formulated an essential paradox for us, one that, as he says, we must accept as it is and that is not for resolution. If the baby is in health, he "creates the object, but the object was there waiting to be created and to become a cathected object. I tried to draw attention to this aspect of transitional phenomena by claiming that in the rules of the game we all know we will never challenge the baby to elicit an answer to the question: did you create that or did you find it?" (1971b,

---

1. Hence the inequality and the heterogeneity of the double analytic discourse. The analyst relies upon a discourse with the absent, namely his own analyst, author of his difference from the analysand.

p. 89). This paradox joins up with another: *the transitional object is and is not the self.*[2]

The qualities peculiar to the transitional object confront us with an unimpeachable double truth. *The analyst is not a real object; the analyst is not an imaginary object.* The analytic discourse is not the patient's discourse, nor is it that of the analyst, nor is it the sum of these two. The analytic discourse is the *relation* between two discourses which belong neither to the realm of the real nor to that of the imaginary. This may be described as a *potential relationship*, or, more precisely, as a *discourse of potential relationships*, in itself potential. Accordingly, the analytic discourse has, in regard to past and present alike, only a potential relationship to the truth. But this does not mean that the analytic discourse may consist in simply anything at all. It must bear an *homologous* relationship to imaginary (or psychic) reality; it forms its counterpart. This implies an approximate correspondence, but an affective approximation, *without which its effect would be nil.* The homology is one we are obliged to construct, for lack of positive evidence. Nevertheless, this construction is not arbitrary, since we cannot help but construct the real, even when it pleases us to think we are doing no more than perceiving it.

In one of his most fundamental papers, inspired by Lacan's work on the mirror phase, Winnicott (1966) analyzes the function of the mother's face as the precursor of the mirror. Here he stresses the importance of the baby's initial communication not only with the breast but also with the mother's face. We know that the baby at the breast (or bottle) sucks while looking not at the breast but at his mother's face. Winnicott rightly points out that while this is going on the baby may see in the mother's gaze either himself or herself. If, too precociously, it is the face of the mother/object that he perceives, he cannot form the subjective object, but will prematurely evolve the object objectively perceived. The result is that he must organize a false self, as an image conforming to the mother's desire. He must then hide away, in secret, his true self, which cannot and indeed must not be allowed expression. With his false self, he can achieve only an external identity. But this is a pathological solution. In the normal progress of events, a compromise is obtained through the creation of the transitional area of experience.

"If the baby is in health . . ." said Winnicott. Some babies, we know, are not. And among these some will later impress us with the intensity of their negative therapeutic reaction. It is striking that Winnicott found it necessary to add, in *Playing and Reality*, a supplement to his original paper on the transitional object. The difference between these two pieces of work is considerable, the fruit of twenty years' experience. In the later version Winnicott discusses what he calls the *negative side of relationships*. In certain borderline cases, the absence of the mother is felt as

---

2. What Winnicott in fact said was that the transitional object is and is not the breast, but the same formulation may be applied to the self.

equivalent to her death. Here the time factor must be duly weighed, since it is in terms of temporal accretion (x + y + z quantity of deprivation, expressed as the accumulated moments of the mother's absence) that Winnicott imagines how the baby can move from distress to "unthinkable anxiety" by way of a traumatic break in life's continuity ("The location of cultural experience"). For such infants *"the only real thing is the gap*; that is to say, the death or the absence [in the sense of non-existence] or the amnesia" (1971b, p. 22 italics mine). While analyzing a patient of this kind, Winnicott arrived at the conclusion that from the point of view of the child *the mother was dead*, regardless of her absence or presence. It occurred to him that in the transference "the important communication for me to get was that there could be a blotting out, and that this blank could be the only fact and the only thing that was real" (ibid). This remark bears out precisely my own observations about the importance in psychosis of the negative hallucination of the subject. For Winnicott's patient, who had had previous analysis, the negation of the first analyst was more important than the fact of the existence of the second analyst. "The negative of him is more real than the positive of you." Such vengefulness is particularly severe with respect to an object which has failed. Here retaliation is a negative response to a negative trauma; in other words, the trauma is not only something which has occurred—in the classical sense of a traumatization (through sexual seduction or an aggressive act)—but that which *did not occur, owing to an absence of response on the part of the mother/object*. "The real thing is the thing that is not there." A very true statement, revealing how the thing that is not there, the symbol, is taken as reality; which recalls Hanna Segal's idea of symbolic equation, but in an exactly contrary sense. In Segal's example, violin = penis. But in Winnicott's example, and here he meets up with Bion, *the non-object is the object*. The non-object, in this context, means not the representation of the object but the non-existence of the object. Winnicott speaks of symbols which disappear. Patients in whom structures of this type are found can seem mentally disabled, and in my own initial encounters with such analysands I have come away with a strong impression of their psychic and intellectual poverty. Their motto is : "All I have got is what I have not got."

This line of speculation, which Winnicott adds in 1971 to his original hypothesis about transitional objects and not-me possessions, is crucial, as it opens the way to a new conceptual theme, *negative investment*. I have postulated (1967, 1969) the existence of a negative narcissistic structure characterized by the valorization of a state of non-being. Striving for that state of quietude which follows satisfaction with an object, but finding himself in a state where satisfaction has not occurred within limits tolerable for his psychic apparatus, the subject seeks to attain the same state as if satisfaction had been achieved, through the strategy of renouncing all hope of satisfaction, through inducing in himself a state of psychic death not unrelated to Jones's idea of *aphanisis*.

In his paper on the mirror-role of the mother's face, Winnicott uses the illustration of the patient who said to him, "Wouldn't it be awful if the child looked into the mirror and saw nothing?" The anxiety of the negative hallucination is truly unthinkable. In my opinion, all the defensive maneuvers described by Melanie Klein's advocates amount to nothing but an awesome strategy for avoiding this fundamental and primordial anxiety.

If "negative symbolization" can provide an extreme (and very costly) solution, another kind of solution is adopted in borderline cases. In my own experience, what I have most often observed is a need to hold on to and to preserve at all costs a bad internal object. It is as if, when the analyst succeeds in reducing the power of the bad object, the subject has no other recourse than to make it reappear, in fact to resurrect it, in its original or in an analogous form, as if the thing most dreaded were the *interval between the loss of the bad object and its replacement by a good object. This interval is experienced as a dead time, which the subject cannot survive. Hence the value for the patient of the negative therapeutic reaction, which ensures that the analyst will never be replaced, since the object which would succeed him might never appear or might only appear too late.*

In another section of *Playing and Reality*, "The use of an object and relating through identifications," Winnicott discusses the patient's ability to *use* the analyst. For this to be possible, the analyst must allow himself to be destroyed as frequently as the subject wishes, so that the latter may be reassured that the object has the capacity to survive his destruction of it. Winnicott makes the interesting comment that destructiveness of this kind is not related to aggressiveness. This states yet another paradoxical truth. It must be understood that what is here in question is not the fantasied activity of an experience of mentally acted-out destruction; rather it is a radical decathexis. Hence what we are concerned with is a succession of libidinal or aggressive cathexes and of decathexes which abolish the preceding cathexes and the objects linked to them. When carried to an extreme, such decathexes lead to psychic death, just as anarchic cathexes deeply pervaded by aggressiveness lead to delusion. Thus the fundamental dilemma becomes: delusion or death (physical or psychic). The work of the analyst is aimed at transforming these alternatives into something less extreme, so that delusion may become playing, and death absence. In this context absence does not mean loss, but *potential presence.* For absence, paradoxically, may signify either an imaginary presence, or else an unimaginable non-existence. It is absence in this first sense which leads to the capacity to be alone (in the presence of the object) and to the activity of representation and of creating the imaginary: the transitional object, constructed within that space of illusion never violated by the question. Was the object created or was it found?

Freud, as I remarked above, sometimes compared the analytic situation to chess. If Winnicott is the master-player of psychoanalysis, it is surely not chess that he plays with his patient. It is a game with a cotton reel, with a piece of string, with a doll or teddy bear. Finally, with children Winnicott plays the squiggle game, in which each partner takes a turn drawing a scribble, which is then modified by the other (Winnicott 1971a). The spontaneous movement of a hand which allows itself to be guided by the drive, a hand which does not act but rather expresses itself, traces a more or less insignificant and formless line, submitting it to the scrutiny of the other, who, deliberately, transforms it into a meaningful shape. What else do we do in the analysis of difficult cases? The beautiful clarity of the chess game, unfurling itself under the open light of day, is absent there. Instead we find ourselves in a murky night pierced by flashes of lightning and sudden storms. Meaning does not emerge complete as Aphrodite rising from the waves. It is for us to construct it. Viderman believes that, prior to the analytic situation, the meaning that we seek has never existed; it is the analytic process which constitutes it *as such* for the first time. Meaning is not discovered, it is created. I prefer to describe it as an absent meaning, a virtual sense which awaits its realization through the cuttings and shapings offered by analytic space (and time). It is a potential meaning. It would be wrong to think that like Sleeping Beauty it merely waits there to be aroused. It is constituted in and by the analytic situation; but if the analytic situation reveals it, it does not create it. It brings it from absence to potentiality, and then makes it actual. To actualize it means to call it into existence, not out of nothing (for there is no spontaneous generation), but out of the meeting of two discourses, and by way of that object which is the analyst, in order to construct the *analytic object*.

This theory implies that mental functioning has to be taken into consideration. In chess, there is only one kind of material at stake; the pieces have different *values* and an unchangeable mode of progression. The analytic situation, on the contrary, brings varying materials to light: drives, affects, representations (of things or of words), thoughts, actions. Their specific modes of functioning—to be the plaything of a drive (directed toward the body or toward the world), to feel, to imagine, to say, to think, to act—all these modes are capable of an ultimate exchange of function. The vectorization of drive into language is placed in check here. For speaking could become tantamount to acting, acting to evacuating, imagining to filling up a hole, and thinking could, at the extreme verge, become impossible (cf. "blank psychosis," Donnet and Green 1973).

Here we have evidently reached the limits of Freudian practice and theory. There is urgent and growing need for another system of reference which gives pride of place to the countertransference and clarifies its elaborative potentialities. The analyst ought either to use his imagination, or resign, for the unconscious creates its own structure only by way of the Imaginary.

The importance of the analytic setting arises from the fact that it allows the development of a *metaphoric* regression which is a double, an analogue of infantile regression. In the same way, the response of the analyst, comparable to holding, is itself only a double of maternal care. It is as if, out of the totality of physical and psychic maternal care, only the psychic aspect were to be admitted into the analytic situation. The part which is not given play in analysis is the one that is missing when the analytic object is constituted. This object, which takes shape through the communication of psychic maternal care, leaves in abeyance any actual regression to the past on the part of the patient, and any physical care on the part of the analyst.

But we must go yet further. And here my agreement with Winnicott reaches its limit. When Winnicott pointed out that there is no such thing as a baby, reminding us of the couple that it forms together with its cradle or with its mother in the holding situation, his observation, as we know, caused quite a stir.

I would maintain, for my part, that there is no such entity as a baby with his mother. No mother-child couple exists without a father somewhere. For even if the father is hated or banished by the mother, erased from her mind in favor of somebody else, of her own mother or father, the child nevertheless is the product of the union of the father and mother. Of this union he is the *material, living, irrefutable* proof. There are mothers who want to wipe out any trace of the father in the child. And we know the result: a psychotic structure. Thus we can assert that ultimately *there is no dual relationship.* There can be no dual exchanges, but there is always some link establishing the possibility of duality, in the form of areas of reunion and separation within the dual relationships.

In the analytic situation, this third element is supplied by the analytic setting. *The work of the analytic setting is comparable to the mirror-work, without which it is impossible to form an image from an object.* This induces the thought that reflection is a fundamental human property. Probably this attribute is innate, but we do now know that an object is indispensable in order to transform this *innate potentiality into its actual realization, failing which, the potentiality dies out and is lost. The analyst is the object necessary to such a transformation, but he can bring it about only with the help of the work of the not-me, which is the analytic setting defined spatially and temporally. What answers for the setting is the combined discourse of the analysand and the analyst, doubles of their respective experience.* Without affect there is no effective language. Without language there is no effective affect. The unconscious is not structured like a language (Lacan); *it is structured like an affective language, or like an affectivity having the properties of language.*

Winnicott was much blamed, and is still being blamed, for his delight in distorting the classical analytic setting. Since I am not prepared to endorse any and every deformation of the analytic setting, I must distinguish between those I would find acceptable and those I would have to reject. It seems to me that the only acceptable variations of classical analysis are *those whose aim is to facilitate the creation of optimal conditions for symbolization.* For classical neurosis, classical analysis serves this function. With borderline patients (taking this term in its broadest sense), the analyst must preserve in each case the minimum conditions requisite to the maximum development of symbolization. Today the analyst's major difficulty lies in this area. No one can decide for him the modalities or the extent of the variations required by such cases. This predicament has several possible results:

1. The cynicism of the analyst who, exploiting for personal ends his patient's need for dependence, gains a pseudo-independence through such shameless manipulation.
2. The collusion involved in a mutual dependency.
3. Guilt connected with the feeling of having transgressed the implicit analytic law.
4. Freedom in analysis based upon the principle that analysis is the construction of the analytic object.

A protective device is necessary here: the analyst's constant awareness of his countertransference and his full employment of it by way of the transference of the analysand. By the term *countertransference* I mean to take into account not only the affective effects, positive or negative, of the analysand's transference, not only the analyst's capacities for antipathy or for sympathy, but also his total mental functioning, including his reading and his exchanges with colleagues. Having said this, I would still agree with the restrictions that Winnicott imposed upon the countertransference in limiting it to the professional attitude. However far we may wish to extend our identification with the patient, this human identification is still a professional one. Hypocrisy is quite out of place here. We terminate the session and do not yield to the patient who wishes it would go on indefinitely. We leave for vacation without him and are paid for our work. We do our best to listen to him, but we see and hear only what we are prepared to see and hear, just as the patient can only understand what he was already on the verge of understanding, although he could not arrive at it all by himself.

In our activity as analysts, our real work does not lie in a mere receptivity to what the patient is communicating, nor on the other hand is it wholly determined by those preconceptions and presuppositions which are necessarily prior to all communication. The analyst's creativity takes shape within the time and space of the communicative exchange where the analytic object is formed by continuously and discontinuously constructing itself.

Analysts listen more easily to their patients than they can to each other. Doubtless because – and this is the final paradox – a colleague is more an-other than he is an a-like, and a patient is more an a-like than he is an-other. Alter ego.

REFERENCES

Donnet, J. L., and Green, A. (1973). L'Enfant DE CA: a Psychose Blanche. Paris: Editions de Minvit.

Green, A. (1967). Le narcissisme primaire: structure ou "état." *L'Inconscient* 1, 2.

_____ (1969). Le narcissisme moral. *Revue Français Psychanalytique* 33.

Viderman, S. (1970). La Construction de L'Espace Analytique. Paris: Donoël.

Winnicott, D. W. (1963a). Communicating and not communicating leading to a study of certain opposites. In *The Maturational Processes and the Facilitating Environment.* London: Hogarth.

_____ (1966). The mirror-role of mother and family in child development. In *Playing and Reality.* London: Tavistock, 1971.

_____ (1971a). *Therapeutic Consultations in Child Psychiatry.* London: Hogarth.

_____ (1971b). *Playing and Reality.* London: Tavistock.

25

THOMAS OGDEN: ON
POTENTIAL SPACE

WINNICOTT'S LANGUAGE

I will begin by presenting in Winnicott's words his concept of the nature of
potential space. I will not attempt at this point to explicate or interpret, and for the
moment will honor Winnicott's admonition to allow the paradoxes "to be accepted
and tolerated and respected . . . and not to be resolved" (Winnicott 1971d, p. xii).
For Winnicott, as for perhaps no other analytic writer, it is crucial that we begin
with his ideas in his own words. For Winnicott, meaning lies in the form of the
writing as much as in the content: "The whole forms a unit" (Winnicott 1967a,
p. 99).

1. "Potential space . . . is the hypothetical area that exists (but cannot exist)
   between the baby and the object (mother or part of mother) during the
   phase of the repudiation of the object as not-me, that is, at the end of being
   merged in with the object" (Winnicott 1971e, p. 107).
2. Playing, creativity, transitional phenomena, psychotherapy, and "cultural" experience ("the accent is on experience," 1967a, p. 99) all have a place
   in which they occur. That place, potential space, "is not *inside* by any use

of the word. . . . Nor is it *outside*, that is to say it is not part of the
repudiated world, the not-me, that which the individual has decided to
recognize (with whatever difficulty and even pain) as truly external, which
is outside magical control" (1971b, p. 41). Potential space is an intermediate area of experiencing that lies between (a) the inner world, "inner
psychic reality" (1971a, p. 106), and (b) "actual or external reality" (1971b,
p. 41). It lies "between the subjective object and the object objectively
perceived, between me-extensions and not-me" (1967a, p. 100).

3. "The essential feature [of this area of experiencing in general and the
transitional object in particular] is . . . *the paradox and the acceptance of the
paradox*: the baby creates the object, but the object was there waiting to be
created. . . . In the rules of the game we all know that we will never
challenge the baby to elicit an answer to the question: did you create that
or did you find it?" (1968, p. 89).

4. This "area is a product of the *experiences of the individual person*
(baby, child, adolescent, adult) in the environment that obtains" (1971a,
p. 107).

5. Potential space both joins and separates the infant (child, or adult) and
the mother (object). "This is the paradox I accept and do not attempt
to resolve. The baby's separating-out of the world of objects from the
self is achieved only through the absence of a space between [the infant
and mother], the *potential* space being filled in in the way that I am
describing" [i.e., with illusion, with playing and with symbols] (1971a,
p. 108).

It seems to me that within the framework of the metaphors and paradoxes
that Winnicott has generated to convey his conception of potential space, there is
little if anything I can add to clarify or extend what he has said. It is very difficult
to find words of one's own to discuss the extremely complex set of ideas that
Winnicott has managed to condense into his deceptively simple, highly evocative
metaphorical language. Winnicott's ideas are entrapped, to a far greater degree
than is ordinarily the case, in the language in which they are presented. The result
is a peculiar combination of clarity and opacity in Winnicott's thinking about
potential space that has given it popular appeal (the concept of the transitional
object in particular) while at the same time insulating the ideas from systematic
exploration, modification, and extension.

It is one of the tasks of this chapter to use language not used by Winnicott to
discuss the phenomena addressed by the concept of potential space. The new
terms, it is hoped, will not alter the essential meanings of the original language and
may provide access to understandings of potential space not provided by Winnicott.

THE PHENOMENON OF PLAYING

It might be useful at this point to present some of the experiential referents for the abstract set of ideas involved in the concept of potential space. In the following example, the state of mind required for playing (i.e., potential space) is at first absent and then made present.

> A two-and-a-half-year-old child, after having been frightened by having his head go underwater while being given a bath, became highly resistant to taking a bath. Some months later, after gentle but persistent coaxing by his mother, he very reluctantly allowed himself to be placed in four inches of bath water. The child's entire body was tense; his hands were tightly clamped onto his mother's. He was not crying, but his eyes were pleadingly glued to those of his mother. One knee was locked in extension while the other was flexed in order to hold as much of himself out of the water as he could. His mother began almost immediately to try to interest him in some bath toys. He was not the least bit interested until she told him she would like some tea. At that point the tension that had been apparent in his arms, legs, abdomen, and particularly his face, abruptly gave way to a new physical and psychological state. His knees were now bent a little; his eyes surveyed the toy cups and saucers and spotted an empty shampoo bottle, which he chose to use as milk for the tea; the tension in his voice shifted from the tense insistent plea, "My not like bath, my not like bath," to a narrative of his play: "Tea not too hot, it's okay now. My blow on it for you. Tea yummy." The mother has some "tea" and asked for more. After a few minutes, the mother began to reach for the washcloth. This resulted in the child's ending of the play as abruptly as he had started it, with a return of all the initial signs of anxiety that had preceded the play. After the mother reassured the child that she would hold him so he would not slip, she asked him if he had any more tea. He did, and playing was resumed.

The foregoing is observational data and does not emanate from a psychoanalytic process. Nonetheless, the observations do convey a sense of the way in which a state of mind was generated by the mother and child in which there was a transformation of water from something frightening to a plastic medium (discovered and created by the child) with meanings that could be communicated. In this transformation, reality is not denied; the dangerous water is represented in the playing. Nor is fantasy robbed of its vitality—the child's breath magically changed dangerous water into a loving gift. There is also a quality of "I-ness" that is generated in play that differs from the riveted stare and desperate holding-on that had connected mother and infant prior to the beginning of play. In the course of this chapter the significance of each of the features of the state of mind noted here will be discussed.

POTENTIAL SPACE AND THE DIALECTICAL PROCESS

A dialectic is a process in which each of two opposing concepts creates, informs, preserves, and negates the other, each standing in a dynamic (ever-changing) relationship with the other (Hegel 1807, Kojève 1934–1935). The dialectical process moves toward integration, but integration is never complete. Each integration creates a new dialectical opposition and a new dynamic tension. In psychoanalysis, the central dialectic is that of Freud's conception of the relationship between the conscious and the unconscious mind. There can be no conscious mind without an unconscious mind and vice versa; each creates the other and exists only as a hypothetical possibility without the other. In mathematical language, the conscious mind and unconscious mind independent of one another are empty sets; they become full only in relation to one another. The unconscious mind acquires psychological contents only to the extent that there is a category of psychological event that has the quality of consciousness and vice versa.

The dialectical process is centrally involved in the creation of subjectivity. By subjectivity, I am referring to the capacity for degrees of self-awareness ranging from intentional self-reflection (a very late achievement) to the most subtle, unobtrusive sense of "I-ness" by which experience is subtly endowed with the quality that one is thinking one's thoughts and feeling one's feelings as opposed to living in a state of reflexive reactivity. Subjectivity is related to, but not the same as, consciousness. The experience of consciousness (and unconsciousness) follows from the achievement of subjectivity. Subjectivity, as will be discussed, is a reflection of the differentiation of symbol, symbolized, and interpreting subject. The emergence of a subject in the course of this differentiation makes it possible for a person to wish. The wish to make oneself unaware of an aspect of one's system of meanings sets the stage for the differentiation of conscious and unconscious realms of experience.

Paradoxically, "I-ness" is made possible by the other. Winnicott (1967b) describes this as the infant's discovery of himself in what he sees reflected in his mother's eyes. This constitutes an interpersonal dialectic wherein "I-ness" and otherness create one another and are preserved by the other. The mother creates the infant and the infant creates the mother. (In discussing dialectics, we are always considering concepts [e.g., the concept of mother and the concept of infant] and not material entities.)

Meaning accrues from difference. There can be no meaning in a completely homogeneous field. The existence of the homogeneous field itself could not even be recognized, because there would be no terms other than itself to attribute to it. One cannot have a dictionary with only one word; in theory, one can have a dictionary with two words, because each word would supply the contrast necessary for the recognition and definition of the other. From this perspective, the unconscious mind *in itself* does not constitute a system of meanings. There are no negatives and no contradictions in the unconscious (Freud 1915), simply the static coexistence of opposites that is the hallmark of primary process thinking. The system Conscious is required to generate unconscious *meaning* and the system Unconscious is required to create conscious *meaning*.

At the very beginning (perhaps only a hypothetical moment), the subjectivity of the mother–infant unit is only a potential held by the aspect of the mother that lies outside of the mother–infant. Winnicott (1960a) can be taken quite literally when he says that there is no such thing as an infant (without a mother). I would add that within the mother–infant unit, neither is there any such thing as a mother. The preoccupation of the mother (what an observer would see the mother) with fitting herself into the place of the infant would be considered an illness if this type of loss of oneself in another were to occur in a different setting (Winnicott 1956).

The mother–infant (in isolation from the part of the mother that is outside this unity) is incapable of subjectivity. Instead, there is the "illusion"[1] (in most ways closer to a delusion) that the mother and infant are not separate and in fact do not exist. The mother exists only in the form of the invisible holding environment in which there is a meeting of the infant's needs in a way that is so unobtrusive that the infant does not experience his needs as needs. As a result, there is not yet an infant.

If there is a good-enough fit between mother and infant and such an illusion/delusion is created, there is no need for symbols, even of the most primitive type. Instead, there is an undisturbed state of "going on being" (Winnicott 1956, p. 303) that will later become the background of experience, but at present is invisible because there is nothing with which to contrast it; it is both background and

---

1. The term *illusion* is used at different points by Winnicott to refer to two quite dissimilar phenomena. The first is the illusion of the subjective object (more accurately described as the illusion of the invisible subject and object), where the mother's empathic responsiveness protects the infant from premature awareness of the self and of the other. This illusion provides a protective insulation for the infant (Winnicott 1948).

The second (developmentally later) form of illusion is the illusion that fills potential space, e.g., the form of illusion encountered in playing. Here, the experience of oneness with the mother and separateness from her coexist in a dialectical opposition (Winnicott 1971b).

foreground. Symbols are required only when there is desire; at the stage of development being discussed, there is only need that is met; the satisfied need does not generate desire (i.e., wishing) for which symbols are required.

The undisturbed, harmoniously functioning mother–infant unit may be only a hypothetical entity, because of the inevitable imperfection of fit between mother and infant.[2] The well-dosed frustration that results provides the first opportunity for awareness of separateness.

At this point, the task for the aspect of the mother who is not a part of the mother–infant unit is to make her presence (the mother as object) known in a way that is not frightening and therefore does not have to be denied or in other ways defended against by the infant. It is this period of the very earliest awareness of separateness, beginning at "about four to six to eight to twelve months" (Winnicott 1951, p. 4), that has been the focus of Winnicott's work on potential space. He has proposed that, in order for this transition from mother–infant unity to a state in which there is mother-and-infant to be nonpathogenic, there must be a potential space between mother and infant that is always potential (never actual) because it is filled in with the state of mind that embodies the never-challenged paradox: The infant and mother are one, and the infant and mother are two.

The movement from mother–infant unity (invisible environmental mother) to mother and infant (mother as object) requires the establishment of the capacity for a psychological dialectic of oneness and of separateness in which each creates and informs the other. At first the "twoness" (that coexists with oneness) cannot be distributed between the mother and the infant in a way that clearly demarcates the two as separate individuals; rather, at this point twoness is a quality of the mother–infant. This is what Winnicott (1958a) is referring to when he talks about the infant's development of the capacity to be alone in the presence of the mother. The transitional object is a symbol for this separateness in unity, unity in separateness. The transitional object is at the same time the infant (the omnipotently created extension of himself) and not the infant (an object he has discovered that is outside of his omnipotent control).

The appearance of a relationship with a transitional object is not simply a milestone in the process of separation–individuation. The relationship with the

---

2. The research findings of Brazelton (Brazelton and Als 1979), Sander (1964), Stern (1977), and others reveals an active "dialogue" between mother and infant from the first days of life. This suggests the possibility of an early, nontraumatic sensing of otherness. Grotstein (1981) has pointed out that it is not necessary to decide if there is mother–infant unity or if there is early awareness of otherness. The two may coexist as separate "tracks" of a dual consciousness.

transitional object is as significantly a reflection of the development of the capacity to maintain a psychological dialectical process.

The consequences of this achievement are momentous and include the capacity to generate personal meanings represented in symbols that are mediated by subjectivity (the experience of oneself as subject who has created one's symbols). The attainment of the capacity to maintain psychological dialectics involves the transformation of the unity that did not require symbols into "threeness," a dynamic interplay of three differentiated entities. These entities are the symbol (a thought), the symbolized (that which is being thought about), and the interpreting subject (the thinker generating his own thoughts and interpreting his own symbols). For heuristic purposes, the original homogeneity of the mother–infant unit can be thought of as a point (Grotstein 1978). The differentiation of symbol, symbolized, and interpreting subject creates the possibility of triangularity within which space is created. That space between symbol and symbolized, mediated by an interpreting self, is the space in which creativity becomes possible and is the space in which we are alive as human beings, as opposed to being simply reflexively reactive beings. This is Winnicott's potential space.

This transformation of unity into threeness coincides with the transformation of the mother–infant unit into mother, infant, and observer of mother-and-infant as three distinct entities. Oneness (the invisible mother–infant) becomes threeness, since at the moment of differentiation within the mother–infant unit, not only are the mother and infant created as objects, but also, the infant is created as subject. The infant as subject is the observer of mother and infant as (symbolic) objects; the infant is now the creator and interpreter of his symbols.

PSYCHOPATHOLOGY OF POTENTIAL SPACE

Winnicott states that symbols originate within potential space. In the absence of potential space, there is only fantasy; within potential space imagination can develop. In fantasy, "a dog is a dog is a dog" (1971c, p. 33), while imagination involves a layering of symbolic meanings. In these very brief statements, Winnicott points to a theory of the psychopathology of the symbolic function, a theory that remains to be completed. In this section, I will attempt to begin to fill in that theory of the psychopathology of symbolization by studying various forms of incompleteness or collapse of the capacity to maintain a psychological dialectical process. As will be seen, the symbolic function is a direct consequence of the capacity to maintain psychological dialectics, and the psychopathology of symbolization is based on specific forms of failure to create or maintain these dialectics.

As was discussed earlier, when there is a good-enough fit between mother and infant, in the very beginning (in the period of the invisible mother–infant), there is no need or opportunity for symbols. Within the context of the mother–infant unit, the person whom an observer would see as the mother is invisible to the infant and exists only in the fulfillment of need that the infant does not yet recognize as need. The mother–infant unity can be disrupted by the mother's substitution of something of herself for the infant's spontaneous gesture. Winnicott (1952) refers to this as "impingement." Some degree of failure of empathy is inevitable and in fact essential for the infant to come to recognize needs as wishes. However, there comes a point at which repeated impingement constitutes "cumulative trauma" (Khan 1963, Ogden 1978).

Cumulative trauma is at one pole of a wide spectrum of causes of premature disruption of the mother–infant unity. Other causes include constitutional hypersensitivity (of many types) on the part of the infant, trauma resulting from physical illness of the infant, and illness or death of a parent or sibling. When premature disruption of the mother–infant unity occurs for any reason, several distinct forms of failure to create or adequately maintain the psychological dialectical process may result:

1. The dialectic of reality and fantasy collapses in the direction of fantasy (i.e., reality is subsumed by fantasy) so that fantasy becomes a thing in itself as tangible, as powerful, as dangerous and as gratifying as the external reality from which it cannot be differentiated.
2. The dialectic of reality and fantasy may become limited or collapse in the direction of reality when reality is used predominantly as a defense against fantasy. Under such circumstances, reality robs fantasy of its vitality. Imagination is foreclosed.
3. The dialectic of reality and fantasy becomes restricted when reality and fantasy are dissociated in such a way as to avoid a specific set of meanings, e.g., the "splitting of the ego" in fetishism.
4. When the mother and infant encounter serious and sustained difficulty in being a mother–infant, the infant's premature and traumatic awareness of his separateness makes experience so unbearable that extreme defensive measures are instituted that take the form of a cessation of the attribution of meaning to perception. Experience is foreclosed. It is not so much that fantasy or reality is denied; rather, neither is created.

These four categories are meant only as examples of types of limitation of the dialectical process. In no sense is this list meant to be exhaustive.

Reality Subsumed by Fantasy

The first of the forms of failure to create and maintain a psychological dialectical process is that in which the "reality pole" of the psychological dialectic is not established on an equal plane with the "fantasy pole" or is weakened by actual experience that is felt to be indistinguishable from, and therefore powerfully confirmatory of, fantasy. The term *reality* is not used to denote something independent of one's processing of perception, since even at our most "realistic," we organize, and in that sense create, our perceptions according to our individual psychological schemata. The term *reality* is used here to refer to that which is experienced as outside of the realm of the subject's omnipotence.

When the "reality pole" of the psychological dialectic collapses, the subject becomes tightly imprisoned in the realm of fantasy objects as things in themselves. This is a two-dimensional world which is experienced as a collection of facts. The hallucination does not sound like a voice, it *is* a voice. One's husband does not simply behave coldly, he *is* ice. One does not feel like one's father, one's father *is* in one's blood and must be bled out in order for one to be free of him. The form of transference generated when the psychological dialectic of reality and fantasy has collapsed in the direction of fantasy is the delusional transference (see Little 1958, Searles 1963): the therapist is not like the patient's mother, he *is* the patient's mother.

A borderline patient experiencing the form of collapse of potential space under discussion became terrified of department store mannequins, feeling that they were living people. For this patient there was no concept of mannequins being "life-like"; either they were alive or they were not. One thing does not stand for another. Things are what they are. (Segal [1957] uses the term *symbolic equation* for this relationship of symbol and symbolized.)

As one approaches the state where nothing is felt to represent anything but itself, one becomes more and more imprisoned in the realm of the thing in itself. Little that one experiences can be *understood*, because understanding involves a system of layering of meanings, one layer forming the context by which the other layers take on significance. For example, the past, the present, dreams, and transference experiences, each provides a context for the understanding of the others and is understandable only in terms of the others.

With limited capacity to distinguish symbol and symbolized, that which is perceived is unmediated by subjectivity (a sense of oneself as creator of meanings). The upshot is that perceptions carry with them an impersonal imperative for action and must be gotten rid of, clung to, concealed, hidden from, put into someone else, worshipped, shattered, etc. What the person cannot do is understand. This is so, not because the person does not wish to understand his experience; rather it is so because as one approaches the realm of the thing in itself, everything is what it is, so that the potential for understanding simply does not exist.

A borderline patient *knew* that the therapist, who had begun the hour three minutes late, did so because he preferred the patient whose hour preceded this patient's. The patient told the therapist that she had decided to terminate therapy, something she had been thinking about doing for a long time but had not previously told the therapist. Attempts on the part of the therapist to understand why the patient interpreted the lateness in this particular way were met with exasperation. The patient accused the therapist of relying on textbook interpretations to deny the obvious.

For this patient, feelings are facts to be acted upon and not emotional responses to be understood. There is no space between symbolized (the therapist's lateness) and the symbol (the patient's emotionally colored representation of the therapist). The two (the interpretation and the external event) are treated as one. A patient recently told me, "You can't tell me I don't see what I see." With the collapse of the distinction between symbol and symbolized, there is no room in which to "entertain" ideas and feelings. Transference takes on a deadly serious quality; illusion becomes delusion; thoughts become plans; feelings become impending actions; transference projections become projective identifications; play becomes compulsion.

Understanding the meaning of one's experience is possible only when one thing can stand for another without being the other; this is what constitutes the attainment of the capacity for symbol formation proper (Segal 1957). The development of the capacity for symbol formation proper frees one from the prison of the realm of the thing in itself.[3]

Reality as Defense against Fantasy

A second form of pathological distortion of the psychological dialectical process is that in which "the reality pole" of the dialectical process is used predominantly as a

---

3. Lacan (1949–1960) has pointed out that the individual, having attained the capacity for symbolization, becomes freed of one form of imprisonment (that of unmediated sensory experience) only to enter a new prison, that of the symbolic order. In the realm of the symbolic order, language provides us with symbols that long preexisted us and in that way determines our thoughts, even though we labor under the illusion that we create our own symbols.

defense against fantasy. Whenever the potential for a psychological dialectical process is limited for defensive purposes (i.e., to exclude, modify, or diminish the significance of a given group of possible thoughts), a price is paid. In this case, the price is the foreclosure of imagination.

When a relatively unrestricted psychological dialectical process has been established, a little girl playing house is both a little girl and a mother, and the question of which she is, never arises. Being a little girl who feels loved by her mother (*in reality*) makes it safe for her to borrow what is her mother's (*in fantasy*) without fear of retaliation or fear of losing herself in her mother, and, as a result, disappearing as a separate person. Being a mother (*in fantasy*) gives the little girl access to and use of all the richness of the cultural, familial, and personal symbols (e.g., in relation to what it means to be a female, a mother, and a daughter) that have been consciously and unconsciously conveyed in the course of *real* experience with her mother, father, and others.

On the other hand, if the little girl is *only* a little girl, she is unable to play; she is unable to imagine and will be unable to feel she is alive in any full sense. Such a situation arises when reality must be used as a defense against fantasy.[4]

A boy who had been allowed to witness his parents having intercourse, as well as the very painful delivery of his younger brother, had developed by the age of 6 a precocious intelligence and a "grown-up" mode of relating that was marked by a profound skepticism. He was interested in finding "logical" explanations for "amazing" things, in particular, television stunts. When as a 7 year old he was taken to a marionette show, his parents became concerned because the boy found nothing pleasurable about the show and instead was preoccupied by his awareness of the fact that the characters were only wooden, carved figures dangling on strings that were manipulated by people behind the screen. Of course, his perception was "accurate," but the powerful awareness of this reality prevented the dialectical interplay of fantasy and reality that generates the possibility for imagination. For this child, the danger of wishes and fears "coming true" in a destructive and terribly frightening way had in all likelihood been made too real by his interpretation of what he had witnessed ("behind the scenes") earlier in his life. Such dramatic early experiences are neither a necessary nor a sufficient condition for fantasies to be experienced as frightening things that need to be controlled through an exaggerated appeal to reality.

---

4. If the little girl is *only* a mother, she is psychotic and will in time become terrified by her fantasied possession of adult sexuality and adult (omnipotent) power over life and death. Here, the reality pole of the dialectic has collapsed into the fantasy pole of the dialectic as discussed earlier.

Patients chronically experiencing this form of collapse of the dialectical process present few if any dreams, dismissing the ones they do present as "senseless," "crazy," "stupid," "weird," and the like. When dreams are presented by these patients, the dreams are often barely distinguishable from their conscious thoughts, e.g., the dreams may depict embarrassing situations that the patient regularly thinks about consciously. Associations to the dreams are often a cataloging of which parts of the dream did or did not "really" occur and precisely what the real situation was that is alluded to or depicted in the dream.

Some of these patients are keen observers and will notice when a single book has been moved in a large bookshelf in the therapist's office. When the patient is asked about his response to a detail that has been noticed, the patient will be extremely skeptical about what benefit could possibly accrue from a discussion of such a trivial thing. I have been told at such moments that looking for some personal significance in the observed detail would be "like trying to get blood from a stone." The fixity of the patient's focus on reality is in fact designed to "drain the blood out" of fantasy. The dialectical resonance of realistic and fantastic meanings is foreclosed, leaving the patient incapable of imagination.

Dissociation of Reality and Fantasy

Fetishes and perversions can be understood as representing a particular form of limitation of the dialectical process in which the reality and fantasy poles become dissociated from one another. Freud (1927) pointed out that fetishes involve a "splitting of the ego" in such a way that the subject both knows and does not know that women do not have penises. This psychological state does not constitute a true psychological dialectic, because it has been constructed largely in the service of denial and as a result involves a severe limitation of the way in which one pole of the dialectic is allowed to inform and be informed by the other. A dialectical process becomes limited when one imposes restrictions upon it: all possible combinations of meanings are possible except those leading to the thought that women do not have penises. That thought, or any derivative of it, must never be thought. To the extent that there is such a limitation placed on a dialectical process, reality and fantasy no longer inform one another and instead stand isolated in a state of static coexistence. A dialectical relationship allows for resonance of meanings, for example, conscious and unconscious meanings. Splitting of the type involved in perversions and fetishism can be understood as involving not only denial, but also the foreclosure of dialectical resonance that might generate meanings that one feels are dangerous.

Foreclosure of Reality and Fantasy

The final form of failure to achieve the capacity to create and maintain a psychological dialectical process that will be addressed is more extreme than those discussed thus far. The forms of dysfunction described previously have all involved a limitation of (metaphorically, a "collapse" of) a dialectic that had to a significant degree been established and was secondarily becoming limited. What will be discussed now is a primary failure to generate a psychological dialectical process manifesting itself as a "state of nonexperience" (Ogden 1980). In a state of nonexperience there is perception, but perception remains raw sensory data that is not attributed meaning. Meanings are not denied, they simply are not created. This state has been described variously as a "foreclosure" of the psychological (McDougall 1974), as an "absence" analogous to that seen in a petit mal seizure (Meltzer 1975), as "blank psychosis" (Green 1975), psychotic "not-being" (Grotstein 1979), and as "death in life" (Laing 1959). In the context of intensive psychotherapeutic work with chronic schizophrenic patients, I have described the state of nonexperience as a state in which.

> . . . all experience is emotionally equivalent, one thing is just as good or just as bad as anything else; all things, people, places and behavior are emotionally interchangeable. . . . Everything can be substituted for everything else, creating a situation analogous to a numerical system in which there are an infinite number of integers but all are equal to one another in value. Addition, subtraction and all other operations would be formally possible, but there would be no point in any of them, since you would always arrive at the same value with which you had begun. [Ogden 1980, p. 520]

As I have discussed elsewhere (Ogden 1980, 1982a, 1982b), I view the state of nonexperience as a superordinate defense resorted to when all other defensive operations have proved insufficient to protect the infant against sustained, overwhelming psychological pain. Under such circumstances the infant ceases to attribute meaning to his perception, thus failing to generate emotional significance (personal meaning) of any type. In the context of the present discussion, this amounts to the foreclosure of the possibility of generating both realistic and fantastic meanings, thus denying the infant the elements from which he might construct a dialectical process involving fantasy and reality.

THE SYMBOL, THE SYMBOLIZED, AND SUBJECTIVITY

As has been discussed, the establishment of the psychological dialectical process creates conditions wherein experience is attributed meanings that can be understood as opposed to simply constituting a pattern of facts to be acted upon. The establishment of the distinction between the symbol and the symbolized is inseparable from the establishment of subjectivity: the two achievements are two facets of the same developmental event. Paraphrasing Winnicott, one could say that potential space lies between the symbol and the symbolized. To distinguish symbol from symbolized is to distinguish one's thought from that which one is thinking about, one's feeling from that which one is responding to. For symbol to stand independently of symbolized, there must be a subject engaged in the process of interpreting perceptions. One might ask what is new in this supposed developmental advance, because logically there has always been a person interpreting his experience. That is, of course, so from an outside observer's point of view, but it has not been so from the subject's point of view. In fact, a subject did not exist when symbol and symbolized were undifferentiable.

The achievement of the capacity to distinguish symbol and symbolized is the achievement of subjectivity.[5] From this point on, symbolic function always involves the threeness of the interrelationship of three distinct entities: (1) the symbol (the thought); (2) the symbolized (that which is being thought about); and (3) the thinker (the interpreting self), who is creating his thoughts and who stands apart from both the thought and the thing being thought about. Potential space ceases to exist as any two of these three elements become dedifferentiated: the thinker and the symbol, the symbol and the symbolized, or the thinker and the object of thought (the symbolized).

There are important implications in the foregoing discussion for a theory of the development of the capacity for symbolization. The period prior to the establishment of the dialectical process (prior to the period of the transitional phenomenon) is characterized not by internal objects as things in themselves, as Melanie Klein (1946) would have it, but, rather, by an absence of the need for symbols at all. In the period of the "invisible" mother–infant unit there is neither a mother nor an infant since the environmental mother exists only as the invisible fulfillment of the infant's needs before they become desires.

As discussed earlier, Winnicott's conception of development can be thought of as a movement from an original state of "oneness" that is not experienced as oneness because the homogeneity of the situation precludes an appreciation of difference and, therefore, the delineation of meanings. The developmental progression, in the context of good-enough mothering, is to "threeness," wherein there is a relationship between symbol and symbolized that is mediated by an interpreting subject. The invisible mother–infant has become a mother-and-infant as (symbolic) objects, and infant as interpreting subject. The infant as subject makes it possible for the infant to become aware of the mother's subjectivity. This then allows for the development of "ruth" (Winnicott 1958b), the capacity for concern for another

---

5. This parallels the Kleinian conception of the creation of psychic reality in the depressive position (Klein 1958).

person as a whole and separate human being capable of feeling *like*, not the same as, one's own. With the development of this awareness of the subjectivity of the other comes the capacity for guilt, for mourning, for empathy, and for the desire to make reparations as opposed to magical restoration of the damaged object.

From this perspective, the breakdown of the dialectical process generating the realm of the thing in itself can be understood to have a specific place in the development of object relations: twoness (infant and mother as objects in the absence of infant as interpreting subject) corresponds to the realm of the thing in itself. There are only objects and no subjects. This is always a product of the breakdown of threeness (the dialectic of fantasy and reality, symbol and symbolized mediated by a subject) and not the normative progression from the invisible oneness of the original mother–infant unit.

Winnicott thus implies that he views the normal development of fantasy as being from its inception part of a dialectical process in which fantasy creates and is created by reality. Such a conclusion runs counter to Melanie Klein's (1946, 1952) notion of the place in normal development of the paranoid–schizoid position prior to the depressive position. In the paranoid–schizoid position, fantasy, symbolic equation, and part–object relatedness predominate. For Klein the depressive position (threeness consisting of subject, symbol and symbolized) develops out of the twoness of the paranoid–schizoid position (symbol and symbolized in the absence of a subject capable of awareness of psychic reality.) For Winnicott, the form of fantasy that Klein associates with the paranoid–schizoid position (a form of fantasy using symbolic equation as the mode of symbolization) always represents a breakdown of threeness. There are inevitable breakdowns in the development of threeness because of inevitable and necessary failures in the mother–infant relationship. This leads the infant to defend himself psychologically in a paranoid–schizoid mode. Pathological development ensues only when the failures in the mother–infant relationship (leading to the breakdown of threeness) are extreme or chronic.

REFERENCES

Brazelton, T. B., and Als, H. (1979). Four early stages in the development of the mother–infant interaction. *Psychoanalytic Study of the Child* 34:349–369. New Haven, CT: Yale University Press.

Freud, S. (1915). The unconscious. *Standard Edition* 14:159–215.

———— (1927). Fetishism. *Standard Edition* 21:147–157.

Green, A. (1975). The analyst, symbolization, and absence in the analytic setting. (On changes in analytic practice and analytic experience.) *International Journal of Psycho-Analysis* 56:1–22.

Grotstein, J. (1978). Inner space: its dimensions and its coordinates. *International Journal of Psycho-Analysis* 59:55–61.

———— (1979). Who is the dreamer who dreams the dream and who is the dreamer who understands it. *Contemporary Psychoanalysis* 15:110–169.

———— (1981). *Splitting and Projective Identification*. New York: Jason Aronson.

Hegel, G. W. F. (1807). *Phenomenology of Spirit*. Trans. A. V. Miller. London: Oxford University Press, 1977.

Khan, M. M. R. (1963). The concept of cumulative trauma. *Psychoanalytic Study of the Child* 18:286–306. New York: International Universities Press.

Klein, M. (1946). Notes on some schizoid mechanisms. In *Envy and Gratitude and Other Works, 1946–1963*, pp. 1–24. New York: Delacorte, 1975.

———— (1952). Some theoretical conclusions regarding the emotional life of the infant. In *Envy and Gratitude and Other Works, 1946-1963*, pp. 61–93. New York: Delacorte, 1975.

———— (1958). On the development of mental functioning. In *Envy and Gratitude and Other Works, 1946–1963*. pp. 236–246. New York: Delacorte, 1975.

Lacan, J. (1949–1960). *Ecrits*. Trans. A. Sheridan. New York: W. W. Norton, 1977.

Laings, R. D. (1959). *The Divided Self*. Baltimore: Pelican, 1965.

Little, M. (1958). On delusional transference (transference psychosis). *International Journal of Psycho-Analysis* 39:134–138.

McDougall, J. (1974). The psychosoma and the psycho-analytic process. *International Review of Psycho-Analysis* 1:437–459.

Meltzer, D. (1975). The psychology of autistic states and of post-autistic mentality. In *Explorations in Autism*, ed. D. Meltzer, J. Bremner, S. Hoxter, et al. pp. 6–29. London: Clunie.

Ogden, T. (1978). A developmental view of identifications resulting from maternal impingements. *International Journal of Psychoanalytic Psychotherapy* 7:486–507.

———— (1980). On the nature of schizophrenic conflict. *International Journal of Psycho-Analysis* 61:513–533.

———— (1982a). *Projective Identification and Psychotherapeutic Technique*. New York: Jason Aronson.

———— (1982b). Treatment of the schizophrenic state of nonexperience. In *Technical Factors in the Treatment of the Severely Disturbed Patient*, ed. L. B. Boyer and P. L. Giovacchini, pp. 217–260. New York: Jason Aronson.

Sander, L. (1964). Adaptive relations in early mother–child interactions. *Journal of the Academy of Child Psychiatry* 3:231–264.

Searles, H. (1963). Transference psychosis in the psychotherapy of chronic schizophrenia. In *Collected Papers on Schizophrenia and Related Subjects*, pp. 654–716. New York: International Universities Press.

Segal, H. (1957). Notes on symbol formation. *International Journal of Psycho-Analysis* 38:391–397.

Stern, D. (1977). *The First Relationship: Infant and Mother*. Cambridge, MA: Harvard University Press.

Winnicott, D. W. (1948). Paediatrics and psychiatry. In *Collected Papers: Through Paediatrics to Psycho-Analysis*, pp. 157–173. New York: Basic Books, 1975.

_____ (1951). Transitional objects and transitional phenomena. In *Playing and Reality*, pp. 1–25. New York: Basic Books, 1971.

_____ (1952). Psychoses and child care. In *Collected Papers: Through Paediatrics to Psycho-Analysis*, pp. 219–228. New York: Basic Books, 1975.

_____ (1956). Primary maternal preoccupation. In *Collected Papers: Through Paediatrics to Psycho-Analysis*, pp. 300–305. New York: Basic Books, 1975.

_____ (1958a). Psycho-analysis and the sense of guilt. In *The Maturational Processes and the Facilitating Environment*, pp. 15–28. New York: International Universities Press, 1965.

_____ (1958b). The capacity to be alone. In *The Maturational Processes and the Facilitating Environment*, pp. 29–36. New York: International Universities Press, 1965.

_____ (1960). Ego distortion in terms of true and false self. In *The Maturational Processes and the Facilitating Environment*, pp. 140–152. New York: International Universities Press, 1965.

_____ (1967a). The location of cultural experience. In *Playing and Reality*, pp. 95–103. New York: Basic Books, 1971.

_____ (1967b). Mirror role of mother and family in child development. In *Playing and Reality*, pp. 111–118. New York: Basic Books, 1971.

_____ (1968). The use of an object and relating through cross identifications. In *Playing and Reality*, pp. 86–94. New York: Basic Books, 1971.

_____ (1971a). Dreaming, fantasying, and living. In *Playing and Reality*, pp. 26–37. New York: Basic Books.

_____ (1971b). Playing: a theoretical statement. In *Playing and Reality*, pp. 38–52. New York: Basic Books.

_____ (1971c). Playing: creative activity and the search for the self. In *Playing and Reality*, pp. 53–64. New York: Basic Books.

_____ (1971d). *Playing and Reality*. New York: Basic Books.

_____ (1971e). The place where we live. In *Playing and Reality*, pp. 104–110. New York: Basic Books.

26

PHILIP GIOVACCHINI: ABSOLUTE AND NOT QUITE ABSOLUTE DEPENDENCE

INTRODUCTION

At the onset of analysis, patients frequently ask what treatment will do to help them. When such questions are asked they may be understood as curiosity about an unfamiliar procedure. They may, however, imply something entirely different. The analyst is viewed as acting upon the patient, doing something to him or for him. This seemingly makes the therapist responsible for the patient's progress and, perhaps, the patient's sense of well-being.

My understanding of, and reaction to, this type of question has varied. When asked: "What will you do for me to make me better?" I often think of resistance. The patient is making me responsible for the success of his treatment and thereby denying, or at least deemphasizing, his own internal processes and responsibility. The question may be a defense, designed to keep internal processes unconscious.

It may be more useful at times to view these questions as statements of the patient's helplessness. He is saying, in effect, "I see myself as helpless to effect any change in my life or to participate in the analytic process, so I will make *you* responsible for my well-being and for a satisfactory treatment outcome." The adaptational attempt is evident. The patient may feel incapable of controlling or, at least, influencing his destiny, so he enlists the therapist as his mentor to help him—

or in the extreme, to do for him what he feels he cannot do for himself. We may, through analysis, trace the genetic roots of such feelings to early relationships with the parents, and work with the subsequent reenactments. The "helplessness" of early childhood is re-created. The omissions and errors of the parent-infant relationship persist in the patient's character.

I believe that with a certain group of patients, helplessness is central to their pathology, and they may demand that the therapist accept the helplessness as reality, insisting that the therapist "take over" the patient's decision-making processes and "run" the patient's life. In *Treatment of Primitive Mental States* (1979), Peter Giovacchini discusses in detail the analysis of a "helpless patient," and emphasizes the helplessness as an attempt at adaptation. His patient is "trying to establish herself as a person who could receive good things from the outside world" (p. 193) as well as use her helpless disorganization to prevent the release of "powerful destructive forces that terrified her because she did not have the psychic strength and organization required to control them" (p. 194).

Giovacchini understood the patient's need to be heard and to express her helplessness without being challenged, and he recognized that this helplessness was not simply a defense or resistance, but the result of a persistent ego defect. Insomuch as he was able to provide a setting in which her helplessness could be freely expressed and acknowledged, he provided a setting in which she could incorporate positive and creative elements of the therapeutic relationship, integrate adaptive experiences, and achieve sufficient psychic structure to be able to function.

There is another group of patients who are similar to the patient discussed, but different in some important respects. They have learned to deal with their helplessness by insisting that people who are emotionally significant to them behave with rigid consistency so that their environment is perfectly predictable. Otherwise these patients are helpless to deal with their surroundings and thus may panic and experience themselves as being overwhelmed by disintegrating regression.

Winnicott writes of a "holding environment" in which a "continuity of being" develops in the child. "The alternative to being is reacting, and reacting interrupts being and annihilates" (1960a, p. 47). The holding environment's main function is to significantly reduce traumatic impingements. Otherwise the child will experience annihilation of personal being, a terror that Winnicott calls "unthinkable anxiety." Under favorable conditions the child establishes a continuity of existence and then begins to develop sufficient psychic integration, which makes it possible for impingements to be gathered into the area of omnipotence.

Winnicott further states, "In healthy development, the infant retains the capacity for re-experiencing unintegrated states, but this depends on the continuation of reliable maternal care or on the build-up in the infant of memories of maternal care" (p. 47). Failure of maternal care leads to terror in this group of patients, and any variance from a rigidly consistent environment produces panic. They are not equipped to deal with anything new or novel (Moraitis 1988), and what little mastery they have has been achieved with tremendous pain.

Such a patient's fear of lack of consistency also makes its way into the therapeutic frame. The therapist cannot make the same mistakes as the mother, and thus must be totally consistent. Any variation in the therapist is felt as an attack, and the patient is overwhelmed with nihilistic anxiety. (Indeed, with this type of patient there is a history of a hostile and traumatic infantile environment. The mother has not only failed to provide protection but represents an attacking, destructive force.)

This places the therapist in a precarious position. He cannot deal directly with the patient's often conscious assertions of helplessness, and yet he cannot abandon his patient to terror. Furthermore, he is incapable of becoming the rigid character that the patient demands, and that he believes he needs. This may cause a "split" in the therapist. He is forced to temporarily accept the patient's helplessness and rigidity, whereas he must, at the same time, maintain a foothold in his own reality. It is the patient's ability to tolerate this split that enables treatment to proceed, and the analytic process itself is deeply involved with the resolution of this split.

The therapist must maintain his own reality; he cannot conform to the patient's demand of absolute consistency. to the therapist, this demand could mean rigidity beyond his capacity. Whatever attempts he makes to meet the patient's demands will be viewed as grossly inadequate. In some instances the patient experiences the analyst as totally failing, at best, or as viciously attacking, at worst.

From the patient's perspective, what he requires of the therapist is reasonable. He experiences the world as volatile and dangerous. He knows that only certain very constricted behavioral patterns can be safe. He needs an omnipresent, omnipotently benign and protective nurturer and comforter, a perfect therapist, because he feels so depleted and vulnerable. This places the therapist at odds with himself because he does not want to fail the patient, or hurt and terrify him. He may understand what the patient needs and part of him might want to provide it, but he realizes that this is not realistic. Again, we see a split in the therapist's viewpoint. At some level, he would like to have the power to help the patient by giving him what he wants. The therapist's narcissism is involved.

But the therapist never really caters to the patient's needs. A collusion exists when the two are convinced that the therapist really has taken over the role of the mother in the primitive setting. He must be prepared to delve into and be consumed by madness, as Winnicott (1952) would state, yet maintain his own sanity. He understands both his and the patient's frame of reference at the same time. This stands in contrast to some other authors, such as Searles (1975), who have talked of the need to "restore the capacity for understanding" after having merged with the patient (Flarsheim 1975). My point is that the merger must occur, but that while the therapist feels disrupted he must nonetheless simultaneously maintain his own objectivity throughout the process.

THE THERAPEUTIC INTERACTION

The patient was a 35-year-old woman who had been in treatment all her adult life, had seen many psychotherapists, and usually had left each therapist after numerous stormy encounters. She presented herself as helpless and completely unable to deal with the world. She lived in a small apartment with her mother, a retired clerk in her seventies, with whom she had lived most of her life. Her father had left before she was born. The mother had no feelings toward him and viewed his departure with indifference.

The patient depicted her mother as having been financially and emotionally inadequate to care for her. She was described as a bitter, spiteful woman who blamed the world, including her daughter, for her misfortunes and misery. The mother saw the child as an intrusion into her world, a thorn to be rid of. She sent her, from the ages of 2 to 4, to live with her maternal grandmother, who, at least, made an attempt to raise her.

But the grandmother also treated the child sadistically. She would publicly embarrass her, stopping people on the street and telling them, in a maniacal manner, how naughty her granddaughter was when she soiled herself. She frequently locked the child in the house and left her unattended for hours; the child would look out the window and see her peers playing, and wonder what it was like to play or have toys. She was lonely and helpless, totally alienated from the outside world and unequipped to deal with it, or even to conceptualize "playing." At the same time she was terrified of the grandmother (who "did this for my own good," the patient stated sarcastically), and would withdraw from her whenever possible.

When she returned to her mother she was consumed with rage, not only in response to the mother's and grandmother's hatred but also at the mother's inadequacy as a mother. Years later, she realized that her mother had totally failed to prepare her for the world.

Twenty-five years later, this rage emerged during our first session when she became furious with me because of the way I took her history. If I did not take her history precisely as did her previous therapists, I was not only stupid and ignorant but also too uncaring about her to "do it properly." I realized that I was in an untenable position. Her complaints completely ignored the variability of history-taking techniques and my own needs and reasons for using my particular style. There was a "right" way for a history to be taken and I was not using it. "How should I take your history?" I asked. "You're the doctor, you're supposed to know," was her response. She also denounced my approach to treatment. In later sessions, it made matters worse if I told her that her feelings toward me were exactly the same as those she had reported having toward her mother. She remarked, "I don't want you to analyze me. I want your help."

Nevertheless, she insisted on a rigid schedule of frequent sessions. This was somewhat surprising to me, but I agreed. I felt that her need to make me useless was part of the therapeutic process and that I should not interfere with her protestations. She needed me to be wrong, no matter what I did.

Early in her treatment, the patient told me of seriously debilitating symptoms. Unless accompanied by her mother, she could not venture from her apartment. Should she attempt to do so, she would be overcome by panic. She would freeze, unable to move for brief periods of time. When she regained enough composure, she would run for shelter in doorways and under awnings. She also experienced a numbing paralysis of her limbs, feeling as if they not only could not move, but had ceased to exist. These symptoms persisted, fluctuating in intensity until she either returned home or was rescued by her mother.

I do not think this is agoraphobia in the classical sense. Defense against libidinal drives seems to have played a less important role in the clinical picture than it usually does in cases of agoraphobia. Sexual thoughts in this patient's associations were infrequent and, when expressed, bizarre in content. I was more impressed with the struggle to maintain ego integration rather than the construction of a phobic defense. Her symptoms recurred periodically, usually precipitated by concern over her mother's health. There were also periods, sometimes of several months' duration, during which she held jobs, socialized to some degree, and appeared somewhat independent.

Soon the patient began comparing me to a previous therapist who, in her mind, could do no wrong. She believed that he completely understood her and was absolutely empathic; he had never failed her, his advice was always correct, and she was in love with him. The only reason she was not seeing him was that he had suffered a "nervous breakdown" and would no longer see her. She idealized him, and I was left with her rage. She felt safe in attacking me inasmuch as it did not matter what happened between us; she had the hope that she could return to him.

Simply put, I had to "help" this patient. I later learned that what this meant to her was that I had to completely take over all nurturing and supportive functioning. I was to omnipotently satisfy all her needs, protect her, and generally make the world a place in which she could exist. I was to be absolutely consistent. I was never to be late, never to take a vacation; I was to be available to her at all hours of the day and night, be absolutely accurate in my interpretations, and have total recall of her background and history. I was, of course, destined to fail and to totally misunderstand her. She already had her magical mother in her former therapist. But despite this seeming impasse, the treatment was proceeding and, indeed, seemed vital to her.

The paradox was that I could not really agree nor disagree with her. Her demands were disruptive and provocative but, in view of her traumatic background, they were understandable. I would lose her as a patient if I did not, in some way, respond. Her previous treatment relationships had included several incidents in which therapists reacted negatively to her demands and she then either left them or provoked them to reject her as a patient. The progression of the present treatment depended on her having the ability to see her demands as "not quite" absolute. This appeared to be the case, for while she demanded all along that I agree with her, something within her permitted her to not be so adamant as to actually destroy the treatment relationship. This, I believe, was our ability to see her demands on me as being "not quite" as absolute as she would assert.

I am not referring to the development of an "observing ego" (Sterba 1934). I do not believe she had any particular wish to understand herself. She was not in analysis to gain any particular insight into intrapsychic dynamics. All this was useless to her. She truly felt my silence and my inability to respond to her demands as an affront, a denial of the seriousness of her plight. The interaction was too primitive to encompass a higher order of understanding. I was there simply to nurture and support her. That I could not or would not do so meant that I hated her and was no better than her mother or grandmother. It also meant that she could not use me to help her deal with the world, and insofar as she had to deal with it alone, she was terrified.

Winnicott (1963) writes of "absolute dependency." He refers to the ability of parents to provide an environment in which their infant can mature, and in which the parents themselves must adapt to the "infant's maturational processes." He refers to a "special state" in which, toward the end of pregnancy and lasting several months afterward, the "mother is preoccupied with the care of the baby . . . , is identified with the baby and knows quite well what the baby is feeling like . . . , for this she uses her own experiences as a baby" and is herself dependent and vulnerable. He refers to the mother's state as "primary maternal preoccupation" (1956) and the baby's as "absolute dependency" (1963). It is here that the "holding environment" is more profound, allowing the infant to proceed with "going-on-being." The patient in the case under discussion seemed fixated at this point, expecting me to produce the "magic" that could only come from the earlier infantile state.

From a different viewpoint, I felt the patient was correct. Her history was such that it seemed appropriate to demand that someone "take care of her." I could see a certain logic to her feeling that she had a right to have had a reasonable mother, and, not having had one, her sense of being unequipped to deal with the adult world. I could also understand the rationale of her need to make me a failure. She needed to express her anger at the "spiteful" mother now, since she would have been destroyed as a child had she attempted to do so then. She was seeking the revenge she could not have exacted from her hostile and ineffective mother. I think her devaluation of me was also important. A useless, impotent mother was a less impinging, less dangerous one. I was to feel as helpless in dealing with her as she felt in dealing with the world.

It was paradoxical that while I was exactly what she had created and needed, her reproduction of the maternal figure was so exact that I appeared to be truly useless and evil to her. I believe the patient viewed herself as so completely damaged by her mother that no reasonable intervention would suffice. Interventions had to be magically perfect, I believe, to counteract the extreme damage she had suffered. The patient used the former therapist as a vehicle to tell me what she thought she needed, but she made it quite obvious that her demands were inherently impossible. Even the therapist held up to me as her example of perfection was also depicted as a tragic failure.

Over a period of about three years there was a gradual lessening of the intensity of her feelings. Early in the treatment she would sit in the corner of my office with a "boom box" blasting me out of the scene. She would revile me for not being able to tell her how to make friends, find work, and resolve conflicts with her mother. Eventually, however, the overall mood of our interaction lightened. Now, "What will you bring back for me?" was asked in an only half-joking manner when I went away on vacation. "What will you give me for my birthday?" was another question. Should I have attempted to act on these requests, the presents would undoubtedly have been perceived as wrong or inadequate, or otherwise devalued. Demands that I run her life became demands that I give her presents. I began to feel, at times, that the patient was playing with me.

Over this three-year period, I was also aware that my feelings toward the patient were changing. I had moved from a position of bewilderment to one of frustrated anger, and then to acceptance and curiosity. This was by no means a linear and progressive movement. My feelings could change from session to session, but in general they moved in a progressive sequence. My bewilderment, starting with the first session, I think is understandable. I had never been attacked in such a manner so suddenly or spontaneously. I was somewhat frightened as well, in that I was not convinced of her ability to maintain control. Nevertheless, there was something in her manner that reassured me. I cannot be specific; perhaps she detected my uneasiness, maybe there was something in her infrequent smile, but somehow I felt sufficiently reassured to have decided to continue treating her.

It was just a matter of months before I found myself getting angry at her. All my efforts seemed to have been of no use to her—even seemed vile and destructive, despite my best intentions. I began to see her as an intrusion in my life. I began to dread her appointments and felt irritated by her phone calls. I became aware that she was allowing me to experience her mother's hatred toward her, and that she seemed to know how far to push. As treatment progressed, I eventually felt a gradual lessening of my frustration as the devalued mother.

I was aware of two decidedly different sets of feelings toward her. I wanted to help her and I understood the source of her panic; yet I was frustrated and angered at the devaluation of my attempts to do so. I too had to "play" in a transitional zone in which neither her reality nor mine was overtly rigid. She, furthermore, had to permit me to do so.

It is important to understand what I mean by "play." I am referring here to a part of the analytic process in which the patient begins to question and then modify her ideas about the world. As previously stated, these ideas are at first rigid, and the analyst's role, in the patient's mind, is equally rigidly defined. This rigidity is designed to protect the patient from the hostile, intrusive mother. The analytic environment, a holding environment, provides a safe setting in which the patient may begin (unconsciously) to question the need for such a rigid protective device.

At first, in the patient's mind, the analyst has an equally rigid view of the world. The patient does not see herself as having a place in the analyst's world, much as she did not have a place in her mother's. The patient believes that the analyst does not want her in his world, and that the analyst is self-serving and uninterested in her needs.

However, the patient must have some capacity to feel safe within this setting. The patient must relax enough to begin to "let her guard down" so that she may question and become curious about the analyst. Her rigid demands of him, and her expectations that he be rigid, must give way to curiosity concerning him and his actual views. She must give up her rigid demands of him, at least to the extent that she may begin to perceive him as having some characteristics different from the ones she has assigned to him. It is the "holding environment" of the treatment setting that permits this. The patient's developing curiosity about the analyst calls the patient's own views into question. The analyst becomes something novel (Moraitis 1988), and this fact opens the door to interpretation by the analyst. The patient may accept, reject, or in some way mold the interpretation to suit her needs, but she is able to establish some sense of control over the interpretation, the analyst, and her own environment. She is now dealing with the world rather than shielding herself from it. With the increasing sense of control, she feels safe to incorporate the interpretation, in that it too is now safe. She thus acquires new psychic structure that she uses to further modify her own ideas about the world. The resulting sense of control provides her with a joyous relief that sharply contrasts with her previous terror of the environment; and the patient using the continuing interpretations, then manipulates, modifies, and changes her formerly rigid ideas. I refer to this as "play" in that she can allow her fantasies to mingle with reality. She can make up stories; she can twist, mold, and manipulate ideas much as transitional objects, and doing so is safe. She exerts some feeling of control over the previously uncontrollable. More importantly, she creates what she needs, rather than subjecting herself to another's intrusiveness.

The analyst, in term, also "plays" in that he experiences pleasure in the patient's growing sense of mastery over her views and feelings. The analyst's comments and interpretations change in accordance with the patient's progress and developing psychic structure. The analyst, being less rigid than the patient expects and demands, changes his view of her with the deepening of his understanding and with the patient's "molding" of his interpretations. This, I think, gives the analyst pleasure and also a feeling of some mastery over the interaction.

It is the ability to modify, experiment with, and manipulate (in a controlled fashion) one's previously rigid beliefs about the world that gives pleasure and is hence tantamount to "play." Thus, once this patient felt she could play with me, I was less threatening and more under her control. In the same way that playing is "not quite" reality, her ideas about me were "not quite" true. Her developing ability to use me as a transitional object with which she could play—one she could control, accept, and reject—heralded the development of a transitional zone between my reality and her rigid demands. That this zone was able to develop at all is surprising, as it is similar to the transitional phenomenon of normal development, with some important differences. I could not state precisely how and when this transitional zone developed. Retrospectively, I think it was able to develop because the "holding environment" of the therapy was indeed different from the chaotic intrusion and pervasive solitude of the patient's infantile home.

As treatment progressed, her rigid demand that I agree with her ideas seemed to abate. My responses felt more relaxed and less as if I were fighting off an intrusion. I believe I was able to remain calm, in part, because she did not intrude to the degree that I felt totally disrupted. As I relaxed, I did not fully reproduce the infantile environment.

The playing aspect of treatment first began when she tested me to ascertain how much intrusion I could tolerate. (Retrospectively, I believe she was testing me even during the first session.) She was indeed able to be disruptive in a contained way. She would, for example, bring knives into the consultation room, threatening to "accidentally" cut my furniture, creating an agitation in me that I had to first recognize and then recover from. At this time we had been merged. She was allowing me to experience her disruption, which I had to resolve within myself before I could help her, as her mother could not. As I learned this and survived it, I became less a threat and more a plaything, as a transitional object would become. This occurred because she was able to tolerate the idea that demands did not have to be absolute, that an area of compromise could exist between her needs and my reality. She could allow me my reality despite the intensity of her feelings and their link to her survival.

The patient was apparently attempting to establish a feeling of mastery over her nihilistic anxiety, fearing that she would be obliterated if she had to deal with any aspect of me that did not conform to her rigid control. I was unable to accept such total control. The patient had to give up her attempt to rigidly control her world. She needed a new perspective on her environment, but she risked annihilation if she relinquished her defenses. On the other hand, should she not relinquish her defenses she would destroy the treatment setting and therefore perpetuate her symptoms. As an alternative, she was infusing me with her agitation, letting me struggle with it much as the attentive mother has to make peace within herself before she can soothe her child.

I very much had to "play with" my fears and master them as I struggled to be an effective therapist. I had to understand my anxieties concerning the possibility of failing her, and concerning her insistence that I was responsible for her fate. I questioned myself as to what it would mean if she left, and why it would threaten me. Would it really make me a bad therapist? Had I truly hurt her? With such questions, I was able to regain my objectivity and analytic posture. My ability to relax allowed the "holding environment" to be established and I was able to view her demands as "not quite" so rigid or so disturbed. I could now question their purpose and seek deeper understanding of them. (It was, thus, equally important for *me* to feel the impact of the holding environment.) She became aware of my growing flexibility, which contrasted with her mother's rigidity, and was able to relax and feel safer. We had entered a relationship in which annihilation was not quite annihilation, absolute control was not quite absolute, and "play" could be established because deeper understanding had become my goal (though not necessarily hers). I was able to establish some flexibility by not taking her demands at face value.

I am referring to the transition away from a structure that is similar to a false self, one that functions more like a fixed shield rather than by compliance. The difference between the transitional phenomenon and the "not quite" zone that occurred in the foregoing analysis is that the former is an aspect of normal development, a phase in which the mother protects the child from the impinging environment, and the child, using the transitional zone, begins to master the environment. By contrast, the "not quite" zone serves an adaptive function in that it allows the construction of a shield to protect the vulnerable inner self.

The patient's ability to enter a therapeutic "transitional" zone or "not quite" zone in which she could progressively relinquish the stern, concrete, and absolute control implied by her initial rigid demands of me, replacing them with the products of our interaction – products that were modified and molded by the two of us – was essential to her therapeutic progress. I think this ability (which had to develop from within the confines of the treatment's "holding environment") to view her own demands as "not quite" as rigidly absolute as they were when entering treatment, paralleled the development of her view that my reality was "not quite" as rigid as she had originally perceived it to be. It was the creation of a not quite zone in between us that allowed her to tolerate the treatment setting. A not quite is gradually transformed into a transitional space.

To elaborate, the not quite zone is not something that merely occurs; it is a process that develops as the result of a specific interaction within the therapeutic frame, a process that has its own course and outcome. It begins with the establishment of a holding environment that the patient experiences as different and safe in a novel way. Once within the safe environment the patient can begin to play with the increasingly evident paradoxes of her rigid reality. The motivation to do this is clear. Once paradox is seen as paradox, a perspective must develop that enables the patient to appreciate a deeper understanding of herself and of her surrounding environment. The rigid reality dissolves and is replaced by the transitional phenomenon typical of normal development.

In normal development, a transitional zone develops between the ego and the environment. The child constructs reality at the outermost borders of this zone. With maturation, the zone decreases, bringing reality closer to the ego.

With my patient, this normal transitional zone had failed. A rigid, defensive reality was constructed to protect her from an assaultive mother. The rigidity had provided a protective barrier in which (to the patient's mind) the mother was trapped, neutralizing her and bringing her within the daughter's control. The attempt to trap me in this same rigid reality, however, not only neutralized and controlled me, but made me useless to her. A zone had to develop in which her relationship with me was "not quite" the relationship with her mother, and her dependence upon me "not quite" absolute. Through "play" in this zone, reality outside the zone could be reconstructed as relatively nonrigid. The less rigid her reality became, the more the not quite zone was transformed into a transitional zone.

I wish to repeat and emphasize that the not quite zone is initially a defensive adaptation that is constructed within the therapeutic setting. It is an aspect of a developmental achievement that begins as a pathological mode of relating but, under optimal conditions, reaches a developmental pathway that reproduces the course of ordinary emotional maturation.

At first the patient's ego boundaries represent an interface between the inner world of the psyche and an external rigid reality. Then, as treatment progresses, the patient constructs a "not quite" zone between the ego boundaries and external reality. This is similar to the transitional zone. As also occurs with the transitional zone, the patient perceives her ego boundaries as located on the periphery of the not quite zone. There is a significant difference, however, in that in ordinary development the transitional zone represents the means by which reality is constructed, whereas the not quite zone is formed within the context of a relatively well-perceived and constructed reality; the latter course is opposite to that of the formation of the transitional zone. The not quite zone *reconstructs* rather than constructs reality, and when this occurs, the not quite zone becomes converted into a transitional zone, a developmental achievement.

FURTHER THERAPEUTIC CONSIDERATIONS

Other patients have been unable to construct a "not quite" zone. A woman in her thirties sought treatment, not to be cured, but to be maintained. This was not obvious at first. Her motives emerged as the setting deteriorated. Again, the childhood setting had been tragic and damaging, but this patient had survived it by becoming religious, and she believed she was on a mission from Jesus. She would spend her sessions preaching to me about her "greatness" as she was trying to convert me. Despite her conviction of greatness, there were frequent episodes of panic during which I was called upon to rescue her from her environment. These episodes occurred when the environment successfully challenged her megalomania. Later, when I interpreted rather than rescued, I fell into disfavor.

The illogic of her thinking eventually became evident to her. If I were needed to rescue her, her greatness was challenged. Actual rescuing did not challenge her megalomanic belief as long as she could later deny she had been rescued. Only when I pointed out the fragility of her beliefs did her grandiose view of herself become no longer convincing to her. She tried to reestablish that view of herself by continuing to preach to me, and trying unsuccessfully, to convert me. Eventually she terminated treatment.

The treatment was not a total loss. While she was unable to fully enter a not quite zone she parted from me in a friendly manner, leaving me for another therapist who, I think, she will also try to convert. I believe she had originally sought treatment because she was aware of the failings of her delusional system and was asking for a reinforcement of her delusions. The terror created by her infantile environment, however, was too intense to allow her to enter into "playful" transference interactions. Therefore, I was preserved as a "good" therapist who perhaps could be returned to at a later date. I still hear from her occasionally.

This patient's need to adhere rigidly to her own reality had been insurmountable. I believe this is because the safety of the analytic setting could not overcome the catastrophic terror that had made her incapable of "playing" with her rigid views. In some cases, a crucial juncture is reached in which the patient must choose between entering a not quite zone and dismantling the treatment setting.

There are numerous focal points at which the treatment is usually challenged. The patient's rigidity is called into question and pitted against the motivation to recover. This conflict needs to be resolved repeatedly by further movement into the not quite zone.

The patient in the first of the foregoing case histories repeatedly reenacted the incident in which she brought a knife into my office and threatened to "accidentally" cut my furniture each time I left town, but the threat was made with decreasing intensity, frustration, and upheaval. The knife episode marked a crucial entrance into the "not quite" zone. This was the point in treatment at which she had to choose between becoming intolerably disruptive (and thus dismantling the treatment setting) or allowing me to resolve my agitation to the extent that I could help her with hers. The patient in the second case history never really entered this zone, insisting rather that I accept her reality and not just understand and tolerate it.

This distinction is important, not merely in that the second patient was (for me at least) untreatable, but also in that we are differentiating between a psychotic and a nonpsychotic transference. The second patient insisted that I accept and support her delusion. A nonjudgmental stance was not sufficient. I had to maintain doubt at least to the degree to which I could ponder the psychic origins of her belief system in order to work with her. With the first patient, on the other hand, the potential existed to develop a tolerance of a different viewpoint.

Winnicott writes about a continuum of the false self, "ranging from the healthy, polite aspect of the self to the truly split-off, compliant, false self that is mistaken for the whole person" (1960b, p. 150). He speaks of the false self evolving from a seduction into compliance with the "not good enough mother." Both of the patients I have discussed could not "comply" inasmuch as they perceived their mothers as so assaultively intrusive that repeated attacks from them had to be actively defended against by the construction of a rigidly predictable environment, which included the mother.

There is a similar continuum from being actively curious to being rigid and intolerant. At which point patients function along this continuum determines their treatability. Their ability to temporarily overcome their nihilistic anxiety and step into the not quite zone parallels where they function on this continuum. There are patients who are willing to play with their ideas from the very beginning, actively soliciting the therapist's participation. These patients are at the most treatable end of the continuum. I think the "helpless" patient who wants the therapist to "do it for me" may fall somewhere in the middle; and the panicky, vulnerable patient, who is even more difficult to engage in a therapeutic process in that he needs to have his needs met rather than analyzed, falls at the least treatable end of this continuum.

This is not a developmental continuum, but rather one determined by the patient's perception of the intrusiveness and assaultiveness of the mother. It extends from playful to helpless, and on to rigid and then to delusional. Children of negligent, nonprotective, but not very intrusive or assaultive mothers may be less rigid in their demands of the outside world; yet they still feel helpless and inadequate. In treatment they do want to be nurtured, but they do not feel particularly threatened by their therapists.

CONCLUSIONS

I have presented the case of a helpless patient who stressed her attempts to adapt to her milieu and to internalize helpful experiences from the outside world. Winnicott views the "holding environment" as a setting in which impingements upon the infant are reduced; he believed that the failure of this environment (and of the mother) is tantamount to annihilation. I have discussed two patients who dealt with traumatic impingements (in these cases, their intrusive mothers) by demanding a rigidly predictable environment, thus putting the therapist in the dubious position of having to maintain and participate in this environment, while realizing simultaneously the impossibility of doing so. This produces a "split" in the therapist created by his two different frames of reference—first, his view of what he can realistically provide in terms of the therapeutic setting; and second, his appreciation and wish to provide for and cater to the patient's rigid but – in view of the traumatic past – seemingly justified demands. Toleration of this split by patients allows their entrance into a "not quite" zone, where the rigidity of their demands can be questioned and "played" with.

A not quite zone is a space that is constructed within the treatment frame. It has a logical progression and outcome, beginning with the establishment of a holding environment and ending with its conversion to a transitional zone. It involves the dissolution, through play, of the patient's rigid perception of reality, and the reconstruction of a less rigid, less defensive reality. This is facilitated when the patient experiences his dependence on the therapist as "not quite" absolute.

Rigid reality, an adaptation designed to protect the patient from an assaultive mother, is gradually modified as it becomes more flexible. A formerly pathological mode of relating reaches a developmental pathway that reproduces the course of ordinary emotional maturation. The patient constructs a not quite zone between the ego boundaries and external reality, which is similar to a transitional zone but exists specifically for the *reconstruction*, rather than the construction, of reality. As this process progresses, the "not quite" functions more and more "transitionally."

I have hypothesized the existence of focal points at which the analytic frame is periodically challenged (with decreasing intensity) and at which the patient's need to be rigid is pitted against the motivation to recover. Resolution repeatedly occurs by moving into the not quite zone.

There is a continuum spanning from a fixed delusional viewpoint to an openly curious attitude. The patient's position on this continuum is determined in part, at least, by the degree of the mother's assaultiveness, rather than mere intrusion, and is a significant determinant of the patient's ability to participate in the treatment interaction.

REFERENCES

Flarsheim, A. (1975). The therapist's collusion with the patient's wish for suicide. In *Tactics and Techniques in Psychoanalytic Therapy: Countertransference*, vol. 2, ed. P. Giovacchini, pp. 155–195. New York: Jason Aronson.

Giovacchini, P. L. (1979). *Treatment of Primitive Mental States*. New York: Jason Aronson.

Moraitis, G. (1988). Transference repetitions and the pursuit of novelty. Paper presented at the meeting of the Chicago Psychoanalytic Society, October.

Searles, H. (1975). The patient as therapist to his analyst. In *Tactics and Techniques in Psychoanalytic Therapy: Countertransference*, vol. 2, ed. P. Giovacchini, pp. 95–151. New York: Jason Aronson.

Sterba, R. (1934). The fate of the ego in psycho-analytic therapy. *International Journal of Psycho-Analysis* 15:117–126.

Winnicott, D. W. (1952) Anxiety associated with insecurity. In *Collected Papers: Through Paediatrics to Psycho-Analysis*, pp. 97–101. New York: Basic Books, 1958.

_____ (1956). Primary maternal preoccupation. In *Collected Papers: Through Paediatrics to Psycho-Analysis*, pp. 300–306. New York: Basic Books, 1958.

_____ (1960a). The theory of the patient–infant relationship. In *The Maturational Processes and the Facilitating Environment*, pp. 37–56. New York: International Universities Press, 1965.

_____ (1960b). Ego distortion in terms of the true and false self. In *The Maturational Processes and the Facilitating Environment*, pp. 140–153. New York: International Universities Press, 1965.

_____ (1963). From dependence towards independence of the individual. In *The Maturational Processes and the Facilitating Environment*, pp. 83–93. New York: International Universities Press, 1965.

27

RENATA DE BENEDETTI GADDINI: REGRESSION AND ITS USES IN TREATMENT:

An Elaboration of the Thinking

of Winnicott

INTRODUCTION

Very cogently, Phyllis Greenacre has noted the following:

> With extraordinary intuition Freud gradually fashioned the methods
> for psychoanalytic therapy after the principles of growth. This was the
> more remarkable in that the new method of treatment involved the
> undoing of strictures of the past which impeded and distorted normal
> psychic development, so that the latter might emerge and proceed by
> itself. This was in contrast with the most advanced theories of the day
> which depended largely, but often unofficially, on support, suggestion,
> and direction in the current situation against a background of neuro-
> logizing hypotheses without much consideration for the individual's
> historical background.
>
> Free association, one of the cornerstones of the psychoanalytic
> method, is somewhat comparable to the fluttering, seemingly random
> activity of the child before he reaches a new stage. It also resembles the
> pondering rumination which goes on in the preconscious dreamy states
> of the creative individual when he is in the process of arriving at some

new idea, formulation or discovery. In the analysand it naturally finds its way back to the sources of his difficulties in the past as well as his disappointments of the present and his hopes for the future. Since he is already caught in an inner nexus of binds, he might arrive at a state of unproductive brooding with obsessional repetition or rationalization if he were left entirely to himself. The analyst having travelled these or similar pathways in himself and with others recognizes the road signs and at appropriate times may point out the significances of the patient's being drawn to the familiar path, even though in the past it has led to pain and frustration. He may even indicate the presence of paths which have been previously bypassed. Gradually then courage for new development emerges. [Greenacre 1968, p. 214]

REGRESSION AND GROWTH

The regression of the analyst to pregnancy and infancy, through his or her reverie with the patient, should be mentioned. It could be mentioned also that pregnant patients, through their primary maternal preoccupation with the baby conceived but not yet born, regress to their own embryonic beginning. In patients of pregnant analysts we expect even more regression to primary, even envious, states through projective identification with the baby in utero. This is, at least, what a number of authors have implied. Interesting examples of regression in the course of pregnancy have been described by Conforto (1988) and, in four cases of women who became pregnant while in analysis, by Lester (1988). On the other hand, patients of pregnant analysts have been observed to undergo regression (Fenster et al. 1988).

Notably, regression is often observed in our patients when they feel the approach of therapeutic termination. In a patient's dream of an attempt at premature termination, the analyst is said to have come to represent the degraded, discarded, devalued part of the patient's self representation. In other words, there has been a regression from a differentiated to an externalizing transference" (Novick 1988, p. 310).

Facilitating regression as a way to progression is an innovation in technique that has recently met the interest of many analysts. We owe the little we know about technique to the study of the fusional states of early development in the natural growth process (R. Gaddini 1987, Mahler 1968), and to our attempts at using them in treatment, mostly connected with looking and with the mother's eyes. Looking, in Ballesteros's (1977) view, is for the infant like grabbing at the mother's eyes as if they were a breast, a part object. In Eissler's (1978) view, also, *looking* establishes a concrete continuity. E. Gaddini (1986) had described a very sensorial quality of looking in the early stages, a sensorial quality that is not yet a perception. The question is: Has a self been built or not? In the latter case, subject and object are still the same. Looking, in this case, has more to do with touching and tactile contact than with the perception of the image.

From severely disturbed patients we have, in fact, learned that what is needed is a very complex situation in which these patients can regress and in which the psychoanalyst can help them make use of their regression to dependence. The patients return emotionally to a very early state of development in which the analyst finds himself in the place of an early mother figure, one that is prior to the patient's objectively perceived mother. There is no longer a differentiated transference. It is a time—that of the subjective object—when sense-related data, mostly connected with looking and with the mother's eyes (Ballesteros 1977, Eissler 1978), are the basis for frustration.[1] The infant, at this time, experiences frustration that may lead to feelings of being overwhelmed and annihilated. When the mind develops, mental pain takes the place of these "primary agonies" (Winnicott 1949). Ideas and thoughts do not produce the same sort of frustration as they did before. As E. Gaddini (1982) pointed out, the mind may therefore well be seen as a rescuer of the body, a way of saving the growing child from the fears of self-loss.

THE LESSON COMING FROM THE "TOO SICK PATIENTS"

In his well-received "Fragment of an Analysis," Winnicott (1972) gave us an intimate glimpse into his technique of handling a seriously emotionally regressed patient.

Another example of working with a temporarily regressed patient, and of handling regression and progression while sharing both with anxious (yet very collaborative) parents, may be seen in the moving case of "Piggle." This was a child who was 2 years, 4 months old, and who had begun at the age of 21 months, with the birth of a sister, to have fears of "the black mummy" (black, for her, meant hate); she subsequently suffered serious anxieties on the basis of disillusionment (Winnicott 1977).

A major contribution toward a better understanding of the work with regressed patients may be found further in Winnicott's letters (Rodman 1987). The

---

1. Quoting Eissler's essay, Harrison (1988) notes, on the matter: "Eissler did not raise the possibility that Freud's work may have been an antidote for the kind of gaze that destroys. While Freud was conscientiously at work, he was spared the critical scorn of Brücke's terrible blue eyes. Also, his own eyes were doing no harm" (p. 370). (Ernst Brücke was the Professor of Physiology at the University of Vienna, whose laboratory Freud eagerly attended while planning an academic career after attaining his medical degree in 1881.)

topic of regression and of treating the regressed patient comes up repeatedly in these letters, mostly in a stimulating and clarifying way. No doubt Winnicott is the person who, most of all, got close to the understanding of regression in a comprehensive way, and who gave value to this process. In his view, the transitional object, which is composed of early sensations to which later developing affects and symbolic meaning are attached, is no less typical of regression than it is of creative reparation. In Winnicott's (1954) view, the gradual construction of the capacity to feel guilty and of the *capacity for concern* (Winnicott's term for Klein's depressive position) has, for him, its corollary in the way regression appears as a necessary condition to rescue basic data and feelings that are originally stored as part of the individual's growth. The capacity for concern and the regression to dependence both heavily influence the whole growth process.

When I say that Winnicott gave value to regression, I mean to regression in the psychoanalytic process, that is, in the treatment of the regressed patient. Like Freud, who "vigorously repudiated the idealization of regression towards oneness with the universe, just as he did other mystical and religious beliefs" (Harrison 1988, p. 372), he was keen in discovering pathology and in understanding the fears of breakdown that were at the basis for these surceases.

FROM WINNICOTT'S LETTERS

In a letter of March 1953 to Clifford Scott, "recapturing some of his remarks to a paper presented the previous night,"[2] Winnicott mentions that "regression was not a simple return to infancy, but contained the element of withdrawal and a rather paranoid state needing a specialized protective environment." "I do believe, however," he added, "that this can be said to be normal in a theoretical way, if one refers to a very early stage of emotional development, something which is passed over and hardly noticed at the beginning, if all goes well" (Rodman 1987, p. 49). He continues, further in this letter:

> In regard to the duration of regression, I could not, of course, predict its length. I had indications, however, which perhaps are rather subtle, and I might have been absolutely wrong. I took as my main platform the relatively normal first two years, and following this, the way in which it started at the age of two by using the mother and by his technique of living in a slightly withdrawn state. In regard to this particular point I am now very much strengthened by my experience of

---

2. "The Management of a Case of Compulsive Thieving."

having allowed a psychoanalytic patient to regress as far as was necessary. It really happened that there was a bottom to the regression and no indication whatever of a need to return following the experience of having reached the bottom. . . . In ordinary analysis one tries to make it unnecessary for regression to have to take place, and one succeeds in the ordinary neurotic case. I do believe, however, that the experience of a few regressing cases enables one to see clearly what to interpret. As an example I would say that since experiencing regression I more often interpret to the patient in terms of need and less often in terms of wish. In many cases it seems to me sufficient that one says, for instance: "At this point you need me to see you this weekend," the implication being that from any point of view I can benefit from the weekend, which indirectly helps the patient, but from the patient's point of view at that particular moment there is nothing but harm from the existence of a gap in continuity of the treatment. If, at such a moment, one says "You would like me to give up my weekend" one is on the wrong track and one is in fact wrong. [pp.49–50]

Regression to persecution is taken up in another letter (November 6, 1953) to Esther Bick, who had used that expression in her paper, "Anxiety Underlying Phobia of Sexual Intercourse in a Woman" (1953): "Your term *regression to persecution* means nothing at all as it stands, I expect you would agree with me that this was some kind of shorthand that you have evolved and that you had not time to say what you were meaning. . . . I suppose you are referring to Melanie Klein's concept of a paranoid position in emotional development, which I consider to be one of her less worked out theories, but in any case your term regression to persecution would not be able to convey any meaning to most of the people listening" (Rodman 1987, p. 51).

The discussion on technique goes on, with Clifford Scott (February 2, 1954) referring to Winnicott's paper on regression:

There is progress and regression and . . . for regression there has to be a rather complicated ego organization. I suggest that the word reversal is not so bad when applied to the word progress, whereas I agree that it is not sensible when applied to the word process. . . .

Regression is an attempt to use previous types of behaviour or abnormal as a defence against present conflict. . . .

Reversal should be kept for attempts on the part of the patient to reverse something, for instance, growth. When you compare impulses and wishes with needs you are stating the change of outlook that I am asking for. It seems difficult to get analysts to look at early infancy except in terms of impulses and wishes. Betty Joseph . . . takes wishes as the beginning of everything. I can agree . . . that a bad breast is a fantasy of the infant; even when using judgment we can see a mother is failing. . . . Rage and depression refer to defensive techniques which also belong to a later stage of development. There is no state of frustration, because the individual has not yet become able to stay frustrated. The failure situation as I am referring to it results in a massive reaction to impingement; at the same time something that could have become the individual becomes hidden away; hidden where I cannot say, but separated off and protected from further impingement by the developing false self which is reactive as a main feature. . . . Difficulties in the classification of psychological disorders in young children and indeed in infants is due to the fact that we have not yet made full use of this concept of the false self developing reactively and more hiding the true impulsive self which might under more favourable circumstances have been gathering strength through experience on a non-reactive basis. [Rodman 1987, p. 59]

In a letter of April 1954 to Betty Joseph, still referring to his presentation of his paper on regression, Winnicott goes into the problem of the infant's fantasy of a bad breast and a bad mothering technique. He wonders, with Scott: "Cannot any bad experience be made worse by the patient's fantasy? . . . It is not the fantasy of a good or bad breast I am trying to draw attention to in the very early stages, quite apart from the fantasy. . . . I find it difficult to get people to leave for a moment the infant fantasy of a bad breast and to go to a *stage further back*, to the effect of a bad mothering technique, such as for instance rigidity (mother's defence against hate) or muddle (expression of mother's chaotic state)" (Rodman 1987, p. 59). Winnicott continues:

What happens to the bad breast in the good state of regression? I think I dealt with this in my first letter when I was saying that I was trying to get to something earlier than the presentation of what can be felt by the infant as a bad or good breast. . . . The bad mothering technique comes out with extreme clearness in the sort of treatment that I was describing. . . . I want to emphasize . . . that the bad mothering is an, essential thing in the sequence in the technique that I described . . . after a good experience which corrects the bad one the next thing is that the patient uses one's failures and in this way brings into the present each original mothering technique inadequacy. [Rodman 1987, pp. 59–60]

Special attention is given to "regression to sleep," a point that was touched upon by Scott in a presentation to the British Society (January 27, 1954) in such a way that "the little bit of truth which was in . . . [this] reference gets lost." Winnicott wonders whether sleep is the "right word" to be used for both "the sort of sleep that most of us have at night, in which any dissociation between sleeping and waking is very markedly lessened by the dream that we, more or less, remember on waking, even if only for a second," as well as ". . . the sort of sleep that you are referring to [which] seems to me to be more of the nature of a depersonalisation or an extreme dissociation or something awfully near to the unconsciousness belonging to a fit" (Rodman 1987, p. 56). He takes here the example of a patient "who is dangerous just after expressing genuine love. In this case the oscillation between love and hate seemed to have been most measurable, but what is more important, they were painful to the patient. I could give other examples, and the one I think of immediately is that of children who are helped rather than hindered by being told that they fear madness, the madness they fear being the oscillation between love and hate" (p.57).

A patient of mine, an anorexic girl of 14, who had become mute and totally negativistic shortly after the beginning of treatment, became aggressive and dangerous first to the analyst's person and afterward—when the girl began to feel attachment to her analyst—to the analyst's properties.

I felt that she wanted to be certified, and surely my understanding and telling her that she was suffering because of her oscillations between love and hate, and that her fears of a catastrophe were fears of madness, helped her in establishing a relationship with me.

About the outcome of regression, this is mentioned in a letter written by Winnicott to Harry Guntrip (August 13, 1954), in which the element of hate in regression is put forward:

> In regard to the future of your woman patient, I certainly think that you are on the right road but there are difficulties ahead. For instance, you have been able to follow the patient's regression to dependence and to be in the place of an early mother figure, that is to say one that is prior to the patient's objectively perceived mother. I would think that there may be very great hate of you because of this position that you have taken, as the patient emerges from the regression and therefore becomes aware of the dependence. If one is not expecting this one may be puzzled at the tremendous hate which turns up within the love relationship in these regressed states. [Rodman 1987, p. 79]

The theory that underlies regression is strongly stated in a letter to Joan Riviere (March 2, 1956): "Unless she [mother] can identify very closely with her infant at the beginning, she cannot 'have a good breast' because just *having* the thing means nothing whatever to the infant. The theme can be developed, and I have frequently developed it, because I know of its great importance not only to mothers with infants, but also to analysts who are dealing with patients who have for a moment or over longer phases been deeply regressed" (Rodman 1987, p. 96). Winnicott's regression theory is elaborated upon further in his letter to Thomas Main (February 2, 1957); Main, at the Cassel Hospital, was offering opportunities to patients to regress while the analyst was actively adapting to their needs. Winnicott wrote: "This work of yours is of importance to psycho-analysis. It may be that psycho-analysis can contribute to your understanding of the problem and that some of the analytic contributions you have not absorbed. . . . The fact remains, however, that your collecting together all the fragments of nursing reactions adds up to a real contribution to psycho-analysis" (p. 112). And, further on: "The characteristic of this kind of patient is that hope forces them to bang on the door of all therapies which might be the answer. They cannot rest from this; as you know so well their technique for mobilizing activity is terrific in its efficiency" (p. 113). (We can see here Winnicott's capacity for recognizing hope as an important element for construction and reconstruction of the self in regressed patients on the basis of trust, the way he had been able to do with delinquents.) The letter continues:

> These patients make us try hard because they have hope and because it is the hope which makes them so clever; yet at the same time, the fact that we cannot provide what is needed produces disaster. In other words, it is only contributing a little if one can show that what these patients need is a very complex situation in which they can regress and in which the psycho-analyst can help them to make use of regression. Whatever can be done here must be only a small bit of what would have to be done to neutralize the destructive potential of this group of people. Indeed I would like to say that the more psychoanalysts become able to do this kind of work with a few patients the more patients there are who will begin to have hope and therefore will begin to bash around in a ruthless search for a life that feels real. I do consider therefore that if psychoanalysts ignore the problem . . . they are ignoring a group of forces that could destroy psychoanalysis and in practice could account for the deaths of analysts and psychiatric nursing staff, and the breakup of the better type of mental institution. [Rodman 1987, p. 114]

To Masud Khan (June 26, 1961), the theme of integration is mentioned in connection with regression: "The word *integration* describes the developmental tendency and the achievement in the healthy individual in which he or she becomes an integer. Thus, integration acquires a time dimension (depressive position). The state prior to integration I call unintegration. . . . Unintegration seems to me to describe a primitive state that is associated clinically with regression to dependence. Dissociation (like disintegration and splitting) seems to be a defence organization . . ." (Rodman 1987, p. 132).

In Winnicott's view, the original environment is reproduced by the psychoanalytic treatment, in which the analyst is concerned with the patient's state of mind, and it becomes especially important when the patient is regressed. As Rodman (1987) puts it:

> Starting from this early area of pleasure-in-illusion, human experience expands to include play, creativity, and cultural life in general. These categories of experience all provide a resting place where strict definition of self and others is not only not required, but is a hindrance to fulfillment. They all occur in the area of overlap between what comes from within and what is given from without . . . [in the] regression to dependence severely disturbed patients return emotionally to a very early state of development of which one feature is their absolute dependence on a caretaking person. [p. xxxi]

This brings to mind a patient of mine—a psychotic woman almost 40 years old—who, after a profound withdrawal in childhood and adolescence, oscillated between catatonia and intense motor excitement, manic testing-out, bulimia, and delusions of various nature. She came to analysis after a number of psychiatric admissions, which unconsciously she had promoted. Her defiant attitude to failure and rejection (which had been heavily experienced in her early life), as well as her search for a need-satisfying process that she had missed, was expressed in her soiling herself, annoying her neighbors, and demanding extensive motherly care.

In Rodman's already quoted letter (October 1, 1969), where technique is discussed, Winnicott points to the dangers analysts run with regressed patients:

> The relief that comes from not having to be so artificially adaptive, quite beyond that which I will do in private life, is so great that I begin to swallow the bait the patient offers and find myself talking about things in general and acting as if the patient had suddenly become well. This is a very great danger area in the treatment of borderline cases where regression to dependence is a prominent feature. Perhaps you would agree on this. On the other hand, I do not want to say that even this kind of mistake is quite useless, if the case survives the experience. Undoubtedly it does show the patient to what an extent one was under strain. The awful thing when a patient commits suicide at this stage is that this leaves the analyst forever holding the strain and never able to

misbehave just a little. I think that is an inherent part of the revenge that suicide of this kind contains, and I must say that the analyst always deserves what he gets here. I say this having just lost a patient through being ill. I could not help being ill, but if I am going to be ill then I must not take on this kind of patient. It is almost mechanistic when we think how things work in this area. [Rodman 1987, p. 182]

MATERNAL CARE, SEDUCTION, AND COUNTERTRANSFERENCE

Freud never abandoned the seduction theory, as Jeffrey M. Masson claims in his notorious volume, *Freud's Assault on Truth: Suppression of the Seduction Theory* (1984). In fact, he gradually modified it and integrated it on the basis of his discovery of infant sexuality, and of the potential phylogenetic meaning that this had on adult neuroses and psychoses. In this book, Masson quotes only a part of Freud's (1905) formulation of the role played by external and internal reality on the etiology of neurosis, and, in so doing, alters its meaning. Freud's formulation indeed stresses the following:

The reappearance of sexual activity is determined by internal causes and external contingencies, both of which can be guessed in cases of neurotic illness from the form taken by their symptoms and can be discovered with certainty by psycho-analytic investigation. I shall have to speak presently of the internal causes; great and lasting importance attaches to the accidental external contingencies at this period. In the foreground we find the effects of seduction, which treats the child as a sexual object prematurely and teaches him, in highly emotional circumstances, how to obtain satisfaction from his genital zones, a satisfaction which he is then usually obliged to repeat again and again by masturbation. An influence of this kind may originate either from adults or from other children. I cannot admit that in my paper on The Aetiology of Hysteria [1896] I exaggerated the frequency or importance of that influence, though I did not then know that persons who remain normal may have had the same experiences in their childhood, and though I consequently overrated the importance of seduction in comparison with the factors of sexual constitution and development. Obviously seduction is not required in order to arouse a child's sexual life; that can also come about spontaneously from internal causes. [Freud 1905, pp. 190–191]

On the other hand, when Freud abandoned Breuer's theory on hypnosis, he turned his eyes on new facts. A new theory generates new techniques, even within its own ambit, and these, in turn, lead to new discoveries. Freud gave evidence of the identity, in the unconscious, of something that lay between internal and external space. After fifty years, Winnicott was thus able to speak of an intermediate space located between the "boundaries" of the inner and the outer worlds, a space where the sense of self begins. It is in this space—a space in which one can relax and get strength—that regression takes place, in my view. With regression to early care, however, seduction comes in as a possible inducer.

MATERNAL SEDUCTIVE CONFIGURATION

As Winnicott wrote in a letter to W. C. Scott on the theme of delinquency, on May 11, 1950 (Rodman 1987, p. 22), "Any kind of sentimentality is worse than useless . . . it is a sort of weakness to be guarded against." Winnicott's view was that aggression, which is intrinsic to human nature, must be given its due outlet. "A sentimental idea is one that does not leave room for hate or, at least, for aggression. . . . To elucidate this point, I may say that any type of sentimentality must be looked upon, in my opinion, as a disturbing, seductive element, whether same appears in maternal care or in analysis; it is an element to be carefully watched" (1987, p. xxiv).

In another letter (to V. Smirnoff, November 19, 1958), commenting on a proposed translation into French of his work on transitional objects, Winnicott writes, "The word *tender* is rather good but it emphasizes an absence of aggression and destruction, whereas the word *affectionate* neither emphasizes or denies it. One could imagine a hug, for instance, being affectionate and yet far from tender" (Rodman 1987, p. 121).

The asserted seduction of Melitta on the part of her mother (Rodman 1987) made me think of a patient of mine—seriously borderline—now in her seventh year of analysis. She "remembered" her breast-feeding, which lasted until she was 7 months old, as a forced feeding, particularly during the last months. "My mother forced me to take her breast and I felt like vomiting. . . ." This feeling of "disgust" and "nausea" arose in the patient every time she was confronted with a certain type of emotion. For instance, she felt this way when she discovered that her younger brother was a homosexual.

She spoke of "milk" in her stomach as something inconsistent, and not as something she drank that satisfied her hunger:

> I often have this feeling when I drink milk. . . . I mix it with baby food, the
> Mellin powdered food for example . . . too much milk must have given me

this feeling of inconsistency. Nausea is something much easier to deal with. . . . You can solve the problem by vomiting. . . . This feeling of being swollen . . . of floating . . . you can't do away with it by provoking vomit. . . . It is something that must be absorbed . . . (one thinks of merging). It is a sensation that I seek, no matter what. After dinner I take my milk with these things in it.

In countertransference, I often felt that this fear of merging with her mother had its counterpart in the patient's fear of being manipulated and in her tendency not to accept interpretations at the time they were offered.

Later in life she forced her own son—the last child after two daughters—to the point of abuse. She forced her breast into him, and then forced him to let go by squeezing his nose to the point of suffocation. The son is now a seriously ill asthmatic, with difficulties in relating to reality. Twenty-two years old, without girlfriends, he is often in my patient's dreams in incestuous situations, sometimes with his head resting in his mother's lap, and she feels guilty. "So grown up . . ." she tells herself in the dream. When interpreting, I made her notice how she, at 47 years old, felt too grown up to rest her head on the analyst's lap, complacently and without the strength to oppose the analyst. She spoke of the correspondence between Marcel Proust and his mother and how the mother called him "Mon petit loup." Then she went on to speak of her own son: "Last night I surprised myself telling him, 'Take this darling,' The soup was on the table, and I was not sure he wanted it. I insisted, 'Will you have this soup, love?' as though he were a child. . . . He gladly plays along with these tender attitudes. On many occasions, as I was sitting on the sofa, speaking to his two sisters, he would come and rest his head on my lap and ask that I caress his hair."

She continued:

I recall a dream. Anna and Federico [the patient's friend and the friend's son] are there . . . a tender and seductive relationship between them. . . . Anna always tended to Federico's bodily care until he was 9. . . . I tried to oppose harshness and indifference to the tenderness and affection that I felt for Giuseppe [the patient's own son]. . . . I was afraid of spoiling him. . . . I tried to protect myself . . . the wrong way . . . through compensation. . . . I wanted him to be autonomous. . . . I had mistreated him in all sorts of ways when he was small . . . and . . . I carried with me the image of myself as a 6-months baby seduced into taking mother's milk, when there were all sorts of things out there which I could have perceived. . . . It was humiliating, it was like being cut off from new things . . . everything was filtered through my mother, a caged-in, unnatural way, indirect, manipulative. . . .

Once again I found myself feeling that as a patient's seduction results in a negative therapeutic reaction, so does the seduction of a child on the part of the mother lead to an interference in basic trust, and, one could say, a negative reaction to life and to relations with others.

The patient continued: "There are attitudes I see in others and, above all, in myself, that have something to do with seduction . . . childish attitudes . . . wanting to be seduced . . . not to break the fusional state . . . often my reaction is abrupt, of a forced estrangement . . . or it may be tender and seductive . . . two extremes. . . ."

Many times I thought how difficult it had been for her to deal with all that she was bringing up in her transference throughout those passing years. In time, I have come to understand that seduction, for her, meant intrusion, "impingement" in Winnicott's sense, the tendency that certain mothers have to thrust themselves into the going-on-being of their children, above all during the first months of their child's life when the formation of a sense of self is taking place. Thus their natural development is hindered. As we have just mentioned, Winnicott believed in the real object as an influencing factor of growth, and so do I. We have discussed it, and while both of us have thoroughly accepted Freud's revolutionary concept that it is the unconscious that organizes and shapes our perception of the external world, and have learned that babies are self-propelling beings in respect to their mothers, we have never accepted entirely the concept that excluded external reality from any determining value either in the construction of the Basic Mental Organization (E. Gaddini 1982) or in early mental processes. This is particularly true for the "concrete subject matter" that Freud (1923) described apropos of early sensations. Thus, clinical experience has taught us that, as analysts, we are never to "intrude" on our patients, particularly on the very sick ones who seem more needy and dependent, lest we should interfere with their possibility of regressing, which we have found to be beneficial in certain stages of the analytic process.

The respect and trust that I have come to place in the natural developmental process—which should manifest itself in an authentic way in every individual, interwoven as it is with instinctual development and early care, and in opposition to every type of seduction—may be found in this 1952 letter of Winnicott to Melanie Klein: "If he were growing a daffodil [referring to a colleague] he would think that he was making the daffodil out of a bulb, instead of enabling the bulb to develop into a daffodil by good enough nurture" (Rodman 1987, p. 35). In another letter, written to a correspondent in Tanzania, he said: "We cannot even teach children to walk . . . but their innate tendency to walk at a certain age needs us as supporting figures" (p. 186). The image of parents as "supporting figures" who facilitate walking recalls both the earlier inclination of the mother to be aware of the needs of her baby, and the analyst's awareness of his patient's needs. Such support excludes every form of intrusion and manipulation that provides narcissistic gratification to the mother and to the analyst. In this view, anything that goes beyond active adaptation—that is, beyond the analyst's letting himself be used according to need—in the patient's search for mental sense and an emotional color for his life's vicissitudes, is already seduction and almost inevitably brings with it, in life and in therapy, a negative reaction. The patient feels trapped: basic trust is at stake.

Within this context, on the topic of regression, another example comes to mind. It is a case reported by Limentani (1987) in his introduction to "Perversions, Treatable and Untreatable":

A patient had brought the analyst a dream: "Tim [her homosexual companion] menstruated at the same time I did. He said, 'Well, now we can make love.' " The analyst reminded her that only the day before she had told him that she could not even think of making love to a woman. If she had, she was afraid she would lose her sense of identity. The patient, restless, answered him, "Even you would be afraid to lose your sense of identity if you had spent your childhood with my mother. My mother was erotic with me, you know, because I've observed her with small children. Even now she's seductive [with me] until my brother enters the room. I never let anyone touch me until I was 2½ years old. I can't forget those first years." The analyst said it was certainly because she seemed to have a compulsive need to re-enact the same situation which was that of coming into contact with someone, of getting excited and, at the same time, going toward frustration in the hope of maybe freeing herself. Much to his surprise, the patient said yes, that was possible, but how could she free herself? [p. 428]

We can therefore conclude, on the basis of what I have reported in these pages, that the true nature of individual relating and its vicissitudes depends more on the quality than the quantity of care, be it the mother's care or the analyst's. The possibility of regression as "the reverse of progress" derives from it, as "for regression there has to be a rather complicated ego organisation. . . . The earlier and more primary mothering techniques, if inadequate, fail to meet needs and therefore destroy the continuity of development in the individual" (April 13, 1954, Rodman 1987, pp. 60–61). The case of this patient, whose prolonged breast-feeding was experienced by her as an abuse, has been presented to illustrate this concept.

The theme of seduction as an inducer of regression, as well as of fear to grow, is a topical subject in today's culture as well as in the most recent studies of psychoanalytic techniques.

Seduction is of such strong interest today because we are living in times of great losses and deprivations of primary needs, and consequently an increased fragility of basic mental organization, with resulting distortions of the early mental processes necessary for autonomy and for a mature identity (E. Gaddini 1982, 1984). Our young people—who instead of having received good enough early maternal care have suffered all forms of intrusion and impingement and are thus afraid to grow—do not want to be autonomous; they want to remain puppies. A stepmother—consumerism—has too often replaced adequate maternal care and has therefore also replaced a true culture of infancy and childhood.

From the repetition compulsion Freud arrived at the concept of the death instinct. With his studies on imitation, E. Gaddini (1969) has made us see an early compulsion to repeat as an attempt to endlessly relive and re-enact the sensory experiences of early being. If seduction was part of this primary bonding—which is being, for the infant (seduction that always "serves to compensate," as one of my patients said)—then we cannot but find ourselves faced by cases of intrapsychic seduction; and this paves the way for the many false idols of today's youth. The underlying fear is self-loss.

REFERENCES

Ballesteros, G. R. (1977). El ojo de la madre como objecto parcial. *Revista de la Sociedad Colombiana de Psicoanalisis* 2:27–51.

Bick, E. (1953). Anxiety underlying phobia of sexual intercourse in a woman. Paper presented at the British Psychoanalytic Society, June 10.

Conforto, C. (1988). Note sul trattamento psicoanalitico di una donna in gravidanza. *Patalogia E Clinica Ostetrica E Ginecologica.*

Eissler, K. (1978). Creativity and adolescence. *Psychoanalytic Study of the Child* 33:461–517. New Haven, CT: Yale University Press.

Fenster, S., Philips, S., and Rappaport, E. (1988). *The Therapist's Pregnancy: Intrusion in the Analytic Space.* Hillsdale, NJ: Analytic Press.

Freud, S (1896). The aetiology of hysteria. *Standard Edition* 3:197–224.

_____ (1900). A note in the prehistory of psychoanalytic technique. *Standard Edition* 18:213–265.

_____ (1905). Three essays on sexuality. *Standard Edition* 7:123–143.

_____ (1923). The ego and the id. *Standard Edition* 19:3–68.

Gaddini, E. (1969). On imitation. *International Journal of Psycho-Analysis* 50:475–484.

_____ (1982). Early defensive fantasies and the analytic process. *International Journal of Psycho-Analysis* 63:379–388.

_____ (1984). Changes in psychoanalytic patients up to the present days. *International Psycho-Analytic Association Monograph Series No. 4.*

_____ (1986). La maschera e il cerchio. *Rivista Italiana di Psicoanalisi* 2:172–186.

_____ (1987). Notes on the body–mind question. *International Journal of Psycho-Analysis* 68:315–329.

Gaddini, R. (1987). Early care and the roots of internalization. *International Review of Psycho-Analysis* 14:321–333.

Greenacre, P. (1968). The psychoanalytic process: transference and acting out. *International Journal of Psycho-Analysis* 49:211–218.

Harrison, I. (1988). Further implications of a dream of Freud: a subjective influence on his theory formation. *International Review of Psycho-Analysis* 15:365–373.

Lester, E. (1988). Towards a profile of maternal functions. Panel presentation at Second Delphi International Psycho-Analytic Symposium. New York, July.

Limentani, A. (1987). Perversions, treatable and untreatable. *Contemporary Psychoanalysis* 23:415–437.

Mahler, M. S. (1968). *On Human Symbiosis and the Vicissitudes of Individuation*. New York: International Universities Press.

Masson, J. M. (1984). *Freud's Assault on Truth: Suppression of the Seduction Theory*. Boston: Farrar & Farrar.

Novick, J. (1988). The timing of termination. *International Review of Psycho-Analysis* 15:307–318.

Rodman, R. F. (1987). *The Spontaneous Gesture: Selected Letters of D. W. Winnicott*. Cambridge MA: Harvard University Press.

Scott, W. C. (1954). Regression to sleep. Unpublished.

Winnicott, D. W. (1949). Mind and its relation to the psyche-soma. In *Collected Papers: Through Paediatrics to Psycho-Analysis*, pp 243–254. New York: Basic Books, 1975.

———— (1954). Withdrawal and regression. In *Collected Papers: Through Paediatrics to Psycho-Analysis*, pp. 255–261. New York: Basic Books, 1958.

———— (1972). Fragment of an analysis, annot. A. Flarsheim. In *Tactics and Techniques in Psychoanalytic Therapy*, vol. 1, ed. P. Giovacchini, pp. 455–493. New York: Science House.

———— (1977). *The Piggle: An Account of the Psychoanalytic Treatment of a Little Girl*. New York: International Universities Press.

28

ARNOLD H. MODELL: "THE HOLDING ENVIRONMENT" AND THE THERAPEUTIC ACTION OF PSYCHOANALYSIS

AT THE CONGRESS IN MARIENBAD in 1936, Glover (1937) observed that "it is essential that out theory of therapeutic results should keep pace with the complexity of ego development and with the complexity of our etiological formulae" (p. 127). This paper is an attempt to respond to Glover's succinct advice, for, as we enlarge the scope of psychoanalysis to include an ever-increasing range of people who are said to suffer from disorders of ego development, we are forced to consider for these people a theory of the therapeutic action of psychoanalysis different from that we use with the so-called "classical case."

The isolation of those factors which underlie therapeutic change in psychoanalysis is not a secure area of knowledge; it is easier to identify the forces that interfere with the progress of an analysis than to understand what contributes to its therapeutic success. Our theory of therapeutic change in psychoanalysis may itself be constantly changing due to the changing nature of the neuroses. This theory is obviously linked to the subject of transference where a final understanding also seems continually to elude us. A thorough examination of the theory of therapeutic action of psychoanalysis is beyond the scope of this paper: it should be understood that the following account is necessarily cursory and simplified.

I believe that most analysts would accept James Strachey's description (1934) that structural growth is effected by means of sparingly employed mutative interpretations. Interpretations are only effective when certain conditions are met:

in Strachey's words, "every mutative interpretation must be emotionally 'immediate'; the patient must experience it as something actual" (p. 286). He says further that the interpretation must be directed to the "point of urgency." This means that very precise conditions must be present regarding the state of the patient's affects. It must be assumed that the patient is in a state of affective relatedness so that the "point of urgency" can be perceived by means of the psychoanalyst's empathy—that is to say, there must be an affective bond. It must further be assumed that the patient's affective experience is of a certain intensity—that is, intense enough to experience the immediacy of feeling but not so intense as to overwhelm him. We know that Strachey believed that the transference interpretations are likely to have the greatest "urgency" and that mutative changes are most likely to occur through the interpretation of a transference. Differences of opinion exist regarding this point: there are those who would place transference interpretation at the very center of the therapeutic process, while others, such as Anna Freud (1969), would give equal weight to interpretive reconstruction utilizing memory, free association, and dreams. Further controversy exists over the effectiveness of interpretation in the presence or absence of a therapeutic alliance: a majority opinion would believe that transference interpretations are mutative, that is, that they produce structural change only when self/object differentiation has been achieved so that the patient can accept the analyst as a separate person and can collaborate actively (Zetzel 1956). Kleinian analysts would take a minority view, believing that transference interpretations can be effective in the absence of a therapeutic alliance. (For a discussion of this controversy see Greenson 1974, Rosenfeld 1974.)

But if we leave these controversies aside, all analysts are united in the view that interpretations can be effective only when there is, in Strachey's terms, a "point of urgency," that is to say, affect that is genuine and communicated.

It is further believed that mutative interpretations lead to structural change by means of a series of innumerable small steps. This results in a growing identification of the patient with the analyst's "analytic attitude" (Bibring 1937). Strachey emphasized the modification of the patient's superego, but we would now include the modification of the ego and the sense of self.

The theory that the therapeutic action of psychoanalysis requires a certain state of affective relatedness would have to be modified as it applied to the psychoanalysis of narcissistic character disorders. For in the opening phase of the psychoanalytic treatment (a phase which may last for a year or more) there is a persistent state of affective nonrelatedness.

We can confirm Kohut's (1971) description of a syndrome defined operationally by the development of a transference consisting of externalizations of part of the self or the undifferentiated self-object, which he called the mirror transference, and the idealizing transference. The uniformity of this particular transference manifestation, in contrast to the transference neurosis, whose content is unique, is of special interest and will be discussed later in this paper. We agree with Kohut that this group is essentially neurotic and not psychotic and can be distinguished from borderline patients (see also Kernberg 1974, Modell 1975b). The diagnosis of this syndrome is also aided by a particular form of the countertransference response (Modell 1973), which is the result of the patient's state of nonrelatedness. The analyst reacts with a sense of boredom and sleepiness to this massive affect block and to the realization that he is continuously in the presence of another person who does not seem to be interested in him. Although the analyst's withdrawal may be defensive, I do not believe it is necessarily neurotic—it is a human reaction to the patient's state of nonrelatedness. The patient's speech usually has a monotonous, dry, or empty quality, traumatic events are related with such absence of feeling that the analyst must struggle against becoming indifferent. Dreams are also shorn of affect and can only rarely be interpreted. Strachey's criterion for interpretation— the state of affective relatedness—"the point of urgency" is lacking, and further, there is an absence of a therapeutic alliance. In the absence of both transference neurosis and a therapeutic alliance, and without a point of affective urgency that permits mutative interpretations, what then provides the motive for the therapeutic action of psychoanalysis in these patients (Kohut 1971)?

Kohut attributes the structural growth that occurs in these cases to a process that he calls "transmuting internalization." He describes it as follows (1971): "Preceding the withdrawal of the cathexis from the object there is a breaking up of those aspects of the object imago that are being internalized" (p. 49). And further, "there takes place . . . a depersonalizing of the introjected aspects of the image of the object" (p. 50). I find Kohut's concept of the "transmuting internalization" an unsatisfactory explanation of the therapeutic action of psychoanalysis in narcissistic personality disorders. It is not that I question that "transmuting internalizations" occur, for this has long been recognized: my principal objection is his theoretical frame of reference—one that focuses nearly exclusively on changes in the self, and described these changes in terms of a distribution of narcissistic object libido. Kohut does not make use of the psychoanalytic theory of object relations; to describe qualitative differences in libido is reminiscent of Freud's 1914 paper, "On Narcissism," a paper that preceded structural theory. Although Kohut does employ structural concepts, narcissism is separated from the development of object relations, a view antithetical to object-relations theory. (For a similar criticism see Loewald 1973, Kernberg 1974.)

Theory has a selective influence upon what we choose to observe. Kohut's theoretical position that narcissism and object relations proceed along separate developmental lines would minimize the interplay of the human environment upon the vicissitudes of development and the sense of self. This is not a minor theoretical disagreement, but a radically different model of the mind. Object-relations theory describes intrapsychic processes in the content of a human environment. Such a view is consistent with contemporary biological theory in that it views the world around the organism with the organism in it. This is what, in psychanalytic jargon, has come to be called a "two body" theory.

It is our contention, therefore, that the syndrome of the narcissistic character disorder that Kohut has so accurately described requires a theory of object relations for its fuller understanding. There is a theory of the therapeutic action of psycho-analysis that derives from the object-relations point of view. We are referring to those analysts who view the analytic setting itself as containing some elements of the mother-child relation. This point of view includes the contributions of Winni-cott (1965), Balint (1968), Spitz (1956), Loewald (1960) and Gitelson (1962), among others. It is view that would see the analytic setting as an open system, a view in which the ego must be considered in relation to its human environment.

We have adopted Winnicott's term, "the holding environment," as an evocative description of this human environment, but it should be understood that in applying Winnicott's term we are emphasizing a theory that is not exclusively Winnicott's. Winnicott introduced the term "holding environment" as a metaphor for certain aspects of the analytic situation and the analytic process. The term derives from the maternal function of holding the infant, but, taken as a metaphor, it had a much broader application and extends beyond the infantile period—where the holding its literal and not metaphorical—to the broader caretaking functions of the parent in relation to the older child (Khan 1963). We suggest that the mother, or more accurately, the caretaking adults, stand between the child and the actual environment and that the child and its caretaker are an open system joined by means of the communication of affects. As Winnicott (1963) put it, ". . . the analyst is *holding* the patient, and this often takes the form of conveying in words at the appropriate moment something that shows that the analyst knows and under-stands the deepest anxiety that is being experienced, or that is waiting to be experienced" (p. 240). The holding environment provides an illusion of safety and protection, and illusion that depends upon the bond of affective communication between the caretaker and the child. We are reminded of the war-time experience of children who remained with their mothers, contrasted with those who were separated. The study made by Anna Freud and Burlingham (1943) demonstrated that the mothers' affective signals took precedence over the actual, the external, reality: the children remained calm when the mothers were unafraid, despite the real danger. The holding environment suggests not only protection from the dangers from without, but also protection from the dangers from within. For the holding implies a restraint, a capacity to hold the child having a temper tantrum so that his aggressive impulses do not prove destructive to either himself or the caretaker. In this regard it is not uncommon to observe at the beginning of an analysis that patients will test the analyst's capacity to survive aggressive on-slaughts. The holding environment provides, in Sandler's (1960) terms, a background of safety. When there is a loss of this holding environment, which may occur for a variety of reasons, such as the illness of the parents or their emotional unavailability, the child is forced into a premature maturation and, in a sense, for a period at least, ceases to be a child, for to have a childhood requires the presence of a holding environment. A child who is forced into a premature self-sufficiency does so by means of an illusion (Modell 1975b), an illusion for which the ego pays a price.

THE HOLDING ENVIRONMENT AND THE ANALYTIC SETTING AS AN OBJECT RELATIONSHIP

Others, however, have questioned whether the analytic situation does in fact recapitulate an early mother-child relation. Anna Freud (1969) states:

> There is, further, the question whether the transference really has the power to transport the patient back as far as the beginning of life. Many are convinced that this is the case. Others, myself among them, raise the point that it is one thing for the preformed object-related fantasies to return from repression and be redirected from the inner to the outer world (i.e., to the person of the analyst); but that it is an entirely different, almost magical expectation, to have the patient in analysis change back into the prepsychological, undifferentiated, unstructured state, in which no division exists between body and mind or self and object. [p. 40]

Leo Stone (1961) is also skeptical about whether the analytic setting can reproduce aspects of an early object relationship.

As Anna Freud indicates, it would be foolish to insist that regression in analysis goes back to structurally undifferentiated states of the first or second year of life. Nevertheless, there are actual elements in the analyst's technique that are reminiscent of an idealized maternal holding environment, and these can be enumerated: the analyst is constant and reliable; he responds to the patient's effects; he accepts the patient, and his judgement is less critical and more benign; he is there primarily for the patient's needs and not for his own; he does not retaliate; and he does at times have a better grasp of the patient's inner psychic reality than does the patient himself and therefore may clarify what is bewildering and confusing.

Strachey (1934) underlined an important paradox that is implicit in psychoanalytic technique. He stated: "It is a paradoxical fact that the best way of ensuring that his [the patient's] ego shall be able to distinguish between phantasy and reality is to withhold reality from him as much as possible" (p. 285). This paradox is also relevant to our consideration of the "holding environment." For although there are "real" caretaking elements in the analyst's customary activity, if he does in fact assume an actual protective role (such as might be necessary in certain emergencies), this will interfere with the analytic process. We wish to reiterate, therefore, that the caretaking elements we have described are implicit in the classical analytic technique itself (in Eissler's terms, without parameters). If active measures are introduced into the analytic situation, there is the paradoxical effect of weakening the analytic holding environment. (The same point has been made by Rosenfeld 1972, and Gitelson 1962.)

It should also be made clear that when we speak of "real" elements in the object relation between patient and analyst as part of the caretaking function, we are not referring to the very different issue of the patient's perception of the analyst and a "real" person (Greenson and Wexler 1969). The word "real" is used here in a different context. Again, to refer back to Strachey's paradox, the introduction of special measures to reveal to the patient the "reality" of the analyst's personality may, in the treatment of the neuroses at least, have the opposite effect. The use of this technique in borderline and other psychotic illnesses is a separate issue.

We have discussed the so-called "actual" elements in the object tie between the patient and the analyst. We know that the situation is further complicated by the fact that this actual object tie is penetrated by the products of fantasy. That these fantasies may be primitive and may occur in young children does not mean that the patient has in fact regressed in a structural sense to the age of one or two, as Anna Freud has questioned. The fantastic elements include the magical wish to be protected from the dangers of the world and the illusion that the person of the analyst in some way stands between these dangers and shields the patient. It is the illusion that the patient is not "really in the world." There is the wish that the patient's being required to do any work — that mere contiguity to this powerful analyst will transfer the analyst's magical powers to himself.

A patient in the termination phase dreamed that she was lying on the floor holding a life-sized doll while I was seated watching her. The patient identified the doll as the analytic process that she was in danger of losing. What is of interest here is that the analytic process itself was invested with the qualities of a transitional object, apart from the person of the analyst. Although the qualities of the holding environment are generated by the analyst's technique, they may become separated from the analyst and take on a life of their own. The analytic process is not infrequently observed in dreams as a more or less protective container, such as a house or an automobile.

The gratifications that result from the analyst's functioning as a "holding environment," we must again emphasize, are not the consequence of the analyst's special activity, that is, actively giving reassurance, love, or support, but are an intrinsic part of "classical" technique. Here, gratification appears to contradict the rule of abstinence, but the nature of the gratification is quite different from that associated with libidinal or aggressive discharge. It moves silently, it is not orgastic. I have suggested elsewhere (Modell 1975a) that the instinctual backing of object relations is of a different order from what Freud described as the instincts of the id. While this assertion remains controversial, it is not controversial to assume that the healing forces of the "holding environment" have biological roots.

THE PSYCHOANALYTIC PROCESS IN NARCISSISTIC CHARACTER DISORDERS

The First Phase – The Cocoon: Transference and the "Holding Environment"

Kohut's description of the idealizing and mirror transference in the narcissistic character disorder is now widely known and we have accepted his description as an operational method of defining the syndrome itself. What we are to describe now are other facets of transference that can be observed if we shift the focus from the self to the broader context of object relations – that is to say, the self in an environment. The complexity of the analytic process is such that what we can offer here are only partial approximations. We have the impression that the early part of the first phase of analysis, as we shall describe it, corresponds to Kohut's description of the idealizing transference. Kohut's mirror transference in its less archaic forms occurs toward the end of the first phase and the beginning of the second or middle phase of analysis. It is also to be understood that the separation of these phases is a fluid, dynamic process; the boundaries between phases are not sharp and, due to progressive and regressive movements, their sequence may be interrupted. The situation is not unlike the changing of seasons.

The initial period usually extends for a year or a year and a half, or may persist longer. It is a period of great frustration for the psychoanalyst: the patient behaves in the main as if there are not two people in the consulting room – the patient remains essentially in a state of nonrelatedness. This state of affective nonrelatedness induces a particular countertransference response that has been widely observed (Kernberg 1974, Kohut 1971, Modell 1973). It is one of boredom, sleepiness, and indifference. In contrast to borderline patients who make intense demands upon the analyst and consequently induce intense countertransference affects, these patients attempt to maintain an illusion of self-sufficiency. They report an intrapsychic perception of this state of self-sufficiency and feel encased in a "plastic bubble" (Modell 1968, Volkan 1973) or behind a sheet of glass (Guntrip 1968) or feel that they are a mummy in a case or, as I have described earlier (Modell 1968), they feel encased in a cocoon.[1] I have chosen the cocoon metaphor because

---

1. Slap (1974) has also described this phenomenon, but has mistakenly associated it with Lewin's dream screen.

it implies a potential for life. A cocoon, unlike a mummy or a plastic bubble, contains something alive and must be attached to something else that is essential for its nourishment.[2] The illusion of self-sufficiency and disdainful aloofness that these people display defends against the very opposite—that is, yearnings that are intense and insatiable. Patient's descriptions of feeling as if they were inside a plastic bubble attest to their endopsychic perceptions of deadness. It should also be obvious that these analogies may be variations of a womb fantasy—a state where one is cut off from interaction from the environment, where one is not "really in the world"; where there is an illusion of self-sufficiency and yet a total dependence upon the caretaking functions of the maternal environment.[3]

During this phase of the analytic process, although the analyst may experience boredom and indifference, the patient may be enjoying the analytic experience. With some patients we have the impression of a child playing happily by himself content to know that his mother is in the next room. The patient is talking to himself, but he does experience a sense that he is safe in the analytic setting.

Although the analyst in the initial period may have a feeling that nothing is happening, we believe that the analytic process is set in motion by the holding environment and the tie to the analyst himself. During this period there cannot be said to be a therapeutic alliance, for this requires a sense of separateness that has not yet been established. Instead of a therapeutic alliance, we see a magic belief reminiscent of what has been described in borderline patients as a transitional-object relationship—the object stands between them and the dangers of the real world. It is as if the patient really believes that he is not "in the world" and that there is no need for him to obtain anything for himself—there is a denial of the need to work. Implicit here is the belief that the analyst can rescue the patient in spite of himself and that the analyst has sufficient power to preserve the analysis in spite of the patient's efforts to sabotage it. In this idealizing phase, the analyst implicitly possesses some powerful qualities so that change may be effected merely by being in his presence. It is a sense of magic based on contiguity: merely to be in the presence of the powerful object is to share his power. What I am describing corresponds, of course, to some aspects of Kohut's idealizing transference. This positively toned transference gradually gives way, for reasons to be described, to negative transfer-

2. Some patients, if they are able to, will come very early to their appointments to obtain the feeling of safety and pleasure of remaining alone in the waiting room with the knowledge that I am next door.
3. Freud used the analogy of an egg in another context (1911): "A neat example of a psychical system shut off from the stimuli of the external world, and able to satisfy even its nutritional requirements autistically (to use Bleuler's term), is afforded by a bird's egg with its food supply enclosed in its shell; for it, the care provided by its mother is limited to the provision of warmth" (p. 220n).

ence. For a cocoon is also similar to a fortress, where nothing leaves and nothing enters. The analyst begins to observe that his comments tend to be forgotten or not even heard—nothing seems to get through. The analyst's emotional position is one of acceptance, patience, and empathy—he must be able to wait. Winnicott has observed (1969): "For instance, it is only in recent years that I have been able to sit and wait for the natural evolution of the transference arising out of the patient's growing trust in the psychoanalytic technique and setting, and to avoid breaking up the natural process by making interpretations" (p. 86). Interpretations at this stage tend to be either dismissed, not heard, or resented as an intrusion. (We will return in a later section to discuss the function of interpretation.)

The Middle Period: The Emergence of Rage and the Development of the Therapeutic Alliance

In this portion of the analysis the positively toned transference gradually changes into its opposite. We begin to enter the period that can be described as one of narcissistic rage. The time of onset of this phase may be due in part to the emotional capacities of the analyst, that is, how long he can tolerate the patient's prolonged state of nonrelatedness. But we suspect that even with the most tolerant and accepting analyst the process would shift of its own accord, for, as the regression deepens, the insatiable demands that have been warded off by denial will become more manifest. The analyst becomes more aware of the patient's insatiable needs for admiration and total attention and, in turn, becomes more confronting. This is not simply the empathic acceptance of the patient's grandiose self that Kohut has described. Here I share the observation of Loewald (1973) who states: "To my mind a not inconsiderable share of the analytic work consists of more or less actively and consistently confronting these freed narcissistic needs of the narcissistic transferences" (p. 447) (see also Kernberg [1974] on confrontation). The confrontation of the patient's grandiosity gradually gives way to a systematic interpretation of the cocoon fantasy itself. With this activity on the part of the analyst, the affect block and state of nonrelatedness is gradually and imperceptibly altered and gives way to genuine affects, albeit that of intense rage. We have arrived at the "point of urgency" that Strachey described as the necessary precondition for giving mutative interpretations. This rage in some patients takes on murderous proportions or may lead to a defensive indifference, a regressive movement back to the earlier cocoon fantasy. I believe, with Winnicott (1969), that the rage itself supports the process of individuation. In contrast to the rage that accompanies the Oedipus complex, the wish to destroy the parent of the opposite sex, this rage is not aimed at the analyst as a parental imago. It is less definite and more diffuse. For example, as the analyst is equated with the environment itself, he becomes the target of rage directed against external reality. This rage may also be fueled by envy—the envy itself is again diffuse and nonspecific: the patient may envy the analyst for what he is and for what he has, that is, his knowledge. As one moves through this stormy period in the analysis, a period that may occupy months or perhaps a year or longer, one observes that the cocoon transference has been gradually dissolving—the patient no longer believes in his self-sufficiency, he is able to acknowledge his demands more directly, his extreme dependency is no longer denied. With this, comes the beginning of individuation, a sense of separateness, and the development of the therapeutic alliance. Although this may be a difficult and painful period, there is a sense that two people are present. The patient gradually, although reluctantly, begins to accept the fact that he has a responsibility for the work in the analysis.

We believe that the holding environment of the first phase has led to sufficient ego consolidation to permit a shift in the focus of therapeutic action of psychoanalysis in the second phase. And we believe that the motive force for the therapeutic action of psychoanalysis in the second phase is interpretation. Interpretation effects the dissolution of the cocoon transference in a manner analogous to the use of interpretation to effect the dissolution of a transference neurosis. It should be understood that, in contrast to the classical case, the dissolution of the cocoon transference permits the establishment of a therapeutic alliance. We can say that at the end of this middle phase the patient is emerging from the cocoon—he is beginning to hatch. With this there is a greater sense of aliveness. As patients report it—they feel as if they are beginning to live their own lives.

Third Phase—The End Phase

In this phase the analysis approximates that of a classical case. This is not to say that it is identical to that of a classical case, in that the potentiality for regressive movement is ever-present. During weekend separations for example, there may be a renewal of the cocoon transference. Elements, however, of the historically idiosyncratic transference neurosis begin to emerge—that is, there is a repetition of imagos of whole persons and not the externalization of parts of the self.

We have now entered the realm of the Oedipus complex. In the male, indications of castration anxiety appear in the transference, which has shifted from the conflict with the environment to recapitulate historically determined facets of the transference neurosis. Correspondingly, there is a shift of focus, both within the transference and outside of it, from dyadic to triangular relationships. While the vicissitudes of the Oedipus complex may not emerge as completely as in a "classical" case, they are unmistakably present.

Affects are now experienced with great intensity—now it is only rarely that the analyst experiences the sense of boredom and sleepiness that so characterized the opening phase. In short, during this period the analysis is not unlike that of a classical neurosis, with the exception that there is the readiness to establish a narcissistic affect block that characterizes the cocoon transference.

Because of extreme dependency, it can be understood that the phase of termination may be prolonged. It should be clear that a true termination can be achieved only if the cocoon transference has been resolved through interpretation. In some patients with narcissistic character disorders, this middle and stormy phase in which the cocoon transference is resolved is never traversed. Consequently, the patient remains unanalyzed and persists in a state where the analytic situation itself is used as a transitional object. It can be said with some truth that such patients become addicted to the analytic process.

EMPATHY AND MUTATIVE INTERPRETATION

We have suggested that interpretations only become mutative during the second phase of the treatment of narcissistic character disorders, that is, when there is a state of affective relatedness. Interpretations are, of course, not confined to the second phase of analysis, and we suspect that their therapeutic action in the first phase may be of a different order. Interpretations may function principally as a sign of the analyst's empathy and understanding—that is, they may function as part of the analytic holding environment. I believe Rycroft (1956) had something of the same idea in mind when he stated: "In addition therefore to their symbolic function of communicating ideas, interpretations also have the sign-function of conveying to the patient the analyst's emotional attitude towards him. They combine with the material setting provided by the analyst to form the analyst's affective contribution to the formation of a trial relationship, within which the patient can recapture the ability to make contact and communication with external objects" (p. 472).

It is unlikely therefore that interpretations can be mutative until there is sufficient maturation of the ego for the acceptance of self/object differentiation. In the opening phase, the analyst's interpretations, although accurate, may not be distinguished by the patient from the analyst's general empathic response (see also Gedo and Goldberg [1973] for a discussion of the hierarchy of treatment modalities).

THE NARCISSISTIC TRANSFERENCE AND THE TRANSFERENCE NEUROSIS

It is the underlying assumption in this paper that, as our psychoanalytic nosology is broadened to include syndromes of varying disturbances of ego structure, we will correspondingly have broadened our understanding of the analytic process and the process of transference. This is the point of view developed by Gedo and Goldberg (1973). We believe it is important to resist a tendency to blur the nosological distinction between the transference neurosis and the narcissistic character disorders. We suspect that the increased attention to the narcissistic disorders may reflect an actual increase in their frequency—a shift in the ecology of neuroses—and that a shifting nosology of neurosis may be the manifestation of yet unidentified psychosocial processes. Fenichel (1938) observed that "neurotics who demand analytic treatment today differ from those that went to Freud thirty or forty years ago." And we now say that the neurotic who seeks treatment today differs from those who consulted Fenichel in 1938. For we have now come to view the capacity to form a transference neurosis as a sign of health. Elements of the transference neurosis appear only after a certain degree of ego growth and consolidation has been achieved. The development of the transference neurosis requires a capacity for illusion (Khan 1973). (For a more general discussion of the transference neurosis, see Blum 1971.) As Greenson has noted (see Workshop 1974), it is fluid, changeable, and different in every patient. This is in marked contrast to the narcissistic transferences, which are uniform to the extent that they can be said to form an operational basis for defining the syndrome. This is not to say that the delineation of the narcissistic transferences occurs regardless of the analyst's technique or skill. Nevertheless, their uniformity suggests that they are based upon the externalization of psychic structures, that is, various portions of the self, or self-object, and that they do not require a condition of basic trust for their emergence. This suggests that the more familiar externalization of the superego is also a noncreative structural transference element, to be distinguished from the transference neurosis.

EGO DISTORTION AND THE EGO'S CONFLICT
WITH THE ENVIRONMENT

In his paper, "Neurosis and Psychosis," Freud (1924) suggested that the ego's conflict with the environment was characteristic of psychosis: "... *neurosis is the result of a conflict between the ego and its id, whereas psychosis is the analogous outcome of a similar disturbance in the relations between the ego and the external world*" (p. 149). Our psychoanalytic experience with narcissistic character disorders has shown us that Freud's formula no longer applies, for this syndrome, where the ego is in conflict with the environment, must be categorized as a neurosis. Yet in the same paper Freud suggests a solution to this apparent contradiction, for he states that it is possible for the ego to avoid a psychotic rupture by "... deforming itself, by submitting to encroachments on its own unity and even perhaps by effecting a cleavage or division of itself" (pp. 152–153). Freud had a specific form of ego distortion in mind, which he elaborated in later papers (1927, 1940). This is the ego's capacity, such as in cases of fetishism, to maintain two opposite views simultaneously, with a resultant loss in its synthetic functions. An example given was that of the fetishist's accurate perception of the female genitals held in the mind side-by-side with the belief in the existence of a female penis. Splitting of this sort, with a loss of synthetic functions, exists in narcissistic character disorders which Kohut described as a "vertical" split.

In our description of the cocoon transference we have suggested that the underlying fantasy of self-sufficiency is defensive and is the consequence of the ego's conflict with the environment. The belief in a state of omnipotent self-sufficiency exists side-by-side with an intense and overwhelming dependency expressed as a craving hunger for admiration and approval. This deformation of the ego is also a split, as Freud described, whose content follows directly from the ego's conflict with the environment. As we have depicted earlier, the specific deformation provides the basis for a specific transference response in which the ego's conflict with the environment is relived in the analytic setting.

We are led to a closer consideration of the nature of the trauma and the resultant ego disturbance or distortion. It would be naïve to suggest that there is a simple or direct relationship between developmental trauma and a specific characterological syndrome. We know of many instances where the developmental trauma is similar and the resultant characterological response quite variable. In questions of this sort Freud (1937) has emphasized the factor of the quantitative strength of the instincts at the time of the environmental trauma, so that it is ultimately a question of inner rather than outer reality.

Further, we know that the reconstruction of childhood trauma from the analytic material of an adult patient is on a less firm footing than our direct observations of the psychoanalytic process itself. Nevertheless, we are not able to minimize the importance of trauma in the etiology of the narcissistic character disorder, which in a very general way may be described as a developmental failure of the "holding environment."

In our patients we can infer through historical reconstruction that there has been a relative failure in the parental holding environment which takes several forms. The child's sense of safety and ultimately his sense of basic trust depends on his reliance on the parents' judgments in their dealings with him and the external world. Intelligent children can easily perceive that their parents' judgment is "off." We were able to determine that several of our patients who suffered from narcissistic character disorders had mothers who were at times childishly fatuous and silly or extremely unpredictable in their judgments of reality. Kohut has described that the mothers of these patients are lacking in empathy and are overly intrusive, an observation we were able to confirm. This failure of empathy can also take the form of a relative failure of the parents' protective function, that is, to protect the child from excessive stimulation. This may mean the failure to protect the child from sadistic or bullying attacks from other members of the household, as well as a failure to protect the child from excessive sexual stimulation. For there to be a failure of the holding environment, we believe that it is necessary that both parents in some way be involved. We have the impression that in the older child the father's role is significant either in opposing or augmenting the maternal element.

Although the specific form of the failure of the parental shield may vary, we believe there is a common denominator in that it induces the formation of a precocious and premature sense of self, a sense of self that retains its fragility and must be supported by omnipotent, grandiose fantasies (Modell 1975b). It is this defensive structure that we see re-emerging in the psychoanalytic processes – the cocoon transference. The conflict with the environment that emerges in the middle period of the analytic process reaches a climax when there is a breaking up of the cocoon transference so that the hatred transferred to the analyst is the patient's hatred of reality.

To return to our question – that of the failure of the holding environment in the "classical" case. Trauma and conflict with the environment are of course not absent in the histories of our so-called classical case, but do not lead to a structural deformation of the ego. We have the impression that such traumas may be reflected in periods of "acting in" during the early phase of psychoanalysis and in the relative abandonment of the therapeutic alliance, as if the patient needs to experience regressively the illusion of the magical protection of the analytic setting. In contrast to the patients with narcissistic character disorders, such episodes do not require any lengthy period of ego consolidation before yielding to interpretation.

It should be clear that we approached the problem of the "holding environment" from several points of view. We believe that there are elements of caretaking functions implicit in the object tie of the patient to the analyst, functions that are part of ordinary psychoanalytic technique. Loewald (1960) has said that the analytic setting represents a *new* object tie. In addition to these "real" elements, there is the fantasy that the analytic setting functions in some magical way to protect the patient from the dangers of the environment, a fantasy similar to that of perceiving the analyst as a transitional object (Modell 1968). These fantasies commonly appear in the termination phase and are no different from other transference fantasies that can be dealt with by interpretation. In so-called classical cases, the analytic setting functions as a "holding environment" silently; it is something that is taken for granted and can be described as part of the "confident" transference. Where there is ego distortion, the analytic setting as a holding environment is central to the therapeutic action.

CONCLUSION

The therapeutic action of the holding environment in the transference neuroses can easily be contrasted to that in the narcissistic character disorders. In the former, the holding environment functions in the manner of a vessel or container that permits the unfolding of the transference neurosis—it provides the necessary background of safety to support illusion. With the narcissistic character disorders, in contrast, the analytic setting facilitates necessary ego consolidation so that mutative interpretations may be eventually effective and a therapeutic alliance may be established. It is only then that elements of the transference neurosis emerge in a form that can be analyzed.

Interpretation leads to the dissolution of magical fantasies associated with the holding environment in a manner analogous to the dissolution of the transference neurosis. If these fantasies associated with the holding environment are not sufficiently analyzed, there is a danger, in the narcissistic character disorder, that the analytic process itself may become a transitional object and the patient would then be addicted to an interminable analysis.

REFERENCES

Balint, M. (1968), The Basic Fault. London: Tavistock Publications.
Bibring, E. (1937), Symposium on the theory of the therapeutic results of psycho-analysis. International Journal of Psycho-Analysis, 18:170–189.
Blum, H. (1971), On the conception and development of the transference neurosis. Journal of the American Psychoanalytic Association, 19:41–53.
Fenichel, O. (1938), Ego disturbances and their treatment. In: Collected Papers, second series. New York: Norton, 1954, pp. 109–128.
Freud, A. (1969). Difficulties in the Path of Psychoanalysis. New York: International Universities Press.
Freud, A., and Burlingham, D. (1943). War and Children. New York: International Universities Press.
Freud, S. (1911). Formulations on the two principles of mental functioning Standard Edition 12:218–226.
_____ (1914). On narcissism: an introduction. Standard Edition 14:67–102.
_____ (1924). Neurosis and psychosis Standard Edition 19:149–153.
_____ (1927). Fetishism. Standard Edition 21:149–157.
_____ (1937). Analysis terminable and interminable. Standard Edition 23:216–253.
_____ (1940). Splitting of the ego in the process of defence. Standard Edition 23:271–278.
Gedo, J., and Goldberg, A. (1973). Models of the Mind. Chicago: University of Chicago Press.

Gitelson, M. (1962). On the curative factors in the first phase of analysis. In *Psychoanalysis: Science and Profession*, pp. 311–341. New York: International Universities Press, 1973.

Glover, E. (1937). Symposium on the theory of the therapeutic results of psycho-analysis. *International Journal of Psycho-Analysis*, 18:125–132.

Greenson, R. (1974). Transference: Freud or Klein. *International Journal of Psycho-Analysis*, 55:37–48.

Greenson, R., and Wexler, M. (1969). The non-transference relationship in the psychoanalytic situation. *International Journal of Psycho-Analysis*, 50:27–39.

Guntrip, H. (1968). *Schizoid Phenomena, Object Relations, and the Self*. New York: International Universities Press.

Kernberg, O. (1974). Further contributions to the treatment of narcissistic personalities. *International Journal of Psycho-Analysis*, 55:215–240.

Khan, M. (1963). The concept of cumulative trauma. In *The Privacy of the Self*, pp. 42–58. New York: International Universities Press, 1974.

——— (1973). The role of illusion in the analytic space and process. In *The Annual of Psychoanalysis*, vol. 1, pp. 231–246. New York: Quadrangle.

Kohut, H. (1971). *The Analysis of the Self*. New York: International Universities Press.

Loewald, H. (1960). On the therapeutic action of psychoanalysis. *International Journal of Psycho-Analysis*, 41:16–33.

——— (1973). Review of Kohut's *The Analysis of the Self*. *Psychoanalytic Quarterly*, 42:441–451.

Modell, A. H. (1968). *Object Love and Reality*. New York: International Universities Press.

——— (1973). Affects and psychoanalytic knowledge. In *The Annual of Psychoanalysis*, vol. 1, pp. 117–124. New York: Quadrangle.

——— (1975a). The ego and the id–fifty years later. *International Journal of Psycho-Analysis*, 56:57–68.

——— (1975b). A narcissistic defense against affects and the illusion of self-sufficiency. *International Journal of Psycho-Analysis*, 56:275–282.

Panel (1971). Models of the psychic apparatus. (S. Abrams, reporter.) *Journal of the American Psychoanalytic Association*, 19:131–142.

Rosenfeld, H. (1972). A critical appreciation of James Strachey's paper on the nature of the therapeutic action of psychoanalysis. *International Journal of Psycho-Analysis*, 53:454–461.

——— (1974). Discussion of R. R. Greenson's "Transference: Freud or Klein." *International Journal of Psycho-Analysis*, 55:49–51.

Rycroft, C. (1956). The nature and function of the analyst's communication to the patient. *International Journal of Psycho-Analysis*, 37:469–472.

Sandler, J. (1960). The background of safety. *International Journal of Psycho-Analysis*, 41:352–356.

Slap, J. (1974). On waking screens. *Journal of the American Psychoanalytic Association*, 22:844–853.

Spitz, R. (1956). Countertransference. *Journal of the American Psychoanalytic Association*, 4:256–265.

Stone, L. (1961). *The Psychoanalytic Situation*. New York: International Universities Press.

Strachey, J. (1934). The nature of the therapeutic action of psychoanalysis. *International Journal of Psycho-Analysis*, 50:277-292.

Volkan, V. (1973). Transitional fantasies in the analysis of a narcissistic personality. *Journal of the American Psychoanalytic Association*, 21:351-376.

Winnicott, D. W.(1963). Psychiatric disorders in terms of infantile maturational processes. In *The Maturational Processes and the Facilitating Environment*; pp. 230-241. New York: International Universities Press.

_____ (1965). *The Maturational Processes and the Facilitating Environment*. New York: International Universities Press.

_____ (1969). The use of an object and relating through identifications. In *Playing and Reality*, pp. 86-94. New York: Basic Books.

Workshop (1974). The fate of the transference neurosis after analysis. (A. Balkoura, reporter.) *Journal of the American Psychoanalytic Association*, 22:895-903.

Zetzel, E. (1956). The concept of transference. In *The Capacity for Emotional Growth*, pp. 168-181. New York: International Universities Press, 1970.

CREDITS

T HE AUTHOR GRATEFULLY acknowledges permission to quote from the following sources:

"Dreaming, Fantasying, and Living," by D. W. Winnicott, from *Playing and Reality*. Copyright © 1971 by Penguin Books Ltd. Reprinted by permission of Routledge Methuen and The Winnicott Trust.

"Hate in the Countertransference," by D. W. Winnicott, from *Through Paediatrics to Psycho-Analysis*. Copyright © 1958 by Basic Books and *International Journal of Psycho-Analysis*, vol. 30, copyright © 1949. Reprinted by permission of Basic Books, a division of HarperCollins Publishers, Inc., the Institute of Psycho-Analysis, and The Winnicott Trust.

"Fear of Breakdown," by D. W. Winnicott, from *International Review of Psycho-Analysis*, vol. 1, pp. 103–107. Copyright © 1974 by the *International Review of Psycho-Analysis*. Reprinted by permission of the Institute for Psycho-Analysis and The Winnicott Trust.

"Fragments of an Analysis," by D. W. Winnicott, from *Holding and Interpretation*. Copyright © 1986 by Grove Press. Reprinted by permission of Grove Press and Chatto and Windus/The Hogarth Press, and The Winnicott Trust.

INDEX

About the Editor

Dodi Goldman, Ph.D., lived for fifteen years on an Israeli kibbutz on the Lebanese border, where he worked as a dairy farmer, teacher, high school principal, and educator in an innovative residential treatment program for adolescents. He has lectured in social history and on the origins of the kibbutz at the research and seminar institute of the United Kibbutz Movement. He served for three years as the administrative and social head of his kibbutz.

Dr. Goldman received his doctoral degree in clinical psychology from the City University of New York and was project coordinator and clinical assessor for multi-site epidemiological studies in psychotic disorders. He is currently in analytic training at the Institute for Psychoanalytic Training and Research in New York City.